Savannah, Charleston

& the Carolina Coast

Randall Peffer, Debra Miller

Contents

SOUTH CAROLINA

GEORGIA

MYRTLE BEACH & THE GRAND STRAND p178

CHARLESTON p144

HILTON HEAD p116

SAVANNAH p62

GEORGIA COAST p92

Destination: Savannah, Charleston & the Carolina Coast

Known to its lovers as the Lowcountry, the lures of Savannah, Charleston and the surrounding coast root in islands, marshes and historic cities that ebb and flow into each other like a watercolor collage.

This is a land of sumptuous images and leisure activities. Live oaks drip with Spanish moss in Savannah's squares. Wild horses graze on the beaches of Cumberland Island. Legions of golfers tee up on seaside courses at Hilton Head, Myrtle Beach and Kiawah and St Simons Islands. It is impossible not to relax as you dabble your toes in the surf at Myrtle Beach or take a lamp-lit carriage ride among the Federal-style town houses of Charleston. For pure grandeur, few experiences can beat a stroll among the Victorian mansions towering over Jekyll Island, or the moment you spot a school of dolphin chasing bait fish through a river of diamonds.

To stroll the grounds of Charleston's plantation houses is to step into the world of *Gone With the Wind*. And when you submerge yourself in Savannah's legendary nightlife, you enter the intrigue and sultriness of *Midnight in the Garden of Good & Evil*.

A boat or kayak trip through the backwaters around Beaufort brings you to a quiet, mysterious place brilliantly described in Pat Conroy's *The Prince of Tides,* while St Helena, Daufuskie and Sapelo Islands preserve the traditions and language of the African American Gullah culture.

Then there is the food. Lowcountry cuisine will rock your palate with the spiced shrimp of a Frogmore stew.

So pick your fantasy, and as they say here: 'Have at it, Bubba.'

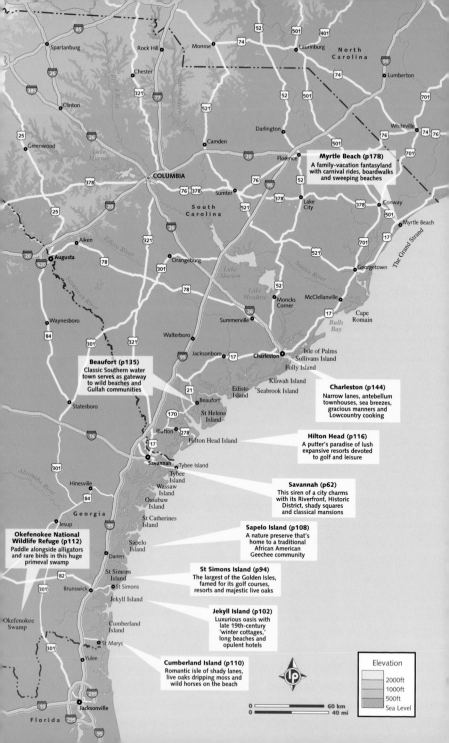

Myrtle Beach (p178)
A family-vacation fantasyland with carnival rides, boardwalks and sweeping beaches

Beaufort (p135)
Classic Southern water town serves as gateway to wild beaches and Gullah communities

Charleston (p144)
Narrow lanes, antebellum townhouses, sea breezes, gracious manners and Lowcountry cooking

Hilton Head (p116)
A putter's paradise of lush expansive resorts devoted to golf and leisure

Savannah (p62)
This siren of a city charms with its Riverfront, Historic District, shady squares and classical mansions

Sapelo Island (p108)
A nature preserve that's home to a traditional African American Geechee community

Okefenokee National Wildlife Refuge (p112)
Paddle alongside alligators and rare birds in this huge primeval swamp

St Simons Island (p94)
The largest of the Golden Isles, famed for its golf courses, resorts and majestic live oaks

Jekyll Island (p102)
Luxurious oasis with late 19th-century 'winter cottages,' long beaches and opulent hotels

Cumberland Island (p110)
Romantic isle of shady lanes, live oaks dripping moss and wild horses on the beach

Elevation
2000ft
1000ft
500ft
Sea Level

0   60 km
0   40 mi

The gracious cities of Savannah and Charleston are the twin jewels of this coastal region, and they're just the beginning of your Lowcountry adventure. Step back in time among the wild horses and plantation ruins on Cumberland Island (p110). Listen to a traditional Gullah storyteller spin yarns on Sapelo Island (p108). Golf, bike and while away your days at a resort on Hilton Head Island (p116). Feast on fresh seafood along Beaufort's historic waterfront (p135). Strut your stuff down the boardwalk or lose your breath on a seaside roller coaster at Myrtle Beach (p178). You'll find thrills galore in the Lowcountry.

Take a twilight stroll under flickering street lamps in Savannah (p62)

Admire the gothic and historic buildings around Savannah's Lafayette Square (p73)

RICHARD CUMMINS

RICHARD CUMMINS

Feast on a Lowcountry boil (a stew made with sausage, corn, shrimp and potatoes) at one of several eateries overlooking the Intracoastal Waterway near Tybee Island (p86)

RICHARD CUMMINS

JOHN NEUBA

Expand your horizons from aboard a windjammer off the coast of Charleston (p144), taking in the panorama of the townscape and historic Civil War forts

Golf, beach-comb and visit the lighthouse museum on St Simons Island (p94)

LEE FOSTER

Get up close to a gator in the Okefenokee Swamp (p112)

LEE FOSTER

Go green with envy touring the ornate mansions of Charleston (p144)

JOHN NEUBAUER

LEE FOSTER

Imagine the former glory of 'King Cotton' at Savannah's Cotton Exchange (p68)

Sip tea with your pinkies up, play a round of croquet, or re-enact scenes from *The Great Gatsby* at the decadent Jekyll Island Club Hotel (p104)

LEE FOSTER

8

LEE FOSTER

Marvel at the time and toil invested in building Savannah's beautiful historic homes (p62)

Shop for the perfect keepsake, like these handwoven sweetgrass baskets (p169)

RICK GERHARTER

Wander the lovingly restored grounds of Middleton Place (p155), west of Charleston

CORINNE HUMPHREY

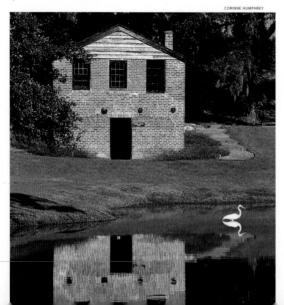

Getting Started

Grab your bathing suit, put a name tag on your golf bag, buy yourself a fresh dress or Polo shirt, splurge on some new dancin' shoes and get ready for Wonderland. The Lowcountry can deliver world-class fantasies. Whether your heart melts for beaches or antebellum cities, golf courses or salt marshes, manor houses or tent sites, shrimp boils or lamb lollypops, a jazz set or a drag show, coastal Georgia and South Carolina are going to take your definition of fun to a whole new level.

WHEN TO GO

The Georgia and South Carolina coast is a four-season destination. Spring and fall are the most temperate and scenic seasons in the Lowcountry and a time of festivals galore, like the St Patrick's Day bacchanal in Savannah, the Spoleto USA festival in Charleston and the Worldcom Classic Heritage of Golf tournament at Hilton Head. Many family vacationers flock like lemmings to the beaches in the summer. The tourist season runs roughly from Spring Break (mid- to late March) to Labor Day (first Monday in September), and some summer attractions close in the off season, especially at Myrtle Beach, Tybee Island and other family-vacation destinations. Lodging prices follow the crowds, meaning that beach hotels drop their rates in cooler months.

See Climate Charts (p198) for more information.

Temperatures for the region range from about 20°F to 93°F. Average precipitation is nothing out of the ordinary: between about 40 and 75 inches per year. Normally only the Upcountry (the region west of I-95 and the marshy lowland of the coast) sees any real snow, but you never know: the winter of 2003 brought the barrier islands a brief dusting. High humidity makes it feel a lot hotter, and drippier (especially in July and August), but sea breezes tend to keep things cooler along the immediate shoreline. The extreme south of Georgia is considered subtropical, with gentle winters in the mid to high 50s and long steamy summers.

The fall generally draws smaller crowds and lower hotel rates, and the temperatures are more pleasant than in summer, but hurricanes spin in from the Atlantic about once every 10 years during that season. Hurricane season is from June to November, with peaks in August and September. South Carolina ranks fifth in the nation for hurricane strikes. For more information on the Lowcountry's hurricanes, see the boxed text 'Big Blows' on p48.

From mid-December to February, the Lowcountry is subject to 'northers' – cold fronts that blast briefly across the South and then dissipate. Except when these chilly winds blow through, the Georgia–South Carolina coast generally enjoys mild winters. Tourism is at its lowest in these months, and hotel and golf rates are exceptionally reasonable.

COSTS

Costs for accommodations on the Georgia and South Carolina coasts vary widely, depending on the season, location, whether or not festivals are happening and the type of accommodations you choose. Generally, rates are highest in the more populated areas, with Savannah, Charleston and Hilton Head at the top end of the spectrum. The cheapest motel rates will usually be in the $40 to $50 range, but prices tend to skyrocket during festivals and other special events. For B&Bs and mid-range hotels, expect to pay $75 to $150, or more. Camping is inexpensive – about $8 per night – but only costlier sites have amenities, such as hot showers.

Food, especially local cuisine, is fairly reasonable. The occasional splurge at a first-rate restaurant will cost anywhere between $25 and $50 per person, but dinner at a good restaurant can be had for $10 – half that for lunch. Shopping at food markets and preparing your own meals will get you by even more cheaply.

If you are camping and cooking the bulk of your own meals, you can manage on $40 per person per day. If you want to eat out and stay in mid-range accommodations, plan on $100 a day (per person and traveling as a couple).

Bargaining isn't a generally accepted practice, but you can arouse competitive instincts to finagle a deal. For example, at hotels in the off season, casually mentioning a rival's rate may prompt a manager to lower the quoted rate. Discount coupons are widely available – check for circulars in Sunday papers and at supermarkets, tourist offices, chambers of commerce and welcome centers.

Urban public transportation is relatively cheap, and buses cost from 80¢ to $1.50. Renting a car costs between $25 and $65 a day, depending on your choice of vehicle, and in some areas a car is the only way of getting around.

HOW MUCH?

Bike rental $12-15

Bottle of beer $2.50

Dinner for one $12-20

Car rental $22-35

Dolphin tour $22

Gasoline $1.50-1.80

Glass of wine $4.50

Hotel double $80

Loaf of bread $1.25

Newspaper $1

Quart of milk $1

Round of golf $85

PRE-DEPARTURE READING

There's a wealth of evocative fiction set in the Lowcountry, but reading a nonfiction book on local culture or history before your visit can also enhance your experience tremendously.

The *Smithsonian Guide to Historic America* for the Carolinas and Georgia includes an exhaustive review of Lowcountry historic sites and lush color photographs. The *Jazz & Blues Lover's Guide to the US,* by Christiane Bird, covers music sights and hundreds of US clubs. Its listings (from 1994) are in need of an update, but its chapters dealing with the Southeast and Lowcountry are very informative. The Sierra Club's *Adventuring along the Southeast Coast* is a useful guide to the Lowcountry, beaches and barrier islands of the region. It describes hikes, backpacking and canoe/kayak trips, and includes bike paths up and down the coast. The gargantuan *Encyclopedia of Southern Culture,* edited by Charles Reagan Wilson and William Ferris, covers everything from agriculture to 'women's life,' with excellent sections on literature and music. Readers who want to delve into the region's culinary delights might pick up Kathryn Tucker's *Southern Cooking to Remember,* which includes seafood recipes.

Charles Hudson's *The Southeastern Indians* is considered the seminal work on the area's Native American history. *Trail of Tears: The Rise & Fall of the Cherokee Nation,* by John Ehle, is a popular history of the tragedy and reads like a novel.

Of the tomes written on the Civil War, a major sourcebook is the three-volume *The Civil War: A Narrative,* written over a 20-year period by Mississippi historian Shelby Foote (whose wry and poignant observations appeared throughout the PBS *Civil War* TV series). The *Civil War Almanac,* edited by John S Bowman and introduced by noted historian Henry Steele Commager, is an authoritative single-volume book with a detailed chronology and biographies of key figures.

Baptized in Blood, by Charles Reagan Wilson, helps readers understand why, for many Southerners, 'the War Between the States' isn't over. Tony Horowitz' *Confederates in the Attic: Dispatches from the Unfinished Civil*

TOP TENS

FAVORITE FESTIVALS & EVENTS

It's almost always party time somewhere in the Lowcountry. Here are the happenings you don't want to miss.

- Jekyll Island Historic District Open House & Festival (Jekyll Island), January (p99)
- Native Gullah Celebration (Hilton Head), February (p125)
- St Patrick's Day (Savannah), March (p74)
- Annual Tour of Homes & Gardens (Savannah), March (p74)
- Worldcom Classic, The Heritage of Golf (Hilton Head) , March (p125)

- Spoleto USA (Charleston), May and June (p162)
- Turtle Talk & Walk (Hilton Head), June (p125)
- Savannah Film & Video Festival, August (p74)
- Annual Celebrity Golf Tournament (Hilton Head), September (p125)
- Christmas in Charleston (Charleston), December (p163)

TOP TEN ACTIVITIES

There's no excuse for getting bored in the Lowcountry. Here are some things you can do to soothe your soul.

- Wandering through shady historic districts of Savannah (p68) and Charleston (p147)
- Antebellum home tours in and around Savannah (p73) and Charleston (p147)
- Discovering the Gullah culture (p55) on the isles of St Helena, Daufuskie and Sapelo
- Dining on Lowcountry cooking (p55) at a backwater crab shack
- Exploring Savannah's wildlife refuge (p90) and Charleston's Cypress Gardens (p171)

- Dolphin and turtle watching at Hilton Head (p120)
- Clubbing in Savannah at City Market, and the Riverfront (p81)
- Kayaking the backwaters of the isles (p141) around Beaufort
- Golfing (p122) the championship courses of Hilton Head and St Simon
- Dancing the shag (p190) in a Myrtle Beach club

MUST-SEE MOVIES

Well over 75 major motion pictures have captured the Lowcountry on film. To get fired up for your visit, consider curling up at home and watching some of these. For more information, see the film section (p36).

- *Gone With the Wind* (1939)
  Director: Victor Fleming
- *Forrest Gump* (1994)
  Director: Robert Zemeckis
- *The Big Chill* (1983)
  Director: Lawrence Kasdan
- *Midnight in the Garden of Good & Evil* (1997)
  Director: Clint Eastwood
- *Conrack* (1974)
  Director: Martin Ritt

- *The Prince of Tides* (1991)
  Director: Barbra Streisand
- *The Patriot* (2000)
  Director: Roland Emmerick
- *Daughters of the Dust* (1991)
  Director: Julie Dash
- *The Great Santini* (1979)
  Director: Lewis John Carolino
- *Something to Talk About* (1995)
  Director: Lasse Hallström

War is a quirky travelogue that explores the phenomenon of Civil War reenactments. The author covers rituals such as 'bloating' – waving the Confederate flag as a symbol of heritage – and issues around racial division.

Stetson Kennedy's 1959 *Jim Crow Guide: The Way It Was* is an eye-opening survey of the jim-crow South. Civil rights history from 1954 to 1965 is chronicled in Juan William's *Eyes on the Prize* (this can also be found as a PBS documentary series by the same name). *Free at Last*, by Margaret Edds, covers the behind-the-scenes struggles for civil rights in several Southern cities.

INTERNET RESOURCES

Brunswick-Golden Isles Visitors Bureau (www.bgivb.com) A primer for living large on St Simons Island, Sea Island, Jekyll Island etc.

Charleston Area Visitors & Convention Bureau (www.charlestoncvb.com) Blows you away with regional travel information.

Gay Savannah (gaysavannah.com) Complete list of gay-run and gay-friendly accommodations, restaurants, bars, clubs and businesses.

Greater Beaufort Chamber of Commerce (www.beaufortsc.org) The official scoop on all things in the land of *The Big Chill*.

Hilton Head Visitors & Convention Bureau (www.hiltonheadisland.org) Golf, golf, golf… and everything else you need for your vacation.

Lonely Planet (www.lonelyplanet.com) Succinct summaries on traveling throughout the USA; Thorn Tree bulletin board; travel news and the subWWWay section, with links to the most useful travel resources elsewhere on the Internet.

Myrtle Beach Area Convention Bureau (www.myrtlebeachlive.com) Where to shag (the dance) and other necessities on the Grand Strand.

Savannah Area Visitors & Convention Bureau (www.savannahvisit.com) The down and dirty for an escapade in the 'garden of good and evil.'

Itineraries

CLASSIC ROUTES

THE BIG THREE   4-7 days

This itinerary makes sure you'll hit the three major Lowcountry destinations: Savannah, Hilton Head and Charleston. After exploring the historic district in **Savannah** (p62) and sampling its sumptuous nightlife, head north on US Hwy 17 over the Savannah Bridge and follow coastal roads through the forest and marshes to the live oaks and antebellum houses of **Historic Bluffton** (p132). From Bluffton it's a short jump (over the Intracoastal Waterway) to **Hilton Head** (p116), where all the world seems at play at historic estates, golf courses and 12 miles of broad beaches. When you've had enough fun in the sun, slip off the island and follow the coastal route north to **Beaufort** (p135), a town alive with historic homes, many of which have appeared in films like *The Big Chill*, *The Great Santini* and *The Prince of Tides*. While in the Beaufort area, take a side trip to **St Helena Island** (p141), where the Penn Center Historic District will introduce you to the African American sea islanders' unique Gullah culture. From here you can take side trips to the resorts on **Kiawah Island** (p173) and **Seabrook Island** (p175), or in less than 1½ hours (by following US Hwy 17 north), you can be in **Charleston** (p144), where spit-and-polish antique inns, town houses and genteel folk await.

Travelers who want to see the Lowcountry's most legendary communities can easily accomplish this trip in four days to a week, as it involves less than 150 miles of driving from one end to the other.

THE GEORGIA COAST   1 week

Spend three days in Savannah (p62), then head south on US Hwy 17.
Just south of Savannah, **Fort McAllister State Historical Park** (p107) has
Confederate earthworks on the banks of the Ogeechee River, as well as
a museum, hiking trails and camping. **Seabrook Village** (p107) is a living-
history museum portraying African American culture. At **Fort Morris State
Historic Site** (p107) you can view an earthen fort used during the British
in the War of 1812. Further south you'll come to a turnoff for the **Harris
Neck National Wildlife Refuge** (p107), where there is good bird-watching
and a long view across the marshes. If you plan ahead, you can make
reservations to take the ferry to **Sapelo Island** (p108) to tour or stay in the
well-preserved African American Geechee community there.

Stop at **Darien** (p107) to watch the shrimpers landing their catch or
nearby **Fort King George State Historic Site** (p107), with its fortifications and
a museum. South of Darien, the **Hofwyl-Broadfield Plantation State Historic
Site** (p107) contains the remnants of a traditional rice plantation. From
here, continue toward **Brunswick** (p106) and the beach-and-golf resorts
at **St Simons Island** (p94) and **Jekyll Island** (p102). Along the way you can
feast on Lowcountry boil (a local stew) at **Mudcat Charlie's** (p107), located
between Darien and Brunswick. The final leg of the drive takes you to
St Marys (p109). Here you can catch the ferry to remote **Cumberland Island**
(p110), where wild horses roam free.

US Hwy 17 and its
tributaries wind
down the Georgia
Coast, passing
through coastal
plains, pine and
hardwood forests
and salt marshes.

CAROLINA BEACHES

1 week

After basking in the historic delights of **Charleston** (p144), follow US Hwy 17 up the coast all the way to the North Carolina border, passing historic sites, some prime coastal wilderness and many of South Carolina's most popular seaside resorts. In **Mount Pleasant** (p171) you'll find historic navy ships to tour at the Patriot's Point Naval & Maritime Museum. Just a short drive further brings you to **Sullivan's Island** (p173), with its public beaches and Civil War–era Fort Moultrie. There's a more commercial beach north of here on the **Isle of Palms** (p172). Once you leave the Isle of Palms, you enter the vast, 250,000-acre **Francis Marion National Forest** (p195), which is rife with hiking, camping and beaching opportunities. Moving north, you return to civilization in the 'shabby chic,' upper-class beach retreat of **Pawleys Island** (p191). You're back in nature at **Huntington Beach State Park** (p191), which not only has beach, hiking and camping opportunities, but also a fortlike historic home to tour. When you cross the bridge to **Murrells Inlet** (p189), you might want to call time out for a deep-sea fishing charter or for a snack of some oysters at a waterside restaurant. Going north from here, you'll see the thick of vacation homes and resorts that dominate **Myrtle Beach** (p180) and the **Grand Strand** (p188). It's beach, boardwalk and amusements till you drop, Jack!

With sun, sand and swimming galore, this coastal jaunt is a perfect getaway.

THE LOWCOUNTRY RAMBLE   2 weeks

If you really want to cover the Lowcountry, you can drive US Hwy 17 and its tributaries from **Cumberland Island** (p110), on the Florida border, all the way to **Myrtle Beach** (p180), near the border with North Carolina. Take the trip north-to-south or south-to-north simply by combining **The Georgia Coast**, **The Big Three** and **Carolina Beaches** trips. Even with all the meandering, the entire trip is less than 350 miles. If you need to return a rental car to one of the area's gateway airports (Myrtle Beach, Charleston or Savannah), you will never be more than a three-hour drive from your airport via I-95.

See all the Lowcountry highlights in this two-week trip.

TAILORED TRIPS

CHARLESTON PLANTATIONS TOUR

The backwaters around Charleston are a particularly good place for plantation viewing. Some grand ones are open for tours; many others along the way remain private estates.

Start with **Boone Hall Plantation** (p171), which is promoted as the inspiration for Tara in *Gone With the Wind*. From Charleston take Ashley Ave north to the Hwy 17 Crosstown Expressway, then north to Mount Pleasant. Follow the sign to your right immediately after the bridge. Nearby, the **Charles Pinckney National Historic Site** (p172) is the former plantation of a famous South Carolinian statesman who helped frame the US Constitution. If you keep going north on US Hwy 17, you'll find **Hampton Plantation Historic Site** (p193), about halfway between Charleston and Myrtle Beach.

Up the Ashley River on Hwy 61, **Drayton Hall** (p155) is a fine brick mansion built c 1738, still in original condition. **Magnolia Plantation** (p155) has a 50-acre formal garden and a swamp garden with alligators and cypresses. Further west, **Middleton Place** (p155) features the country's oldest landscaped gardens, as well as working stables, a slave house and a 1755 guesthouse.

THE GREAT GOLF MARATHON

For many golfers, coastal Georgia and South Carolina are the promised land of Tiger, the Bear, Bobby Jones and Bagger Vance. You could golf at a different course each day for a year in the Lowcountry and still not play every hole. Myrtle Beach alone has 120 courses. For those with only a week to search for the perfect eagle, here are the courses that will make you feel like you're on the pro tour. They're all just a short drive off I-95.

In Myrtle Beach don't miss the four courses at **Wild Wing Plantation** (p184), named top golf resort in the state in 2002, or the extremely popular **Pawleys Plantation** (p184). Then hustle south to Charleston for 18 at the **Wild Dunes Resort** (p172), which has a couple of Tom Fazio numbers.

When you roll into Hilton Head, challenge yourself on the at **George Fazio course** (p123) at Palmetto Dunes – which was named one of the top 50 resort courses in the USA – or hit the **Harbour Town Golf Links** (p123), the site of the Heritage Golf Classic every March.

Savannah's do-not-miss course is right across the river, on Hutchinson Island – the **Club at Savannah Harbour** (p72). It was named one of the 10 best places to play golf for the millennium. Finish up your week at one of two classic Golden Isles courses, the exclusive Seaside course at **Sea Island Golf Club** (p98), or the Oleander course at **Jekyll Island's golf resort** (p103).

The Authors

RANDALL PEFFER

As a boy Randy hopped a freight train out of Pittsburgh, Pennsylvania (his hometown) in search of the King of the Hoboes. He's been traveling ever since. Savannah, Charleston and the Carolina Coast have enthralled him since 1986, when his sailboat broke down near Savannah on a trip up the Intracoastal Waterway, giving him time to explore the local creeks, sounds, backwaters and islands. He decided the fates were trying to send him a message, so he scrubbed the voyage and became a live-aboard in the Lowcountry. Since then Randy has written feature travel stories about the region for *Travel Holiday*, *Sail* and major metro dailies. He is the author of four other Lonely Planet guides, a National Geographic guide, two sailing memoirs and a murder-mystery novel.

My Lowcountry

For me there is nothing like seeing the Lowcountry at sunrise from a shrimper, a sailboat or (especially) a kayak. A maze of tidal rivers and creeks snake before me into the marshes and out to sea from the Intracoastal Waterway. Brown pelicans skim the water in search of fish, pairs of dolphins chase shoals of shrimp, and blue crabs flutter just below the surface of indigo waters. Raccoons forage for oysters at low tide, gators wallow in the reeds, and wild horses survey the scene from the shade of moss-draped live oaks. In wooden skiffs, Gullah fishermen set nets for mullet and chant to each other in their mysterious Creole. The air fills with the melodies of songbirds, and everything smells like spring. When all of this comes together, I find myself yearning for the night and the bluesy clubs of Savannah (p62), Hilton Head (p116), Charleston (p144) or Myrtle Beach (p178) until another sunrise finds me on the water again.

DEBRA MILLER

Deb Miller grew up in Vancouver, British Columbia and worked at Lonely Planet's offices in Oakland for four years before moving to Atlanta, where she now writes about the 'new South' experience as a contributing editor to *Atlanta Magazine*. An avid roadtripper, she's weaved her way through the backroads of the South, watching cotton explode like popcorn, eating barbecue and marveling at Southerners' ability for generous, humorous and lively conversation. Deb writes for several magazines and has contributed to seven books for Lonely Planet, including the USA guide, for which she covered the entire southeastern United States.

My Lowcountry
It's on the periphery of day, when the Lowcountry kicks off her shoes, that I swoon, love-drunk on her salty, sultry air – when she steps out of her laced-up boots and sticks her toes in the pluff mud at dusk, or when she watches the sunrise barefoot on the sandy beach. I love to sit on a bench in Beaufort and watch the tide's ebb and flow dramatically change the world, to spend sunset sipping wine while fishing boats unload their catch at Mount Pleasant's Shem Creek (p172), to slurp early-morning coffee on the white sand in Myrtle Beach (p178), to play tennis and dip in the ocean at Kiawah Island (p173). Every time I tour Savannah (p62) and Charleston (p144), I get transported to a different time in history; these two charming cities seem to encapsulate the entire country's complexity, personality, strife and joy. My Lowcountry is magical and wonderful; she is like a pair of flip-flops that just get better every time you put 'em on.

CONTRIBUTING AUTHOR:

David Goldberg, MD wrote the Health chapter (p209). Dr Goldberg completed his training in internal medicine and infectious diseases at Columbia–Presbyterian Medical Center in New York City, where he has also served as voluntary faculty. At present, he is an infectious-diseases specialist in Scarsdale, New York and the editor-in-chief of the website MDTravelHealth.com.

Snapshot

The sultry air and sandy beaches of the Lowcountry have inspired poets, artists and naturalists ever since the region was first settled. But in recent years, the land's allure has also brought golf fanatics, vacationing lovers and beach-seeking families. As a result, the fragile coastline has been overdeveloped, and what was once a wild, quiet ecosystem today quivers on the brink of destruction.

But there is hope. Although some areas seem too far gone, others – like the wild and pristine ACE Basin, the Cape Romain National Wildlife Refuge and the Okefenokee Swamp – are gradually being protected, and environmentalists are hard at work trying to reverse or at least stem the ecological damage.

Still, the battle between preservation and 'progression' wages on. Pretty, windswept Jekyll Island was purchased by the state of Georgia in 1947 and was protected by a charter allowing only 35 percent of the land to be opened to residents and businesses. While the 99-year lease doesn't expire for almost half a century, state lawmakers have murmured interest in reviewing the charter, potentially opening Jekyll up to further development.

Politics and patriotism play big roles in the South, and it's no different in the Lowcountry. Though the majority of voters in both Georgia and South Carolina are right-leaning conservatives, Democratic leaders have succeeded at the state level – until 2002, when voters in both states replaced their Democratic governors with Republicans Mark Sanford (SC) and Sonny Perdue (GA).

A decidedly hot political potato is the controversy over the Confederate flag. Considered by many to be emblematic of slavery and social inequality, the old flag also tugs at the heartstrings of conservative Southerners, who say its stars and bars represent the pride of the Old South. In 2000, pressure from groups like the National Association for the Advancement of Colored People (NAACP) forced the South Carolina government to remove a Confederate flag that had flown over the statehouse since 1962. In Georgia, debates over the flag continue to fly high: In 2001 the state flag, which closely resembled the Confederate flag, was replaced by a new one – pleasing some Georgians but displeasing others. In the 2002 gubernatorial election, part of Sonny Perdue's winning platform was to let voters choose whether to bring the old flag back – and some politicos believe this gave him the edge.

Like many symbols in the south, the flag is yet another metaphor for the struggle for equal representation. Race relations in the Lowcountry continue to be an issue, as the disparity between poor blacks and affluent whites often seems like a chasm too great to overcome. Although social change is slow in these parts, social awareness is on the upswing. Preservation of the Gullah culture, for example, is viewed by many as a cultural imperative.

It's likely that your only concern about crime in the Lowcountry will be whether you paid too much for fresh shrimp. Still, it's worth noting that Savannah has a high murder rate (among locals; tourists are generally not targets). But things are changing. In November 2003, the city elected Mayor Otis Johnson, who won based in part on his promises to find new methods to deal with crime and poverty.

History

Native Americans, Spaniards, the French, the British, American revolutionaries, Confederates, Yankees and West Africans have put their thumb prints on this land for all eternity. In your travels around the Lowcountry, you will quickly discover how all these various cultures have seen this land of sea islands, rivers and marshes as a prize of great value. And you will learn how deeply today's citizens cherish the relics, history and myths surrounding the cultures that have struggled against each other here.

For something offbeat, *South Carolina: The WPA Guide to the Palmetto State*, written in 1941 under the government-funded writers' program, is an entertaining read for history and colorful tales of the Lowcountry.

NATIVE AMERICAN STRUGGLES

Whether exploring the Indian shell middens on Hilton Head, traveling the backroads or perusing a map of the region, a traveler may well sense the presence of the Native Americans, particularly because of place-names like the Ogeechee River, Okefenokee National Wildlife Refuge or Kiawah Island. These names are almost all that remains of the indigenous culture that once flourished in the Lowcountry. Once, more than 20 separate clans (such as the Yemassee, Ashepoo, Kiawah and Edisto) lived here.

Together they formed a confederation called the Cusabo. Some, like the Yamacraw chief Tomochichi (at Savannah), were friendly and helpful to the first European colonists, but others lost patience with their persistent incursion into traditional hunting and fishing lands. Colonial abuses led to an Indian retaliation known as the Yemassee War (1715). For two years, 15 clans under the leadership of the Yemassee massacred British traders and colonists, driving some (in Beaufort) back to their ships and threatening to overrun the colonial seat at Charles Town.

Eventually the Yemassee alliance fell apart, and by 1750, almost all of the Native Americans fled west from the Lowcountry to seek protection under the powerful Cherokee. In 1827 they formalized their own sovereignty, as the Cherokee Nation, by adopting a constitution based on the US model. But in 1829, the state of Georgia passed legislation annexing a large portion of Cherokee territory and declaring Cherokee law null and void. In 1838, the US Army, along with local militias, made 18,000 Cherokee and the displaced coastal tribes move west to reservations in Oklahoma with little more than the clothes on their backs. More than 4000 Indians died on this forced migration, which is now remembered as the Trail of Tears.

DID YOU KNOW?

When asked by a newspaper reporter to describe the 1838 forced migration of Native Americans, a Chahta tribesman said it was nothing less than a trail of tears. The name has stuck ever since.

SPANISH & FRENCH FIASCOS

The Indians' first encounter with Europeans probably took place in 1521, when the Spanish expedition of Francisco Cordillo poked around the Carolina coast. Five years later, a Spanish judge named Lucas Vásques de Ayllón attempted to found a colony at the mouth of the Cape Fear River and then on Winyah Bay in South Carolina, but disease, poor weather and starvation ended the venture a year later.

Gaining a foothold proved a difficult undertaking. In 1540, Spanish explorer Hernando de Soto landed with an army of 900 soldiers and hundreds of horses in the New World but immediately set off in search of gold. His route led from Georgia through South Carolina to the mountains of western North Carolina and on to the Mississippi River, where he turned south to the Gulf of Mexico. In 1563 a group of French

Huguenots set up camp at Port Royal Sound in South Carolina, but they pulled out after their supplies were destroyed by fire. A few years later a Spanish contingent arrived from Florida and established Fort San Filipe; they endured for 20 years.

The 2000 film *The Patriot*, starring Mel Gibson, is based loosely on the exploits of 'the Swamp Fox,' Francis Marion. Marion gave his name to the vast forest reserve surrounding the Santee River, north of Charleston.

THE CHARLES TOWN COLONY

The appeal of the Lowcountry has always been its fertile marshland. In 1663 and 1665, England's King Charles II granted land between Virginia and northern Florida to eight proprietors, or royal landowners, for agricultural development. Although the proprietors had the final say in their regions, local governments emerged, and the colony of Carolina was founded in 1670. Soon planters and slaves arrived from Barbados to drain the marshes for plantations of rice and indigo.

As the colony grew, the proprietors founded Charles Town (renamed Charleston after the American Revolution) as their commercial and trading center and appointed a colonial governor. In 1672 the colony consisted of about 200 people and 30 houses; by 1720 Charles Town's population exceeded 600. Today, you can see a recreation of that era at Charles Towne Landing.

THE SAVANNAH EXPERIMENT

The first permanent colonial town in Georgia began in 1733, when a group of English investors led by General James Edward Oglethorpe won a charter for a colony that was meant to act as a buffer against Spanish interests in Florida. Oglethorpe's company had a strict code in the beginning – no slaves, liquor or Catholicism, and even land ownership

PIRATES OF THE ATLANTIC COAST

In the late 17th century, piracy started as your standard smuggling – trying to avoid tariffs levied by the British on goods shipped to America. During Queen Anne's War (1701–13), pirates began to plunder vessels on the high seas, which was fine with the British, as long as targets were French or Spanish. Problem is, they kept it up after the war, and the Atlantic Coast was terrorized with increasingly brazen hit-and-run tactics. The stakes were so high that even some highly respected sailors turned to piracy; the notorious Captain William Kidd was commissioned by New York's colonial governor as a legal privateer in 1689 before he went 'bad.'

However, the very worst scoundrels were Stede Bonnet and Edward Teach (aka Blackbeard), who hid in numerous sounds and bays along the Outer Banks. In the summer of 1718, four ships under Teach's command anchored outside Charleston harbor, took hostages and held them for a ransom of medical supplies. When Bonnet – who was called the 'Gentleman Pirate' because of his background as an educated planter in Barbados – pulled the same stunt, Charleston sounded the alarm. A military search party was dispatched, and Bonnet and his men were captured, tried and summarily hanged. For more about Bonnet's illustrious 'career,' see 'The Gentleman Pirate' in the Charleston chapter (p153).

A giant of a man who braided his long locks for maximum effect, the restless Blackbeard – who for a short period managed to settle down with a wife in Bath, North Carolina – met his grisly end a few months later. On November 21, 1718, two Royal Navy ships under the command of Lieutenant Robert Maynard slipped into the Ocracoke Inlet and staged a dawn raid on Blackbeard's sloop. After a fierce battle, Blackbeard and half of his crew were slain, and the pirate's head was stuck on the bow of Maynard's ship for the voyage back to Virginia.

With the demise of Bonnet and Blackbeard, the heyday of piracy was finished, but vestiges of the era survived. Even in the 20th century, regular navy crews still held rights to prizes for captured enemy ships; the US abolished the practice only in 1904, after Admiral Dewey was denied prize money for ships he'd captured in Manila Bay.

was forbidden. The colonists located their town on a high bluff 18 miles upriver from the Atlantic Ocean. Architect William Bull laid out a gridlike pattern of streets, houses and public buildings; in the middle of each ward was an open square. Savannah grew to 24 squares, 21 of which you can still see today. This careful urban design is widely studied and admired for making a livable, beautiful, expandable city.

Early stabs at agriculture on the perimeter of the settlement yielded modest results, but plantings of rice, cotton and indigo were more successful after the ban on slavery was lifted in 1750. Soon plantations dotted the coastal plain south to the Florida border and north to Beaufort and Charleston. And for a time, the Lowcountry, with Charleston as its capital, was considered to be the literary and cultural center of the American colonies, spawning writers like William Gilmore Simms.

REVOLUTIONARY STRIFE

In the 1760s the British placed new duties in the colonies – on goods such as sugar, coffee, paper and tea. In the early stages, groups in the Southeast were divided over how to react to the British 'tyranny.' Many of the settlers were of Anglo-Saxon origin – British, but also Irish, German and Swiss – and while most resented the heavy taxes being imposed, blood ties to Anglo-Saxon roots inhibited support for a war.

But growing revolutionary fervor, climaxing in the Boston Tea Party of 1773, tipped the scale, and in 1776 delegates from South Carolina and Georgia were among the signers of the Declaration of Independence. The British attacked Charleston in the early days of the war but were repulsed and did not return for four years. Under the command of Lord Cornwallis, British forces launched a major offensive in 1780, gaining virtual control over Georgia. Cornwallis assembled his troops in Savannah and began to zigzag north, taking Beaufort and then Charleston.

Backwoods folk turned squarely against the British, organizing effective, guerilla-style militias. Nipping at the heels of the British (particularly to the north of Charleston) were partisan heroes, including Francis 'Swamp Fox' Marion. By 1781 the badgered and surrounded British surrendered in Virginia.

'KING COTTON'

Long after the cities of the North plunged into the Industrial Revolution, coastal Georgia and South Carolina maintained their stately agricultural way of life. Large-scale plantations dominated the economy and politics of the Lowcountry. Rice and indigo were grown in the marshes, but the biggest money-winner was cotton. So predominant was the white, fluffy product that it was matter-of-factly referred to as 'King Cotton.' The climate and soil, enriched by the alluvial sediments in the coastal plains, were ideally suited for growing a highly prized, long-strand variety known as 'sea island cotton,' and in the 18th and 19th centuries, textile factories in Europe acquired a habit for it. Stretching across hundreds of acres of dark fertile soil, massive cotton farms like the still-surviving Boone Plantation were the domain of a privileged class of planters with immense political clout.

Toward the end of the 18th century, cotton profits began to lag because of cheap cotton coming out of Egypt and elsewhere, and its production might have waned if not for the cotton gin, which was invented by Eli Whitney in 1793. Gins mechanized the task of separating seeds and hulls from cotton fibers, thus making production much more efficient. Soon gins were installed on plantations all along the coast. Even with the new technology, cotton was labor intensive and not particularly profitable if those who labored over it were paid a fair wage. But, of course, the planters didn't have that problem.

SLAVERY

Planters exhibited an impressive faculty for self-deception and shared a common perception that their slaves were merely a docile lot, content to remain in servitude for their entire lives. The unhappy reality was that, in addition to being denied the most basic human liberties, slaves were not allowed to maintain their African cultural and religious practices. Many were prohibited from learning to read. Some masters sexually exploited female slaves, and all too often, slaves experienced separations from family members.

South Carolina in particular was the scene of untold barbarity, as Charleston was the main port of entry for thousands of slaves, who were sold at the slave market and put to work almost as soon as they climbed from the holds of incoming ships. While some slaves rose in stature by learning trades or becoming house servants, the great majority were field workers whose legal status was hardly greater than that of domestic animals. After removing a 1733 ban on slavery in 1750, Georgia quickly caught up and surpassed South Carolina in terms of numbers of slaves.

As a consequence of cheap slave labor, many planters enjoyed a genteel lifestyle. The wealthiest planters inhabited impressive classical mansions such as Middleton Place, Magnolia Plantation & Gardens, and Drayton Hall, with household servants attending to domestic needs, including cooking, craftwork, child-raising and even wet-nursing. In this rarified atmosphere, an elitist code of ethics flourished, upholding values like chivalry and honor that by that time might well have seemed old-fashioned to most Northerners.

THE CIVIL WAR BEGINS

By the mid-19th century, slavery was illegal in half of the states that then formed the US. The prevailing argument was for preserving the balance of power as the nation grew – for each new free state admitted to the rapidly expanding Union, Southern lawmakers wanted a new slave state admitted. Meanwhile South Carolina and its elder statesman John C Calhoun were doing everything possible to preserve the 'peculiar institution' of slavery.

The conflict over slavery came to a head in the presidential election of 1860. Republican candidate Abraham Lincoln made public his feelings that slavery was morally wrong. Within a month of Lincoln's victory in the presidential election, South Carolina statesmen drew up the Ordinance of Secession, which was unanimously adopted on December 20, 1860. Six other Southern states, including Georgia, seceded from the Union before Lincoln took office in January 1861. Provoked by Lincoln's

---

THE TRUTH ABOUT TARA

The film adaptation of *Gone With the Wind*, about the Civil War in Georgia and South Carolina, turned a bright spotlight on the Lowcountry, with scenes supposedly set in Charleston and with the figure of dashing Rhett Butler (Clark Gable), the Charlestonian ship captain and blockade runner. But eat your heart out. You won't find the set for Tara plantation or any other part of the famous film in Lowcountry. Producer David O Selznick recreated it all in Hollywood.

decision to resupply troops at Fort Sumpter in Charleston Harbor, the South Carolina militia began shelling Sumpter with cannons. These were the first shots of what would prove the bloodiest war in US history.

Some of the islands and coastal plains of Georgia and South Carolina fell under Federal control following the invasion at Port Royal Sound

THE 'GREAT UNPLEASANTNESS'

When people from elsewhere come to the South, they often wonder why so much attention is given to the Civil War, or as Southerners say, 'the War Between the States.' Visitors find it puzzling that many Southerners are still concerned with events that happened nearly 150 years ago.

But once you've spent some time here, you'll realize that the 'Great Unpleasantness' did much to define the culture, ideologies, opinions and ideas that continue to shape the South and, indeed, the rest of the country.

In essence, the South was a conquered nation, and the accompanying mindset drove – and still drives – a deep wedge between Southerners and Yankees (a term broadly used for anyone living north of the Mason–Dixon Line).

South Carolina and Georgia were the first states of the 'Old South' – a term referring to the mostly English colonists who founded towns like Charleston and Savannah. Isolated from both Britain and the rest of the country, they set to work building slave-labored plantations and getting rich off the bounty of rice and cotton.

When Lincoln came along spouting ideas about freeing the slaves, South Carolina and Georgia were quick to secede from the Union. Their leaders believed a faraway authority, especially one whose ideologies differed so greatly from their own, should not make local decisions. Landowners banded together, and soon the 11 states of the Confederacy became a force to be reckoned with.

The Civil War lasted for four years (1861–65). It was a bloody, face-to-face conflict, the outcome of which would change the course of history. After the war, much of South Carolina and Georgia were left in smoldering ruins.

When you see buildings and plantations that survived the war, you get a strong sense of the glory days of the past. But 'glory' is a relative term. When people refer to the 'Old South,' or the time prior to the Civil War, it conjures up many emotions. To black people, the term represents a time of enslavement, oppression and injustice. To fourth- and fifth-generation whites, whose ancestors owned those homes and plantations, the concept means something else entirely – often it's an indescribable mixture of pride and shame.

Many slaves had stayed on plantations during the war. After the Civil War abolished slavery, a great uncertainty hovered above both blacks and whites. What next? Plantations couldn't survive without slave labor, but the owners couldn't afford the wages. The newly emancipated slaves had no money; most had nowhere to go, nor any idea of what to do next.

A system known as sharecropping replaced slavery, but not by much. White landowners divided up their land and rented acreage to black families. The families were given seed, tools and shelter up front, with the idea that income from future crops would repay the debt. But landowners kept a huge cut when the crops were sold, leaving the blacks so indebted that they couldn't leave, even though they were 'free' to do so.

During the next hundred years, between the Civil War and the Civil Rights movement, there was a dramatic cultural shift. While racial tolerance bloomed in some areas, hatred exploded in others. Many white Southerners resented the blacks, and vice versa. What was happening in this part of the South was an amplification of what was taking place across the country.

Today, many white Southerners will say that race isn't as much of a hot-button issue anymore. Many black people agree. Other people, who see the glaring economic disparity between whites and blacks, think differently. Both the outcome of the Civil War and issues of race remain volatile topics that people in these parts don't like to discuss. Over the last century, the roiling emotions and fevered racism have mellowed to a somewhat steady simmer, like a pot of water that never really boils or cools.

and Hilton Head in late 1861. Meanwhile the port cities of Charleston and Savannah teetered on the edge of Confederate control as Union warships blockaded the harbors, attempting to choke off commerce and resupply.

SHERMAN'S MARCH

The Lowcountry was spared from serving as a major battleground until May 1864. Then Union general Ulysses S Grant called on William Tecumseh Sherman to 'create havoc and destruction of all resources that would be beneficial to the enemy.' Sherman carved a swath of devastation 60 miles wide and 250 miles long through eastern and central Georgia on his infamous 'March to the Sea.' After burning Atlanta, Sherman reached Savannah, where he set up headquarters, offering the city intact as a Christmas present to Abraham Lincoln and sparing the wealth of historic architecture that is now one of the largest historic districts in the country.

Soon Union forces moved up the coast, and burned Charleston. Four months later, on April 7, 1865, the South surrendered.

DID YOU KNOW?

In the early 1960s, Savannah drew on its liberal traditions and became perhaps the first fully integrated city in the South.

RECONSTRUCTION & RACIAL STRIFE

At the end of the war, the Lowcountry lay in ruins. Huge tracts of soil had been laid to waste by advancing and retreating armies. Homes had been looted and torched, fields had been plundered and left fallow, and families had been decimated. Southern blacks – now free – faced an uncertain future.

Emancipation proved not so easy to sort through. Blacks amounted to 40% of the South's population, but in states such as South Carolina, they constituted a majority. In 1867, Congress passed the Reconstruction Acts, which granted blacks the right to vote and divided the South into military districts. Yet little changed for many slaves, who continued to work the plantations as they had before the war – only now as poorly paid laborers. A sharecropper system gradually developed, in which field hands relied on the landowners for supplies and were constantly in debt.

With emancipation, deep-seated hatred rose to the surface. Emancipation was followed by white resistance to black suffrage. Jim crow restrictions, which maintained racial segregation of transportation modes, waiting rooms, hotels, restaurants and theaters, were enforced.

THE DREADED KLAN

During Reconstruction some whites acted outside the law in order to intimidate blacks and reinforce discriminatory standards. Formed in Tennessee after the war, the Ku Klux Klan (KKK) quickly spread to South Carolina and Georgia with the aim of opposing the perceived excesses of Reconstruction. It officially disbanded in 1870, when racist overtones led to a federal crackdown. But it returned in 1915 after the release of the film Birth of a Nation, based on Thomas Dixon's novel The Clansman. By this time, the KKK's unambiguous mission was to keep blacks down. (It also targeted Jews, Catholics and foreigners.)

The Klan reached peak membership in the 1920s. Riding horseback at night and wearing hoods to obscure their identities (many were prominent citizens), Klansmen harassed targeted individuals and groups with impunity. Rampant violence led to the Klan's losing public favor, and membership fell drastically in the 1930s. But the KKK would rear its ugly head again during the Civil Rights movement.

DIFFERENT WORLDS

Immigration to the New World increased sharply in the early 18th century, and settlers of older colonies turned their eyes to the Southeast for opportunities. Anglo-Saxon groups, mainly Scotch-Irish and Germans, loaded up their wagons and headed for the lush valleys of the Appalachians and the Piedmont. Most were Protestant minorities – Moravians, Presbyterians and Quakers – and shared few interests with the rich plantation owners of the east. This led to clear political and socioeconomic divisions between the folks of the Backcountry and Lowcountry (in South Carolina, the common terms are Upcountry and Lowcountry). The split persists to a certain extent today, and depending on where you are, making cracks about hillbillies or city slickers is a time-honored pastime.

Separate public institutions were created, including schools and hospitals, and 'white' and 'colored' signs began to appear over doorways and drinking fountains throughout the region.

A BLESSED RECESSION?

Most of the Lowcountry languished for decades after the Civil War. The collapse of cotton prices in the late 19th century sent Savannah into a severe economic decline. In Charleston prominent families were penniless, and their grand homes were auctioned off to repay war debts or became the boarding-house ancestors of today's B&Bs. Planters abandoned most of their sea-island plantations, leaving the blacks there to survive by subsistence farming and fishing while nurturing their long-repressed West African ways and the Creole language they had developed, known as Gullah.

In the long run, this prolonged economic recession may have been a good thing. Had the Lowcountry prospered, the elegant streets and buildings of Savannah and Charleston that we see today may well have been demolished in the name of development, and Gullah culture would have probably disappeared, a victim of encroaching Northern capitalism.

CIVIL RIGHTS

For most Americans, the Civil Rights movement began on May 17, 1954, when the US Supreme Court handed down its decision in the Brown vs Board of Education case outlawing segregation in public schools. However, some Southern states did not accept this ruling, and the next 11 years saw demonstrations, protests and civil action aimed at desegregation and increased black political representation. Concerned that new businesses would be scared off by racial violence, South Carolina managed a moderately smooth desegregation in the 1960s.

President Lyndon B Johnson signed into law the Voting Rights Act of 1965, despite vigorous opposition from conservative statesmen such as Strom Thurmond, from South Carolina. Enforcing the act has led to sweeping changes in the American political process; by 1992, there were more than 5000 African American elected officials in the formerly segregated states, compared to only 300 in the entire nation in 1965.

HISTORIC PRESERVATION & BOOM

During the 1920s, Charlestonians took a look around their little city and realized that what most folks considered to be a tangle of dilapidated building stock was actually a prize collection of relics from the antebellum

South. The year 1931 saw citizens and government come together to pass America's first historic-zoning legislation, and preservation of the Battery began. After the end of WWII, the preservation movement blossomed, and Charleston evolved into the magnificent living-history attraction it is today.

Savannah followed suit in 1955. When the beautiful Davenport House nearly became a parking lot, preservationists launched a campaign that went on to protect and restore the historic downtown. The 2½-sq-mile historic district now has over 1000 restored Federal and Regency buildings.

Meanwhile a growing number of affluent Americans, golfers and real estate developers discovered the wild beauty, serenity and mild weather of the South Carolina and Georgia sea islands. The first major resort development came in 1961, when the exclusive Sea Pines Plantation opened on Hilton Head with three golf courses. Since then 10 others have followed on the island, with at least a dozen other resort plantations and hundreds of golf courses sprouting up all over the Lowcountry, from Jekyll Island to North Myrtle Beach.

With the emergence of the Lowcountry as a major vacation destination, the region's social profile has altered dramatically. Coastal Georgia and South Carolina have always experienced periodic immigration, but nowadays well-educated people from all over the world are moving to the region to take up skilled occupations. 'New Southerners' could as easily be of Asian or Hispanic descent as of European or African descent. California fusion cuisine has become as popular as boiled shrimp and corn. But some good things never change, and old-fashioned Southern hospitality still reigns supreme in the Lowcountry.

In 1994, John Berendt's hugely successful murder mystery-travelogue, *Midnight in the Garden of Good & Evil* (and the subsequent film, directed by Clint Eastwood) portrayed Savannah as a remnant of the Old South, where tradition battles with debauchery. The book firmly secured the city's celebrity status.

The Culture

From the outset of European colonialism, the coast of Georgia and South Carolina has been a place where people have tuned their activities more to the turning of the tides and the changing of the seasons than to the ticking of a clock. Most of the blacks and the whites who settled and grew up here during the last three centuries were farmers and fishers, and those traditional occupations still bind them together and lay claim to a lot of Lowcountry hearts. These traditions infuse local ritual and celebrations, like the blessing of the shrimp fleet in Brunswick, Georgia and the Lowcountry Oyster Festival in Charleston.

REGIONAL IDENTITY

The British planters who came to the Lowcountry to grow rice and sea-island cotton brought with them an immense love of European cavalier values that placed a high premium on the code of chivalry and its attachment to hospitality, cultural traditions, dignity, honor and patriotism.

Margaret Mitchell's blockbuster novel *Gone With the Wind* depicts these cavalier values during the antebellum days of the Lowcountry. Pat Conroy's *The Prince of Tides* and *The Great Santini* show how those values persist in contemporary families. All these works portray a haunting sense of tragedy and a gothic fascination with the macabre and bizarre – all of which are a part of Lowcountry culture as well.

Because of slavery, South Carolina had more blacks than whites for two centuries, and the slaves and their descendants have infused the Lowcountry with their infatuation with the world of spirits (generally called 'haints'), soulful music and an abundant readiness to laugh in the face of life's misfortunes. Films like *Daughters of the Dust,* about the African American's Gullah culture, and novels like Gloria Naylor's *Mama Day* bear witness to these qualities and are also modern examples of a love and talent for storytelling, both oral and in written form.

To journey beyond the grave with the spirits of Lowcountry, check out *Ghosts of the Carolinas,* by Nancy Roberts.

Today, the Lowcountry still husbands its traditions, and historic preservation is an abiding passion with both longtime residents and newcomers. Still, airports, interstate highways and the discovery of the Lowcountry by tens of millions of travelers has brought waves of recent immigrants to the area. While Charleston, Beaufort and some of the surrounding islands remain bastions of families who trace their roots back seven generations in the same house, Hilton Head, Myrtle Beach and Savannah now seem almost as cosmopolitan as Martha's Vineyard, Miami Beach or San Francisco.

LIFESTYLE

Southern hospitality is legendary in the Lowcountry: most folks are friendly, accessible, hospitable and courteous, and would rather invite you in for lemonade than see you spend one more instant out on that hot sidewalk. However, a few longtime residents can be a bit xenophobic, regarding outsiders as possible 'Yankee invaders.'

Female travelers from less chivalrous parts of the world may be somewhat surprised (or miffed) to find that many local men continue to uphold traditional manners, like holding doors open for women. Male travelers, on the other hand, may risk offending local women by not holding doors open – *c'est la vie.*

Both men and women shake hands when greeting each other, while family and friends embrace and kiss with varying degrees of visible affection. Straight men don't usually hug or kiss each other, and Gallic-style cheek-pecking may be considered pretentious among women. Unless you're introduced to someone as a Mr, Ms, Miss, or Mrs, it's usually fine to use first names.

Many folks in the Lowcountry tend to use formal rules of address ('no sir,' 'yes ma'am'), but they don't necessarily expect outsiders to be so polite. However, such small courtesies will certainly be noticed and appreciated; being extraordinarily polite and not coming on too strong will ease social interaction.

Dos & Don'ts

Be aware that being clean and tidy is important, and visitors who appear unkempt (wearing cut-offs, anything too revealing or – heaven forbid – being unshowered) will draw negative attention. People tend to dress a little more formally when attending the theater or a concert; you may find you're the only one in jeans at *The Nutcracker*. Conversely, a suit and tie will be out of place in most nightclubs. Ask first if you're not sure.

Locals may get edgy discussing racial dynamics. Be cautious about initiating such a discussion until you've established a good rapport with someone.

Further points to consider are that American national pride is particularly strong in the Lowcountry, which is good to be aware of when discussing political and social issues. Critical comments, especially from a non-Southerner, might be construed as a slight to national honor and may provoke a very negative reaction. Other iffy subjects include gun control, religion and the politics revolving around a woman's right to an abortion.

POPULATION

Since the Lowcountry is a subregion spanning two states (Georgia and South Carolina), an accurate population count is at best an esimate. 'About a million folks, more or less' is the answer a number of local authorities give. This number can be broken down into distinct demographic groups, but it should be noted that there has also been much cultural and racial intermixing over the past 200 years, and racial categories and definitions are often not as sharp as they appear, though white people are now the majority along the Georgia and South Carolina coasts.

The majority of black people in the Lowcountry today are descended from the African slaves who were brought here to work on plantations. In 1900, 35 years after the Civil War, more than 90% of African Americans in the US lived in formerly Confederate states.

Beginning around WWI and continuing into the 1950s, millions of African Americans migrated north to escape economic hardship and entrenched racism. Significantly, African Americans are now relocating back to Lowcountry. Today, Georgia and South Carolina still have a significant proportion of African Americans: 30% in South Carolina and 29% in Georgia; and those percentages hold true for the Lowcountry.

In recent years immigration has affected the makeup of the Low-country population. Hilton Head and Myrtle Beach, which are populated largely by whites, have attracted tens of thousands of snowbirds and resort workers from other parts of the country, as well as from overseas.

Latinos now account for about 4% of the region's population and have developed significant communities in resort areas like Hilton Head. Asian Americans are a growing force in Savannah and Charleston. As is true almost everywhere in the US, the Lowcountry was home to Native Americans. However, disease, war and forcible removal wiped out many of the local Native American tribes in the 18th and 19th centuries, and the percentage of people of Native American heritage now living in the area is less than 1%.

EDUCATION

Schools throughout the Lowcountry became a hotbed of civil rights activity after the Supreme Court outlawed segregation in its Brown vs Board of Education ruling in 1954. Many white politicians fought desegregation in the following decade.

White resistance to integration dragged on until the early 1970s, when federal agents, the press and local activists pushed for compliance with the court directive. By the early 1980s, racial issues had taken a back seat to the quest for quality at all levels of education.

Secondary education in coastal Georgia and South Carolina continues to be marked by poor funding and a lack of resources, but state programs and initiatives have started to make up for lost ground. South Carolina, the weakest link in the region on educational matters, has developed a network of regional technical schools that work with businesses to retrain former mill workers in more skilled industries.

In educational achievement rankings, Georgia and South Carolina have improved in recent years and now fall in the upper lower half (ie, below national averages) for per capita government expenditures on education and for percentages of the population earning a bachelor's degree. The vast majority of pupils complete high school, but scores on college-entrance exams such as the SAT remain low, showing that much remains to be done.

Distinguished Lowcountry universities include the Citadel military college, in Charleston, and the Savannah College of Art and Design, which has played an important role in the historic preservation of the city's buildings. Also in Savannah you will find Armstrong Atlantic State University and the historically black Savannah State University. The University of South Carolina has a number of branches in the Lowcountry.

RELIGION

Religious life plays a large role in the culture of the Lowcountry, although its influence has waned somewhat in the last 50 years. Baptists predominate in a region that has been called part of the 'Bible Belt,' where folks take a serious and fundamental approach to their Protestant religion.

In the past, coastal Georgia and South Carolina have been nearly as divided over religion as over race. Protestants did not tend to associate with Catholics or Jews, and intermarriage between faiths, even among different Protestant branches, was scandalous. The Ku Klux Klan persecuted Catholics and Jews along with blacks. Today it's still common for whites and blacks to attend separate churches.

Local residents are very up front about their religious beliefs, and you might be asked about yours. A question like, 'Do you accept Jesus Christ into your life?' may be merely a conversation starter, not an evangelical query.

DID YOU KNOW?

The University of South Carolina campus in Beaufort starred as the Gump Medical Center in *Forrest Gump* and as a nameless college campus in *Something to Talk About*.

During the 1990s mainstream America became better acquainted with Gullah culture and language through the imaginative children's TV show *Gullah Gullah Island* and from the moving feature film *Daughters of the Dust*.

Protestantism
Fire-and-brimstone sermons, creekside baptisms, vacation Bible school and strict blue laws are all part of a standard Bible Belt experience today.

GULLAH CULTURE
Many parts of the US resemble the European cities from which the founding settlers emigrated. Only in the sea islands along the Georgia and South Carolina coast does the US resemble parts of West Africa.

From the region known as the Rice Coast (Sierre Leone, Senegal, Gambia and Angola), African slaves were transported across the Atlantic Ocean to a landscape that was remarkably similar – swampy coastlines, tropical vegetation and hot humid summers. The African slaves, who were in the majority on the plantations, had little contact with Europeans and were able to retain many of their homeland traditions.

After the fall of the planter aristocracy (in the wake of the Civil War), the freed slaves remained on the islands in relative isolation until the mid-20th century. Being cut off from the mainland ensured that African traditions were passed on to the descendants of the original slaves.

Gullahs & Geechees
The result of the black sea islander's isolation was Gullah, which describes both a language (see the next page) and a culture that persists today on Sapelo Island, Georgia and on Johns, James, Wadmalaw, Edisto, Hilton Head, St Helena and Daufuskie Islands in South Carolina, as well as in mainland communities in Georgetown, Charleston and Beaufort, South Carolina and Darien, Georgia.

In Georgia people from the Gullah culture are known locally as 'Geechee' (a corruption of the name of the local Ogeechee River). Once a pejorative term, 'Geechee' is now used with pride by Georgia sea islanders to describe their heritage. Black sea islanders in South Carolina call themselves 'Gullah.'

Sweetgrass Basketry
Enduring traditions include the making of sweetgrass baskets, which has an identical twin in Sierra Leone handicrafts. Sweetgrass basketry involves three types of materials: the marsh grass called sweetgrass, palmetto fronds and longleaf pine needles.

Sweetgrass makes up the bulk of the basket, with strips of the palmetto fronds and pine needles woven into the coiled grass. This tradition is typically passed from mother to daughter, and basket prices are based on the number of hours invested. The Smithsonian Institution, in Washington, DC, displays baskets made by the Forman family of Charleston. For more information on this craft, see 'The Basket Ladies' (p169).

Gullah Stories
Gullah storytellers often related the exploits of Buh Rabbit, more famously known as Brer Rabbit from the Uncle Remus books. This small yet cunning rabbit is a common character in the trickster tales of West Africa. He outwits bigger and stronger animals and is constantly in danger of retaliation.

The following excerpt of a slave tale comes from *Folk-Lore of the Sea Islands, South Carolina*, by Elsie Clews Parsons (Metro Books, 1969).

> Oncet Buh Rabbit an' Buh Wolf buy a cow togeder. Den Buh Rabbit kill de cow, an' Buh Wolf didn' know it. Buh Rabbit take de cow tail an' stick un down in de dirt an' run, gone ter call de wolf. An' tell de wolf 'Le' um pull on de cow tail, see ef he could get 'e cow up!' Den, when dey pull, de cow tail come off. Said, 'Cow gone down in de groun'.' After Buh Wolf gone, Buh Rabbit gone to get de meat to kyarry home for his fader.

The fundamentalist Baptists who are a strong force in this region resulted from a split in antebellum times known as the Great Revival. During the 1840s, debates occurred over the interpretation of religious doctrine

MELODIES OF LOWCOUNTRY SPEECH

In the Lowcountry, dialects vary widely in pronunciation, pace, delivery and, often, vocabulary. They vary not only by geography – accents on the Georgia coast can be markedly different from those you hear in Myrtle Beach – but also by race and social class.

Nevertheless, there is a rich, slow resonance to the speech of all Lowcountry natives that makes your ears perk up. You will find your body drawn closer to these voices, the very melodies of which seem to promise you the imminent disclosure of a strange secret...or the telling of a tale of romance, betrayal, murder and hidden staircases. Of special interest are the linguistic nuances of Lowcountry African Americans.

Most African Americans descend from two linguistic families: the Sudanic, of the West African coast; and the Bantu, in East and Central Africa. Although there are many different languages within these two groups, there remains a structural similarity. Today some of these syntactical features have been retained in the dialect called Black English (also known as Ebonics and African American Vernacular English, or AAVE).

Black English emerged in the 17th century in Africa as a common trading language with English ships, and it was transported to North America via Jamaica. The common colonial policy of dispersing homogeneous groups caused Africans to rely on this lingua franca to communicate with each other.

Primary characteristics include replacing the phoneme 'th' with the 'd' sound ('this' becomes 'dis') and the absence of the verb 'to be' when describing a condition. For example, 'He is black' in Standard English becomes 'He black' in Black English. There is also no obligatory marker for the plural (one cent, two cent) nor for the possessive ('teacher's book' collapses to 'teacher-book').

The Gullah Language

The most traditional and African-sounding speech used among African Americas today is Gullah, which occurs on the coastal islands of the Lowcountry. Gullah is a creole of Elizabethan English and West African languages (mainly Bantu and Wolof) and is spoken by about 500,000 people. It is the only English-derived creolized language used in the United States.

Influenced by various creoles that are spoken by West Indians, and by English dialects used by plantation overseers in the American colonies, Gullah sounds like English, but has the grammar and melodies of the West African coast. Gullah vocabulary is largely English, but with enough African words to stump a nonspeaker. Linguists recognize Gullah as a distinct language rather than a dialect.

Some Gullah words have snuck into the Southern lexicon; words such as 'cooter' (turtle), 'benne' (sesame), 'bubba' (brother) and 'bad mouth' (to talk badly about someone). To get started, here are a few more Gullah words to whet your interest. For further study, look for the pamphlet 'Gullah for You!' by Virginia Mixson Geraty.

Gullah word	Definition	English usage
bidibidi	small bird or chicken	biddy
buckra	white man	— —
guba	peanut	goober
gumbo	okra	gumbo
jiga	insect	chigger
jogal	to rise, to cause to rise	joggling board
jug (juk)	disorderly	juke box
nana	grandmother	nana

concerning slavery, resulting in the establishment of the pro-slavery Southern Baptist Convention in 1845. Baptists and Methodists combined make up about half of the churchgoing population of the Lowcountry.

African American Christianity
During slavery, all expressions of African religious traditions were repressed, and they had to be carried out in secrecy. Slaves were allowed (many were obligated) to attend Sunday services at their slave-owner's church; some early black communities even founded their own churches during slavery. After emancipation, missionaries from Northern churches successfully set up congregations in black communities; the African Methodist Episcopal (AME) church helped found many churches and is now prolific in the Lowcountry.

The church has always been a powerful unifying force in African American communities. Early civil rights leaders, such as Dr Martin Luther King Jr, came from the preacher's ranks. Black churches have been the target of numerous racially motivated attacks, both historically (most well remembered from the Civil Rights era) and in recent years, such as in the rash of arson across the South in 1995, which prompted a federal investigation.

Roman Catholicism
Catholicism has left a relatively small imprint on the Lowcountry. But the Catholic Church played a leading cultural role in the 1960s, when desegregation in Catholic schools moved faster than in the public sector. In the last few decades, the influx of Spanish-speaking immigrants and a relocation of northern Catholics into coastal Georgia and South Carolina has increased the religion's influence.

Judaism
While Judaism is not often associated with the Lowcountry, a significant Jewish community took up early residence here, with Savannah having the oldest Reformed temple in America. Intolerance of Jews in the region occurred at certain times and in certain places; the worst anti-Semitic incident was the 1915 lynching of Leo Frank in Georgia, for the alleged murder of a teenage girl. Over the centuries, however, the relative tolerance among the gentiles allowed Jews of diverse origins and cultural backgrounds to integrate more successfully into the landscape than is commonly supposed.

ARTS
For centuries, the Lowcountry has spawned some of America's most unique artistic creations, particularly in the fields of literature and music.

Literature
The Lowcountry's rich literary offerings are best understood in the context of Southern literature. All influences have their distinct flavors, but all draw on the age-old Lowcountry traditions of oral storytelling – tales told on the porch swing or under the family's live oaks on balmy summer evenings.

THE 19TH CENTURY
Once upon a time in the 1830s in America, when New Englanders were still writing sermons about sinners in the hands of an angry god and New Yorkers had just begun to thrill to the historical romances of

James Fenimore Cooper, Charleston rivaled New York as the literary capital of the new United States. Among the writers to emerge from the cultured and literate Lowcountry society was William Gilmore Simms (1806–70). Even today his novels, like *The Yemassee* (1835), about the Lowcountry Indian wars, and *The Partisan* (1835), about the Revolutionary War hero Francis 'Swamp Fox' Marion, make for entertaining reading. The story in *The Partisan* gave rise to the popular Mel Gibson film *The Patriot.*

Arguably the most famous Southern writer of the 19th century, Edgar Allan Poe (1809–49) made his reputation while a journalist in Northern cities. As a young man, Poe was stationed in the army on Sullivan's Island, off the coast of Charleston, where he set his eerie tale of buried treasure in 'The Gold Bug.' The characters in the latter are all Southern stereotypes.

LOCAL AUTHORS

Oxherding Tales, by sociologist Charles Johnson (1893–1956), is an evocative, entertaining story about a mulatto slave who is educated in the classics and sold to a sex-crazed female plantation owner. He escapes and passes into white society with a slave catcher close at his heels.

Julia Peterkin (1880–1961), from the Murrells Inlet–Pawleys Island area, wrote *Scarlet Sister Mary*, the 1928 Pulitzer Prize–winning novel about a Gullah woman working on a coastal plantation. Peterkin was well qualified: She learned to speak Gullah before English.

Cornelia Walker Bailey, one of the matriarchs of the Geechee community on Sapelo Island, has authored the popular memoir *God, Dr Buzzard, and the Bolito Man*. Gloria Naylor's novel *Mama Day* is a rich depiction of Geechee life.

SOUTHERN RENAISSANCE

As the rest of the US began to enjoy 20th-century prosperity, the South lagged far behind in terms of education, race relations and nutrition – not to mention high art and literature. Yet, sometime early in the century, this region of storytellers came alive with great literature and produced a genre of haunting, macabre and surreal poems, novels and memoirs – generally described as 'Southern Gothic.'

Perhaps the phenomenon was a result of a long period of regional self-analysis brought about by military defeat and Reconstruction; or maybe it was a result of lingering guilt over the treatment of African Americans. In any case, the generation of Southern writers who emerged in the early and mid-20th century remains among the most well regarded in world literature.

Margaret Mitchell's *Gone With the Wind* is the second best-selling book in the world (after the Bible).

The contributions of writers from the Lowcountry to this pool of literature have been considerable. The deep brooding work of Savannah poet Conrad Aiken won a Pulitzer Prize (1930) with highly psychoanalytical poems such as 'The Charnel Rose.'

Flannery O'Connor (1925–64) was perhaps the greatest short story writer of the 20th century. A native of Savannah, O'Connor graduated from the Georgia State College for Women in Milledgeville. She was diagnosed with lupus (a type of autoimmune disorder) in 1950 and moved to her mother's farm where she finished the novel *Wise Blood*. A collection of short stories, *A Good Man Is Hard to Find*, appeared in 1955 to widespread acclaim. She died in 1964, a year before her final collection, *Everything That Rises Must Converge*, came out. O'Connor's characters and themes are traditionally Southern, although seen in a religious framework – no other writer has achieved this to the same degree.

Margaret Mitchell (1900–49) tried writing short stories in the 1920s without success, but went on to compose the most popular Southern novel of all time, *Gone With the Wind* (1936).

CONTEMPORARY WRITING

The Lowcounty's most prolific modern writer is Pat Conroy. His love affair with the Lowcountry has inspired many of his novels and has given rise to popular film adaptations as well. Conroy's first book is the autobiographical *The Water Is Wide* (1972), about his experiences as a teacher in isolated Daufuskie Island, near Hilton Head. Subsequent volumes include *The Lords of Discipline,* about cadet life at the Citadel military college in Charleston, and *The Great Santini* (1976), about a domineering marine pilot and his family, who have just moved to Beaufort. *The Prince of Tides* (1986) and *Beach Music* (1995) are two more recent best-sellers that evoke haunted scenery and families in the Lowcountry.

Josephine Humphries wrote *Rich in Love,* a novel that portrays a young woman's coming of age in Mount Pleasant, a Charleston suburb. You get heaping helpings of Southern-style humor in William Price Fox's *Southern Fried,* which has recently been re-released with six additional stories under the title *Southern Fried Plus Six.*

John Jakes, the best-selling author of Civil War sagas like *North and South Trilogy* and *On Secret Service,* lives on Hilton Head much of the year and is a strong supporter of the arts and preservation on the island.

It is almost impossible to overestimate the celebrity that has come to Savannah from New Yorker John Berendt's nonfiction mystery-travelogue *Midnight in the Garden of Good & Evil* (1994).

Pat Conroy's memoir *My Losing Season* (2002), about playing basketball for the Citadel, is a bittersweet requiem to the game and coming of age in the Lowcountry.

Films

The romantic landscapes and predictable, warm weather of Lowcountry are a filmmaker's dream.

Many films have been made from books listed in the preceding Literature section. Apart from this, the PBS-produced *Civil War* series, available on home video, sheds a drawn-out light on the region's history. Another Civil War epic, *Glory,* about the heroic all-black Massachusetts 54th Brigade, was shot in a number of Lowcountry locations, including Jekyll Island.

Filmed in coastal South Carolina, *The Patriot* features Mel Gibson (a pacifist) playing a character who is a synthesis of Revolutionary War heroes Francis 'Swamp Fox' Marion and Andrew Pickens; the sumptuous footage of swamps, oceans and forests is pure eye candy. Idyllic Beaufort is another popular location for movies: *The Big Chill, The Great Santini, Forrest Gump* and *Forces of Nature* are just a few of the titles filmed in the town.

Almost all of Pat Conroy's novels have been made into movies and were shot in the Lowcountry. The landscape shots in *The Prince of Tides* do a superb job of capturing Conroy's evocative descriptions of this tidewater area.

For a total sea-island experience and a sense of the way it was, don't miss *Conrack,* a film adaptation of Pat Conroy's novel *The Water Is Wide,* in which a young Jon Voight tries to bring commonsense education to a black school on Daufuskie Island, or *Daughters of the Dust,* about life in a Gullah community. Savannah, of course, was the setting for *Midnight in the Garden of Good & Evil* and *Forrest Gump.* John Travolta came to town to make *The General's Daughter;* Julia Roberts and Dennis Quaid were here to make a horse-country opus, *Something to Talk About*. Set largely in Savannah, Bluffton and Jekyll Island, *The Legend of Bagger Vance*, a story about a mythic golfer, shows the region to good effect and stars Will Smith and Matt Damon.

Music

Many Lowcountry musicians draw from the vital African American musical traditions that have long been alive in the Carolinas and Georgia, and the music you hear along the southeast coast is as varied as the interplay between saltwater and land in this region. The strains of R&B, jazz, soul, Southern rock and alternative rock have flowed to the Lowcountry (whose clubs and bars offer a multitude of performance opportunities) from small Upcountry towns and Atlanta. In addition, the coast prides itself in being the originator of one genre: the relaxed rhythms of beach music, as performed in the legendary dance halls of Myrtle Beach. Gospel choirs (like the Hallelujah Singers in *Forrest Gump*) are a staple on AM radio stations, at Gullah church services and at functions as diverse as steamboat tours and Sunday brunches.

JAZZ

Although it's not widely known, the Carolinas spawned several masters of modern jazz, and their music still infuses the jazz caves of Savannah, Charleston, Hilton Head and Myrtle Beach.

John Birks Gillespie (1917–93), better known as 'Dizzy,' was born in Cheraw, South Carolina. He attended the Laurinburg musical institute in North Carolina but moved to Philadelphia when he was 18. In the 1940s, he and Charlie Parker were among the great innovators of the frenetic language of bebop.

'Sheets of sound' were the hallmark of exquisite tenor saxophonist John Coltrane (1926–67), who grew up in a small town near High Point, North Carolina. Coltrane was immortalized on Miles Davis' landmark album *Kind of Blue* (1959) and in cutting-edge groups later in his career, which was cut short by liver cancer. Perhaps his most famous album is *A Love Supreme*.

Memorable jazz standards such as ''Round Midnight,' 'Straight, No Chaser' and 'Misterioso' were penned by Thelonious Monk (1917–82), an eccentric bebop pianist from Rocky Mount, North Carolina. Though something of a self-styled sophisticate, Monk never forgot his Southern roots: Collard greens protruded from his lapel at Big Apple club dates.

SOUL

The unbridled energy of soul grew out of the R&B heard in the Low-country (and throughout Georgia and South Carolina) during 1950s, thanks mainly to the pioneer efforts of Ray Charles.

James Brown, 'the Godfather of Soul,' was the only black R&B artist to make the transition to soul in the '60s, then to funk in the '70s. Born in 1933 to a poor family near Barnwell, South Carolina, Brown led the gospel band The Famous Flames in the mid '40s. In 1956, the Flames cut their 'secularized' gospel song 'Please, Please, Please,' which became a top R&B hit. Brown's stage shows were stunningly professional, with fast-paced dancing, knee drops and his trademark simulated collapse.

Apart from James Brown, Otis Redding (1941–67) embodied the soul sound in the '60s. Born in Dawson, Georgia, but raised in Macon, Redding's style was immediately recognizable for the catch in his voice.

RAY CHARLES

Born into poverty in the backwoods of southern Georgia during the Depression, Ray Charles was four years old when he saw his brother drowned in a bathtub; then he started to lose his sight and went completely blind by the time he was seven.

'Soul is a way of life,' Charles once explained, 'but it's always the hard way.'

Self-taught on the piano, Charles was barely 18 when he cut his first single, 'Confession Blues.' By the summer of 1949 he'd released some 20 singles, mostly in the velvety style of crooner Nat 'King' Cole. In 1955 he recorded the hit 'I Got a Woman,' a gospel–blues tune with churchy piano; this and tunes like it would lay the foundation for a generation of soul vocalists in the '60s.

Charles charted a milestone in 1959 when, in a smoky dancehall near Pittsburgh, he cut 'What I'd Say,' a gospel call-and-response with a Latin beat. Sounding like a re-creation of a revival meeting, the song was condemned as blasphemy and banned by several radio stations – and became a million-seller. In 1962, he cut his greatest crossover ever, the album *Modern Sounds in Country and Western Music* – the first time a black jazz–blues artist had ventured into country, which was considered a white domain. Two of the traditional country songs Charles covered on this album reached the Top 10 in pop R&B charts.

Since then Charles has won just about every meaningful cultural and musical award, including the National Medal of Arts, 12 Grammies and a spot in the Rock and Roll Hall of Fame. He remains a beloved, almost saintly, figure in the Lowcountry and across America, swaying back and forth behind his grand piano, and he performed 'America the Beautiful' at Ronald Reagan's renomination and at Bill Clinton's first inaugural ball.

Among other works, the hit 'Sittin' on the Dock of the Bay' shows Redding's mastery of rhythmic subtlety and timbral variation and captures a lazy Lowcountry mood.

Richard Penniman – aka 'Little Richard' – was a rock 'n' roll singer from Macon who incorporated soul and blues into classics such as 'Tutti Frutti' and 'Good Golly Miss Molly.' Other famous soul artists from Georgia include Gladys Knight (of 'the Pips' fame), who signed with Motown.

SOUTHERN ROCK

Shades of the Confederacy still echo in the Lowcountry with the rhythm and lyrics of Southern rock that emerged from mainstream rock in the early '70s. A blend of R&B, jazz and country, Southern rock was oriented toward concerts, with unusually long (for the era) tunes; some live recordings of a single song covered an entire album side. Its songs idolized individualism, Southern and rural life, and macho behavior – themes that were popular among white Southern working-class teenagers. In Atlanta during the '60s, producer and publisher Bill Lowery oversaw a small but talented corps of artists, including Billy Joe Royal, Ray Stevens and Jerry Reed, but few hits produced a distinctive regional sound.

Enter the Allman Brothers, the first definitive Southern rock band. In 1969, Duane Allman and his brother Gregg, a vocalist and keyboard player, formed the original Allman Brothers Band, which included guitarist Dicky Betts and bassist Berry Oakley. They were among the first to sign with Capricorn Records, a fledgling Georgia company set up by Otis Redding's former manager, Phil Walden. The Allmans produced a rich fabric of hits, but the deaths of Duane Allman and Berry Oakley in motorcycle accidents in 1971 and 1972 – in Macon, within a block of each other – robbed the group of its creative verve. The Allmans' history features prominently in the Georgia Music Hall of Fame, in Macon.

Lynyrd Skynyrd penned the Southern rock anthem 'Sweet Home Alabama' and other hits for the Atlanta-based Sounds of the South label; its famous live recording of 'Free Bird' was made in Atlanta's Fox Theatre. Like the Allmans, Lynyrd Skynyrd suffered a tragic accident – an airplane crash that claimed the lives of four band members.

The heyday of the genre passed with the '70s, but quite a few old Southern rockers just keep on rockin' in the clubs and pubs of Lowcountry. The Marshall Tucker Band, from Spartanburg, South Carolina, still serves up an eclectic mix of jazz, western swing and unusual instrumentation.

POP & ALTERNATIVE

The small towns of South Carolina and Georgia, and the clubs of Savannah and Charleston, have been incubators for celebrity bands. Groups like REM, Widespread Panic, the Indigo Girls and the B-52s got their starts here in the late '70s and early '80s. As for South Carolina, its best-known contemporary rockers are Hootie & the Blowfish.

BEACH MUSIC

Beach music has been around for half a century in the Lowcountry. Its origins lie in the post-WWII soul and R&B of urban black 'streetcorner' music. Purists maintain that beach music isn't surf music and has nothing to do with the Beach Boys or Jan & Dean. Songs of this genre are a relaxed 4/4 shuffle to which dancers can 'shag' – a sophisticated touch dance that's related to the jitterbug (but not to any Austin Powers movies). Fronted by Bill Pinkney, the Drifters were credited with popularizing beach music with their classic 'Under the Boardwalk' (1964), although the form seems to be as much about 1950s nostalgia as anything else. Performing groups tended to be African American and had curiously similar names (the Coasters, the Platters, the Catalinas and so on).

Beach music thrived in the late '50s and early '60s but was somewhat forgotten during the Vietnam War years. Disco nearly killed it, but in 1979, a group called SOS (Society of Stranders) organized a reunion of aging shaggers at Myrtle Beach. A resurgence followed. Considered lewd by parents of the '50s, the shag became such a cultural icon that it was declared South Carolina's state dance in 1985. Today, beach music is usually performed by white groups such as the Embers, who are just as likely to play the governor's mansion as a beachside hall. SOS, meanwhile, still attracts thousands of fans to its zoo-like gathering in North Myrtle Beach. Of course, *Beach Music* is the title of a popular 1995 Pat Conroy novel (soon to be a film).

To get in the groove with beach music and its full history, there is no better place to start than the website www.beachshag.com.

ARCHITECTURE

The architectural style most commonly linked to the Lowcountry is the neoclassical antebellum plantation house, a la Tara in *Gone With the Wind*. The former plantation region along the coasts and rivers holds a great concentration of surviving examples, particularly around Charleston, Beaufort and Savannah.

Many antebellum mansions, like Boone Hall Plantation, are open to public tours. Houses are carefully restored and decorated, both by local historical societies and by individuals, with elaborate interior furnishings in period style; many display the furnishings of the original residents. On guided tours, you'll find that each piece has a story to tell, and the history of the family is at least as important as the house (if not more so). Often, the original architectural craftwork was done by slaves, and a few antebellum houses retain their original slave cabins.

The vast historic districts of Charleston and Savannah show off extraordinary collections of 18th- and 19th-century urban buildings. While Georgian architecture is prevalent (especially in Charleston), many of the structures date from the Federal period. Savannah also sports a collection of immense Victorian town houses (many are now B&Bs), while Jekyll Island's historic district is resplendent with huge Victorian vacation cottages belonging to the rich and famous.

The humble houses of the working class also make a striking impression. In the poorest areas, you can still find the proverbial 'shotgun shack,' which typically has a rusty, corrugated roof, paper-thin walls and about an arm's length between it and the one just like it next door. Their rooms are lined up one after another – behind the small porch there's a living room, then a bedroom, then a kitchen – affording little privacy for whole families. You could stand on the front porch and, from the front door, shoot straight through the back door – hence the term. You'll also notice that many families in poorer communities live out of trailers and keep a 'swept lawn' in the dirt apron out front.

Gardens

Meticulously sculpted gardens, often accompanied by waterfalls, terraces, statuaries and sculptures, are a famous feature of the Lowcountry. Magnolia Plantation, in Charleston, has a horticultural maze, a topiary and a biblical garden. Brookgreen Gardens, 16 miles south of Myrtle Beach, holds the largest collection of American sculpture in North America.

Environment

Watch a heron take off over the salt marsh as the morning sun lifts into the day. Paddle a canoe through the murky and mysterious shroud of a swamp. Walk along a long stretch of white-sand beach at sunset. See American alligators sunning themselves in the middle of a still pond, and spot osprey building their strong, complicated nests. Marvel at the majesty of a thick-limbed ancient live oak, dripping glistening moss like syrup.

The South Carolina and Georgia coasts are active; they are constantly moving and changing and inviting, which is why they're irresistible. This part of the world is best experienced in the quiet hours, at sunrise or sunset – when the croaking of frogs, the humming of insects and the movement of tides all conspire to reinvent the world.

Atlantic and Gulf Coasts, by William Amos and Stephen H Amos, is an excellent field guide, with color photos of birds, plants, fish and other coastal and sea life.

THE LAND

The term 'Lowcountry' refers to the coastal area stretching roughly between Georgetown, South Carolina and St Marys, Georgia, though its boundaries could just as easily be defined by the sometimes sweet, sometimes intense, always present aroma of fish. Though 'Lowcountry' refers to cuisine, culture and even ideology, it also refers to the mushy indefinable blend of land and sea. One minute you could be walking on solid land, the next kayaking through a salt marsh or swimming in the ocean.

The coastal plains are dotted with swamps, marshes and tidal rivers, some of them startlingly wild and primitive. The Atlantic Ocean lapped over this region until the last Ice Age ended, leaving sands and marine sediments. The coastal swamps and bogs of the Southeast are cushioned by layers of peat thousands of years old. Many of the boggy lowlands have been drained for agricultural use, but a good bit of muck remains, much of it now valuable wildlife and nature reserve.

Barrier Islands

A string of slender barrier islands extends from the middle of the South Carolina coast to Jacksonville, Florida, and while several of them are superb vacation spots, many are only accessible by private boat. Millions of years ago, much of this area sat underwater, but compared to the rest of the region, the barrier islands are geological youngsters. The older and innermost set of islands, the Pleistocene islands, harbored beaches 35,000 to 40,000 years ago, before the last great Ice Age. The further offshore Holocene islands were formed 4,000 to 5,000 years ago, with the change of the sea level after the last Ice Age. The barrier islands are a curious feature, as storms and ocean currents can change their shapes overnight. The 1000-plus miles of Atlantic shoreline offer plenty of dunes, sea oats and, of course, white sandy beaches. Unlike elsewhere in the South, there are no bayous.

Lowcountry: The Natural Landscape, by Tom Bladgen, is a beautiful photography book covering the magical underbelly of the tidal rivers, salt marshes, swamp forests and barrier islands.

Salt Marshes

A half-land, half-tidewater ecosystem teeming with shellfish, fish and marine birds, the salt marsh is a combination of salt-tolerant Spartina grasses and herbs. The brackish waters of the salt marshes get flushed twice daily by the tides. Salt marshes thrive in the protected, still waters behind barrier islands, which act as breakers against strong waves and tidal currents.

Productive at converting solar energy into plant tissue, marsh grasses unload vast amounts of nutrients into the waters, which in turn provide a hearty cuisine for shellfish.

Among the salt marshes are muddy flats that get bolstered by the ongoing decay of marsh plants, which form into a goopy but fertile soil the locals call pluff mud. Avoid standing too long in the pluff mud; the brown, rather odiferous muck'll suction you in, and you'll spend your day cleaning it out of your toenails.

Swamps

Similar to marshes, swamps are flooded, deep-water bogs that differ because they grow trees (marshes do not). Bald cypress and water tupelo are the predominant trees in Lowcountry swamps. Tannic acid from the tree roots discolors the water and reduces the potential for photosynthesis. Leaves decompose slowly, and the dense soils harbor hundreds of birds, mammals, reptiles and amphibians. Enchanting swamps are found all along the coast, including Georgia's Okefenokee Swamp, in the Okefenokee National Wildlife Refuge, the largest fresh-water wetland habitat in the US. The protected ACE Basin (named for Ashepoo, Combahee and Edisto Rivers) helps to maintain the unique and diminishing blackwater swamp ecosystem.

DID YOU KNOW?

Tannic acids in cypress-tree roots combine with decomposing peat to make swamp water a tea-colored shade. The dark color reduces the intensity of sunlight for photosynthesis, keeping swamp waters dense and stagnant.

Freshwater

A string of lakes, some of them quite large and deep (and mostly artificial), stud the coastal plain. The upper part of the lengthy Savannah River, which marks the border between South Carolina and Georgia, forms a chain of freshwater lakes and rivers for which the region is famous. Georgia's undammed Altamaha River flows for 140 miles through pristine hardwood bottomlands, cypress swamps and tidal marshes.

Designated by The Nature Conservancy as one of the '75 Last Great Places' in the world, the ecologically diverse watershed is one of the largest river systems in the US. Every second, the river expels about 100,000 gallons of freshwater into the Atlantic Ocean just north of Brunswick. Some 120 species of rare or endangered plants and animals are found in the watershed.

WILDLIFE

Because of so many diverse and nutrient-rich ecosystems, the Georgia and South Carolina coasts are home to a variety of small mammals, a whole universe of birds and a hardy selection of insects. Five species of sea turtles, including the loggerhead, are under threat, as human traffic on the beaches disturbs their nesting grounds. For more information on this, see the boxed text 'Gentle Giants of the Sea' (p46). Georgia has a high proportion of endangered fish species, including four kinds of dasher.

The Georgia Conservancy (www.georgiaconservancy.org) is a statewide environmental organization working to protect air, water, unspoiled places and community green space.

The Southeast has many varieties of huge and colorful butterflies, which are drawn to the region's abundant flowering plants; indeed, some gardens are specially designed to attract butterflies. Dragonflies – your friends because they eat mosquitoes – inhabit the wetlands, and katydids and crickets chirp through the night along the lower shores.

Mosquitoes are the most feared wildlife in the region, especially along the marshy coast or inland along rivers. In the still air of early evening, listen for the soft drone that signals their emergence. You'll also make the acquaintance of nuisance gnats so small they're called 'no-see-ums' but don't let that fool you – they have gargantuan appetites. Having bug spray in your day pack is a good idea.

Huge, brown-winged cockroaches, affectionately called 'palmetto bugs' by locals, are another pest; they grow up to 3 inches long, live both indoors and out, and will even fly in your face if you get too close. Though positively prehistoric looking, cockroaches are as harmless to humans as black flies. Most locals don't flinch at the sight of them, though truth be told, most folks also have a tight relationship with their exterminator.

Animals & Reptiles

In the Lowcountry, small mammals dominate, primarily raccoons, opossums (called 'possums'), rabbits, squirrels, bats and armadillos. Toward the northern stretches, the forests host black bears, bobcats and endangered red and gray foxes.

The Okefenokee Swamp teems with over 200 varieties of reptiles and amphibians. The American alligator is an almost certain sighting in the creeks and lowland marshes along the coast. Once hunted to dwindling numbers for its valuable hide, the alligator has made a comeback due to the protection provided by the Endangered Species Act.

Freshwater turtles are abundant (the soft-shelled variety is considered the most tasty and is marketed commercially), but all of the six sea turtle species found along the coast – loggerheads, Hawksbill, green, leatherback, Kemp's Ridley, and Olive Ridley – are designated either threatened or endangered. Should you encounter a turtle or nest, beat a quick and quiet retreat, as human intervention has put the turtles' fragile lifecycle under serious stress. For more information on this, see the boxed text 'Gentle Giants of the Sea' (p46).

Bottle-nosed dolphins can often be seen accompanying deep-sea fishing boats or passing freighters, and it's not uncommon to see dolphins swim alongside your kayak. Otters are found in the Okefenokee Swamp and some other protected areas.

Poisonous snakes are common but are rarely encountered. Venomous water moccasins – called 'cottonmouths' for the white lining they reveal when extending their jaw – live in the coastal plains. Copperheads and timber rattlesnakes are common in wet, wooded areas, such as swamps. Snakes generally won't bother you, and it's unlikely you'll even come across one.

Birds

So many spectacular species of birds live, mate or migrate along the South Carolina and Georgia coasts that it seems like one long bird sanctuary. Because of its location on the Atlantic Flyway, thousands of migratory birds flock here in winter months. In spring and fall, transient songbirds and shorebirds stop briefly on their way north to and from their nesting grounds. Estimates put the number of bird species at more than 300; the high population is due to the variety of habitats.

Watch for plovers, sanderlings and willets chasing the tides, or look for the American oystercatcher's thick orange bill and distinctive red eye. See eagles soar overhead or watch an endangered wood stork feed its young. See graceful egrets and herons standing motionless in a placid pond, wave at a cormorant drying its wings, or spy an osprey tending its nest in the trees.

DID YOU KNOW?

Despite their nasty reputation, cold-blooded American alligators can go long stretches without eating, needing just 1lb of food a week when they're active. Their acidic stomachs can digest almost anything, including feathers, bones and turtle shells.

The South Carolina Department of Natural Resources (www.dnr.state.sc.us) lists current programs and initiatives, with links to recreation, environment and wildlife sites.

The Georgia Department of Natural Resources (www.dnr.state.ga.us) has links to information about coastal ecology and wildlife.

KUDZU

Throughout the South, you'll often see areas with large trees completely covered by a leafy green vine, looking like impossibly large topiaries. This is kudzu, brought by the Japanese to Philadelphia in the late 19th century as a decoration. Southerners adopted it as a fragrant, shady porch vine. The US Soil Conservation Service discovered that it stopped erosion and planted it throughout the South.

Oops. Growing as much as a foot a day in the hot, moist Southern climate, kudzu took over farmer's fields, climbed electric poles and created electrical outages, derailed trains on steep grades, smothered trees and swallowed porches, billboards, road signs and abandoned automobiles. This 'savior of Southern soil' – as it was once called – blankets 7 million acres from Florida to Maryland and as far west as Louisiana. Once established, the tough vines are difficult to get rid of – the root of a 20-year-old plant can weigh 250 pounds. Construction and road building help spread kudzu – a single root buried in fill material can create an infestation.

Not everyone sees kudzu as completely useless. The Japanese use it in tea, as a health tonic and to make kimono fibers. The Chinese use it to make rope and as a hangover remedy. Enterprising Southerners turn it into art or food – making woven-kudzu baskets, kudzu-blossom jelly or french-fried kudzu. Festivals celebrating the weed are popping up in small towns. Cattle and sheep love it, but there's more of it than them.

So while in Georgia, grab a sharp machete and go looking for your next art project or meal. Just don't fall asleep next to it.

Great spots to bird-watch are at **Huntington Beach State Park** (p191), near Myrtle Beach, at the **Cape Romain National Wildlife Refuge** (p195) or on **Cumberland Island** (p110).

Swamps and marshes harbor a host of birds. **Colonial Coast Birding Trail** (p102), which stretches from Savannah to the Okefenokee Swamp, is composed of 18 car-accessible viewing areas that represent the different habitats of the coast. Staff at visitors centers along the way can offer bird-watching suggestions for both skilled and first-time birders.

Plants

The Southeast is well known for many flowering species of trees, shrubs and flowers, and in the heat of the humid summer months, the native flora bursts with intoxicating fragrance and beauty. Gardening is big here, and landscape architects plan their arrangements as if with an artist's brush and palette. From the blooming of the first tender crocuses in late January and until the last patches of yellow witch hazel in December, blossoms can be seen throughout most of the year. Some of the common flowering species include southern and Fraser magnolias, azalea, rhododendron, dogwood, redbud, wax myrtle and hydrangeas. Jasmine, camellia, lavender, gardenia and honeysuckle sweeten the Lowcountry air.

In the coastal areas you'll glimpse a strange plant long associated with the romantic South: wispy tendrils of Spanish moss draped from the broad limbs of a live oak. Despite its name, Spanish moss is neither moss nor Spanish. Related to the pineapple, the flowering plant is an epiphyte: It sucks all its daily nutrition from the air. The plant's name was supposedly derived from its resemblance to a Spaniard's beard. Live oaks also sport vibrant green tresses of resurrection fern.

In coastal areas, bald cypress, black gum and sweet gum trees give way to maritime forests of oak, cedar and holly, with salt marsh and palmetto palms growing in the subtropical latitudes (South Carolina is the Palmetto State).

NATIONAL & STATE PARKS

Because of the area's important history in the nation's development, many sights have been deemed significant enough for state and federal designation. The parks are more about historical and environmental preservation than they are about recreation, though camping and recreation opportunities abound.

Federal sites overseen by the National Park Service (NPS) on the Georgia coast include the nation's largest swamp (Okefenokee National Wildlife Refuge) and the windswept Cumberland Island National Seashore. Historic sites include Fort Pulaski National Monument and Fort Frederica National Monument. Georgia State Parks along the coast include Skidaway Island State Park, near Savannah, and Crooked River State Park, near St Marys. Except for a small Gullah community, all of Sapelo Island belongs to the government as a state park. Several state-run historic sites are scattered throughout the area.

Along the South Carolina coast, the NPS maintains Charles Pinckney National Historic Site, Fort Moultrie National Monument and Fort Sumter National Monument. Campers and wilderness seekers have a handful of excellent state parks to choose from, including Hunting Island State Park, near Beaufort, and Edisto Beach State Park, on Edisto Island. Near Myrtle Beach is the fabulous Huntington Beach State Park and, closer to town, Myrtle Beach State Park. Preserved historic sites include Charles Towne Landing State Historic Site, near Charleston.

Administered by the Fish and Wildlife Service (FWS), Cape Romain National Wildlife Refuge stretches for 22 miles along the coast north of Charleston. In addition to protecting the fragile ecosystem, the refuge works to relocate threatened loggerhead turtles and to breed and re-release threatened red wolves. Also run by the FWS, the Pinckney Island National Wildlife Refuge protects the fragile salt-marsh habitat between Hilton Head and the mainland. The refuge provides a safe haven for migratory birds and native animals, since it is protected from sea storms by Hilton Head.

For a complete list, or for more information on these national parks, visit www.nps.gov or www.recreation.gov. For state parks in Georgia, go to www.gastateparks.org. For South Carolina state parks, check out www.southcarolinaparks.com.

Longstreet Highroad Guide to the Georgia Coast and Okefenokee, by Richard J Lenz, is chock full of information for nature lovers, hikers, bikers, boaters and history buffs.

ENVIRONMENTAL ISSUES

Coastal areas have been prime real estate ever since humans began trading with one another. Native Americans settled heavily alongside the coast, and the first Europeans created coastal colonies to fish, trade or ship out when they needed to. By the early part of the 20th century, poor land management of the singly important cotton crop had exhausted the soil – Piedmont blues artists sung about 'pickin' cotton low' because plants didn't have the strength to grow higher. Vital wetlands were being drained or filled for agricultural development, and jetties built along the Atlantic caused extensive erosion as ocean currents were redirected.

Growth these days is out of control. Vast land consumption, poor urban planning and coastal sprawl threaten the fragile coastal zone (the band of land stretching 50 miles inland from the ocean).

Experts say that sprawl isn't just due to population growth. In fact, from 1973 to 1994 the population of the Charleston metropolitan region grew 40% but used up a whopping 250% more land area. Growth is inefficient;

The LowCountry Institute (www.lowcountryinstitute .org) partners with local policymakers, landowners and developers to protect the biodiversity of the Lowcountry.

GENTLE GIANTS OF THE SEA

A designated threatened species, loggerhead sea turtles (Caretta caretta) nest on Hilton Head and other southeast beaches between May and August.

Loggerheads live in temperate and subtropical waters throughout most of the world. Adults usually stay close to shore, while juveniles float in the open ocean. Loggerheads prefer to feed in coastal bays and estuaries, or in the shallow water along the continental shelves of the Atlantic Ocean. They live exclusively in the water, and the females only come on land to lay eggs (males never come ashore).

The loggerhead has a massive skull and a body weighing 250lb to 400lb and reaching up to 4 feet long. Primarily carnivorous, they feed mostly on shellfish that live on the bottom of the ocean. They have powerful jaw muscles and a strong beak, which they use to crack the shells of horseshoe crabs, mussels, and clams.

Like all sea turtles, loggerheads have front and rear paddle-like flippers that function like the wings of an airplane, providing propulsion through the ocean. The upper shell of the loggerhead, called the carapace, is usually a reddish-brown color, and the lower shell, called the plastron, is dull brown to yellow.

An adult female will nest once every two to four years, coming to shore up to seven times per season to lay eggs. Nesting occurs at night – the female crawls slowly to a dry part of the beach and begins to excavate a pit with her flippers. Once the cavity is right she deposits 100 to 125 ping-pong ball–sized eggs. She then covers the egg cavity using her rear flippers and packs down sand over the nest to disguise it. When the work is done, the female slowly drags herself to the sea.

About 60 days after the female lays her eggs, the small turtles begin to hatch. They use a sharp tooth to break open the shell. All of the hatchlings join together to dig out of the nest, a job that can take several days. During the cool night, the 2-inch-long hatchlings emerge from their sandy nest and scramble toward the sea. It is during this run to the sea that many hatchlings fall prey to waiting predators. Once in the water, hatchlings swim several miles offshore, where they catch ocean currents. The hatchlings stay in the open water for several years before returning to shore waters.

The life of a loggerhead sea turtle is fraught with danger. Estimates speculate that only 1 of every 10,000 hatchlings survives to adulthood. There are many reasons for this, some natural, some manmade. For example, each year thousands of turtles become entangled and drown in fishing nets. Thousands more are killed each year when they mistakenly eat trash and debris, and the creature is still hunted for its meat.

Lights Out!

The most important way to protect loggerheads is to turn the lights out. Sea-turtle hatchlings usually emerge from the nest at night. They orient themselves toward the brightest horizon (the moonlight sea) and dash toward the light. The artificial lights from buildings and streets near the beach disorient the hatchlings, causing them to wander inland. If they don't make it to the ocean quickly, hatchlings can die of dehydration and exposure, or can be caught by predators such as birds and crabs.

Artificial lights also discourage females from nesting. The town of Hilton Head Island requires that lights on structures visible from the beach be shielded or turned off after 10pm from May 1 to October 31. Any windows facing the beach must also be covered with draperies or shade screens.

Contact one of the following organizations for more information about the loggerhead sea turtle, or to report stranded, injured or dead turtles.

Coastal Discovery Museum (☎ 843-689-6767)
Hilton Head Island Marine Turtle Stranding Representatives (☎ 843-341-4690)
South Carolina Department of Natural Resources Wildlife Hotline (☎ 800-922-5431)

Turtle-Watching Ettiquette

■ If you encounter a nesting turtle, do not shine any lights on or around her – she may abandon her effort to nest.

■ Do not use flash photography.

■ Stay behind the turtle so that she cannot see you.

■ Observe from a distance.

■ Do not harass a turtle.

■ Don't touch or prod her to move.

■ Stay out of the way as she crawls back to the water.

■ If you see a nest, don't disturb it; leave any identification markers in place.

■ If you find a hatchling wandering in daylight, place it on moist sand in a dry container, shade it, and call one of the numbers listed below.

■ Call to report dead or injured turtles.

Safe Turtle Watches

The Coastal Discovery Museum conducts the Sea Turtle Protection Project in conjunction with the South Carolina Department of Natural Resources. The project monitors the nesting of these large reptiles by patroling the beaches from May through October. If nests are found in unsuitable locations, they are moved for the safety of the hatchlings. After the hatchlings leave the nests, researchers inventory each nest to determine how many eggs successfully hatched.

The museum offers a special Turtle Walk & Talk tour. These guided evening beach walks are designed to give participants information about the nationally threatened species. Participating in one of these programs is probably the safest way to view loggerheads and is the best way to learn how to help protect them.

instead of building up, most residential and commercial developers use more land and grow out.

It's no secret that sprawl is offensive to more than just the eye. Undeveloped land is a sponge, whereas developed land – such as golf courses and parking lots – is a surface. Flowing over surfaces and therefore unfiltered by nature, rainwater runs off into creeks, rivers and estuaries. Residential sprawl causes more people to drive, which leads to air pollution, which gets into waterways and starts damaging the food chain (invertebrates and fish, birds, sea and land mammals etc).

Along the South Carolina and Georgia coasts, the frenzied building of resorts and golf courses to keep up with the demands of tourism (the driving force of the economy) have led to haphazard depletion of coastal areas. You'll see this especially in Myrtle Beach. Only 25 years ago it was a one-traffic-light town; now it has grown into a perfect example of sprawl. Georgia has done a better job of slowing growth and protecting some of the coastal islands, though development continues at a rapid clip.

Vestiges of a near-feudal mentality among politicians and industrialists often remain, encouraging a system of patronage that allows predominant industries to go about their business with little oversight from local authorities. There are a few silver linings in this cloud, however, as environmental groups like the Georgia Conservancy and the South Carolina Coastal Conservation League work to encourage the protection of fragile areas and to put pressure on politicians and policymakers to promote responsible development. Environmental groups have also

BIG BLOWS

The hurricane season in the eastern US is from June to November, with most activity occurring in August and September. Hurricanes can also appear outside the official season, but this is much less common. While the annual average is only about five hurricanes per year, the frequency can vary greatly from year to year.

Hurricanes are defined as storms that originate in the tropics and have winds in excess of 74mph. Those that hit the Southeast form off the coast of Africa and whip in a westerly direction across the Atlantic. The winds of these hurricanes revolve in a counterclockwise direction around a center of lower barometric pressure, picking up energy from warm waters and moisture as they approach the Caribbean.

The first stage of a hurricane's approach is called a tropical 'disturbance,' followed by a tropical 'depression' and, when winds exceed 39mph, the system is upgraded to a tropical 'storm.' The system is called a 'hurricane' when wind speed intensifies around a low-pressure center, called 'the eye of the storm.'

The strength of a hurricane is rated from one to five. The mildest is a Category 1 hurricane, and the strongest and rarest hurricanes, the Category 5 monsters, pack winds that exceed 150mph. In 1989, Hurricane Hugo, which left a devastating path of destruction in and around Charleston, was a Category 4. Hurricane Mitch, which killed more than 10,000 people in Central America in late 1998, was a rare Category 5. In 1999, Hurricane Floyd pounded the Bahamas at Category 5 and threatened the entire southeastern US coast. Though Floyd fell to a Category 2 as it hit the coast, Savannah experienced winds at 53mph, Charleston winds gusted at 85mph and Myrtle Beach got more than 16 inches of rain.

Hurricane Names

Ever wonder why hurricanes have human names? Names were given to storms to ease confusion for forecasters and the general public. Apparently, an Australian forecaster was the first to use this method. He named storms after disdainful political figures, so he could say so-and-so was 'causing great distress' or 'wandering aimlessly about the Pacific.'

During WWII, US military meteorologists named storms after women (their girlfriends or wives). In 1979, both men's and women's names came into rotation. Names follow alphabetical order, alternating between masculine and feminine names. Names of particularly brutal hurricanes get retired, while others get reused. The names Hugo, Mitch and Floyd, for example, are all retired.

Hurricane Safety

If you are caught by an approaching hurricane, stay calm and follow local warnings. Hotels are typically of concrete and steel construction, capable of withstanding strong winds with minimal damage. However, in low-lying areas, ocean swells can also pose a hazard – if you have an oceanfront room, it's a wise precaution to relocate to a unit farther inland. The flooding caused by a storm surge has been known to completely cover outlying barrier islands.

Most hurricane injuries are the result of flying debris, so don't be tempted to venture outside in the midst of a storm. If a hurricane warning is announced, stay sober. A hurricane is no time to be partying. You'll need your wits about you both during and after the storm.

Hurricane Information

Hurricanes are tracked by the US National Hurricane Center in Miami. Satellite weather forecasts provide advance warning, but it is difficult to predict a storm's path. For current weather information, you can visit the *Miami Herald* website (www.herald.com) and scan the menu for hurricane and storm information.

Another excellent place to find current English- and Spanish-language tropical-storm information is the National Hurricane Center's Tropical Prediction Center website (www.nhc.noaa.gov), maintained by the US National Oceanic and Atmospheric Administration.

teamed up with longtime local advocates, who know that paving over living ecosystems is permanent – once it's gone, there's no way to get it back.

Natural disasters such as hurricanes wreak periodic havoc on the coast. Hurricane Hugo drove ashore in 1989, causing $8.5 billion in damage (and a whopping $5 billion alone in South Carolina), the second most expensive hurricane in US history. The hurricane cycle is an argument for keeping coastal development of housing and industry to a minimum, but this logic routinely goes unheeded.

The South Carolina coastal Conservation League (www.scccl.org) works to protect the threatened resources of the South Carolina Coastal Plain.

Outdoors

As soon as you see the coast for the first time, the majesty of the long, white-sand beaches seems truly overwhelming. Watching the waves roll in and crash on the shore remains almost a spiritual affair, one that cleanses away any thoughts of traffic or the frenzy of everyday life. The first thing you absolutely must do when you arrive at the coast is jump in the water. Worry about the towel and the beach chair later – just dive into the waves and let the saltwater wash all over you. Swim out a ways and then bodysurf the waves back into shore. Repeat as many times as necessary, until you can taste the salt on your lips, feel the refreshing tingle of the Atlantic in your pores. This is the best way to experience the outdoors on your trip to the Georgia and South Carolina coast. It's free, it's easy and you can do it first thing in the morning, midday or by the light of the moon.

It only gets better. Once you've dived into the ocean, you'll realize that life in these parts is intimately tied to the flow of the waves. If you were to set up a 24-hour video camera overlooking any of the coastal areas along the Georgia and South Carolina coasts and then play it back at high speed, you'd likely be astonished at the drama that occurs twice every day with the ebb and flow of the tides. At low tide a marsh can look like land; at high tide, it can disappear completely. At low tide a broad beach can become a sliver of sand and a boat can seem stranded, only to be bobbing in the water a few hours later. There are many ways to see this, from a kayak or a sailboat, or by simply standing with your feet submerged as the tide swallows your ankles.

Cycle along island paths, swing a tennis racquet or golf club and walk through nature trails in the Okefenokee Swamp, at Cypress Gardens, at Middleton Place or Magnolia Plantation. Stroll the historic cities of Charleston, Beaufort and Savannah, canoe through an estuary or sit on a bench and watch the sunset. Whatever you do, take advantage of the coastal mysteries and learn the Lowcountry secrets by being outdoors.

SWIMMING

Long stretches of white sandy beaches await along the South Carolina and Georgia coasts, and it's a mighty fine thing to jump in the Atlantic any chance you get. Around Charleston, the best beaches are at Sullivan's Island, Isle of Palm and Folly Beach. A little further south and more remote are the shores at Edisto Island, Kiawah Island and at Hunting Island State Park, near Beaufort. Hilton Head's hard-packed beaches are great for biking, jogging or sippin' a cold one from your beach chair.

Around Savannah, sink your toes into the sand at Tybee Island or Skidaway Island State Park. Near Brunswick, St Simons, Little St Simons and Jekyll Island all have beautiful, white, powdery shorelines. The wild, windswept beaches of Cumberland Island are great for hours of strolling. Soft, white Myrtle Beach hugs the coastline for miles. Check out the nice stretches of sand at North Myrtle Beach and Huntington Beach State Park.

KAYAKING & CANOEING

Slip a kayak in the water just about anywhere along the coast, and you'll be a happy paddler, especially when the dolphins swim up to play in the boat's wake. Whether you're experienced or trying a 'yak out for the first time, exploring the Lowcountry's estuaries and sheltered inlets in this way is a must.

Canoeing and kayaking are excellent in spring, summer and early fall, when the weather is gorgeous and the waters relatively calm. In late fall and winter, rains and choppy waves can interfere, but many paddlers cherish the cooler weather and paddle year-round.

Good spots in Georgia include St Marys, from where adventurers even paddle over to Cumberland Island, Tybee Island, St Simons and Sea Island. In South Carolina, slip in the waters around Hilton Head, Kiawah Island, Beaufort and Mount Pleasant. Near Myrtle Beach, Murrells Inlet is perfectly sheltered, and the tributaries around Georgetown make for excellent paddling. The calm waters of the inland swamps are conducive to toodling around in a canoe. Canoe tours and rentals are available at the Okefenokee Swamp and at the Francis Beidler Forest, near Charleston.

Instruction, tours and rentals are all widely available. Two-hour guided kayak tours usually cost about $40 to $45 per person, and full-day trips are usually $85 to $125. Kayak and canoe rentals are about $15 per hour for a single and $25 per hour for a double. For outfitters and organizations, see 'Boating' (p53) and the destination chapters.

GET CRABBY!

Walking along the beach, you'll notice many crabs scurrying away or seeming to simply vanish into the sand. Most crabs have five matching limbs: four pairs of legs and a pair of claws. 'Swimming crabs' have little flippers on their last pair of legs, allowing them to paddle through the water. 'Walking crabs' cannot swim, and their legs end in dainty points. Several types of crabs claw around on these shores – see if you can identify any.

Walking Crabs

- **Fiddler Crab** Found in sandy and muddy environments, the female fiddler crab has a singular large claw she uses to burrow and scrape.
- **Ghost Crab** Zipping along the beach at dizzying speeds, beige-colored ghosts burrow in dry sand.
- **Hermit Crab** Forever finding new homes, these little guys find and move into empty snail shells when they grow. They can carry shells up to five times their body weight. When they grow too big, they just move out.
- **Marsh Crab** These dark-colored, flat-shelled crabs often dart about in the dunes and marshes.
- **Spider Crab** Resembling a large spider, this guy has a bumpy brown shell and long skinny legs. This one is also called the 'decorator crab,' because the rough shell collects bacteria and plankton, helping the crab disguise itself.

Swimming Crabs

- **Blue Crab** Yummy! These are the crabs we most often eat. Only the males should be harvested and can be distinguished from the females by the lack of red 'nail polish' at the tips of their claws.
- **Lady Crab** Found on sandy shoals just offshore, these are identifiable by their red and purple calico spots on the shell. Ladies often bury themselves in the sand, leaving just their eyes and antennae exposed.
- **Speckled Crab** Often found in tide pools, these have white dots all over their brown shells, making them almost indiscernible in the sand.

FISHING

Given that harvesting the sea is the primary industry here, it's no surprise that the coast offers great fishing opportunities. Fishing is a way of life in these parts, and soon after Lowcountry children learn to walk, they learn to fish.

The Intracoastal Waterway winds through the Lowcountry – from Myrtle Beach down through Georgia's barrier islands – and offers some of the richest fishing in the Atlantic. Oysters, shrimps and crabs breed and proliferate in the inshore marsh grasses. You can throw a trap or a line over the side of a pier or bridge, and more times than not, you'll catch something. Fishing at the river mouths, in calm inlets or sheltered bays turns up flounder, bass and trout. To bag biggies like snapper, grouper, sea bass and pompano, take a boat or a fishing charter further offshore. Charter boats also take passengers out to the swift, northeasterly flowing Gulf Stream, where they all fight for game fish like sailfish, marlin, wahoo and tuna. Spring, summer and early fall are the most popular seasons for fishing, though outfitters will take hard-core anglers out year-round and are always happy to hook you up with anything from simple bait to full gear.

All anglers over the age of 16 must possess a fishing license, available at most tackle shops and outfitters. The license is $3.50 a day or $24 for a season. This license is required for hook-and-line fishing, cast netting, seining, crabbing, gigging, sport bait trawling and harvesting shellfish.

SCUBA DIVING

The entire Georgia coastline was submerged more than 10,000 years ago, when bison and mastodons roamed the land. Now a submerged limestone reef about 18 miles off Sapelo Island, **Gray's Reef National Marine Sanctuary** (www.graysreef.nos.noaa.gov) encompasses 17 square nautical miles of a flourishing underwater ecosystem. The reef sits in an ever-changing transition zone between temperate and tropical waters. Divers enjoy exploring the sanctuary's rocky outcroppings, ledges, caves and burrows, where sea life thrives. Dominant invertebrates include sponges, barnacles, sea fans, hard coral, sea stars, crabs, lobsters, snails and shrimp, while fish like black sea bass, snapper and grouper cruise by.

Near Charleston, divers can explore the murky waters of the Cooper and Ashley Rivers, where fossilized shark's teeth are common finds. Farther out, divers can explore a variety of real and artificial wrecks. You can also arrange dive trips from Hilton Head and Savannah.

BIKING

Hopping on a road bike, mountain bike or cruiser is probably the best way to explore coastal islands and towns. The mostly flat roads, the usually slow car traffic and beaches with hard-packed sand let you ride just about anywhere. Excellent trail networks on islands like Kiawah, Jekyll and Hilton Head lead cyclists through forests, past golf clubs and tennis courts, and along the ocean. And nothing is more refreshing than jumping into the cool Atlantic after getting sweaty on a bike ride.

Rentals are available everywhere on the islands and in towns like Charleston, Savannah and Beaufort. Most rentals cost about $15 per hour, or $25 per day. If you're going to be staying put, you might want to look into extended bike rentals, which are usually cheaper.

People looking to cycle-tour will find themselves fairly alone in this area. A cyclist with loaded-down panniers going the distance is an unusual sight in this region, and while folks might look at you funny,

BOATING

In order to understand life in the Lowcountry, one must experience the view from the water. Get a waves-eye view from a kayak, enjoy a dinner cruise on a paddlewheeler, or zip around in an inflatable Zodiac. Join a fishing charter, slip over the ripples in a sailboat, or ply along in a pontoon. There are options for boaters of all experience levels.

To boat in the Lowcountry is to scratch its underbelly, to understand the cultural evolution of its people. Being on the water lets you ponder the days when Native Americans toured these waters by canoe, when explorers shouted the words 'Land Ho!' at the first sight of the mainland, when pirate ships prowled the waters or when slave ships brought West Africans to this new world.

For most coastal locals, having a boat is on par with (or maybe more important than) having a car. For this reason, boat docks and access points are everywhere. Boat rentals – from kayaks and canoes to pontoon boats and sailboats – are also widespread. Anywhere there's a marina, there are outfitters, ready to take people out to the watery world.

The best places to rent boats or take guided boat tours are from the marinas at the big resort areas, like St Simons Island and Hilton Head. Boat tours are plentiful in Charleston, Beaufort and Murrells Inlet, near Myrtle Beach. Following are a few recommended outfitters, although you can literally go boating everywhere.

- **Sea Kayak Georgia** (☎ 912-786-8732, 888-529-2542; www.seakayakgeorgia.com; Tybee Island) Kayak trips to Little Tybee Island and Lazaretto Creek are offered on weekends from March through May and daily June through September. The company also offers a limited number of full-day trips, kayaking classes and camping trips.
- **Southeast Adventure Outfitters** (☎ 912-638-6732; St Simon's Island) The three-hour sea kayak trip is a great introduction. The company also offers guided tours to the Okefenokee Swamp and local rivers, as well as camping trips to Sapelo and Cumberland Islands.
- **Jekyll Harbor Marina** (☎ 912-635-3137; Jekyll Island) Floating docks, dry storage, boat rentals, bicycle rentals and parasail rides are offered. Dolphin tours and fishing charters are offered from the Jekyll Wharf (☎ 912-635-3152).
- **Okefenokee Adventures** (☎ 912-496-7156; Okefenokee National Refuge) One- or two-hour guided boat tours are possible; for a sense of true swamp mystery, try the night tours.
- **Scott's Low Country Nature Tours** (☎ 843-683-0187; Hilton Head) Get up close and personal with the dolphins. Captain Scott Henry's six-passenger open boat departs Shelter Cove Marina for a two-hour private tour.
- **Spirit of Harbour Town** (☎ 843-842-7179; Hilton Head) This large party boat carries passengers through the Intracoastal Waterway and down the Savannah River to Savannah. There are both daytime and nighttime trips; both last five hours.
- **Stars & Stripes** (☎ 843-842-7933; Hilton Head) This agency offers 90-minute day sails and a two-hour sunset cruise aboard a former America's Cup sloop.
- **Lowcountry Rafting Adventures** (☎ 843-986-1051, 877-722-7238; www.lowcountryraftingadventures .com; Beaufort) Fun and informative tours of the ACE Basin and surrounding barrier islands in a motorized raft; tours leave from the downtown marina.
- **ACE Basin Tours** (☎ 843-521-3099; 888-814-3129; Coosaw Island) On this tour you'll ride a 38-foot pontoon through the rivers and estuaries of the ACE Basin.
- **Bohicket Boat Adventure & Tour Company** (☎ 843-768-7294; www.bohicketboat.com; Kiawah Island) Fishing, boating, kayaking and sailing trips, as well as boat and kayak rentals. The 'Sea Island Excursion' is a three-hour trip to shell-filled beaches; the two-hour 'Dolphin Watching' trip follows the playful bottlenose dolphins.
- **Captain Dick's** (☎ 843-651-3676; www.captdicks.com; Murrells Inlet) The good captain rents out pontoons, skiffs and kayaks. Try the 'Cruisin' the Beach' sightseeing cruise, the educational and fun 2½-hour 'Saltwater Marsh Explorer Adventure' or the two-hour 'Gator Tour,' which is conducted in an amphibious vehicle. Deep-sea fishing trips are also available.

they'll go out of their way to get you out of the heat and find out what freakish force of nature pushed you this way.

Low shoulders and almost nonexistent bike lanes along the highways make long-distance cycling a risky business, but there are a lot of great secondary and tertiary roads for road biking. Contact the **Coastal Bicycle Touring Club** (www.cbtc.org) for a list of local rides around Savannah, plus links to cycling clubs in Georgia. In Charleston the **Coastal Cyclists Bicycle Club** (www.coastalcyclist.org) is a coalition of cycling organizations whose website gives ride maps and area information.

Snail's-pace development is under way for the 27-mile **Waccamaw Neck Bikeway**, which will connect Georgetown (north of Charleston) to Murrells Inlet (just south of Myrtle Beach).

TENNIS

Full-service tennis centers are almost as ubiquitous as golf courses along the coast. Most resorts offer clay and hard courts, lighted facilities and excellent instruction. Resorts with noteworthy tennis facilities, where clinics, drills and match play are offered, include Palmetto Dunes Tennis Center and Sea Pines Racquet Club, on Hilton Head; and Kiawah Island Resort Tennis Center, on Kiawah Island. You can usually rent or 'demo' racquets for a nominal fee. Court fees can be anywhere from $3 to $20 per hour, and one-on-one private lessons usually cost about $50 to $65 per hour.

Excellent public facilities include the Van der Meer Tennis Center, on Hilton Head; and the Family Circle Tennis Center, near Charleston. The latter hosts the women's pro Family Circle Cup in April.

GOLF

Oh hear ye, Gods of Golf. The Georgia and South Carolina coast has literally hundreds of courses, making it a veritable shrine to the game. Here you'll find everything from arcade-like minigolf to championship courses. Course architects like Pete Dye, Jack Nicklaus, Robert Trent Jones and the Fazio brothers have whipped up a dizzying array of both public and private courses to suit all ability levels. Still, even with all these courses, competition for tee times can be brutal. It's best to book ahead (up to a month in advance for the busy spring and fall seasons).

Food & Drink

Southerners love to eat, and they take their regional cuisine very seriously. Classic Southern country cooking is often described as 'hearty' – no doubt because it tastes wonderful, it's satisfying, it makes you feel relaxed and, if enjoyed in great quantities, it eventually produces a nice, cushy coat of fat around your arteries. You'll find plenty of that in Georgia and South Carolina, but the Lowcountry coastal cuisine adds its own flair, often taking advantages of fresh food – from the sea or from the garden.

STAPLES & SPECIALITIES
Soups & Stews

Southerners are fond of one-pot meals, where you throw a bunch of ingredients into a pot, let it simmer and hope for the best. These meals are great for long camping trips, beachside parties or for large groups. In fact, many recipes you'll find serve 30 people or more.

Frogmore stew consists of sausage, corn, shrimp, potatoes and seasonings, and was born when a tired fisherman took all of the ingredients out of his cupboard and dumped them into a pot. It's named after Frogmore, South Carolina, an early African American settlement on St Helena Island. Georgia's version of Frogmore stew is called Lowcountry boil and is essentially the same thing.

Charleston Receipts, by the Junior League of Charleston, captures the true flavor of Charleston, intertwining food history and recipes for favorites like she-crab soup and benne crackers.

In and around Charleston, she-crab soup is a delicious, creamy soup that can be heavenly when prepared well. The she-crab's eggs, especially in winter, add a special flavor to the soup – a flavor he-crabs can never replicate. Shrimp chowder is also a popular dish, as is oyster soup. Black bean soup is also a local favorite and is spiced up with Caribbean flavors.

Rice

Going back to the booming plantation days, rice has been a major staple in the Lowcountry diet. Rice recipes from Italy, France, Spain, the West Indies and Africa came into the diet, and many restaurants serve traditional risotto, jasmine rice or jambalaya. Other truly Southern favorites include red rice, which is made with tomatoes, onion and bacon. Though recipes differ slightly, dirty rice is made with chicken livers, ground beef, onions and celery.

A big favorite is hopping John, a hearty stew made with ham and cow peas (the local term for field peas). It was traditionally eaten on New Year's Day to bring good luck; collards usually accompany the meal to represent money. Another rice dish, especially in South Carolina, is pilau (*per*-low), traditionally made with chicken, bacon and tomatoes. In some parts, pilau is called chicken bog.

Seafood

Fresh, just-caught seafood sits at the center of any dinner table or lunch table, or sometimes even breakfast table for that matter. Look out onto the water or stand by the docks, and you'll see trollers, gill netters and seiners hauling in the catch of the day.

All that good shrimp! Boiled shrimp, fried shrimp, steamed shrimp and sautéed shrimp are as common as salad in other parts of the country.

FROGMORE STEW

With everyday life in the sea islands so intricately tied to the sea, it's no surprise that the locals grow up with the knowledge of how to head and devein a shrimp in two seconds. Because seafood is seasonal, Lowcountry natives also learn how to be creative chefs. You work with what you get – and what ya already got.

That's how Frogmore stew was born. It's likely that locals have been cooking some version of it for hundreds of years, but the 'official' stew was born about 45 years ago. The story goes that a soldier on National Guard duty was preparing a cookout for his mates. Of course he had fresh seafood, but all he had was leftovers to serve it with. So he threw everything he had into one big pot – fresh shrimp, crabs, leftover sausage, onions, potatoes and corn on the cob; spiced it all up and – voila! He'd created Frogmore stew, named for the town at the Four Corners Community on St Helena. Here's a sample recipe, but the key to good Frogmore is ample improvisation.

5lb fresh shrimp, headed but not peeled
1lb fresh crab meat (you can throw in whole crabs, but they take up a lot of room in the pot)
3lb sausage, cut into ½-inch pieces
10 ears of sweet corn, husked and cut in half
10 baby potatoes, cut in half
3 onions, chopped
1 beer
2 gallons water
1 package seafood seasoning (readily available at the seafood counter of most supermarkets)

Put water, potatoes, seasoning, and sausage into a large pot. Bring to a boil. Add crab, corn and beer. Simmer for about 15 minutes (until potatoes are cooked). Add shrimp; when the shrimp are pink (about 5 minutes), it's done. Add salt and pepper to taste.

There's nothing quite like a basket of fresh steamed peel-n-eat shrimp dipped in garlic butter. A regional specialty is shrimp 'n' grits – shrimp simmered in butter or bacon fat and served over grits.

Crab is also common and you could spend a lifetime and a lot of delicious meals searching for the very best crab cake. A steak piled high with crabmeat'll make your heart go pitter patter, and a giant plate of fresh crackin' crabs is an excellent way to get into a meal. At your typical crab shack, plates of uncracked shellfish – oysters, crabs, mussels and shrimp – are brought to tables covered with brown paper or newsprint. You'll be offered cracking tools and plastic bibs, and when you're done, the server will collect the whole mess in the paper and toss it away in one quick swipe. Clams and oysters are in season from mid-September to mid-May. Oysters are best slurped up raw with a little lemon and hot sauce. Grouper, snapper and sea bass are just some of the fresh fish available, along with fried catfish.

Southern Cooking to Remember, by Kathryn Tucker Windham, includes recipes for Lowcountry seafood, Appalachian stack cakes and wild duck from Georgia marshlands.

Creative chefs from Myrtle Beach, Charleston, Savannah, Hilton Head and St Simons Island continually add innovative jazz to traditional seafood dishes, while seafood slingers in smaller communities keep old customs alive and well.

Grits

First used in Native American cooking, grits are small broken grains of white corn, or ground hominy. Traditionally a breakfast food (with eggs, bacon and toast), grits are now used in just about everything. Fry 'em up with a bit of bacon fat (a staple in Southern kitchens), top 'em with cheese or gravy, mix 'em with tomatoes and onions, or just eat 'em plain. Grits are an acquired taste, but if you spend much time in the South, you'd better get used to the tasty dish – and never, as much as you want to, say they taste like porridge (although they do).

Barbecue

A particularly revered Southern cuisine is barbecue, which can be made with smoked or marinated meat, which is then grilled and eaten with 'dip' (barbecue sauce). Pork is the meat of choice (offered chopped, sliced, pulled or in ribs), but barbecued chicken and beef are also available. Most Southerners do not use 'barbecue' as a verb; instead they talk about 'grilling,' as in 'We're gonna grill some burgers,' or 'Let's grill out tonight, darlin'.'

In Georgia, barbecue is *always* made from pork (pulled or shredded), with a wide range of sauces. In the Southeast, most barbecue sauces are either vinegar- or tomato-based, though you'll also find mustard-based sauce, a Carolina specialty. Sauce recipes are often closely guarded family secrets.

A plate of barbecued meat (just called 'barbecue') is usually served with a slice of white bread and a side of coleslaw, baked beans or macaroni salad. The classic venue is a no-frills roadside stand with a hickory-smoking chimney out back.

Gullah Cuisine

At first glance, Gullah cuisine seems to have a lot in common with traditional Southern cuisine. You'll see fried chicken, fried whiting, catfish, red rice, white rice, gumbo and okra, collard greens, peas and rice, candied yams and string beans. The big difference is in the flavors. Most Gullah cooks will tell you they never follow a recipe, that 'food asks for what it needs.' Most Gullah foods come from nature and from the necessity to make do with whatever you have. The best places to sample Gullah cuisine are on Hwy 17, just north of Mount Pleasant; on St Helena Island (near Beaufort); or on Sapelo Island.

Other Regional Specialties

A 'meat-and-three' plate means you pick an entree and three of several well-cooked vegetables, typically okra, corn, black-eyed peas, collard greens, mustard greens or turnip greens. You'll often find macaroni-and-cheese listed with vegetables, along with cole slaw, Jell-O salad and mashed potatoes. Most meals come with a flaky biscuit, cornbread or hush puppies, which are small fried rounds of dough, named from what was said to the whining dogs looking for scraps at fish fries.

You might be more inclined to try one of the region's other specialties: peaches. Peaches are one of Georgia's signature crops (brought by the Spanish in the mid-16th century) and can be found fresh or in pies, cobblers and ice cream. South Carolina is actually billed as the 'Peach Capital of the USA,' though most would think, from all the peachy propaganda, that Georgia could claim that title. Watermelons are another common fruit grown locally. The sweet Vidalia onion is grown only in the Georgia town of the same name – Vidalias are a sweet onion used in many Lowcountry recipes.

Peanuts – also known as groundpeas, pinders and goobers – were introduced to non-Southerners during the Civil War, which started an

More than 150 recipes, including shrimp and grits, sweet potato pie and crawfish gumbo can be found in *Hoppin' John's Lowcountry Cooking: Recipes & Ruminations from Charleston and the Carolina Coastal Plain*, by John Martin Taylor.

DID YOU KNOW?

Chitlins are boiled pig intestines typically eaten with cabbage and served alongside pork, coleslaw and sweet potato pie. When the intestines are fried, they're called fried chitterlings.

Sallie Ann Robinson, a former Daufuskie student of Pat Conroy's, wrote *Gullah Home Cooking the Daufuskie Way*, in which recipes are categorized into four food sources: the garden, the river, the sea and the woods.

industry for this little-known, high-protein snack. You'll see them sold throughout the region, especially on chilly winter days. The peanuts are boiled, shells and all, in a big pot of salty water until the shells are soft but not mushy.

DRINKS
Nonalcoholic Drinks

On a hot day, a cool drink of lemonade or iced tea goes down the throat like elixir sent from the heavens. Lemonade is usually sweet and very lemony. If you ask for tea, it'll be assumed you mean iced tea, either sweet or unsweetened. If you opt for 'sweet tea,' be forewarned: 'sweet' often means sugary, syrupy sweet. If you want the kind the Queen of England drinks, you must ask for 'hot tea.' Though Southerners drink coffee in the morning, the coffee craze isn't happening at the same rate as the rest of the US and sometimes it can be hard to find a good, strong brew. It's OK to drink tap water throughout the region.

Alcoholic Drinks

In recent years, wine menus have expanded in coastal restaurants, and you can find some great selections from all over the world. Microbrewed beer is increasingly popular, and you'll find cozy brewpubs in most cities. Hard liquor is widely available, and bourbon and Coke remains a Southern favorite. A mint julep is a tall frosted drink made with bourbon, sugar and ice and garnished with sprigs of mint; although it's as familiar as Tara, you'll see few Southerners actually order one.

The legal drinking age in both South Carolina and Georgia is 21. In Georgia, it is illegal to buy beer, wine or hard alcohol from a store on

A big young white guy and a small old black woman make magic together in *The Gift of Southern Cooking: Recipes and Revelations from Two Great Southern Cooks,* by Edna Lewis and Scott Peacock.

WHAT'S WITH THOSE TINY BOTTLES?

Ordering a cocktail in South Carolina seems awfully similar to ordering a drink on an airplane. Look behind the bar at any pub, bar or restaurant and you'll see hundreds of 1.7oz minibottles, but no sign of a big bottle. The same bedrock conservatism that prompted the teetotaling days of prohibition led lawmakers to pass a law in 1973 that mandated that all liquor be poured from tiny bottles. Someone, somewhere actually thought removing a bartender's ability to 'free pour' out of large bottles would actually deter drinkers.

The opposite has happened. Elsewhere in the country, a shot of booze measures 1oz or 1.5oz, so with minibottles being 1.7oz, South Carolina bartenders actually pour the nation's stiffest drinks.

Be careful what you order, as mixed drinks can cost a fortune. If you order a 'brown cow' for example, you pay for two drink, because they have to open up one bottle of vodka and one bottle of Kahlua. You'll also get drunk faster, because the drink will amount to almost three standard drinks. Don't even think about ordering a Long Island iced tea, which is made with rum, gin, vodka, tequila and triple sec. You'll pay for a small bottle of each of the five liquors, and you'll end up with a drink strong enough to seriously kick your ass – and then there's always the subsequent hangover of monumental proportions.

Minibottles are also tough on bartenders, who develop calluses from twisting so many tiny tops. They are also environmentally disastrous, because none of those tiny bottles get recycled.

Many attempts have been made to repeal the minibottle law, which is part of the state constitution. But proponents for keeping the bottles say the state will lose out on taxation, and that it'll more difficult to control the flow of booze from big bottles. Loose as the logic may seem, so far the law's held strong.

Sunday, though you can buy booze in restaurants. It is illegal in Georgia to buy beer with an alcohol content higher than 6%. While alcohol is sold on Sundays in South Carolina, an arcane liquor law states that all booze served in bars and restaurants must be poured out of minibottles. In both states it's illegal to drive with open containers of alcohol in the car; drunk driving is a serious felony offense. Drinking alcohol outdoors is generally prohibited, but it's tolerated at open-air music festivals…and on the streets of Savannah!

CELEBRATING WITH FOOD

Both Georgia and South Carolina are passionate about their festivals, most of which feature massive amounts of food. Get a sampling of traditional Gullah cuisine at the Gullah Festival in Beaufort in May, and at the Native Gullah Festival on Hilton Head in February. Savannah's Thanksgiving Southern Style brings out the best of local restaurants chefs, as does the Taste of Charleston, held in mid-October at the Boone Hall Plantation. In March, Hilton Head's Wine Fest is a tasting extravaganza. Plates piled high with raw oysters grace the tables at Charleston's Lowcountry Oyster Festival in January.

For recipes of Southern and Lowcountry dishes, along with links to cookbooks and Southern food products, go to www .southernconnoisseur.com.

VEGETARIANS & VEGANS

Strict vegetarians and vegans will have a tough time getting satiated in this region. While many college students in Charleston and Savannah have embraced the benefits, others will be downright stunned to hear you eat no meat at all. Most dishes are made with some form of seafood or meat; get into a conversation about it with any Southerner and they'll likely ask, 'So what *do* you eat?'

Most restaurants offer vegetarian salads and soups, but be sure to ask first; at first glance soups might look vegetarian, but most recipes are made with chicken or beef stock. For example, black bean soup is often made with chicken broth. Others are made with seafood; if you are willing to eat seafood, your options will open up immensely.

Many different rice dishes are available (again, ask whether or not it has been cooked in meat stock), and vegetables are served with almost every meal (though Southerners tend to cook them a long while), so in a pinch you can fill up on veggies and rice.

Though few places would be considered vegetarian restaurants (and vegan restaurants simply don't exist), many delis and cafes in Charleston, Myrtle Beach, Hilton Head and Savannah usually offer good vegetarian options. In Charleston, try **Hominy** (p166) for good Southern vegetarian dishes. In Savannah, **B Matthew's Bakery & Eatery** (p80) has a great selection of sandwiches and soups, many of which are vegetarian.

The *Beaufort Gazette* homepage (www .beaufortgazette.com /features/food/recipes) is filled with Lowcountry and Southern recipes.

WHINING & DINING

Because so many family resorts surround the bigger cities, children are welcome at all but the fanciest restaurants in the region. Family-friendly restaurants usually get packed at around 6pm for dinner, but most have highchairs, crayons and staff that will help you by heating up milk or baby food. Many restaurants offer a special children's menu, which takes a nice bite out of your bill.

Recommended kid-friendly places in Charleston include the Italian restaurant **Bocci**, the yummy **Sticky Fingers**, **Hyman's** and **AW Shucks** for seafood (see Charleston's Eating section p165). In Savannah, good home cookin' with offerings for kids can be found at **Mrs Wilkes' Dining Room** (p80)

BRUNSWICK STEW

Here's a Lowcountry favorite that will make you feel like the prince (or princess) of tides.

3lb chicken
1lb beef
1lb lean pork
3 chopped onions

Place meat in large pot with onions, salt and pepper. Add water to cover the meat and onions, and then cover the pot. Cook until meet falls from the bones (about three hours). Allow to cool. Shred meat and return it to the stock.

Add:
4 cans (16oz) tomatoes
5 teaspoons Worcestershire sauce
14oz ketchup
1 teaspoon Tabasco
2 bay leaves
12oz chili sauces
½ teaspoon dry mustard
½ stick of butter

Cook for an hour; stir occasionally.

Add:
3 teaspoon white or apple vinegar
16oz canned lima beans
15oz canned peas
3 small Irish potatoes, diced
1 box of frozen, sliced okra

Cook until thick. Serve with boiled shrimp, oysters, crab or barbecue.

and **Debi's Restaurant** (p79). In Myrtle Beach, most restaurants cater to families, offering a plethora of all-you-can-eat buffets and theme-inspired décor; the **Nascar Café** (p186) is one such example.

If you're staying in one of the resort areas – like Myrtle Beach Isle of Palm, Kiawah Island, Hilton Head or St Simons Island – and you'd like to cut costs, be sure to find out whether or not you've got a full or partial kitchen in your room. If you do, you can keep staples like milk, breakfast foods and snacks on hand, so you're not tied to the restaurants. Also, be sure to shop in grocery stores in outlying communities. Stores near the resorts tend to jack up prices; peanut butter that costs $3 on the mainland might cost $5 on Hilton Head or Kiawah Island.

Children not used to the rich cuisine might want to ease into it; the amount of butter and oil used in Southern cooking can upset young tummies. Children and pregnant women, who are more susceptible to contaminants, should avoid raw seafood.

HABITS & CUSTOMS

Southern cuisine is inexpensive and typically served up in heaps. Southerners take their time preparing and serving meals, and they heartily avoid the whole concept of rushing. Service in restaurants isn't necessarily slow, but it usually isn't fast, and impatience is looked upon as the ultimate in rudeness.

All-you-can-eat lunch and dinner buffets are common in Myrtle Beach and family resort areas. Some restaurants serve family-style, seating unrelated groups at the same table to pass shared plates around. Note that some families say a prayer before eating; other patrons at the same table would not necessarily be expected to join in (guests at a family's home *would* be expected to do so), but it would be respectful to wait silently until they're done before serving or eating.

Most restaurants offer nonsmoking sections, though smoking is usually permitted in bars and on outdoor patios. In the South, smokers are not thought of as lepers as much as in other parts of the country, though that is slowly changing.

DID YOU KNOW?

Most Southerners consider Miracle Whip (called 'salad dressing' in these parts) to be mayonnaise. If you ask for mayo on your sandwich, you'll most likely get Miracle Whip.

Savannah

CONTENTS

'This place is fantastic. It's like *Gone With the Wind* on mescaline.' Such is the description of Savannah rendered by the protagonist (John Cusack) in Clint Eastwood's film version of *Midnight in the Garden of Good & Evil*. He ain't wrong, Scarlett.

Set on the Savannah River about 18 miles from the coast amid moors and mammoth live oak trees dripping with Spanish moss, the city is steeped in tradition. With about 2.5 sq miles of historic mansions, cotton warehouses and public buildings, Savannah preserves its antebellum history in a way only its Lowcountry sister city Charleston can rival. Walking among the cotton wharves and 21 lush urban squares, you can trace American history from the time of Georgia's first settlement to the moment in the Civil War when the Yankee General Sherman seized the city and offered it as a Christmas present to President Abraham Lincoln.

But while Charleston has always harbored its reputation as a dignified, refined and politically courageous cultural center, Savannah revels in being the bad girl. The town loves its sinful pleasures, be they the brown-sugar and hot-pepper sauce on Lowcountry shrimp or the bump and grind of a drag-queen diva. Five million tourists a year arrive in Savannah looking for the colorful cast of characters featured in *Midnight*. Well, their kindred spirits are still here waiting to escort you to the party. The Marvin Gaye song 'Let's Get It On' is a virtual call to arms here. And the St Patrick's Day celebration is a rite of spring to equal New Orleans' Fat Tuesday.

HIGHLIGHTS

■ **Wining**
The cafés, bars & clubs around City Market (p68) and the Riverfront (p68)

■ **Dining**
Monkey Bar/Fusion Restaurant (p81), on Broughton St

■ **Fantastic Festival**
The city's St Patrick's Day Celebration (p74) on March 17 – a veritable Mardi Gras East

■ **Offbeat Experience**
A drag show at Club One Jefferson (p84)

■ **Wildlife Encounter**
Birding in Savannah National Wildlife Refuge (p90)

■ TELEPHONE CODE: **912**	■ POPULATION: **131,700**	■ AREA: **65 SQ MI**

ORIENTATION

Situated near the northern edge of the Georgia Coast, Savannah is a sprawling port city on the south side of the Savannah River, 20 miles inland from the Atlantic Ocean and about 5 miles east of I-95. The Historic District – which contains most of the Savannah's restaurants, hostelries, nightlife and attractions – is a compact area of about 20 square blocks clustered around the river bank. Bay St, Broughton St and Oglethorpe Ave are the main east–west arteries. Bull St runs north–south and divides addresses in the Historic District between streets with the prefix 'East' and streets with the prefix 'West.' Large Forsyth Park borders the southern side of the Historic District.

Maps

You can snag free maps of the city at hotels and tourist attractions around town. These are good enough if all you plan to do is wander around the Historic District. For more serious exploration of the surrounding area, pick up *Street Maps of Savannah/Chatham County* for $3 at the visitors center.

If you are a AAA member, get their excellent Savannah map, which includes detailed coverage of the entire Georgia coast, as well as Hilton Head, Beaufort and the surrounding area.

INFORMATION

Bookstores

Barnes & Noble (Map pp68-9; ☎ 912-353-7757; Oglethorpe Mall, 7804 Abercorn St)
E Shaver, Bookseller (Map pp66-7; ☎ 912-234-7257; 326 Bull St)
Ex Libris (Map pp66-7; ☎ 912-525-7550; 228 Martin Luther King Jr Blvd) The coffee shop here has filling sandwiches and desserts.
Waldenbooks (Map pp68-9; ☎ 912-927-1408; Savannah Mall, 14045 Abercorn St)

Emergency

AAA Roadside Service (☎ 800-222-4357)
Emergency Numbers (☎ 911) Police, ambulance, firefighters.
Main Police Station (☎ 912-232-4141) Nonemergencies only.

SAVANNAH IN...

Two Days

Start your day with a leisurely breakfast along the river bluff at **B Matthew's Bakery & Eatery** or in the Historic District at **Clary's Café** (everybody's favorite diner in *Midnight*). Visit the **Savannah History Museum** or spend the cool hours of the morning following the **Walking Tour** (p72) or by taking a guided tour of the **Historic District**. Then catch lunch at an outdoor café in City Market. To beat the heat of the day, head for the **Riverfront** for some shopping, ride the *Savannah Belles* **ferry** to Hutchinson Island or take a cruise aboard one of the paddle wheelers of **Savannah Riverboat Cruises**. Spend the cool hours of the evening window-shopping for a restaurant in the Historic District, at City Market or along the Riverfront. Before or after dinner, take a romantic carriage ride (you'll need a reservation) with a bottle of wine (it's legal). Then head to one of the city's jive night spots to let the good times roll.

On your second morning in town, you might want to hit a museum or get serious about shopping at City Market or the Riverfront. Then blast out of town for lunch and the beach at **Tybee Island** or take a wilderness hike or tour. By night, take in the delights wining and dining in an unexplored quarter of the city.

Three Days

Follow the two-day itinerary, but slip into a more relaxed Southern mode and spread these activities over three days. Save time to chill in the garden or pool at your accommodations. Do the Forrest Gump thing and hang out on a park bench in one of the squares and let the world pass you by. Find time for a picnic in a square, in a park or along the river. Join a tour of **Davenport House** or explore the **Telfair Art Museum**. Take in the dueling pianos at **Savannah Smiles** (p83) or one of many jazz acts.

***MIDNIGHT* MADNESS?**

All of the hubbub surrounding the city's role in the book and flick *Midnight in the Garden of Good & Evil* is enough to make a person suspicious that a huge propaganda mill is fanning the flames of *Midnight* at the expense of Savannah's other attractions. But it's not just media hype – a recent sojourn to Savannah put us in touch with lots of first-time visitors, and to our surprise, almost all of them – from conventioneers to biker posses – wanted to talk about Jim Williams, the Mercer House and the time Kevin Spacey came to town to star in the flick. So it does not seem that it is possible to overstate the influence that *Midnight* continues to hold over Savannah. For better or worse, *Midnight* is to Savannah what witches are to Salem, Massachusetts and what Shakespeare is to Stratford-upon-Avon.

Internet Access

Internet cafes come and go rapidly. At the time of publication, Savannah had none. But you can get online at many of the city's hotels. Surfing is free at the **Chatham-Effingham-Liberty Regional Library** (Map pp66-7; ☎ 912-652-3600; 2002 Bull St, btwn 36th & 37th).

Internet Resources

www.savannahvisit.com Things to do, history, restaurants and lodging.
www.savannah-online.com Current news stories and articles.
www.gaysavannah.com Complete list of gay-run and gay friendly accommodations, restaurants, bars, clubs and businesses.

Media

Savannah Morning News The city's major daily newspaper.
Savannah Tribune Daily; focused toward the African-American community.
Connect Savannah Weekly; covering arts and entertainment.
WBMQ 630AM News and talk radio
WIXV 95FM Classic rock
WJCL 96.5FM Country
WSIS 104FM R&B oldies
WSVH 91.1FM National Public Radio

Medical Services

Candler Hospital (Map pp68-9; ☎ 912-692-6000; 5353 Reynolds St)
CVS Pharmacy (Map pp66-7; ☎ 912-238-1494; cnr Bull St & W Broughton St; ☽ 8am-6pm Mon-Fri, 10am-6pm Sat)

Money

There are plenty of ATMs throughout the city. In a pinch, or for a full-service bank, go to Johnson Square, where there are several major banks.

Post

Main post office (Map pp66-7; ☎ 912-235-4653; 2 N Fahm St; ☽ 7am-6pm Mon-Fri, 9am-3pm Sat) Just west of downtown at the intersection with Bay St.
Downtown branch (Map pp66-7; W State & Barnard Sts; ☽ 8am-5pm Mon-Fri) The most convenient post office in the Historic District.

Tourist Offices

Savannah Visitors Center (Map pp66-7; ☎ 912-944-0455, 877-728-2662; www.savannahvisit.com; 301 Martin Luther King Jr Blvd; ☽ 10am-10pm) Excellent resources and services in the restored 1860s Central of Georgia train station. You can pick up walking-tour guides and discount coupons for local accommodations. You can also pick up parking passes for the Historic District. A number of privately operated city tours start here.
Hospitality Center (Map pp66-7; W River St; ☽ 10am-10pm) Racks filled with flyers on attractions, tours, restaurants, entertainment and hotels. There's also a Hospitality Center at the Savannah International Airport.

DANGERS & ANNOYANCES

The Historic District is safe during the day. However, muggings and drug dealing are common in neighborhoods that surround the Historic District, and desperate folks prowl the Historic District after dark. The area south of Forsyth Park is sketchy at night, and in fact, the Historic District south of Oglethorpe Ave can feel lonesome and threatening after sunset. Savannah has its share of murders (one concierge admitted hiding the newspaper when the front-page news was too bad). Be aware too that criminals know where the well-heeled tourists hang out. At night, use common-sense precautions and stay in well-lit, populated areas. The Riverfront and the area north of State St in the Historic District are generally OK.

SAVANNAH

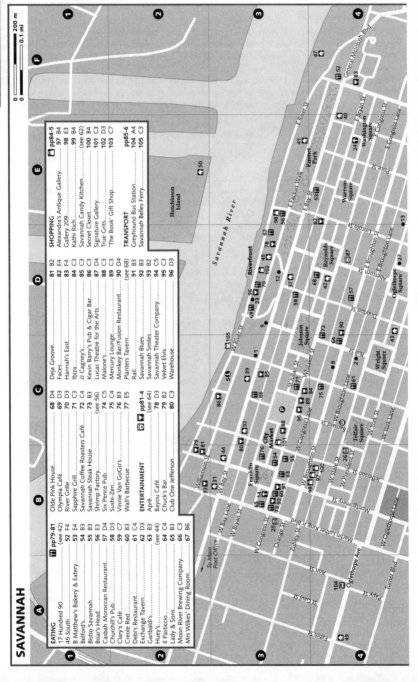

EATING	pp79-81
17 Hundred 90..................	(see 42)
45 South......................	52 F4
B Matthew's Bakery & Eatery..	53 E4
Belford's.....................	54 B3
Bistro Savannah...............	55 B3
Boar's Head...................	56 E3
Casbah Moroccan Restaurant....	57 D4
Churchill's Pub...............	58 D3
Clary's Café..................	59 C7
Creole Red....................	60 B3
Debi's Restaurant.............	61 C4
Exchange Tavern...............	62 D3
Garibaldi's...................	63 B3
Huey's........................	(see 44)
Il Pasticcio..................	64 C4
Lady & Sons...................	65 B3
Moon River Brewing Company....	66 C3
Mrs Wilkes' Dining Room.......	67 B6
Olde Pink House...............	68 D4
Olympia Café..................	69 D3
River Grille..................	70 D3
Sapphire Grill................	71 C4
Savannah Coffee Roasters Café.	72 C4
Savannah Steak House..........	73 B3
Shrimp Factory................	(see 56)
Six Pence Pub.................	74 C5
Sushi-Zen....................	75 C4
Vinnie Van GoGo's.............	76 B3
Wall's Barbecue...............	77 E5

ENTERTAINMENT	pp81-4
Apré..........................	(see 64)
Bayou Café....................	78 D3
Chuck's Bar...................	79 B2
Club One Jefferson............	80 C3

Deja Groove...................	81 B2
Faces........................	82 E4
Hannah's East.................	83 F4
Ibiza........................	84 C3
JJ Cagney's...................	85 C3
Kevin Barry's Pub & Cigar Bar.	86 C3
Lucas Theatre for the Arts....	87 D4
Malone's.....................	88 C3
Mercury Lounge................	89 C3
Monkey Bar/Fusion Restaurant..	90 D4
Planters Tavern...............	(see 68)
Rail.........................	91 B3
Savannah Blues................	92 B3
Savannah Smiles...............	93 B2
Savannah Theater Company......	94 C5
Velvet Elvis..................	95 C3
Warehouse.....................	96 D3

SHOPPING	pp84-5
Alexandra's Antique Gallery...	97 B4
Gallery 209...................	98 E3
Kathi Rich....................	99 B4
Savannah Candy Kitchen........	(see 62)
Secret Closet.................	100 B4
Signature Gallery.............	101 C3
True Grits....................	102 D3
'The Book' Gift Shop..........	103 C7

TRANSPORT	pp85-6
Greyhound Bus Station.........	104 A4
Savannah Belles Ferry.........	105 C3

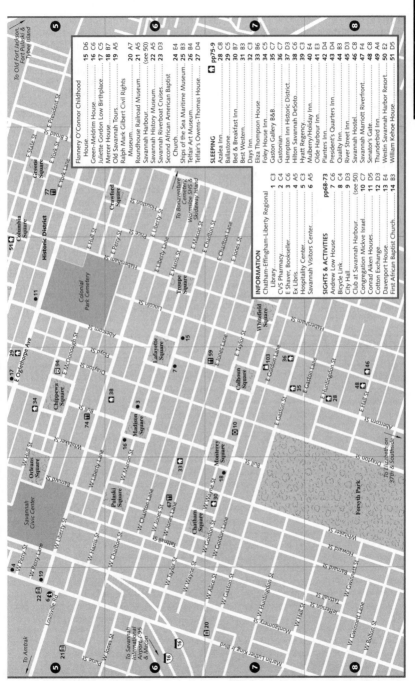

Flannery O'Connor Childhood
House.. 15 D6
Green-Meldrim House...................... 16 C6
Juliette Gordon Low Birthplace...... 17 C5
Mercer House................................. 18 B7
Old Savannah Tours....................... 19 A5
Ralph Mark Gilbert Civil Rights
Museum..................................... 20 A7
Roundhouse Railroad Museum........ 21 A5
Savannah Harbour.................... (see 50)
Savannah History Museum.............. 22 A5
Savannah Riverboat Cruises........... 23 D3
Second African American Baptist
Church....................................... 24 E4
Ships of the Sea Maritime Museum.. 25 B3
Telfair Art Museum........................ 26 B4
Telfair's Owens-Thomas House....... 27 D4

SLEEPING 🔲 pp75-9
Azalea Inn..................................... 28 C8
Ballastone.................................... 29 C5
Bed & Breakfast Inn...................... 30 B7
Best Western................................. 31 B3
Days Inn....................................... 32 C3
Eliza Thompson House.................... 33 B6
Foley House Inn............................. 34 C5
Gaston Gallery B&B....................... 35 C7
Gastonian..................................... 36 C7
Hampton Inn Historic District........ 37 D3
Hilton Savannah DeSoto................ 38 C6
Hyatt Regency............................... 39 C3
Mulberry/Holiday Inn.................... 40 E4
Olde Harbour Inn.......................... 41 E3
Planters Inn.................................. 42 D4
President's Quarters Inn................. 43 D4
Quality Inn................................... 44 B3
River Street Inn............................. 45 D3
Savannah Hostel............................ 46 D8
Savannah Marriott Riverfront......... 47 F4
Senator's Gate.............................. 48 C8
Thunderbird Inn............................ 49 A4
Westin Savannah Harbor Resort...... 50 E2
William Kehoe House...................... 51 D5

INFORMATION
Chatham-Effingham-Liberty Regional
Library... 1 C3
CVS Pharmacy................................. 2 C4
E Shaver, Bookseller....................... 3 C6
Ex Libris... 4 A5
Hospitality Center........................... 5 C3
Savannah Visitors Center................. 6 A5

SIGHTS & ACTIVITIES pp68-73
Andrew Low House........................... 7 C6
Bicycle Link.................................... 8 C4
City Hall... 9 D3
Club at Savannah Harbour........... (see 50)
Congregation Mickve Israel............ 10 C7
Conrad Aiken Houses..................... 11 D5
Cotton Exchange............................ 12 D3
Davenport House............................ 13 E4
First African Baptist Church............ 14 B3

SAVANNAH

SIGHTS

Savannah's **Historic District** is a rectangle bounded by the Savannah River, Forsyth Park, E Broad St and Martin Luther King Jr Blvd. Almost everything of interest to visitors lies within or just outside this area. Twenty-one of Savannah's original 24 squares are the pillars of the district, and each marks an exquisite place to relax among flower gardens and shade trees. Also, there's usually a monument to some notable (like Georgia's first settler, James Oglethorpe) who is buried in the square. The Historic District turns distinctly residential south of York St.

Located along the wharves of the Savannah River on the northern edge of the Historic District, the **Riverfront** is Savannah's most popular tourist attraction. The main pedestrian and auto artery is River St, which is home to dozens of shops, restaurants and nightspots. This brick-and-cobblestone waterside promenade, which runs along a gallery of restored cotton warehouses, is a great place for strolling, shopping and watching your fellow Homo sapiens at play. Here you can bathe in the sights and sounds of a commercial river that's alive with everything from ferries and pleasure craft to huge container ships. Especially in the cool of the evening, the Riverfront attracts some fabulous jazz musicians, who play for donations.

Factors Walk promenade is essentially the upper level of buildings between River and Bay Sts and was the city's business center in the 19th century. Now it is a line of shops. Nearby are the gold-domed **City Hall** and the **Cotton Exchange** building, which is guarded by lion statues and was once one of the world's busiest exchanges.

Set along the western edge of the Historic District, at W St Julian St near Franklin Square, the **City Market** is a pedestrian mall that's filled with shops, cafés, restaurants and pubs in restored warehouses. There are frequently street entertainers and live bands playing here. Folks come to soak up the sun and enjoy

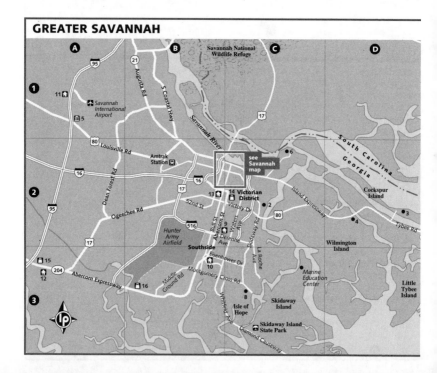

GREATER SAVANNAH

the entertainment, to people-watch and to chill with a snack and beverage on the park benches and at the tables of the open-air cafés. By night, the bars on the fringes of City Market start booming.

South of the Historic District, the **Victorian District** encompasses 50 blocks of two-story wood homes built in the late 19th century. Different areas are in various stages of renovation, and a recently renovated gem can be right around the corner from a sagging eyesore.

Even farther south is the **Southside** (south of Derenne Ave), a modern district rife with shopping malls, fast-food emporiums and hotels. The hotels here, however, are much cheaper than accommodations in the Historic District.

Savannah History Museum

Located just behind the visitors center, this **museum** (Map pp66-7; ☎ 912-238-1779; 303 Martin Luther King Jr Blvd; adult/child $4/3; ☼ 8:30am-5pm Mon-Fri, 9am-5pm Sat & Sun) is a good place to start a visit to the Historic District. The exhibits

document the history of the area's railroads and rice and cotton plantations through illustrations, photography, captions and artifacts. There is also a replica of Forrest Gump's park bench (which, in the film, was in Chippewa Square).

Telfair Art Museum

This small but elegant **art palace** (Map pp66-7; ☎ 912-232-1177; 121 Barnard St; adult/child $8/2; ☼ 10am-5pm Tue-Sat, 1pm-5pm Sun) has the look of a Roman temple and contains several plaster casts of Roman statues, a marvelous rotunda gallery of European paintings and the 'Bird Girl' statue from the cover of the book *Midnight in the Garden of Good & Evil*. There is a strong collection of 18th- and 19th-century paintings and decorative arts as well. The museum is housed in an 1818 mansion in the neoclassical Regency style.

Ralph Mark Gilbert Civil Rights Museum

Standing just south of the I-16 overpass, this civil rights **museum** (Map pp66-7; ☎ 912-231-8900; 460 Martin Luther King Jr Blvd; adult/child $4/2; ☼ 9am-5pm Mon-Sat) tells the story of African Americans in Savannah, focusing on the Civil Rights era. After the first sit-ins in 1960, a 15-month economic boycott and a 'wade-in' at Tybee Island, the city integrated one year before the passage of the 1964 Civil Rights Act. In 1964, Martin Luther King Jr called Savannah 'the most integrated city south of the Mason–Dixon line.'

Roundhouse Railroad Museum

Just to the south of the history museum and visitors center stands this **museum** (Map pp66-7; ☎ 912-651-6823; 601 W Harris St; adult/child $4/3.50; ☼ 9am-4pm), a relic from the days of steam railroading and a must-see for rail fans. The 38-stall roundhouse (dating from 1853), working turntable and repair shops of the now-defunct Central of Georgia Railroad stand just beyond the northern edge of the Historic District. There are more than 17 pieces of historic rolling stock here, including quite a few steam engines. Some engines work, and the museum is negotiating for right-of-way to operate its equipment and carry passengers.

0 ___ 4 km
0 ___ 2 mi

Hilton
Head
Island

80

Tybee
Island

ATLANTIC

OCEAN

Ships of the Sea Maritime Museum

A short distance north of the history museum is this small but engaging **maritime museum** (Map pp66-7; ☎ 912-232-1511; www .shipsofthesea.org; 41 Martin Luther King Jr Blvd; adult/child $5/4; ☑ 10am-5pm Tue-Sat). The attractive exhibits focus on nautical memorabilia and models of ships, particularly ones associated with the city. The SS *Savannah* was the first steamship to cross the Atlantic Ocean; much later, there was the nuclear-powered NS *Savannah*. The collection is housed in one of the South's earliest Greek Revival structures.

Davenport House

If you have time for touring only one house, make it the **Davenport** (Map pp66-7; ☎ 912-236-8097; Columbia Sq; adult/child $7/3.50; ☑ 10am-4pm Mon-Sat, 1-4pm Sun). It was the first of Savannah's historic homes to be restored, and its 30-minute tour is exceptional for both its antique collection, and its knowledgeable guides. The Georgian architecture is some of the finest in the South. It also has a shop with books on architecture, restoration and preservation.

Telfair's Owens-Thomas House

A superb example of the Regency style, this **mansion** (Map pp66-7; ☎ 912-233-9743; 124 Abercorn St; adult/child $8/2; ☑ noon-5pm Mon, 10am-5pm Tue-Sat, 1-5pm Sun) is home to an impressive collection of the Thomas family's heirlooms. Dating from 1816, the mansion operates under the curatorial direction of the Telfair Art Museum, and its carriage house, painted 'haint blue' to repel spirits of the dead, has a substantial collection of African Americana from the slave period.

Mercer House

This **house** (Map pp66-7; 429 Bull St) is the big enchilada for *Midnight* fans. Although Johnny Mercer (see p82) himself never actually lived here, the house was designed for his great-grandfather. In 1969, it became the home of the extravagant socialite antique dealer Jim Williams, then the site of Danny Hansford's murder (1981) and Jim's own death (less than a year later and almost on the same spot). Since Jim's demise, his family has had the house on the market for $9 million. Several Hollywood celebrities have been considering purchasing it, but no one has yet ponied up with the change. Sotheby's auctioned off most of the furnishings (like the Fabergé collection and the Joshua Reynolds paintings, in 2000). Ten years after the publication of *Midnight*, tourists continue to flock here and wonder at the stories this house could tell.

The interior of the home is not accessible to the public, so you'll just have to gawk at it from the street.

Andrew Low House

Built in 1848 by cotton merchant Andrew Low, this **grand home** (Map pp66-7; ☎ 912-233-6854; 329 Abercorn St; adult/child $7/4.50; ☑ 10am-4pm Mon-Wed, Fri & Sat, noon-4pm Sun) is of classical mid-19th-century design. There are guided tours every half hour. The Low House was the first historic house museum and now contains Savannah's most remarkable collection of antebellum antiques.

Other Historic Homes

The **Green-Meldrim House** (Map pp66-7; ☎ 912-232-1251; 1 W Macon St; adult/child $5/2; ☑ 10am-4pm Tue & Thu-Sat, closed Dec–mid-Jan) is the parish house of St John's Episcopal Church. It served as the headquarters for General Sherman after occupying Savannah with his Union troops in December 1864. The house is among the finest examples of Gothic Revival architecture in Savannah.

Dating from 1821, the **Juliette Gordon Low Birthplace** (Map pp66-7; ☎ 912-233-4501; 10 E Oglethorpe Ave; adult/child $8/7; ☑ 10am-4pm Mon-Sat, 12:30-4:30pm Sun) is an upper-middle-class Victorian home that was the childhood abode of the founder of the Girl Scouts of America.

The **Flannery O'Connor Childhood House** (Map pp66-7; ☎ 912-233-6014; 207 E Charlton St; adult/child $2/1; ☑ 1-4pm Sat & Sun) recalls the days before the author of *Wise Blood* turned into the queen of Southern Gothic writers.

The **Conrad Aiken Houses** (Map pp66-7; 228-230 E Oglethorpe Ave) mark the sites where the Pulitzer Prize–winning poet and novelist – who was a contemporary and friend of both TS Eliot and Ezra Pound – spent the first 11 and last 11 years of his life. With the shift of poetry anthologies to include voices from more diverse cultures, Aiken's highly psychoanalytical poems, such as 'The Charnel Rose,' rarely reach print these days.

Historic Houses of Worship

The **First African Baptist Church** (Map pp66-7; ☎ 912-233-6597; 23 Montgomery St; admission free; ⊙ 10am-3pm Mon-Fri) is the oldest African American church in North America. It was built in 1859 by slaves (after completing their normal day's work). Breathing holes in the floor downstairs are said to have been used by slaves fleeing to freedom. There are church services on Sunday.

The **Second African American Baptist Church** (Map pp66-7; ☎ 912-233-6163; 123 Houston St; admission free; ⊙ 10am-2pm Mon-Fri) marks the site of two historic orations. During the Civil War, conquering general WT Sherman read the Emancipation Proclamation to white and black Savannahians here. In the 1960s Dr Martin Luther King allegedly delivered a draft of his 'I Have a Dream' sermon here (although several churches claim this honor) before giving voice to it again at the Civil Rights March on Washington.

At Monterey Square, **Congregation Mickve Israel** (Map pp66-7; ☎ 912-233-1547; 20 E Gordon St; $2 donation; ⊙ 10am-noon & 2-4pm Mon-Fri) is the oldest Reform Judaism temple in the USA (the congregation formed in 1733, though the present Gothic building dates from 1878). The original congregation members came mainly from Spain and Portugal. Inside you will see the oldest Torah in the United States and more than 1800 articles of Judaica.

Universities

From its beginnings in 1979, the **Savannah College of Art and Design** (SCAD; ☎ 912-238-2400; www.scad.edu) has grown to 6000 students. The college has been primary force in renovating buildings in the Historic District, and it now occupies more than 52 structures, which are scattered throughout the Historic District. Its artistic students help give vitality to the downtown area. Many of the tourist industry employees – waiters, hotel clerks etc – are SCAD students.

Armstrong Atlantic State University (Map pp66-7; ☎ 912-927-5211; www.armstrong.edu) in Southside is part of the state university system and has nearly 6,000 students. Historically black **Savannah State University** (☎ 912-356-2336; www.savstate.edu) is also part of that system.

ACTIVITIES

While you might think that visiting Savannah is purely an urban experience, the city offers a surprising number of ways to escape the madding crowd in pursuit of sport, exercise and wildness adventures.

Biking

Biking is an excellent way to get around the Historic District, but be careful around the squares – cars may not always yield the right of way. **Old Savannah Tours** (Map pp66-7; ☎ 912-234-8141; 250 Martin Luther King Jr Blvd; ⊙ 9am-5pm), across from the visitors center, rents bicycles for $16 a day, including a lock and helmet. **Bicycle Link** (Map pp66-7; ☎ 912-233-9401; 22 W Broughton St; ⊙ 9am-5pm Mon-Sat), a full-service bike shop, rents bicycles for $20 a day or $80 a week.

DETOUR: BONAVENTURE CEMETERY

Although you have to drive 10 minutes east of the Historic District to find this place, fans of *Midnight* claim that this **burial ground** (Map pp68-9; ☎ 912-651-6843; admission free; ⊙ 8am-5pm), on Bonaventure Rd, is a must see, and they are right! The cemetery was the site of the voodoo rituals in the popular movie. Here you can walk at the edge of the Wilmington River amid the historic statues, moss-covered oaks, wisteria and azaleas.

Songwriter Johnny Mercer (see p82) and poet Conrad Aiken (see p70) are buried here. The Aiken tomb (look for the bench gravestone) was the site of a macabre martini party (in the book version of *Midnight*) at which a local character, Miss Harty, tells a somber tale of how Aiken's father killed his wife and then himself.

To get there from downtown, take E Liberty St east. The street turns into Wheaton St and then Skidaway Rd. Make a sharp left onto Pennsylvania Ave and then a quick right onto Bonaventure Rd, and follow that to the cemetery.

Golf

You don't have to go to Hilton Head or Georgia's Golden Isles for world-class golf. Just head right across the Savannah River to **Club at Savannah Harbour** (Map pp66-7; ☎ 912-201-2007; ☼ sunrise-sunset), on the grounds of the Westin Savannah Harbor Resort. Here you'll find a championship 18-hole course designed by Robert Cup and Sam Snead. The Club at Savannah Harbour's course was recently named one of the 'top 10 places to play in the United States for the millennium' by Golf & Travel magazine. A round will run you about $85 if you stay at the Westin; $115 if you don't. But take heart: the course offers winter specials (January 1 to March 15) for as low as $55.

Tennis

Forsyth Park (Map pp66-7; ☎ 912-351-3852; South of Gaston St; ☼ sunrise-10pm) is the place to go if you are staying in town. There are four lighted courts, and access is free.

WALKING TOUR

For a stroll among the historic homes and squares of the Historic District, start your walk at **Reynolds Square (1)**, on Abercorn St at E Bryan St. This lush square dates from 1754. Once the site of a public filature (a reel for drawing silk off cocoons), the square is now home to a statue of John Wesley, who was the first religious leader of Oglethorpe's Georgia Colony (1736–37) and a founder of Methodism.

The **Olde Pink House (2)** on the western side of the square dates from 1771. Today this classic Georgian mansion is a popular restaurant, but in earlier times it was a planter's mansion, a bank and a headquarters for occupying Federal officers during the Civil War. It is also known for being haunted by the feisty spirits of slave children.

Walking south on Abercorn St, you soon come to **Oglethorpe Square (3)**, which is the burial site of General James Edward Oglethorpe, founder of the Georgia Colony.

On the east side of the square is **Telfair's Owens-Thomas House (4)**, a Regency-style mansion with a carriage house painted 'haint blue' to repel spirits of the dead.

A block east of here, on E State St, lies **Columbia Square (5)**, which once marked the eastern limit of Savannah when it was a walled city. The western side of the square is the site of **Davenport House (6)**, which offers the best house tour in the city.

From here follow Lincoln St south to **Colonial Park Cemetery (7)**. The old graveyard at Abercorn St and E Oglethorpe Ave served as the city's graveyard from 1750 to 1853; several Revolutionary War heroes are buried here. During the Civil War, bored Union soldiers changed dates on some of the headstones as a joke, creating impossibly long lives. A number of the ghost-walk tours leave from here, and the place exudes an appropriate nighttime spookiness when bathed in lamplight or moonshine.

After taking Abercorn St south to **Lafayette Square (8)**, named for the Marquis de Lafayette, you reach the **Andrew Low House (9)**, the first house museum in the Historic District.

You are now among the most gracious homes in Savannah, particularly after you travel two blocks south on Abercorn St and head west on **E Jones St (10)**, the most prestigious street name in the Historic District. The owners of town houses on this street have a tradition of keeping their curtains drawn back from the mammoth front windows as if to taunt passersby with images of the opulent interiors.

From E Jones St it is just a quick jog south on Bull St to **Monterey Square (11)**, the site of the most infamous mansion in Savannah. **Mercer House (12)** was a major setting for events in *Midnight*.

Zigzagging back north among more 19th-century mansions via W Gordon St, Whitaker St, W Jones St and Bull St, you come to **Chippewa Square (13)**, where Tom Hanks, as Forrest Gump, sat on a park bench and told the story of his quest for the love of his life, Jenny.

SAVANNAH FOR CHILDREN

While Savannah is best known as a center for adult entertainment, the city is quite kid-friendly.

Forsyth Park (p72) has 30 acres of greenery, as well as a summertime wading fountain and playgrounds.

Tybee Island (p86), located 18 miles east of town, is where Savannahians have gone to the beach for 200 years. It's a great place for building sandcastles.

Just east of town, **Old Fort Jackson** (p90) has battlements and alcoves for exploration, and sometimes there are reenactments. **Fort Pulaski** (p90), an island fort on the way to Tybee Island, has a moat and a drawbridge. **Skidaway Island State Park** (p89) has gobs of stuff for family fun – trails, a pool, a lookout tower, and the Georgia Marine Education Center and Aquarium. **Savannah National Wildlife Refuge** (p90) is a massive wilderness, with hiking trails and gators basking in the sun.

Savannah Belles **Ferry** (p86), running between the Riverfront and Hutchinson Island, is a cheap, three-minute river tour. **Roundhouse Railroad Museum** (p69) is great for any kid who likes trains.

ORGANIZED TOURS

Few excursions are more romantic than a sunset carriage ride around the city on a fair, warm evening. The visitors center is the best place to book tours, whether by foot, trolley, minibus or horse-drawn carriage ($17 for 50 minutes). Most of the city's tour operators begin and end their excursions from the center's parking lot. The top four operators are **Carriage Tours of Savannah** (☎ 912-236-6756), **Old Savannah Tours** (☎ 912-234-8128), **Gray Line** (☎ 912-234-8687) and **Old Town Trolley Tours** (☎ 912-233-0083). Most of the tours are similar in that they take you around the Historic District in an open trolley, highlighting historic sites and sets from *Midnight, Forrest Gump* and more recent films, while the driver explains local history and sites. Each company has departures every 20 minutes or so between 9am and 9pm daily (a good indication of Savannah's popularity as a tourist destination). The basic 90-minute tour is $17, or you can get on and off the trolley all day for $21 – each admission price includes entrance fees to one historic house.

It has been said that every story in Savannah begins with someone who is dead. No question, Savannah's fascination with its ghosts borders on fetish. Well

---

GAY & LESBIAN SAVANNAH

With many gay and lesbian merchants, innkeepers, college students and military personnel, Savannah has a lively queer scene. John Berendt's book *Midnight in the Garden of Good & Evil* opened the closet doors on Savannah's gay scene a decade ago with a big ka-boom, but the city had a rich gay underground for decades. 'Before *Midnight,* you could do anything in Savannah, as long as you didn't advertise; now you can advertise,' says one longtime observer of the gay scene. Check out www.gaysavannah.com for a complete list of gay-friendly inns, bars and clubs. See p84 for some choice entertainment picks. **Club One Jefferson** is not to miss.

---

over a half-dozen different tours of the historic district use ghosts as their theme for unfolding the city's grand and tortured history. See the bulletin board at the visitors center for current options. You can be a player in the **Creepy Crawl** (☎ 912-238-3843), a walking and drinking tour of haunted pubs. There are also many other specialized tours, including black-heritage tours. Naturally, **'The Book' Gift Shop** (☎ 912-233-3867) sponsors 'Midnight in the Garden of Good & Evil' tours. Reservations are often required. The **Scandals Tour** (☎ 912-234-3571) is a walking tour starting at the Colonial Cemetery; it really gives you the down-and-dirty of the city's sins.

Although Savannah is largely an urban experience, its magnificent river and related creeks reach into some extraordinary wilderness, some of which can be accessed from the city itself. For more wilderness-type tour options, see the Around Savannah section (p86).

Savannah Riverboat Cruises (Map pp66-7; ☎ 912-232-6404; www.savannah-riverboat.com; 9 E River St; 1hr cruise adult/child $14/9, theme cruises $26-36; ☉ 9am-8pm) gives tours on classic paddle boats. The one-hour daytime cruise will allow you to see the Lowcountry marshes and learn the history of the Savannah River. The theme cruises have a lot more to offer. Consider the Sunday Brunch Cruise or, better yet, the Monday Gospel Dinner Cruise (two hours of live gospel music) or

the Murder Afloat Cruise (you solve the case).

Wilderness Southeast (☎ 912-897-5108; www.wilderness-southeast.org; half/full-day tours $60/110; ☉ 9am-5pm) offers a range of wilderness adventures, including birding, canoeing and gator-watching. The company will pick you up at your hotel or meet you at a convenient rendezvous point.

Low Country River Excursions (☎ 912-898-9222; Bull River Marina, US Hwy 80 E; adult/child $15/10; ☉ 9am-5pm) offers 90-minute cruises on 40-foot pontoon boats to view gregarious bottle-nosed dolphins.

FESTIVALS & EVENTS

Savannah has a nearly endless list of festivals and special events. A complete list is available from visitors centers or online at www.savannahvisit.com.

JANUARY
First Friday for the Arts Stages an art exhibit in City Market.

FEBRUARY
Annual Black Heritage Festival Has dance, art, music and lectures.

MARCH
St Patrick's Day Takes on the dimensions of a rite of spring as wild and crazy as New Orleans' Mardi Gras.
Annual Tour of Homes & Gardens Your chance to see inside all those legendary mansions and secret gardens.

APRIL
Tour of Hidden Gardens in Savannah Takes you into eight private gardens.

MAY
Savannah Shakespeare Festival Brings a medley of dramas, dance and children's' plays to City Lights Theatre.

JUNE
Savannah Asian Festival Celebrates with art, music, dance and food.

JULY
Fourth of July Celebrated with fireworks over the river.

AUGUST
Savannah Film & Video Festival The premier Savannah College of Art & Design (SCAD) event, attracting nationally known artists to show their stuff.

SEPTEMBER
Savannah Jazz Festival Brings world-class performers to the city's clubs and stages.

OCTOBER
Coastal Empire Fair A major carnival, with rides, a petting zoo and other entertainment.

NOVEMBER
Thanksgiving Southern Style Showcases the talents of local restaurant chefs.

DECEMBER
Christmas on the River Features a parade, Santa, food, crafts and live entertainment.

SLEEPING

If your idea of a great escape is a plush bedroom with a window on a wild and mysterious city, you're going to love Savannah. The city has a dizzying array of accommodations for romantic get-aways and family adventures – there are about 60 options in the historic district alone.

Dozens of historic inns and B&Bs beckon those yearning to live in the champagne-and-caviar opulence of songwriter Johnny Mercer. For those searching for more modern conveniences (like workout rooms, room service, spas and pools), the city has an extraordinary collection of respected chain and boutique hotels, as well as one major resort, complete with championship golf.

Though most rates start at above $100 a night and the fancier places run well over $200, many of the historic inns and B&Bs have a wide range of rates. When making a reservation, you may want to ask why. Cheaper rooms can be a tiny space in the basement with no view, or they may face an unattractive and noisy parking garage. Most of the inns are totally nonsmoking; some do not allow children under 12.

While you will find familiar chain hotels located on Bay St, in the heart of town near the Riverfront, these can be a bit pricey for somewhat generic lodging, because you're paying for the location. If you want standard, decent budget chain hotels and don't mind driving to the Historic District, you must travel 5 miles south of Forsyth Park on Abercorn St to an area of

Savannah known as Southside. Another concentration of reasonably priced chain hotels is around I-95 exit 94, about 5 miles from downtown. You can find seaside accommodations 20 minutes away (see Tybee Island p86).

Whatever type of accommodations you choose, rates tend to be cheaper midweek. The visitors center and various visitors guides contain discount coupons for the inns and hotels and are probably your best bet for finding a deal.

The **Savannah Area Convention & Visitors Bureau** (www.savannahvisit.com) is helpful and lists many accommodations options, with links. **Sonja's Bed & Breakfast Reservation Service** (☎ 800-729-7787, www.bandbsavannah.com) represents over 20 inns with pictures and descriptions on her website. **Romantic Inns of Savannah** (www.romanticinnsofsavannah.com) is a similar operation.

Savannah adds a 2% local option tax to the 4% state tax, plus an additional 6% hotel tax.

Budget

Savannah Hostel (Map pp66-7; ☎ 912-236-7744; 304 E Hall St; dm/d $19/36-46; P ✗) Gregarious Brian Sherman runs this restored mansion at Lincoln St near the edge of the Historic District. He offers dorm beds and one private double. The carriage house next door has a shared bath between the adjoining rooms and is a good bet for couples. Guests can use the kitchen in the mansion, and there's a large Kroger's grocery store across the street. The CAT shuttle stops nearby on Habersham St, between Hall and Gwinnett Sts. The office is open 7am to 10am and 5pm to 10pm; guests are expected to leave during the day. The hostel is closed January and February, and sometimes in December and late November.

Thunderbird Inn (Map pp66-7; ☎ 912-232-2661; 611 Oglethorpe Ave; d $55; P ✗) Set in a less desirable location near the Greyhound bus station, 'the Bird' is a worn but serviceable motel for dedicated budget travelers only. Rates drop on weekdays.

For the best values in accommodations, head to the Southside, a 10-minute drive from the Historic District. **Best Western** (Map pp68-9 ☎ 912-355-1000; www.bestwestern.com;

SAVANNAH

45 Eisenhower Dr; d $55-65; (P) (🔁) (🔁) (✕) (🖵)), **Baymont Inn & Suites** (Map pp68-9) ☎ 912-927-7660; 8484 Abercorn St; d $50-63; (P) (🔁) (🔁) (✕)) and **La Quinta** (Map pp68-9) ☎ 912-925-9505; 6 Gateway Blvd; d $55-65; (P) (🔁) (🔁) (✕)) are at I-95 exit 94.

If you are in tenting or RV mode, your best bet is to head out to Tybee Island. For a more secluded experience, try Skidaway Island State Park. See the Around Savannah section (p86) for details on both places.

Mid-range
HOTELS

If you favor moderately priced hotels, Savannah has a good variety. Many well-respected national chains have hotels here.

Savannah Marriott Riverfront (Map pp66-7; ☎ 912-233-7722, 800-228-9290; www.marriotthotels.com; 100 General McIntosh Blvd; d $130-190; (P) (🔁) (🔁) (✕) (🖵)) Set on the river and connected to the shops and restaurants of River St via the River-

---

AUTHOR'S CHOICE

Westin Savannah Harbor Resort (Map pp66-7; ☎ 912-201-2000, 800-937-8461; www.westinsavannah.com; 1 Resort Dr; d $180-285; (P) (🔁) (🔁) (✕)) What a view! From the top floors of this 16-floor palace set on Hutchinson Island, you can see the Riverfront and Historic District buzzing just across the river and watch mammoth ships (how do they turn around?) with their tugs parading to and from the commercial port north of the city. The ambiance of the Westin is old-school opulence, with tall ceiling and lots of crystal, polished mahogany, brocade and leather. Rooms have the predictable Westin top-drawer fabrics, bed and art. The huge pool and Jacuzzi overlooks the river scene, and there is a spa, tennis and a championship golf course on the property. You also get Kids Club services and three restaurants. A three-minute ferry ride gives you immediate access to the city.

Hampton Inn Historic District (Map pp66-7; ☎ 912-231-9700, 800-426-7866; www.hotelsavannah .com; 201 E Bay St; d $135-170; (P) (🔁) (🔁) (✕) (🖵)) Wow. Not your average Hampton Inn, Debbie Jo. Built of red bricks – some of which were taken from local demolitions – the inn fits in with the character of other turn-of-the-century commercial buildings on Bay St. Public rooms mimic an antebellum saloon, with pine flooring from an old sawmill. The rooms, of course, have no-nonsense, modern décor. The sundeck and small pool on the roof can't be beat for families with kids who want a break from the city.

Azalea Inn (Map pp66-7; ☎ 912-236-2707, 800-582-3823; www.azaleainn.com; 217 E Huntingdon St; d $130-250; (P) (🔁) (✕)) You'll find this 1880s Italianate charmer, decorated with period and contemporary pieces, a block east of Forsyth Park. The friendly owners create a casual and unpretentious atmosphere. The inn consists of seven rooms and a two-bedroom carriage house, all with four-poster beds, and some with Whirlpools.

Senator's Gate (Map pp66-7; ☎ 912-233-6398; www.thesenatorsgate,com; 226 E Hall St; d $150-200; (P) (🔁) (✕)) With only four rooms and with friendly, gracious owners living on the premises, you really get personalized treatment here. Opened in 2000 after two years of renovations, this elegant 1885 Italianate house has lots of huge windows, a spacious parlor, 1880 French wallpaper, 12-foot ceilings and original heart-pine floors. The modern bathrooms all have hot tubs and heated towel racks. There's a two-night minimum.

Days Inn (Map pp66-7; ☎ 912-236-4440; 201 W Bay St; www.daysinn.com; d $80-120; (P) (🔁) (✕) (🖵)) The dark-brick façade of this 253-room hotel dates back 160 years and fits in with the character of the surrounding architectural heirlooms. Set at the northwest corner of the Historic District, the Days Inn has an excellent location, its within a two-minute walk of all the shops, restaurants and nightlife of City Market and the Riverfront.

Under the Rainbow (Map pp68-9; ☎ 912-790-1005; www.under-the-rainbow.com; 104-106 West 38th St; d $125-135; (P) (🔁) (✕)) This inn is a great place for gay couples and singles. The B&B is in a restored Belgian-block double-house complete with raised porches and second-story verandas. All five rooms have private baths, fireplaces and porches. Besides the full breakfast, you get a cocktail hour in the evening. The hospitality is fabulous.

walk, this hotel is within easy walking distance of the Historic District. It's a large hotel with eight floors and about 400 rooms. The indoor/outdoor all-weather pool makes it an attraction to families with children. In the off season, rates are discounted.

Hyatt Regency (Map pp66-7; ☎ 912-238-1234, 800-233-1234; www.hyatt.com; 2 W Bay St; d $145-205; **P** ✖ 🅿 ✕ 🖳) This hotel has an exit directly onto River St. It offers luxurious, business-class accommodations, but its ugly boxy exterior is a slap in the face to the area's historic feel. It's very popular for business conferences. Breakfasts are part of the deal, but the Sunday brunch (about $12), in a dining room with picture windows overlooking the river is the real treat.

Hilton Savannah DeSoto (HSD; Map pp66-7; ☎ 912-232-9000, 800-445-8667; www.desotohilton.com; 15 E Liberty St; d $100-136; **P** ✖ 🅿 ✕ 🖳) Near Madison Square, the HSD has modern business-class rooms, an outdoor pool and convention facilities. This hotel often offers discounted rates, which can be a good value, considering you get friendly service and Hilton's legendary attention to detail, but be careful to avoid the silly $50 cancellation fee for leaving before your scheduled departure date.

Quality Inn (Map pp66-7; ☎ 912-236-6321; www.qualityinn.com; 300 W Bay St; d $89-129; **P** ✖ ✕ 🖳) On the edge of the Historic District, between Montgomery and Jefferson Sts, the Quality Inn is near the Riverfront and is a good value if you want to be in the heart of Savannah's action. Its generic exterior belies its 52 modern rooms. You're paying for the location, not ambiance or the simple continental breakfast. But you pay quite a bit less here than in most neighboring establishments.

Also recommended are the following:

Best Western (Map pp66-7; ☎ 912-233-1011; www.bestwestern.com; 412 W Bay St, $83-115; **P** ✖ ✕ 🖳)

Clubhouse Inn & Suites of Savannah (Map pp68-9; ☎ 912-356-1234; 6800 Abercorn St; d $70-80; **P** ✖ 🅿 ✕)

Fairfield Inn Savannah Airport (Map pp68-9; ☎ 912-965-9777, 800-228-2800; www.marriott.com; d $65-75; **P** ✖ 🅿 ✕)

B&BS

Having a B&B experience in a historic home is a major reason that travelers visit Savannah.

Bed & Breakfast Inn (BBI; Map pp66-7; ☎ 912-238-0518; bedbreakfast@travelbase.com; 117 W Gordon St; d $80-150; **P** ✖ ✕) Among Savannah's historic inns, the BBI stands out for its value. Located adjacent to Chatham Square, the inn is an 1853 Federal row house. Its 16 rooms aren't as posh as those in some other inns, but then BBI is less expensive. It's decorated with antiques, period reproduction pieces and Oriental carpets, and it has a relaxing private garden and deck. You get hearty breakfasts, with eggs and fresh fruit.

Eliza Thompson House (Map pp66-7; ☎ 912-236-3620, 800-348-9378; www.elizathompsonhouse.com; 5 W Jones St; d $110-255; **P** ✖ ✕) Here's a B&B that is less formal than some other inns. The Thompson House is an 1847 Federal-style home with 25 gracious rooms decorated with antiques, Oriental carpets and heart-pine floors. The beautiful courtyard is a great place to relax. You get breakfast in the morning, wine and cheese in the evening, and coffee and dessert at night.

Olde Harbour Inn (Map pp66-7; ☎ 912-234-4100, 800-553-6533; www.oldeharbourinn.com; 508 E Factors Walk; d $130-230; **P** ✖ ✕) Once a cotton warehouse on the bluff above the Riverfront, this small inn rents 24 comfortable suites, each with a fully equipped kitchen. Ask for one of the rooms with a balcony overlooking the river.

River Street Inn (Map pp66-7; ☎ 912-234-6400, 800-253-4229; www.riverstreetinn.com; 115 E River St; d $145-270; **P** ✖ ✕) This spot has a great location in a converted cotton warehouse on the river, in the midst of the River St restaurants, gift shops and nightspots. The 86 spacious rooms come with wood floors, brick walls and four-poster canopy beds; some rooms have a view of the Savannah River. The game room and proximity to the attractions of the Riverfront make the inn attractive for visitors with children.

President's Quarters Inn (Map pp66-7; ☎ 912-233-1600, 800-233-1776; www.presidentsquarters.com; 225 E President St; d $140-225; **P** ✖ ✕) A Federal period townhouse near Wright Square, this inn features 19 large rooms tastefully furnished with four-poster beds and working fireplaces. Presidential pictures are a motif throughout, and there's a verdant courtyard for chilling. Rates include breakfast, wine, fruit and afternoon hors d'oeuvres.

Planters Inn (Map pp66-7; ☎ 912-232-5678, 800-554-1187; www.plantersinnsavannah.com; 29 Abercorn St; d $150-240; ℗ ❊ ✖) Set on Reynolds Square, this large 1890 historic inn has a great lobby and 60 rooms furnished with antique reproductions. One side of the inn faces a noisy parking garage, so ask for a view of the square.

Top End

HOTELS

Mulberry/Holiday Inn (Map pp66-7; ☎ 912-231-1200, 800-465-4329; www.savannahhotel.com; 601 E Bay St; d $175-245; ℗ ❊ ✖) Set in a restored stable and cotton warehouse at the eastern edge of the Historic District, this hotel sparkles with the feel of a classic Savannah mansion, where 19th-century antique reproductions are the rule in both public spaces and guest's rooms. There is no better place for a romantic interlude in Savannah than the Mulberry's rooftop Jacuzzi in the moonlight, with the sounds of sultry jazz echoing up from the nightspots on Bay St.

B&BS

Foley House Inn (Map pp66-7; ☎ 912-232-6622, 800-647-3708; www.foleyinn.com; 14 W Hull St; d $177-290; ℗ ❊ ✖) On Chippewa Square, Don and Beryl Zewer are the gracious hosts of this B&B. Their 1896 five-story Victorian brick house exhibits a fusion of continental and Southern styles. Its 18 spacious rooms are decorated in antiques and Oriental rugs, and many have fireplaces, balconies and Jacuzzis. Rates include a full breakfast, tea and cookies, and evening hors d'oeuvres; the cheaper rooms are in a carriage house and in the basement.

Gastonian (Map pp66-7; ☎ 912-232-2869, 800-322-6603; www.gastonian.com; 220 E Gaston St; d $223-380; ℗ ❊ ✖) One of Savannah's premier inns, the Gastonian occupies two adjacent 1868 Italianate Regency mansions. The romantic setting includes a working fireplace in each room, a lush formal garden, a pleasant deck and huge Whirlpool baths. Rates include a gourmet breakfast and afternoon tea.

Ballastone (Map pp66-7; ☎ 912-236-1484, 800-822-4553; www.ballastone.com; 14 E Oglethorpe Ave; d $250-470; ℗ ❊ ✖) Welcome to Savannah's grandest and most elegant historic inn. Situated in the heart of the Historic

---

HOME BREW...SAVANNAH STYLE

About 150 years ago, when it was party time in Savannah (but then again, when has it not been?), the good old boys would clamor for a local nectar called 'Chatham Artillery Punch.' As legend has it, the punch takes its name from a cadre of pre–Revolutionary War gunners who had a talent for spiking a rather genteel fruity beverage concocted by local society ladies for their cotillions. The 'suave and deceitful brew' gained national recognition after Savannahians served it to President James Monroe in 1819 during a truly festive sightseeing tour on the river. One version of the legend claims the punch took the legs out from under the president as surely as well-placed cannon fire. Quite possibly. Check out the recipe!

1.5 gallons Catawba wine	2.5lb sugar
1.5 gallons strong tea	½ pint Benedictine
1 gallons rum	juice from 18 lemons
1 quart gin	juice from 18 oranges
1 quart brandy	1 bottle of Maraschino cherries
1.5 quart whiskey	

Chill and store for 48 hours, add one case of champagne...and party!

If you have the courage, you can sample a mug of the 'suave and deceitful brew' by stopping by the bar at the **Shrimp Factory** (Map pp66-7; ☎ 912-236-4229; 313 E River St). A mug of punch costs $8, and you get to keep the glass.

District, the 1838 building is rife with antiques and rich hardwoods complementing the Scalamandre wallpaper, modern baths, a full bar and a beautiful garden. Rates for the 17 rooms include a full breakfast, afternoon tea and evening hors d'oeuvres.

William Kehoe House (Map pp66-7; ☎ 912-232-1020, 800-820-1020; www.williamkehoehouse.com; 123 Habersham St; d $200-275; P 🞐 🗶) You'll find this stately, four-story Victorian with 15 rooms on Columbia Square. Yep, it looks a little like a funeral home…because it was one, and you may want to ask the owners about some of the playful spirits that allegedly cruise the halls.

Gaston Gallery B&B (Map pp66-7; ☎ 912-238-3294, 800-671-0716; www.gastongallery.com; 211 E Gaston St; d $200-215; P 🞐 🗶) This 19th-century Italianate town house on peaceful Gaston St offers exceptionally spacious public areas, a front porch and a garden.

EATING

Get ready to feast! Savannah offers a legion of fine-dining experiences, from gourmet Southern food to wild fusion combos with fresh seafood. Many restaurants are concentrated along the waterfront and in City Market, on W Congress St; both are great places to window-shop for an eatery that fits your mood. Restaurants are also scattered throughout the Historic District.

Budget

Savannah Coffee Roasters Café (Map pp66-7; ☎ 912-232-5282; 7 E Congress St; sandwiches $4-7; 🞐 🗶) Overlooking Johnson Square is this clean, well-lighted coffeehouse right out of a Hemingway story. It's a good place to chill with a latte and newspaper. There's good people-watching inside and out, gourmet coffee and thick turkey sandwiches ($6).

Debi's Restaurant (Map pp66-7; ☎ 912-236-3516; 10 W State St; dishes $4-9; 🞐 🗶) If you're looking for a place that serves solid, home-style meals, sandwiches and burgers (less than $5), this may well be it. Although the ambiance is rather basic, the grub is popular with locals. The efficient service and super-friendly staff are as good as it gets.

Wall's Barbecue (Map pp66-7; 515 E York Lane; sandwiches $4-7; 🞐 🗶) Set in an alley between

E York St and Oglethorpe St, this is a hole-in-the-wall that serves very tangy, tender barbecue and enough vegetables to satisfy vegetarians. A BBQ sandwich with two veggies costs $6.

Sushi-Zen (Map pp66-7; ☎ 912-233-1188; 41 Whitaker St; sushi $3-9; 🞐 🗶) Largely a take-out place, this sushi bar has seating for about 20 customers on two floors. It is popular with the hippest of the SCAD students and is a fresh place to get off the tourist path. There are about 50 different varieties of rolls. Quite a few are highly imaginative: consider the Savannah Roll, with crab, cucumber and four kinds of smelt eggs – excellent with Pinot Grigio.

Creole Red (Map pp66-7; ☎ 912-234-6690; 409 W Congress St; mains $6-12; 🞐 🗶) This funky little place near City Market wins our vote for cheap, authentic Creole eats. And it has the feel of a Bourbon St dive in the Big Easy – small and dark, with splashes of red light and the scent of the bayou. You can face off with a plate of jambalaya for just $7. The deviled crabs (Savannah blue-crab meat spiced with a 'secret seasoning' and packed in the half shell) run $10…and are fab-you-loss!

Mid-range

Six Pence Pub (Map pp66-7; ☎ 912-233-3156; 245 Bull St; mains $8-16; 🞐 🗶) If this place looks familiar, it may be because you saw it in the tavern scene where Julia Roberts throws a hissy fit in the 1995 movie *Something to Talk About*. Cultured Savannahians (like those in the movie) favor this cozy little pub for long lunches of drinks, stories and ale-and-mushroom pie. There's live beach music, soul or jazz on weekend evenings.

Lady & Sons (Map pp66-7; ☎ 912-233-2600; 311 W Congress St; mains $17-21; 🞐 🗶) is a Savannah institution. The exceedingly popular Southern-style restaurant serves delicacies like candied sweet potatoes, butter beans and fried chicken. You can go for the outstanding buffet or order off the menu. If you don't want to wait in line for dinner, come at 11:30am for the lunch menu, which echoes the dinner offerings at half the price ($9 to $11).

Casbah Moroccan Restaurant (Map pp66-7; ☎ 912-234-6168; 118 E Broughton St; mains $15-25; 🞐 🗶) The inside of the Casbah looks like

SAVANNAH

a Moroccan ceremonial tent and shimmers with the scents of braised lamb, couscous and incense. The Moroccan sampler called 'The Royal Treat' ($26) is the way to go; it will feed two. Don't miss the belly dancer, who does her thing in the dark with a tray of candles balanced on her head.

Bistro Savannah (Map pp66-7; ☎ 912-233-6266; 309 W Congress St; mains $16-23; ⚏ ⚔) Here's one of the top seafood restaurants in Georgia. The place uses organically grown local and regional produce. Choose from garlic sautéed mussels and asparagus, or barbecued black grouper with peach and pear chutney.

Garibaldi's (Map pp66-7; ☎ 912-232-7118; 315 W Congress St; mains $10-23; ⚏ ⚔) Here's a northern Italian restaurant serving pasta,

veal, shrimp, fish and chicken dishes in an intimate but casual setting. The chicken Milanese is a good value ($13).

Churchill's Pub (Map pp66-7; ☎ 912-232-8501; 9 Drayton St; mains $9-15; ⚏ ⚔) This is the oldest bar in Savannah. Built in England in 1860 and moved to its current location in the Roaring Twenties, Churchill's still has English owners to complete your time-and-space warp to the UK. It's very popular with a middle-aged crowd, who come for the fish and chips ($11) and bangers and mash ($9).

Moon River Brewing Company (Map pp66-7; ☎ 912-447-0943; 21 W Bay St; dishes $5-15; ⚏ ⚔) You'll find this aromatic brewpub in an 1821 building just one block from the Riverfront. Heavy with the scent of hops

---

TOP FIVE FEASTS

B Matthew's Bakery & Eatery (Map pp66-7; ☎ 912-233-1319; 325 E Bay St; pastries $2-4; sandwiches $4-6; ⚏ ⚔) There is simply no better place to spend a lazy morning in Savannah than this sensuous café at the east end of the Historic District. Brian Caroll and Charles Becton have converted a run-down bar (dating from 1791!) into an attractive mix of tables and window seats overlooking the river. The bakery cases tempt with spinach croissants, rugelach (pastry made with cream-cheese dough) and apple tarts. Pick one, get a fresh espresso and kick back to the soft tones of Etta James seeping from the stereo. When it starts to feel like picnic weather outside, have Charles build you a deli sandwich of Italian roast beef, snag a small bottle of vino and score one of the loaner picnic blankets. Then head across the street into the park overlooking the river for lunch and a nap. Sweet.

Sapphire Grill (Map pp66-7; ☎ 912-443-9962; 110 W Congress St; mains $22-28; ⚏ ⚔) Yes, Dog! Chef Chris Nason fires up quite a feast in this converted warehouse near City Market and has gotten the attention of major-league food critics from Atlanta who have called the grill 'Savannah's most exciting eatery' – cool in its bare woods, metallic fixtures and contemporary art. The menu is highly eclectic, ranging from bouillabaisse in champagne ($27) to Colorado lamb lollipops ($26) Don't miss the buttermilk-marinated calamari appetizer ($9).

Mrs Wilkes' Dining Room (Map pp66-7; ☎ 912-232-5997; 107 W Jones St; $12-20; ⚏ ⚔) A longtime favorite for sociable Southern breakfasts and lunches, this family-style eatery packs its guests around long tables for three meals a day. We favor lunch, served 11am to 3pm, which includes black-eyed peas, turnips, fried chicken, sweet potatoes, green beans and rice for a fixed price of $12. The gentle Mrs Wilkes passed on in 2002. But her cuisine lives on through her family and loyal customers, who infuse the restaurant with her friendly, fun-loving spirit. No credit cards here.

Il Pasticcio (Map pp66-7; ☎ 912-231-8888; 2 E Broughton St; mains $14-25; ⚏ ⚔) Wildy popular with trendy couples, this spot on the corner of Bull St is a great date restaurant, serving authentic, abundant Italian food in a lively atmosphere. The scene is a large, open, dimly lit dining room looking out on the street through plate glass. Handmade pastas are the rule, but you've got to consider the baked sea bass ($23) and the grilled lamb chops with a port-wine reduction ($25). Young professionals meet at the bar after work.

Olympia Café (Map pp66-7; ☎ 912-233-3131; 5 E River St; mains $7-18; ⚏ ⚔) Remember the restaurant in *My Big Fat Greek Wedding*? The Olympia is as close as you'll come to that in Savannah. There's great family-style Greek cooking here. The staff actually shouts 'Opa!' just like the movie. To hell with the diet; don't miss the baklava ($1.50).

from the vats, it attracts a young crowd with its homemade brews and local artwork on the walls. The menu ranges from buffalo-wing appetizers ($8) and corn and crab chowder ($6) to burgers and sandwiches ($7). You can tie on a serious feed bag with the baby back ribs ($15).

Huey's (Map pp66-7; ☎ 912-234-7385; 115 E River St; mains $7-18; 🤖 ⊠) At this eatery in the River Street Inn, lunch consists of filling, authentic Cajun cooking, and the crowd is not too touristy. Try the blackened-tuna sandwich with red beans and rice ($10) or grilled chicken smothered with provolone and onions ($7).

Vinnie Van GoGo's (Map pp66-7; ☎ 912-233-6394; 317 W Bryan St; pies $9-16; 🤖 ⊠) Right across from Franklin Square, this is a popular place for college students. You can get a killer 14-inch New York–style pizza with two toppings for $12. They also sell pizza by the slice, calzones and domestic and imported beers. This hangout isn't much to look at, but the tables outside are great for people-watching. They accept cash only.

Clary's Café (Map pp66-7; ☎ 912-233-0402; 404 Abercorn St; dishes $4-16; 🤖 ⊠) OK, this is the diner on the corner of Jones St, where Luther used to hang out with his pet houseflies (pinned to his shirt on strings) in *Midnight*. And it hasn't changed much since then (or since its founding in 1903), except that tourists now wait in line to bathe in its funkiness. Chicken pot pie ($9) is a good bet. So are the soups ($4). Breakfasts are moderately priced.

Also recommended are the following:

Belford's (Map pp66-7; ☎ 912-233-2626; 215 W St Julian St; brunch $7-12; 🤖 ⊠) Indoor/outdoor seating for champagne brunch at City Market

Boar's Head (Map pp66-7; ☎ 912-651-9660; 1 N Lincoln St; mains $14-24; 🤖 ⊠) Imagine BBQ shrimp in a tangy peach sauce in a Riverfront cotton warehouse

Savannah Steak House (Map pp66-7; ☎ 912-232-0092; 423 W Congress St; mains $16-33; 🤖 ⊠) Very exotic cuisine, such as antelope medallions

River Grille (Map pp66-7; ☎ 912-234-5588; 21 E River St; mains $7-22; 🤖 ⊠) The décor smacks of Depression-era Texas; ribs, ribs and more ribs

Exchange Tavern (Map pp66-7; ☎ 912-232-7088; 201 E River St; mains $9-20; 🤖 ⊠) Pub fare with gusto – great shish kebabs

17 Hundred 90 (Map pp66-7; ☎ 912-236-7122; 307 E President St; mains $18-26; 🤖 ⊠) Located in a haunted cellar in the President's Quarters Inn; try the bourbon chicken

Top End

Elizabeth on 37th (Map pp66-7; ☎ 912-236-5547; 105 E 37th St; mains $25-32; 🤖 ⊠) Consistently one of Savannah's top restaurants, Elizabeth is housed in an elegant 1900 mansion. The cuisine is modern Southern (flounder and softshell crab are staples) and changes with the season. The wine list is impressive, and Savannahians claim the desserts are the best in the city.

Olde Pink House (Map pp66-7; ☎ 912-232-4286; 23 Abercorn St; mains $16-28; 🤖 ⊠) Only in Savannah. This 1771 building, on every haunted-house tour, is also a dignified restaurant serving contemporary Low-country seafood and Southern cuisine. You can eat in the elegant dining room or the more casual tavern and piano bar downstairs. Folks who have dined on the exceptional pork tenderloin ($23) talk about it for weeks

Also recommended are **Monkey Bar/Fusion Restaurant** (Map pp66-7; ☎ 912-232-0755; 8 E Broughton St; mains $16-26; 🤖 ⊠), which offers up glam, blues & American–Asian fusions like cilantro-sake chicken (also see the Entertainment listing p82), and **45 South** (Map pp66-7; ☎ 912-233-1881; 20 E Broad St; mains $22-33; 🤖 ⊠), featuring intimate, candlelit gourmet Southern cuisine.

ENTERTAINMENT

There is a reason John Berendt called Savannah 'the Garden of Good and Evil.' And that reason is nightlife. Not only does Savannah draw locals and tourists to its night scene, but it is also a mecca for biker clans and off-duty military folk from nearby bases. One base alone has 17,000 enlisted personnel, and when the troops are not on deployment, they head for the bars and clubs to act out the rituals you may have seen in *The General's Daughter*. An open-container law permitting adults to wander the streets with alcoholic beverages in hand, and bars and clubs can stay open until 3am.

For an up-to-date list of events at clubs and bars, check out Thursday's *Savannah Morning News* and the weeklies *Connect Savannah* and *Creative Loafing*, which you can find for free in many bars, restaurants and accommodations.

SAVANNAH

Jazz

Savannah has many good jazz venues. Local performers to look for include Gail Thurmond and Ben Tucker.

Savannah Blues (Map pp66-7; ☎ 912-447-5044; 411 W Congress St; 🍴 ✗) Here's a spot to heal your broken heart and muddled brain. The club draws the city's most devoted jazz aficionados. And there are a lot of them, because this joint is just what you want when you think of Miles, Coltrane, Ella, Muddy and their descendants: sultry, below-the-belt rhythms, the scents of Camels and Jim Beam, and a funky blend of fresh and weathered faces, white and black.

Hannah's East (Map pp66-7; ☎ 912-233-2225; 20 E Broad St; 🍴 ✗) Set on Bay St, Hannah's East is another legendary jazz bar with an intimate atmosphere and simple bar foods. Local legend Emma Kelly, the Lady of 6000 Songs, made an appearance in *Midnight*, but hasn't let celebrity wreck her groove. She gets down at Hannah's on Tuesday and Sunday evenings.

Planters Tavern (Map pp66-7; ☎ 912-232-4286; 23 Abercorn St; 🍴 ✗) Classic jazz piano is the rule in this intimate, crowded cellar tavern that attracts a middle-aged, up-scale crowd. You can order food from the Olde Pink House upstairs (p81). Be prepared to wait for a seat. But the wait is worth it when Gail Thurmond is at the keyboard.

Bars & Clubs

Monkey Bar/Fusion Restaurant (Map pp66-7; ☎ 912-232-0755; 8 E Broughton St) It rocks! Just

---

JOHNNY MERCER: THE MAN FROM MOON RIVER

Called the king of pop music before Elvis inherited the crown, Savannah's Johnny Mercer still haunts the hearts of generations of Americans with songs like 'Moon River.' And with well over 1100 published songs, he was the most prolific lyricist of the 20th century.

John Herndon Mercer was born November 18, 1909 in Savannah, where his father was a prominent attorney and real estate entrepreneur. The Mercers traced their American ancestry back to before the Revolutionary War, in which Hugh Mercer served as a brigadier-general under George Washington. Johnny Mercer developed his interest in music early, studying piano and trumpet, before going off to boarding school in Virginia.

In the 1920s Mercer moved to New York. His first song was 'Out of Breath and Scared to Death of You,' for a Broadway show in 1930. By 1932 he was a singing and writing for the Paul Whiteman Orchestra. He also recorded many songs with Benny Goodman and Eddie Condon. Mercer's list of songwriting collaborators reads like a who's who of composers. He worked with Hoagy Carmichael, Harold Arlen, Jerome Kern and Henry Mancini.

He had hit songs with Bing Crosby in the late 1930s and with Jo Stafford ('Candy'). His own hit recordings include 'Accentuate the Positive,' 'Blues in the Night,' 'That Old Black Magic,' 'One for My Baby,' 'Come Rain or Come Shine' (all with Harold Arlen); and 'Lazy Bones' and 'Skylark' (with Hoagy Carmichael). He also wrote 'I'm an Old Cowhand,' 'I Remember You,' 'PS I Love You,' 'Jeepers Creepers,' 'You Must Have Been a Beautiful Baby,' 'When a Woman Loves a Man,' 'Too Marvelous for Words,' and 'Fools Rush In.'

He won Academy Awards for 'The Atchison, Topeka and the Santa Fe' (1946, with Harry Warren), 'In the Cool, Cool, Cool of the Evening' (1951, with Hoagy Carmichael). Two songs from the end of Mercer's career also won Academy Awards, 'Moon River' (1961, with Henry Mancini) and 'Days of Wine and Roses' (1962, with Mancini). It only takes one night of watching a rising moon cast a silver path on the Savannah River to understand how the romance and sensuality of Savannah infused Mercer's work.

As president and co-founder of Capitol Records, Mercer was instrumental in the recording careers of musicians like Peggy Lee and Nat 'King' Cole. He died in Los Angeles in 1976, but is buried in Bonaventure Cemetery (p71) in Savannah.

Mercer released a fine album later in his life called *My Huckleberry Friend*. Also check out the many Mercer tribute albums, like Susannah McCorkle's *The Songs of Johnny Mercer*, Ella Fitzgerald *Sings the Johnny Mercer Songbook* and Lorenz Alexandria's *The Songs of Johnny Mercer*.

rocks. Owner Wendy Snowden, who ushered the Six Pence Pub to fame a decade ago, launched this gloriously retro place in early 2003. Wendy and her clientele ooze an authentic artsy glam, giving the Monkey Bar the feel of an Indy film party. And the cuisine is just as far out there (see Eating p81). But even though Wendy serves some killer fusion grub, MB/F really stands out as a party site, thanks to the down and dirty sounds of fabulous soul and blues divas (don't miss Elijah). Couples get up right in the middle of dinner and start dancing. Plenty of folks never eat at all. They just keep groovin'. Whew!

Savannah Smiles (Map pp66-7; ☎ 912-535-6453; 314 Williamson St) You'll find this venue tucked behind the Quality Inn. Just listen for the dueling pianos belting out classic rock anthems at the request of the audience. Visitors of all ages love this foot-stompin', table bangin', hand-clappin' sing-along place. This is the spot to find some serious therapy for the Beach Beat and Big Chill generations.

Warehouse (Map pp66-7; ☎ 912-234-6001; 13 E River St) Advertising the 'coldest, cheapest beer in town,' the 'House' appeals to serious and financially challenged hedonists from all corners of the human spectrum. Both suits and short-shorts belly up for $1 drafts and well drinks during 'happy hour,' Monday to Friday 4pm to 7pm. And you can eat for almost nothing while catching a buzz. Wings and oysters are 25¢ each.

Kevin Barry's Pub & Cigar Bar (Map pp66-7; ☎ 912-233-9626; 117 W River St) Located just west of the Hyatt Regency, Kevin's has live Irish music Wednesday to Sunday and food such as shepherd's pie ($8). It's like St Paddy's Day every night here. The crowd, a mix of locals and travelers, comes in all ages.

JJ Cagney's (Map pp66-7; ☎ 912-233-2444; 17 W Bay St) Here's an excellent place to spot both up-and-coming local bands and singer–songwriter types. Local 20-somethings flock here. T-shirts and blue jeans rule.

Bayou Café (Map pp66-7; ☎ 912-233-6411; 14 N Abercorn St) Between Bay and River Sts, the Bayou is a gritty place, popular with partying students. It also has live music every night, mostly alternative, country-rock and blues.

Malone's (Map pp66-7; ☎ 912-234-3059; 27 Barnard St) At the east end of City Market, this popular bar draws customers from a wide range of ages. It has indoor and outdoor seating and live acoustic music occasionally. The café tables outside are great for people-watching.

Mercury Lounge (Map pp66-7; ☎ 912-447-6952; 125 W Congress St) Ten-ounce martinis (just imagine!) attract a college crowd. The house band covers mostly classic rock and alternative tunes…but sometimes gets downright fresh and edgy.

Velvet Elvis (Map pp66-7; ☎ 912-236-0665; 127 W Congress St; cover $4-10) In City Market, Velvet Elvis has live music on weekends, geared toward a seriously alternative crowd of head bangers and goths. Hollywood types (like Kevin Spacey) passing through town sometimes slip in here incognito.

Dance Clubs

Apré (Map pp66-7; ☎ 912-238-8888; 2 E Broughton St; cover $10) Set above Il Pasticcio restaurant (see p80), Apré is currently the hippest club in town. The music is hard house, and the clientele is largely SCAD students during the week. On weekends the crowd gets fancier and older (25 to 35), and on these days, jackets and dresses are not out of place. The club gets packed, particularly between midnight and 1:30am, when the booze is *free*. In addition, you get a free bottle of champagne with a party of six; it's free vodka for a party of eight. Rock 'n' roll!

Deja Groove (Map pp66-7; ☎ 912-644-4566; 302 Williamson St; cover $5) Head for Williamson St behind the Quality Inn near the river to find this hot singles' dance club. The DJ spins a lot of classic rock and Top 40 tunes for a crowd of under-30s. You will see a fare number of GI Joes and Jills here trying to shake off the mili-base blues. Here's the place to break out your leather pants or red bodice and do 'The Electric Slide.'

Ibiza (Map pp66-7; ☎ 912-495-9001; 121 W Congress St; cover $5) Rising from the ashes of a totally wild establishment called The Zoo, this three-story club has a different scene on each floor. On the ground level you've got a bluesy jazz cave. On the 2nd floor the DJ's got a Top 40 groove going. The 3rd floor rumbles with techno jazz.

Gay & Lesbian Venues

Club One Jefferson (Map pp66-7; ☎ 912-232-0200; www.clubone-online.com; 1 Jefferson St) Savannah's premier gay venue, Club One features drag shows, pool tables and a large dance floor. Although its clientele is mostly gay, straight party animals also come here to dance and see the most excellent dragon ladies. Lady Chablis – the sassy drag queen featured in *Midnight* – still hides her candy here about once a month. Don't miss the country-music queens. Dolly and Shania? Eat your heart out, boyfriend.

Chuck's Bar (Map pp66-7; ☎ 912-232-1005; 301 W River St) Chuck's brings two words to mind – 'good cruising.' Kind of hard to believe you'd find a hot gay bar cheek-by-jowl with the tourist traps on River St. But, hey, Savannah isn't your average, white-bread kind of place. Come after 11pm on the weekend, when the lights are low and the air is thick with testosterone.

Faces (Map pp66-7; ☎ 912-233-3520; 17 Lincoln St) Check out this laid-back neighborhood bar with a pool table in the back. Even though Faces is really a locals' hideout, the gang is very welcoming and willing to show you the way to Savannah's velvet underground.

The **Rail** (Map pp66-7; ☎ 912-238-1311; 405 W Congress St) This intimate little pub used to be a popular bar with the enlisted military personnel, and little by little it became a comfortable hangout for women soldiers and sailors, as well as alternative college kids. The word spread, and now the bar has become popular with lesbians. Some have worn the uniform; some never will.

Performing Arts

Lucas Theatre for the Arts (Map pp66-7; ☎ 912-232-1696; 32 Abercorn St; tickets $15-25) A recently renovated theatre, the Lucas offers a nearly continuous slate of plays, concerts, musicals and classic films.

Savannah Symphony Orchestra (☎ 912-236-9536) fades in and out of financial troubles, but this professional orchestra nevertheless perseveres. It has a number of free events at Forsyth Park and River St and also plays at the Savannah Civic Center's **Johnny Mercer Theater** (Map pp66-7 ☎ 912-651-6556; tickets $20-30), on Orleans Square.

Savannah Theater Company (Map pp66-7; ☎ 912-233-7764; 222 Bull St; tickets $30) Head for Chippewa Square for this community theater, which presents comedies, musicals and dramas like *Lost in the '50s* in its art deco movie theater.

SHOPPING

Given Savannah's fascination for the dead-and-gone, the exotic, and the temptations of the flesh, it is no surprise that antique dealers, art galleries, gourmet food vendors and sweet shops dominate the commercial landscape. Boutiques exist, particularly along Broughton St, where you will find some big-name chains such as Banana Republic and The Gap. But clothiers are not major players in downtown commerce. Antiques rule. With more than 100 registered dealers (which once included Jim Williams, the accused murderer in *Midnight*), Savannah offers first-rate shopping for heirlooms. There are a number of art galleries run by Cooperatives of Artists, including students and faculty at SCAD. Try to get your hands on a copy of the *Georgian Guardian*, the SCAD newspaper, to find out about current art openings and exhibitions.

River St and the associated **Factors Walk** (p68) boast a collection of about 40 shops, galleries and restaurants. An equally attractive commercial zone in the Historic District, the **City Market** area (p68) in the vicinity of Franklin Square and W St Julian St, is packed with venues rich in antiques, fresh art, boutiques and sinful scents.

Antiques & Galleries

Alexandra's Antique Gallery (Map pp66-7; ☎ 912-233-3999; 320 W Broughton St) In the Historic District, you'll find 65 dealers in this four-story restored mercantile building.

Abercorn Antique Village (Map pp68-9; ☎ 912-233-0064; 201 E 37th St) If you head south into the Victorian District, you will find this large gallery with about 40 dealers.

Gallery 209 (Map pp66-7; ☎ 912-239-4583; 209 E River St) Featuring the work of 30 Lowcountry artists, Gallery 209 displays work in ceramics, jewelry, prints and painting.

Signature Gallery (Map pp66-7; ☎ 912-233-3082; 303 W St Julian St) Here's a vibrant gallery option in City Market.

Clothing & Gifts

Kathi Rich (Map pp66-7; ☎ 912-236-7424; 317 W Broughton St) For those who like eclectic designer gear for both males and females, don't miss this hip little shop.

Secret Closet (Map pp66-7; ☎ 912-447-1044; 321 W Broughton St) To wrap (or unwrap) yourself in romantic luxury, you may want to dip into the fine lingerie selection here. There are also dresses by Lilli, Betsey Johnson and Casabella.

Savannah Candy Kitchen (Map pp66-7; ☎ 912-233-8411; 225 E River St) You can score handmade pecan pralines and fudge that some people claim are better than sex. Just pop in here for the smell of boiling sugar and melting chocolate.

True Grits (Map pp66-7; ☎ 912-234-8006; 107 E River St) This is your stop for Civil War artifacts like reproduction swords and firearms, recovered shipwreck treasures, Lowcountry cookbooks, Southern sauces and gourmet foods. The Scorned Woman hot sauce is killer.

'The Book' Gift Shop (Map pp66-7; ☎ 912-233-3867; 127 E Gordon St) You guessed it. The shop sells all manner of memorabilia related to the book and film *Midnight in the Garden of Good & Evil*. This is the place to pick up a video, signed copies of the book, and replicas of the iconic statues of Bird Girl and Rebecca. The shop is also offering a number of *Midnight*-related tours (see Organized Tours p73).

Markets & Malls
If you need a mall fix, head for **Oglethorpe Mall** (Map pp68-9; ☎ 912-354-7038; 7804 Abercorn St) or the **Savannah Mall** (Map pp68-9; ☎ 912-927-7467; 14045 Abercorn St) in the vast Southside. You will find outlet shopping with 25 factory stores like Bass, Wamsutta Van Husen and Reebok at the **Festival Factory Stores** (Map pp68-9; ☎ 912-925-3089; 11 Gateway Blvd S Abercorn), at exit 84 off I-95.

GETTING THERE & AWAY
Air
The **Savannah/Hilton Head International Airport** (Map pp68-9; ☎ 912-964-0514) is about 5 miles west of downtown off I-95. American Eagle, Delta, United, US Airways and Continental Express have direct flights to and from Atlanta, Charlotte, Miami, New York, Newark, Washington DC, Cincinnati, Chicago, Dallas and Houston.

Here are some sample budget fares: Atlanta ($140), Charlotte ($240), Cincinnati ($215), Chicago ($200), Dallas ($280), Houston ($215), Miami ($210), New York ($200), Newark ($200) and Washington, DC ($175).

Bus
The **Greyhound bus station** (Map pp66-7; ☎ 912-232-2135) is just west of downtown at 610 W Oglethorpe Ave.

More than 30 buses depart per day. Connections include:

destination	cost	duration	frequency
Atlanta, GA	$48	5½ hrs	25 daily
Augusta, GA	$35	2½ hrs	24 daily
Brunswick, GA	$16	1½ hrs	26 daily
Charleston, SC	$27	3 hrs	2 daily
Columbia, SC	$36	4 hrs	4 daily
Jacksonville, FL	$25	2½ hrs	12 daily
Macon, GA	$44	4 hrs	4 daily

Car & Motorcycle
Savannah's Historic District lies an easy 5-mile drive east of I-95. I-16 is your connecting route, which brings you virtually to the doorstep of the visitors center on Martin Luther King Jr Blvd.

The Savannah International Airport has most of the major car rental agencies, including **Budget** (☎ 912-964-4600; ☿ 8am-10pm), **Economy** (☎ 912-352-7042; ☿ 8am-10pm) and **National** (☎ 912-964-2628; ☿ 8am-10pm).

Train
The **Amtrak station** (Map pp68-9; ☎ 912-234-2611, 800-872-7245) is 4 miles from City Hall and is served only by taxis ($7). Three 'Silver Service' trains per day go south to Jacksonville, Florida, (one-way $43 to $52, 2½ hours), continuing on to Miami ($68 to $130, 12 hours). Northbound, there are two trains per day to Charleston ($19 to $25, two hours).

The station can be difficult to find. From downtown, go west on Louisville Rd, turn left on Telfaire Rd, then look for signs on the right.

GETTING AROUND
Savannah is so pedestrian-friendly that you don't need a car to enjoy it. In fact, if you have one, it's best to park it and walk or take tours around town.

To/From the Airport

Coastal Transportation (☎ 912-964-5999) provides a shuttle downtown for $21. Taxi service costs about $20 to downtown, plus $5 for each additional passenger. The flat rate to Tybee Island is $42. There's no public bus to/from the airport.

Car & Motorcycle

Parking is difficult. As you can imagine, the Historic District is packed with resident, commercial and tourist vehicles. Fortunately, many hotels, inns and restaurants have private lots or valet parking for guests. For short-time visitors, municipal parking garages and lots will accommodate you; there's one at City Market (200 W Congress St) and Bryan St, and four lots on River St. Rates run $5 weekdays, $7 weekends for unlimited hours. The garages are open from 7am to 3am.

Visitors can buy a 48-hour parking pass for $8 at the visitors center and at the Bryan St Garage. The pass works at the municipal garages, River St lots and one-hour meters.

Bus

Chatham Area Transit (CAT; ☎ 912-233-5767; www .catchacat.org) operates local buses, including a **free shuttle** that makes its way around the Historic District and stops within a couple of blocks of nearly every major site. This is a cheap way to see the city without paying for the tourist trolleys. It circulates about every 20 minutes (every 40 minutes on Sunday). For the location of stops, call or check the website. You can also look for it at the following places: the visitors center, Forsyth Park at Bull St, on Congress St in front of Franklin Square, or on Bay St in front of the Hyatt Regency.

CAT also has a comprehensive system of buses outside the Historic District. The fare is 75¢ (exact change). The website has complete route information.

Ferry

Savannah Belles Ferry (Map pp66-7; ☎ 912-447-4000; $3 round trip; ☉ 7am-11pm) operates ferries between the Riverfront and Hutchinson Island to the north, the site of the Westin Savannah Harbor Resort & Spa (p76) and the Trade & Convention Center. The ride lasts about three minutes, and ferries leave about every half hour.

Taxi

The taxi rate is $1, plus 25¢ each 1/5 mile, and $1 for each additional passenger. You'll need to call for a cab; try **Yellow Cab** (☎ 912-236-1133).

AROUND SAVANNAH

Don't miss the local outback. Quite a few destinations around Savannah offer surprising, relaxing, rural and historical alternatives to the city scene. The surrounding historic sites, state parks, beaches, national wildlife refuges and forts give you an opportunity to learn some history, explore the marshes, view wildlife and hike among ruins constructed of tabby (a building material made of oyster shells, lime and sand, mixed with water). Whether you are a child at heart or traveling with children, a visit to the Savannah area takes on more texture when it includes an escape to the beach at Tybee Island, a trek through the Lowcountry wilderness on Skidaway Island or the Savannah National Wildlife Refuge, or a climb to the ramparts of Fort Pulaski.

TYBEE ISLAND

Taking its name from the local Indian word for 'salt,' Tybee's the place to come if you like standing at the base of a gargantuan lighthouse and watching it flash its message out to a nearly constant parade of ships. It's also the local in-spot for folks who like to party in their beach gear.

Lying about 18 miles east of Savannah, at the end of US Hwy 80, Tybee Island is a small beach community sitting on a lot of history. In an important strategic location near the mouth of the Savannah River, the island has attracted Spanish and French explorers, pirates and British settlers. Later Tybee hosted a hospital for contagious diseases and a quarantine station for slaves and other ship passengers. During the Civil War, Union forces on Tybee fired on Fort Pulaski in April 1862. After the war, the island became a resort area for local Savannahian families, and it has remained so for 130 years.

Despite the island's long history, most of the homes and business here look like they were built about 50 years ago, during the resort-construction boom that struck most of the Atlantic Coast following WWII. In other words, don't expect Nantucket quaint, Jekyll Island opulence or Hilton Head spaciousness at Tybee. This is simply a middle-class beach community that attracts a mix of families and party animals. During the colder months of the year, Tybee is nearly a ghost town during the week. By contrast it is packed and rocking out during the summer months and during school vacations.

Hollywood types (who come to town to make movies) fall in love with the place. Ben Afleck, John Travolta and Tom Hanks all own island property. Sandra Bullock lives here part of the year.

Orientation & Information

About 5 miles long and 2 miles wide, the island's main attraction is the 3 miles of wide, sandy beach, good for swimming, castle building and surfing. The most popular public access is on the southern side of the island near the Tybee Pier and Pavilion, where parking costs $7 a day. The pier makes for a relaxing strolling or fishing spot. Another public-access point is at the northern end of the island, near the lighthouse; parking costs $5 a day. Shops and restaurants cluster near the village at the southern end of the island (around 14th to 16th Sts).

The **Tybee Island Visitors Center** (Map pp68-9; ☎ 912-786-5444, 800-868-2322 802; 1st St/US Hwy 80; www.tybeevisit.com; 9:30am-5pm) is on the right as you come into town.

Sights & Activities

On the northern end of the island is the 154-foot-tall **Tybee Island Lighthouse** (Map pp66-7; ☎ 912-786-5801; adult/child $5/4; 9am-5pm Wed-Mon Apr-Aug), the oldest in Georgia and still in use. The 178 steps to the top reward you with views of the Lowcountry islands, Savannah and the ocean, which is a breeding ground during the winter for the rare and endangered Northern Atlantic right whales. The neighboring **Tybee Island Museum** is in the basement of Fort Screven, which was in use from 1897 to 1947. The simple museum, which is part of the same attraction as the lighthouse, has exhibits

and vintage photographs that illuminate the island's history.

Tybee and the surrounding beaches, creeks, marshes and islands are ripe for outdoor adventuring. Note the outfitters listed below have irregular hours in the off-season (October to March).

You can rent bicycles from the **Sundance Bicycle Shop** (☎ 912-786-9469; $25/day; 9am-6pm), on 16th St. **Alakai Outfitters** (☎ 912-786-4000; 1213 US Hwy 80; single/double kayak $28/50, surfboard $20/day; 10am-5pm Mon & Wed-Fri, 9am-6pm Sat & Sun), 1.5 miles past the Tybee Island bridge, rents sit-on kayaks. They also offer surfing lessons and lead bike tours to nearby destinations.

Sea Kayak Georgia (☎ 912-786-8732, 888-529-2542; www.seakayakgeorgia.com; 9am-5pm) offers kayak trips to nearby Little Tybee Island and Lazaretto Creek ($55, three hours) on weekends March through May and daily June through September. The company also offers a limited number of full-day trips ($95), kayak instruction and longer camping trips to Sapelo Island, Ossabaw Island and the Okefenokee National Wildlife Refuge (see the Georgia Coast chapter p112). The company is located 1.8 miles past the Tybee Bridge, on the right.

Sleeping

Tybee offers more than two dozen hotels, motels and B&Bs, as well as rental agencies listing condos and beach houses for stays of a week or longer. For an up-to-date list and links, consult www.tybeevisit.com. **Tybee Beach Vacation Rentals** (☎ 912-786-8805, 800-755-8562; www.tybeebeachvacationrentals.com) gets high marks from local renters. Expect to pay $500 to $2000 a week.

HOTELS & MOTELS

A number of hotels stand on the main drag, Butler Ave.

Best Western Dunes Inn (☎ 912-786-4591; www.dunesinn.com; 1409 Butler Ave; d $59-91; P 🐾 🛒 🗙) Here's a popular spot for families, offering 53 rooms and a pool amid lush, landscaped grounds. Rooms include a kitchenette, and some have Jacuzzis.

Ocean Plaza Beach Resort (☎ 912-786-7777, 800-215-6370; www.oceanplaza.com; d $105; P 🐾 🛒 🗙) Set on the oceanfront off Butler Ave at 15th St, the Ocean Plaza is the queen-bee accommodation in town, with 199 large but generic rooms, some overlooking the ocean. There are two pools, a conference center, a restaurant and a bar on the property. The restaurant here also has a good view of the beach.

Beachside Colony Resort (☎ 912-786-4535; www.beachsidecolony.com; 404 Butler Av; d $95; P ⚄ ⛵ ✗) Although this is another concrete box on the beach, families flock here for the price and the convenience. With 66 rooms packed with other families, you can be sure your kids will find friends here. The soundproofing ain't bad…considering.

B&BS

Lighthouse Inn (☎ 912-786-0901, 866-786-0901; www.tybeebb.com; 16 Meddin Dr; d $155-185; P ⚄ ✗) You gotta love this place. The inn, built in 1910, is on the Historic National Register and was the home of the Fort Screven bandmaster. All three guest rooms in this lovely yellow frame cottage have private baths, some with claw-footed iron soaking tubs and all with cable television, VCR, telephone, and a small refrigerator. Public rooms have a casual urbanity, with lots of original art and a grand piano. Of course, a delicious complimentary breakfast is served each morning. The beach is about a two-minute walk.

Beach Dreams Bed & Breakfast (☎ 912-786-9090, 877-786-8866; www.beachdreamsbandb.com; 4 13th St; d $140-215; P ⚄ ✗) With only three rooms in a spacious summer cottage, this B&B calls to couples in search of a romantic escape. The views over the sand dunes to the ocean are exceptionally serene, as are the gauzy fabrics and soft colors in the bedrooms.

CAMPING

River's End Campground & RV Park (☎ 912-786-5518, 800-786-1016; 915 Polk St; sites $26-32; P ⛵) is on the northern side of the island, just three blocks from the ocean. Tent sites on the northern part of the campground are the prettiest but are close to the noisy pool pump. Sites on the southern side are in a large grassy area near the road and RVs.

Eating

Tybee has quite a few beach, beer and burger joints along Butler Ave that can supply your basic cravings. But a few

restaurants in town and on the road into town (US Hwy 80) stand out.

Breakfast Club (cnr Butler Ave & 15th St; breakfast $4-10; ⚄ ✗) The crew serves a good breakfast here, including standard and specialty omelets ($5 to $10), chorizo and waffles.

Crab Shack at Chimney Creek (☎ 912-786-9857; 40-A Estill Hammock Rd; mains $11-35; ⚄ ✗) Here's a lively restaurant, where huge platters piled with shellfish are served on an outside deck lit up with hundreds of Christmas lights. Customers shovel the shells into a garbage can via a hole in the table's center. The specialty is the sampler platter ($22/35 for one/two people). The Lowcountry boil – a moderately spicy mix of boiled shrimp, sausage, potatoes and corn – is also very good ($12). To get here, turn right at the Chimney Creek sign and go almost a mile past the bridge.

North Beach Grill (☎ 912-786-9003; 41A Meddin Dr; mains $4-20; ⚄ ✗) Tucked away behind the Tybee Lighthouse Museum, this grill is worth the search. Access is through the beach parking lot. You can soak up the island atmosphere on the patio or inside. Jamaican dishes and seafood are the dinner specialties – jerk chicken, red beans and rice, grilled okra, sweet potatoes and fruit salsa. The lunch menu is simpler – sandwiches and portobello burgers.

Outback Café (☎ 912-786-7394; 725 First St; mains $7-14; ⚄ ✗) Locals try to keep this place for themselves. They come for the butterfly shrimp and massive plates of chicken fingers. Try the deviled crabs.

Bars & Clubs

Tybee is well known for attracting a party crowd. Among the gin joints and karaoke caves, there are two places you gotta see.

The Grill (☎ 912-786-4745; 404 Butler Ave) Islanders, Savannahians and travelers gather here at happy hour for free food and half-price domestic beer. The place really gets packed at quittin' time on Friday.

Doc's Bar (☎ 912-786-5506; 10 Tybrisa St) This is an institution. Featured in the novel *The Republic of Love,* Doc's has a dance floor and live jazz, blues and beach beat. The crowd is totally eclectic but favors over-30 slicks and slims. People will tell you it's a great pick-up joint…and they ain't lyin' one single bit. Come to play or come to watch. You won't be disappointed.

Getting There & Around

You'll be driving this one, Bubba. US Hwy 80 E brings you the 18 miles to and from Savannah. Just take the President St Extension out of Savannah from E Bay St and follow the Hwy 80E signs.

As for getting around, it is impossible to get lost on Tybee. US Hwy 80 E becomes Butler Ave once you get on the island. This is the main drag, and it curves through the settlement and runs along the beach until it reaches a dead end at the island fishing pier.

There are six-hour parking meters at the Tybee Island Museum and throughout town.

WORMSLOE STATE HISTORIC SITE

Ten miles southeast of Savannah's Historic District, this **historic site** (Map pp66-7; ☎ 912-353-3023; www.gastateparks.org; 7601 Skidaway Rd; adult/child $2.50/1.50; ⏲ 9am-5pm Tue-Sat, 2-5:30pm Sun), on the Isle of Hope, preserves the tabby ruins of a colonial estate. It was built by Noble Jones, one of Georgia's first settlers, and provides a reminder of the difficult wilderness that met the colonists upon their arrival. An interpretive center presents a film on the founding of Georgia and the Wormsloe site, reminding visitors that the colony was *not* settled by convicts from debtor's prison.

Entry to the site is lined with more than 400 live oaks, planted by Jones. A short (less than a mile) trail leads through the forest to tabby ruins, a family gravesite and an overlook of the marsh. Colonial living skills and crafts are demonstrated during special programs throughout the year.

From downtown, take Liberty St east to Wheaton St (veers to right), then take Skidaway Rd. Wormsloe is just past Norwood/Ferguson Aves on the right.

MIGHTY EIGHTH AIR FORCE HERITAGE MUSEUM

Classic combat aircraft aficionados, history mavens and descendants of WWII combatants will find this **museum** (Map pp68-9; ☎ 912-748-8888; www.mightyeighth.org; I-95 exit 102; adult/child $8/6; ⏲ 9am-5pm) a powerful lure. The 90,000-sq-foot complex honors the men and women who helped defeat Nazi aggression via the greatest air armada the world had ever seen – the Eighth Air Force. Having been activated in Savannah in 1942, the Eight Air Force has had more than 350,000 members. During WWII, 26,000 were killed in action, and 28,000 became prisoners of war.

Opened in 1996, the museum features three theaters in addition to the **Mission Experience**, which takes you along for the actual sights and sounds of a B-17 bombing mission. The Battle of Britain Theater, the Mighty Eighth Theater, and the Freedom Theater run continuously during museum hours and present topics ranging from the early history of the Eighth Air Force to Cold War air-defense strategy. Displays include galleries showing the rise of Nazi fanaticism in Germany, the Holocaust and the Mighty Eighth's role in the supersonic age of Vietnam and the Cold War. The combat gallery, with its restored war birds and replicas, is one of the high points of the museum, as are the outside exhibits of an F-4 Phantom jet and a B-47 bomber. The museum also has a **restaurant** on the premises.

SKIDAWAY ISLAND STATE PARK

Known as a haven for campers and hikers, this barrier island also features a Marine Education Center & Aquarium. While part of the island has been developed as a gated residential community, 588-acre **Skidaway Island State Park** (Map pp68-9; ☎ 912-598-2300; ⏲ 8am-sunset; admission/sites $2/18; Ⓟ Ⓖ) keeps the feeling of the wild. Here you will find two nature trails (1 mile and 3 miles) that wind through salt marshes, live oaks, cabbage palmettos and longleaf pines. Wildlife here includes fiddler crabs, shorebirds and rare migrating birds. The trails lead to an observation tower overlooking the salt flats and marsh. You can pick up interpretive brochures at the park office. The park's 88 camping sites are in a flat, somewhat exposed area. Flush toilets, showers and laundry facilities are provided.

To reach Skidaway Island, follow the directions to Wormsloe State Historic Site, but turn south on Ferguson Ave, then left onto Diamond Causeway. After you cross the Skidaway River, the state park is on the left.

Also on the island, the University of Georgia **Marine Education Center & Aquarium** (Map pp68-9; ☎ 912-598-2496c; adult/child $2/1; ☺ 9am-4pm Mon-Fri, noon-5pm Sat) has a dozen or so small tanks containing aquatic species such as stingrays, turtles, nurse sharks, spiny lobsters, octopuses and cowfish. Also on display are handmade Native American baskets and regional historical photos. Hiking loops of ½-mile or 1 mile wind through the maritime forest and beside the salt marsh. The scenic location overlooks the Skidaway River.

From downtown, take E Liberty St, which turns into Wheaton and then Skidaway Rd. Make a right onto Ferguson Ave, then a left onto the Diamond Causeway (Spur 204). Once you've crossed the water, you're on the island. To get to the Marine Education Center & Aquarium, turn left at the stop sign after the light onto McWhorter Rd. Make another left on Modena Island Rd. The center is at the end of the road.

SAVANNAH NATIONAL WILDLIFE REFUGE

This 27,771-acre **wildlife refuge** (Map pp68-9; ☎ 912-652-4415; US Hwy 17; www.savannah.fws.gov; admission free; ☺ sunrise-sunset) is part of a string of habitats along the coast administered by the Savannah Coastal Refuges office of the US Fish & Wildlife Service. The refuge consists of freshwater marshes, tidal rivers and creeks and bottomland hardwoods. Once part of an 18th-century rice plantation, the system of dikes is still maintained to provide habitat for migratory waterfowl.

The plentiful wildlife here includes alligators, Southern bald eagles, great egrets and blue herons. Migratory birds on the Atlantic Flyway also stop here, including mallards and other ducks, warblers and sandpipers. Birding is best from October through April, but is good year-round.

Hikers and **bicyclists** can wander more than 25 miles along the dike system. The **Cistern Trail** leads to Recess Island.

The 4-mile, one-way gravel **Laurel Hill Wildlife Drive**, off US Hwy 17, offers access into the park along the earthen dikes. Portable toilets and an information board are at the entrance. Look for the alligator pond with the jumping fish a mile down the drive. From Savannah, take US Hwy 17 Alt across the Eugene Talmadge Bridge into South Carolina; after 5 miles, turn left on US Hwy 17 and follow it for 2 miles. The entrance to Laurel Hill Wildlife Drive will be on the left. This is your only entrance to the refuge by car.

OLD FORT JACKSON

Georgia's oldest standing brick fortification, **Old Fort Jackson** (Map pp68-9; ☎ 912-232-3945; www.chsgeorgia.org; Fort Jackson Rd; adult/child $3.50/2.50; ☺ 9am-5pm) began as an earthen fort during the Revolutionary War. Overlooking the Savannah River, it served as headquarters for the Confederate river defenses during the Civil War.

The fort is still intact, with barracks, a blacksmith shop, and a cannon and muskets on display. A number of scheduled events and Civil War reenactments occur here, so call or check online for a schedule if you want to see the South rise again and smell gun smoke. Sometimes a gun crew fires the fort's huge 32lb (that's the size of the shell!) cannon.

From downtown Savannah, go east on Bay St for 2.2 miles (it merges with President St) to Woodcock Ave, turn left and follow the signs for 1.2 miles.

FORT PULASKI NATIONAL MONUMENT

Laborers built this **fort** (Map pp68-9; ☎ 912-786-5787; www.nps.gov/fopu; US Hwy 80; adult/child $3/free; ☺ 9am-5pm) on Cockspur Island in 1847 to guard the mouth of the Savannah River from invaders from the sea. Military engineers thought that such a huge masonry fort, with 7½-foot-thick walls, was impenetrable. Yet the fort was seized by Georgia state troops before the state even seceded from the Union.

A year later, on April 10, 1862, the Union opened fire on Fort Pulaski from Tybee Island, 1 mile away, using experimental rifled cannons, which fired bullet-shaped projectiles with great accuracy at long range. The projectiles bore through Pulaski's brick walls, exposing the fort's powder magazine to direct attack. The Confederates surrendered 30 hours after the bombardment began. Prior to the Civil War, the heaviest ordnance from smoothbore cannons and mortars was effective on heavy masonry walls only within 700 yards. But the Union's experimental cannons changed all that.

The rapid fall of Fort Pulaski marked the end of conventional masonry fortifications throughout the world. More immediately, its fall tightened the Union blockade, preventing Savannah from exporting cotton and importing military supplies.

After the Confederate surrender, Union commander Major General David Hunter announced that all slaves in Fort Pulaski and on its island were 'confiscated and declared free.' Several of these freed slaves served in the 1st South Carolina Volunteers, one of the earliest African American units in the US Army.

Visitors can view the well-preserved fort, complete with moat and drawbridge. From the parapets, you can see the Savannah River, Atlantic Ocean and salt marshes. The visitors center includes a museum, film and bookstore. Trails lead through the dikes surrounding the fort, and there are occasional Civil War reenactments.

To get here, travel about 15 miles east of Savannah on US Hwy 80 (the road to Tybee Island) and look for signs directing you off to the left; from downtown, head east on Bay St.

The Georgia Coast

CONTENTS

It's hard not to fall under the spell of Georgia's coastline and its isles. Southeast of Savannah lie a hundred miles of coastline protected by 13 large and small barrier islands. Many of these are uninhabited and inaccessible to the traveler. Some – notably Wassaw, Ossabaw, St Catherines, Blackbeard, Sapelo, Wolf and Cumberland – are private compounds and/or nature preserves for waterfowl, migratory birds, alligators, nesting sea turtles and wild horses.

At the southern end of the coast, several islands that were once the retreats of America's mega-rich are now favorites of beachcombers, bicyclists, golfers and history buffs. These islands – St Simons Island, Jekyll Island, Sea Island and Little St Simons Island – have become known as the Golden Isles. Sapelo Island's Hog Hammock community is one of the best-preserved examples of African American sea-island culture (see 'Gullah Culture' p32 and 'Melodies of Lowcountry Speech' p33).

All of this variety is set amid a coastal plain of startling beauty – the omnipresent live oak trees; small streams cutting through tidal marshlands with fiddler crabs and great egrets looking for their next meal; and mile after mile of cordgrass swaying with the wind.

Historically, this coast was strategically important in the colonization of both Georgia and America, in the Revolutionary War, in the slave trade and in the Civil War. It is still home to numerous military installations, including the Kings Bay nuclear submarine base on the Georgia–Florida border near St Marys. The wonders of the vast Okefenokee Swamp lie just to the west.

THE GEORGIA COAST

HIGHLIGHTS

- **Wining**
  Ziggy Mahoney's (p101), on St Simons Island, for beach music, rock, blues, country and disco – yeehah!

- **Dining**
  Courtyard at Crane (p104), on Jekyll Island, for alfresco dining like in *The Great Gatsby*

- **Sporting Event**
  A kayak expedition to Sapelo Island (p108) or Cumberland Island (p110)

- **Wildlife Encounter**
  The wild horses of Cumberland Island (p110)

- **Offbeat Experience**
  Sapelo Island coastal wilderness and the Geechee community (p108)

- TELEPHONE CODE: **912**
- POPULATION: **64,000**
- AREA: **1100 SQ MI**

ST SIMONS ISLAND & AROUND
pop 14,000

Famous for its golf courses, resorts and landscape of majestic live oaks, **St Simons Island** is the largest and most developed of the Golden Isles and is home base for many travelers exploring the Georgia Coast. St Simons lies 75 miles south of Savannah and just 5 miles from Brunswick. But while the southern half of the island is a thickly settled residential and resort area, the northern half and adjacent **Sea Island** and **Little St Simons Island** offer vast tracts of coastal wilderness amid a tidewater estuary.

During the late 17th century, Native Americans on the island traded with the French, who were conquered by the Spanish. In 1736, General James Oglethorpe established Fort Frederica, Georgia's first military outpost, and in 1742 he defeated invading Spanish forces in the Battle of Bloody Marsh. The plantation era began in the late 19th century – sea-island cotton, indigo and rice were grown on large plantations using slave labor. The loss of that labor after the Civil War made growing cotton unprofitable, but the pleasant climate and proximity to the sea ushered in the age of tourism in the 1870s.

With the island's rich history and plentiful recreation options, summers can be very crowded; the low season (October to March) is more relaxed, and prices are easier on the wallet.

Orientation

Demere Rd is the main artery leading from the causeway onto the island to the Village. Set on the southern end of the island, and surrounding the crossroads of Ocean Blvd and Mallery St, the Village is a bustling center of good restaurants, shops and entertainment. The nearby fishing pier is popular with locals for fishing, crabbing and strolling. Frederica Rd is the major north–south route for the island, and much of the island's commerce surrounds the intersection of Frederica Rd and Demere Rd.

Sea Island lies off the east side of St Simon and can be reached via the Sea Island Causeway. To reach Little St Simons Island, off the northeast tip of St Simons, you must take a private boat from the north end of St Simons. The free map available at the two visitors centers is a useful tool for getting around.

Information
BOOKSTORES
GJ Ford Bookshop (☎ 912-634-6168; cnr Sea Island & Frederica Rds)

EMERGENCY
Emergency numbers (☎ 911) Police, ambulance, firefighters.
Police Station (☎ 912-554-7560) For nonemergencies.

INTERNET ACCESS
St Simons Public Library (☎ 912-638-6234; 530 Beachview Dr; $3 per 30min)

INTERNET RESOURCES
www.bgivb.com Maps, activities, restaurants, lodging and entertainment.
www.brunswickexperience.com Activities, restaurants and lodging.

MEDIA
Brunswick News The area's primary daily.
Golden Isles Weekender A free weekly rife with advertisements and current entertainment happenings, available at restaurants, bars and lodgings.

MEDICAL SERVICES
For any serious medical problems, your best bet is to head west 5 miles to the hospitals in the city of Brunswick.

Glynn Immediate Care (☎ 912-267-7600; 3400 Parkwood Dr, Brunswick)
Southeast Georgia Regional Medical Center (☎ 912-466-7000, 2415 Parkwood Dr, Brunswick)

MONEY
Banks are along Frederica Rd between Demere Rd and Sea Island Rd.

POST
Main post office (☎ 800-275-8777; 1705 Frederica Rd; ☽ 8am-5pm Mon-Fri, 8am-1pm Sat)

TOURIST OFFICES
Visitors Center (☎ 912-638-9014; ☽ 9am-5pm) Tucked away in the library complex east of the fishing pier, this place has excellent maps of the island and of bike routes, as well as information on lodging.
Brunswick-Golden Isles Visitors Bureau (☎ 912-265-0620; www.bgivb.com; US Hwy 17 & FJ Torras Causeway; ☽ 8:30am-5pm Mon-Fri) There's a really helpful staff here and an amazing array of restaurant, activity and lodging brochures, many with discount coupons.

Sights

St Simons Island Lighthouse & Museum of Coastal History

(☎ 912-638-4666; Beachview Drive; adult/child $3/1; ☺ 10am-5pm Mon-Sat, 1:30-5pm Sun), near the Village on the southern side of the island, contains exhibits on the lighthouse, a lighthouse keeper's life and island history. The first lighthouse on this spot was burned in 1862 by retreating Confederate soldiers. The current structure was built in 1867, and it remains a navigational aid to boats entering St Simons and Doboy Sounds. The view from the top is well worth the 129 steps.

The **Battle of Bloody Marsh** (admission free; ☺ 8am-4pm) occurred on the eastern side of the island. In 1742, the British (including English and Scottish immigrants and Southeastern Indians) ambushed and defeated invading Spanish soldiers (aided by Indians and emancipated slaves). It is said that the water turned red from the blood of the dead. The Spanish permanently evacuated the island a week later and relinquished plans to colonize the eastern coast of North America. There are no facilities here, just an interpretive sign and an overlook of the now peaceful marsh. The signed gate is off Demere Rd.

Toward the northwestern side of the island, 7 miles from the Village, the **Fort Frederica National Monument** (☎ 912-638-3639;

THE GEORGIA COAST

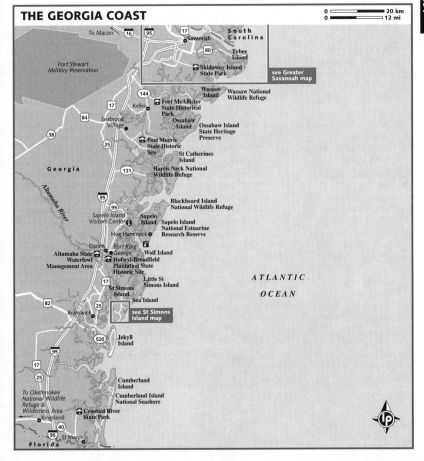

THE GEORGIA COAST

0 ——— 20 km
0 ——— 12 mi

To Macon 16
95
17
Savannah
South Carolina
80
Tybee Island
Fort Stewart Military Reservation
Skidaway Island State Park
see Greater Savannah map
Wassaw Island
Wassaw National Wildlife Refuge
144
Keller
Fort McAllister State Historical Park
17
84
Seabrook Village
Ossabaw Island
Ossabaw Island State Heritage Preserve
38
25
Fort Morris State Historic Site
St Catherines Island
Georgia
131
Harris Neck National Wildlife Refuge
95
Blackbeard Island National Wildlife Refuge
99
Sapelo Island Visitors Center
Sapelo Island
Sapelo Island National Estuarine Research Reserve
Hog Hammock
Darien
Fort King George
Wolf Island
Altamaha State Waterfowl Management Area
Hofwyl-Broadfield Plantation State Historic Site
17
Little St Simons Island
St Simons Island
Sea Island
ATLANTIC
OCEAN
82
Brunswick
25
see St Simons Island map
520
Jekyll Island
17
25
Cumberland Island
To Okefenokee National Wildlife Refuge & Wilderness Area
Cumberland Island National Seashore
Crooked River State Park
Kingsland
40
95
St Marys
Florida

THE GEORGIA COAST

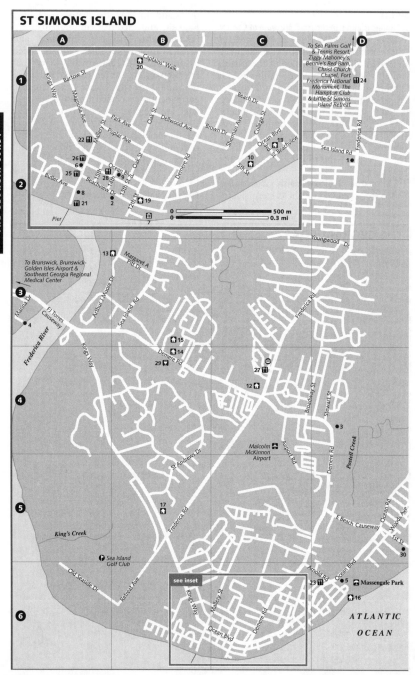

ST SIMONS ISLAND

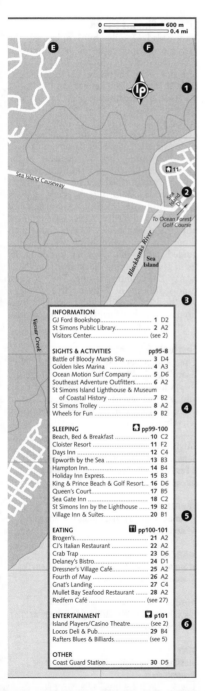

0 ————— 600 m
0 ————— 0.4 mi

adult/car $2/4; 🕙 8am-5pm) protects the tabby ruins of a fort and town established in 1736 by General James Oglethorpe. Residents of the town once numbered 11,000. Included in the admission fee are a 25-minute film and interpretive signs on colonial life.

Near Fort Frederica, **Christ Church Chapel** (donation suggested; 🕙 2-5pm) is a simple but beautiful structure built in 1886. You can visit the inside and wander around the old graves. It's a feast of color in the spring, when the blossoms and flowers are in bloom.

The **St Simons Trolley** (☎ 912-638-8954; Mallery St near the pier; 90min tours adult/child $13/7) offers historical tours, which include the lighthouse, Bloody Marsh site, Fort Frederica and Christ Church. Tours leave from the pier in the Village at 1pm daily, with an additional tour at 11am in the summer.

Activities

The **beaches** on St Simons are sandy and long, but they tend to disappear at high tide. One of the best is near the **Coast Guard station** on the eastern side of the island, at the end of 1st St. There's parking and restrooms here, but no food. **Massengale Park** also has beach access.

Bicycle paths lead across the flat landscape to many of the island's sights. You can rent beach cruisers from the **Ocean Motion Surf Company** (☎ 912-638-5225; 1300 Ocean Blvd; hourly/daily $5/15; 🕙 9:30am-6pm). This company also offers kayak tours of the marshes and creeks. **Wheels for Fun** (☎ 912-634-0606; 532 Ocean Blvd; hourly/daily $5/15; 🕙 9am-6pm) is another good deal and is near the Village.

This is a good place to learn **sea kayaking** because of the area's low wave energy and high water temperatures. **Southeast Adventure Outfitters** (☎ 912-638-6732; www.gacoast.comnavigator/sea.html; 313 Mallery St; 🕙 10am-6pm) offers kayak tours, rentals and sales. The best introduction is owner/guide Michael Gowen's three-hour sea kayak trip for $40. The company also offers guided tours to the Okefenokee Swamp and local rivers, as well as camping trips to Sapelo and Cumberland Islands. The store has complete outdoor supplies, maps and nautical charts. Rental costs are $25 per day per cockpit for a kayak, and $25 per day for a canoe. If you strike out in your own kayak, keep in mind that the tides are 8 feet, and the coastal rivers change direction twice a day.

Golden Isles Marina (☎ 912-634-1128; FJ Torras Causeway at Frederica River Bridge; ☻ 8am-6pm) has dive shops, boat rentals and dolphin tours. For information on charter fishing, call the **Golden Isles Charter Fishing Association** (☎ 912-638-7673; ☻ 8am-5pm), at Golden Isles Marina.

St Simons and Sea Island boast 99 holes of challenging **golf courses**. Greens fees run $55 to $80, depending on the course and the time of day. **Sea Island Golf Club** (☎ 912-638-5118; Frederica Rd at Kings Way; ☻ 8am-5pm) has three 18-hole courses, including the famous Tom Fazio–designed Seaside and the Rees Jones–designed Plantation course. Golfing is for club members and guests of the Cloister Resort and the Lodge at Sea Island who want to make the trek to the south end of the island to play. **Sea Palms Golf & Tennis Resort** (☎ 912-638-9041; 5445 Frederica Rd; ☻ 7:30am-5pm) has 27 holes open to the public. The **Hampton Club** (☎ 912-634-0255; 100 Tabbystone Lane; ☻ 8am-5pm), located on the northern end of St Simon, has a Joe Lee–designed course that features marsh and island holes.

Sea Island

On the northeastern side of St Simons and connected by the Sea Island Causeway, narrow Sea Island is largely the preserve of the luxurious **Cloister Resort** (☎ 912-638-3611, 800-732-4752; www.seaisland.com; d $250-650 meals included; Ⓟ ⌧ ⌧ ⌧). Dating from the 1920s, this classic island resort caters to celebrities, old money and the jubilant members of America's leisure class. With buildings echoing classic Mediterranean (stucco and terra-cotta tile roofs), antique and repro-duction furnishings, lavish fabrics and a butler staff of 10, the Sea Island experience is top drawer. In addition to three premier golf courses (like the Ocean Forest Course, at the north end of the island), the resort offers four restaurants, two pools, a beach club, tennis, spa, water sports, bikes, skeet shooting, horseback riding, lawn games and nightly entertainment. In 2000, Cloister Resort opened the so-called 'ultimate golf retreat,' the oceanfront Lodge at Sea Island, and in 2003 the resort started a $200 million renovation. Here's an exceptional place to pamper yourself.

Little St Simons Island

This island (2 miles by 3 miles) off the extreme northern tip of St Simons is accessible only by private boat. There's just one very charming old resort here, **Little St Simons Island Retreat** (☎ 912-638-7472, 888-733-5774; www.littlestsimonsisland.com; d $375-700 meals included; Ⓟ ⌧ ⌧ ⌧). Since the retreat only accommodates 30 guests, the experience here evokes the simplicity and exclusiveness that robber barons must have felt when coming here to 'rusticate' in the 1920s. The 10,000-acre island has nearly 7 miles of undisturbed beaches and marshes and woods. Wild horses, deer, gators, otters, sea turtles, raccoons and armadillos roam free, and bird-watchers have counted upwards of 200 species. Guests divide their time between swimming, beach walks, guided nature tours, biking, kayaking, fly fishing and kicking back over meals of hearty Lowcountry cuisine. The 15 guest rooms are spread between five cottages, like the 1917 hunting lodge, with its huge fireplace, wicker furniture and decorative hunting trophies.

Festivals & Events

The Golden Isles (St Simons Island, Jekyll Island and Brunswick) work together to sponsor a number of annual festivals and special events. A complete list is available from visitors centers or online at www.bgivb.com.

JANUARY
Annual Jekyll Island Historic District Open House & Festival Shows off the mansions of the rich and famous.

FEBRUARY
St Simons Island Players Production Brings live theater to the island.

MARCH
St Simons Annual Tour of Homes & Gardens Opens up some amazing pleasure domes.

APRIL
Jekyll Island Civil War Military Encampment Brings hundreds of reenactors to the island.

MAY
Blessing of the Shrimp Fleet Party time at the Brunswick docks.

JUNE
Jekyll Island Musical Theatre Festival Productions
Presents opera under the stars.

JULY
St Simons Sunshine Festival Crafters, food and
entertainment at seaside.

AUGUST
Jekyll Island Beach Music Festival Draws shagsters
from all over the coast.

SEPTEMBER
Brunswick Coastal Heritage Festival Showcases
Lowcountry seafood and Geechee culture.

OCTOBER
St Simons by the Sea Arts Festival Draws a large
collection of folk and fine artists.

NOVEMBER
**Jekyll Island Community Christmas Tree Lighting
Festival** Brings the holidays to the Historic District.

DECEMBER
**St Simons and Jekyll Island Christmas Tours of
Homes** Gives a taste the Yuletide season, Southern-style.

Sleeping

Hotel tax in St Simons is 11%. Prices vary
drastically between high season (May to
September) and low season. Rooms with
a view will cost more than rooms without.
For beach-front condo rentals, check out
Atlantic Land & Development Corp (☎ 912-634-
9941; 1002 Ocean Blvd). **Trupp Hodnett Enterprises**
(☎ 912-638-5450, 800-627-6850; 520 Ocean Blvd)
offers more than 350 privately owned
vacation properties, including oceanfront
condos, villa and Victorian-style cottages.

BUDGET

St Simon has few accommodations for
budget travelers, but two are memorable.
Queen's Court (☎ 912-638-8459; 437 Kings Way; d
$55-60; P ⊠ ⊠ ⊠) Near Mallery St in the
Village, the Queen's Court is a conveniently
located, family-owned budget hotel within
easy walking distance of restaurants. The 23
rooms are clean, reasonably furnished and
an excellent value for this prime location.
The lodge is set on grounds with live oaks
draped with Spanish moss, and there's an
outdoor pool. Suites and kitchenettes are
available.

Epworth by the Sea (☎ 912-638-8688; www
.epworthbythesea.org; d $50-85; P ⊠ ⊠ ⊠) Just
off Sea Island Rd north of the causeway is a
Methodist conference and retreat center, but
it's open to anyone. The cheaper rooms are
older and simpler; the highest rates get you
a modern apartment with a separate kitchen.
It's popular with religious groups. Its
strength is its serene setting on the banks of
the Frederica River, overlooking the Marshes
of Glynn. There's an on-site cafeteria.

MID-RANGE

You might want to examine the location and
features of the mid-range accommodations
carefully before making your selection, since
a number of these offers are located in the
middle of the island, far from the beach
Beach, Bed & Breakfast (☎ 912-634-2800; www
.beachbedandbreakfast; 907 Beachview Dr; d $105-165;
P ⊠ ⊠ ⊠) Imagine breakfast on the
porch, with a spectacular view of Jekyll
and Cumberland Islands across the sound.
This three-story pink and white inn near
the Village has ocean-view and oceanfront
rooms, each with a complimentary stock of
beverages in the fridge, a telephone and a
sound system. Guests get 'Lucille's Tea by
the Sea' every afternoon.

St Simons Inn by the Lighthouse (☎ 912-638-1101;
609 Beachview Dr; d $70-100; P ⊠ ⊠ ⊠) Across
from the lighthouse, this Mediterranean-
style stucco inn with red-tile roof doesn't
have any sea views, but it is a clean,
modern hotel in a great location, near all
the action in the Village. All rooms have a
fridge and microwave. You can also rent
fully equipped detached apartments and
king suites with Whirlpools. Continental
breakfast is included.

Sea Gate Inn (☎ 912-638-8661, 800-562-8812;
www.seagateinn.com; 1014 Ocean Blvd; d $70-155;
P ⊠ ⊠ ⊠) This modern inn, about a half
mile east of the Village, has 48 large, well-
appointed rooms with decks and sliding-
glass walls, most facing the ocean or pool.
Many rooms come with a kitchenette. The
inn also has a separate Ocean House, where
all rooms have ocean views, starting at $145.
Families with children love this place.

Several chain hotels are located at the
center of the island. **Days Inn** (☎ 912-634-
0660, 800-870-3736; www.daysinn.com; 411 Longview
Plaza; d $70-100; P ⊠ ⊠ ⊠), **Hampton Inn**
(☎ 912-634-2204, 800-426-7866; www.hamptoninn.com;

2204 Demere Rd; d $80-130; (P X X X) and **Holiday Inn Express** (☎ 912-634-2175, 800-787-4666; www.holidayinnexpress.com; 299 Main St; d $80-100; P X X X) have lodgings off Demere Rd, in the heart of the island's business district.

TOP END

At the island's big-budget places, you either pay for exclusive ambiance or a plethora of activities.

The **King & Prince Beach & Golf Resort** (☎ 912-638-3631, 800-342-0212; www.kingandprince.com; 201 Arnold Rd; d $150-190; P X X X) Here's a great place for a family vacation. Amenities include indoor and outdoor pools, tennis courts, a fitness center, a dining room and a lounge. The oceanfront resort features Spanish Colonial architecture, and some of the 187 comfortable rooms have ocean views. The resort also rents two- and three-bedroom villas starting at $310. Its golf course, the Hampton Club (p98), is on the northern end of the island.

Village Inn & Suites (☎ 912-634-6056, 888-635-6111; www.villageinnsuites.com; 500 Mallery St; d $130-170; P X X X) Park your car and throw away the key. Shaded beneath centuries-old live oaks in the heart of the Village, this lodge's public area and bar are located in a restored 1930s beach cottage that still has its original stone fireplace. From here, it's an easy stroll to the beaches, lighthouse, pier, restaurants and night spots. Each of the 28 guest rooms has a 27-inch television, and most feature private balconies overlooking the courtyard pool or the Village.

Eating

BUDGET

Eating cheap on St Simon doesn't mean eating poorly.

Fourth of May (☎ 912-638-5444; 4444 Ocean Blvd; mains $7-15; X X) Standing on the corner of Ocean Blvd and Mallery St, this packed little place with green-and-white checkered tablecloths and a major-league dessert case is popular with locals and tourists for good reason. Menu items include home-style Southern vegetables, casseroles, sandwiches, soups, salads, seafood and scrumptious desserts. Veggie plates are $1.15 per vegetable, sandwiches are $5 to $7, and daily specials run about $7. Indoor and outdoor seating is available.

Try the pepper shrimp ($11) or come for the daily potluck specials ($7); on Friday, its shrimp jambalaya or chicken and dumplings. Decent wine is only $4 a glass, and kids eat for under $4.

Dressner's Village Café (☎ 912-634-1217; 223 Mallery St; breakfast/lunch $4/6; 🕒 7:30am-2:30pm Mon-Fri, 8am-2:30pm Sat; X X) Here's another little (blue-and-white) checkered-tablecloth spot, smack in the middle of the Village. Dressner's is a particularly cheery place to linger over a breakfast of omelets, pancakes or French toast at reasonable prices (under $5).

MID-RANGE

While many of St Simons' mid-range eateries are in the Village, near the pier, don't miss the ones in the middle of the island.

Gnat's Landing (☎ 912-638-7378; 310 Redfern Village; mains $7-15; X X) This onetime BBQ restaurant has been revamped into a totally new structure that reeks of a chill Key West attitude (beyond casual). There's a covered porch, and the clientele turns out in cut-offs and flip-flops. Good old American fare dominates the menu with daily specials including fresh seafood, fried pickles, Mrs Slappy's famous seafood gumbo and the $8000 margarita (you *gotta* ask about this one).

Brogen's (☎ 912-638-1660; 200 Pier Alley; mains $5-15; X X) Set near the fishing pier, this laid-back bar and grill with indoor/outdoor seating gets a lot of votes for 'best burger on the island.' The menu is largely pub salads and sandwiches, but another great way to go is the large veggie pizza ($14) and a pitcher of beer ($4), enjoyed on the upper deck.

CJ's Italian Restaurant (☎ 912-634-1022; 405 Mallery St; mains $7-15; X X) Locals can barely speak the name of this place without openly salivating. Like one of the tiny cafes you find in New York, this is a narrow and deep space serving moderately priced pizzas, subs and pastas. The bread sticks are awesome! Kids love this place.

Bennie's Red Barn (☎ 912-638-2844; 5514 Frederica Rd; mains $14-22; X X) If you had visited Bennie's back in 1954, you would have enjoyed the best steak and seafood served in the Golden Isles. Some things never change. The steaks are cut fresh and cooked over an old-fashioned wood fire. Fresh local seafood is brought in daily. You will not soon forget the rare filet mignon ($20). Kids' meals run $7, and you get great service from the professional wait staff.

Mullet Bay Seafood Restaurant (☎ 912-634-9977; 512 Ocean Blvd; mains $10-18; ☒ ☒) Just around the corner from Mallery St, in the heart of the village, is this favorite local dining venue. Go for the blackened-tuna salad ($9) for lunch on the shady porch. Kids' meals start at $2. Butcher paper and crayons on the tables keep the little ones busy.

Crab Trap (☎ 912-638-3552; 1209 Ocean Blvd; mains $11-16; ☒) Just south of Arnold St, the Crab Trap looks a lot like a shack. The atmosphere is alive with a holiday crowd, but there's no nonsmoking section. Seafood specialties – mostly shrimp and oysters – are the big attractions.

TOP END

Locals on St Simons favor two venues for gourmet dining.

Redfern Café (☎ 912-634-1344; 200 Redfern Village; mains $16-25; ☒ ☒) The scrumptious dinners here are creations of a chef from the Culinary Institute of America. Offerings include tender veal prepared differently each evening, grouper with fresh oyster sauce, Portuguese-style roasted pork tenderloin, rack of lamb and crab cakes with oysters on a bed of smoky cheese grits. The Friday night special is bouillabaisse. You can dine inside or on the patio.

Delaney's Bistro (☎ 912-638-1330; 3415 Frederica Rd; mains $15-26; ☒ ☒) Join local Chef Tom Delaney, who conjures up selections from the freshest seafood, poultry and certified Black Angus beef. Lunch includes Delaney's own sautéed crab cakes ($10) and fabulous portobello pizza ($10) For dinner, try the shrimp provençal ($19).

Entertainment

Ziggy Mahoney's (☎ 912-634-0999, 5514 Frederica Rd) This joint has been an island institution for more than 20 years. Adjacent to Bennie's Red Barn (p100) Ziggy's has the most popular live entertainment and dance music on St Simons Island. Presiding over the party is the legendary duo Ziggy Mahoney. They play everything from beach music and classic rock to blues, country and disco. The crowd is made up of preppy 30-somethings who come to crowd 'round

the bar, suck suds, pack the dance floor and catch some fresh air on an open deck under the oak trees. Live music and dancing take place Thursday, Friday and Saturday nights.

Brogen's (☎ 912-638-1660; 200 Pier Alley; mains $5-15; ☒ ☒), Can you say 'meat market'? During the summer and on weekends, this bar and grill by the beach oozes a 'Why Don't We Get Drunk and Screw' ambiance on its upper deck, when Pabst draft is $1 a glass or $4 a pitcher. The crowd is largely under 25, and while the sound system pumps out classic rock and hip hop, some partiers inevitably take to dancing on the bar. A local tradition has it that you haven't really done St Simons until you have gotten toasted at Brogen's, then scrambled next door into the park to launch your shoes (tied together by their laces) into the branches of a massive live oak. The so-called 'Shoe Tree' sports scores of party sneakers. Also see this listing under Eating (p100).

Locos Deli & Pub (☎ 912-634-2002; 2463 Demere Rd) There's live rock Thursday to Saturday and a late-night grill here, with quesadillas ($5) and Philly cheesesteaks ($7) – just the things to pull you back into party mode after a pub crawl. There's even a veggie menu.

Rafters Blues & Billiards (☎ 912-634-9755; 315½ Mallery St) The sign on the door says 'This is a club of love,' and it ain't lyin'. Head up the stairs from Mallery St to rub shoulders with young hard-bodies and to get down with some mean blues.

Island Players (☎ 912-638-3031; tickets $15-30) This troupe presents plays in the summer near the visitors center in the Casino Theatre, next to the St Simons Public Library and visitors center.

Getting There & Away

AIR

On Glynco Pkwy, 2 miles off I-95 at exit 38, is **Brunswick-Golden Isles Airport** (☎ 912-265-2070). There are currently three flights a day to/from Atlanta on **Delta Connection** (☎ 800-221-1212) for $140 and up.

CAR & MOTORCYCLE

A 5-mile **FJ Torras Causeway** leads from Brunswick on the mainland to St Simons Island. From I-95, exits 29 through 42 will eventually take you to the causeway.

JEKYLL ISLAND

Pop 1200

This place oozes the luxury of a robber baron's oasis, and for good reason – it was an exclusive refuge for millionaires in the late 19th and early 20th centuries. The film *The Legend of Bagger Vance* captures that epoch, and many scenes were shot in and around the Jekyll Island Club Hotel (p104).

Jekyll is 7 miles long and 2 miles wide, with 10 miles of beaches. French, Spanish and British explorers and pirates have all visited the island, and it was once the site of sea-island cotton plantations. Slaves were imported to work on the cotton plantations; the schooner *Wanderer* unloaded 490 slaves from Africa on the northern end of the island in 1858, 50 years after the importation of slaves was outlawed in the US.

In the late 19th century, a group of millionaires who called themselves 'the Twenty-Seven' – including JP Morgan, William Rockefeller, Joseph Pulitzer and William Vanderbilt – established an exclusive club on the island where they could play golf, 'rusticate' and be rich together; many of their winter 'cottages' are still intact. The club began declining in popularity when the income tax was introduced, during the Depression. It closed during WWII, when labor and supplies were low, and the US government feared that such a high concentration of wealth and power in one place invited attacks by enemy subs off the coast.

The island is now owned by the state of Georgia, and while there are many private residences on land that are leased from the state, much of the island remains wilderness, replete with hiking trails and 20 miles of bike paths.

Jekyll has plenty of wildlife, including deer, wild turkeys, hawks, egrets, herons and shorebirds. Good bird-watching sites are indicated by the **Colonial Coast Birding Trail** signs; a list of these is available at the Welcome Center.

Information

BOOKSTORES

Island Bookstore (☎ 912-635-3077; Stable Rd, in the Historic District; ☽ 9am-5pm)

EMERGENCIES

Emergency numbers (☎ 911) Police, ambulance and firefighters.

INTERNET RESOURCES

www.jekyllisland.com Links to most island attractions.
www.bgivb.com Activities, restaurants, lodging and history.

MEDICAL SERVICES

See p94 for a listings of hospitals in Brunswick.
Jekyll Pharmacy (☎ 912-235-2246; Jekyll Island Shopping Center, Beachview Dr; ☽ 10am-5pm Mon-Sat)

MONEY

First Bank of Brunswick (☎ 912-635-9014; Jekyll Island Shopping Center, Beachview Dr) Your only convenient ATM on the island.

POST

Jekyll Island Post Office (☎ 912-235-2625; Jekyll Island Shopping Center; ☽ 9am-5pm Mon-Fri)

TOURIST OFFICES

Jekyll Island Welcome Center (☎ 912-635-3636, 877-453-5955; ☽ 9am-5pm), on the causeway to the island, has maps and good brochures on activities and lodging. Another spot that's good for information is the **Brunswick-Golden Isles Visitors Bureau** (☎ 912-265-0620; www.bgivb.com; US Hwy 17 & FJ Torras Causeway; ☽ 8:30am-5pm Mon-Fri). The **Jekyll Island Museum** (☎ 912-635-4036; Stable Rd, in the Historic District; admission free; ☽ 9am-5pm) has free biking and walking-tour maps.

Dangers & Annoyances

Herds of deer roam the island and frequently wander into the roads at night. The north end of the island is particularly dense with deer. Drive slowly so as not to be one of the dozens of motorists who hit these animals each year.

Sights & Activities

The 240-acre **Historic District** is a good place to just wander about among the oaks and fancy cottages, although you cannot go inside the houses, except on a tour. The **Jekyll Island Museum** (☎ 912-635-4036; Stable Rd, in the Historic District; admission free; ☽ 9am-5pm), on Stable Rd, is the hub of activity for the Historic District and sells walking-tour maps. Exhibits explain the history of the island and its conversion to a state-owned resort.

Tram tours (☎ 912-635-4036; adult/child $10/6; ☽ 10am-3pm) leave from the museum center and pass through the millionaires' Historic District. Several houses have been renovated with period furniture and decorations; the tours take visitors inside three of the houses, which are in various stages of renovation, to marvel at the opulence.

Alternative ways of touring the district include the Jekyll Island Museum's horse-drawn **carriage rides** (☎ 912-635-9500; adult/child $10/5; 10am-4:30pm). The **Live Oaks and More Tour** (☎ 912-635-5032; adult/child $5/3; 9:30am-5pm) is a guided walking tour of the Historic District, focusing on the gardens and plant life. Tours depart at 1pm Monday from Faith Chapel, in the Historic District.

You can get access to the 10 miles of beach at several locations, including the **Central Dunes Picnic Area**, which has bathrooms. Note that parts of the beach are completely covered at high tide.

Jekyll Island has 20 miles of dedicated, paved **bicycle paths** around the entire island, including in the Historic District, along the beach and within some of the natural areas. The Welcome Center (p102) distributes maps. Many accommodations rent bikes, but you can also get them at **Miniature Golf & Bicycle Rentals** (☎ 912-635-2648; Beachview Dr; hr/day $5/11; 9am-8pm) and the **Jekyll Harbor Marina** (☎ 912-635-5032; tandems hr/day $6/13; 9am-5pm).

The **Tidelands Nature Center** nature walks (☎ 912-635-3636; adult/child $5/3; 9am Mon, Wed, Fri) take you to a different destination each day and include the marsh and beach areas.

The **Clam Creek Picnic Area & Fishing Pier,** on the northern end of the island, is worth a visit to gaze across St Simons Sound at the St Simons Lighthouse. You can have a picnic while viewing the wading birds in the marsh, and later, stroll along secluded **Driftwood Beach.**

Loggerhead sea turtles nest on the island from May through August. Turtle walks are offered by the **Sea Turtle Project** (☎ 912-635-2284; Jekyll Island Museum; adult/child $6/4; 8:30pm & 9:30pm in season).

The island has Georgia's largest public **golf resort** (912-635-2384; Captain Wylie Rd; fees $35/45; 8am-6pm), with three 18-hole courses and one 9-hole course. In 2001 the **Pine Lakes** course had a $3.2 million redesign by Clyde Johnston; the **Oleander** is ranked among the state's best courses.

The **Jekyll Island Tennis Center** (☎ 912-635-3154; $16/hr; 9am-6pm) was selected as one of the 25 best municipal tennis facilities in the country. Of the 13 courts, seven are lighted. Eight United States Tennis Association–sanctioned tournaments are held here every year.

The **Jekyll Harbor Marina** (☎ 912-635-3137), south of the Jekyll Island Bridge, has floating docks, dry storage, boat rentals, bicycle rentals and parasail rides. **Dolphin tours** are offered from the **Jekyll Wharf** (☎ 912-635-3152; adult/child $17/8; 9am-6pm). Fishing charters are also available.

Summer Waves (☎ 912-635-2074; adult/child $15/12; Riverview Dr; 10am-6pm Sun-Fri, 10am-8pm Sat) has more than a million gallons of water in 11 acres of rides. It's open Memorial Day to Labor Day.

You can catch a horseback ride on the beach at **Victoria's Carriages & Trail Rides** (☎ 912-235-9500; Stable Rd; $35/hr; 9am-5pm).

Sleeping

In spite of its reputation as an oasis for the rich and famous, Jekyll has accommodations for travelers of all budgets. But except for the historic Jekyll Island Club Hotel, all buildings are long and low to blend in with the natural environment. For a complete list of accommodations, check out www.jekyllisland.com or www.bgivb.com.

Jekyll Realty (☎ 912-635-3301, 888-333-5055; www.jekyll-island.com; Jekyll Shopping Center) rents houses on a weekly basis. The houses are individually owned and decorated. Rates range from $450 a week for a simple two-bedroom house accommodating four people to $2800 for a beachfront house with five bedrooms.

Jekyll Island Campground (☎ 912-635-3021; www.jekyllisland.com; 1197 Riverview Dr; tents/RV $20/25; P) What a location! Set on the undeveloped, northern end of the island, this campground has 158 sites and sits right across the street from the trails of the Clam Creek Picnic Area & Fishing Pier. Driftwood Beach is also nearby. RVs are packed closely together on the main part of the campground; some tent sites are well away from the RVs. Amenities include a camp store, bicycle rental and a coin laundry.

Quality Inn & Suites (☎ 912-325-2202, 800-281-4446; www.imichotels.com; N Beachview Dr; d $60-200; P) Here's a great location and a good value for families with kids. This 71-room wonder sits right across from the beach and was totally renovated in 2002. Rooms have sturdy motel furniture and functional fabrics, and each room includes a microwave and fridge. It has an outdoor pool, guest laundry and a small continental breakfast. It is also walking distance to the restaurants in the Jekyll Island Plaza. Golf and tennis facilities, as well as minigolf and bike rentals, are on offer. For $150 you get a two-bedroom apartment with a kitchen (cookware not included). Many guests rent by the week here, for under $400.

Villas by the Sea Resort Hotel (☎ 912-635-2521, 800-841-6262; www.jekyllislandga.com; N Beachview Dr; d $90-260; P X R X) Here's another great value for families. This upscale resort village of 176 condos (with patio or balcony) spans 17 landscaped acres of live oaks and gardens, as well as 2000 feet of beach. In addition to the pool, there is a playground, baby-sitting services and the best bar scene on the island (see Entertainment p105).

Jekyll Inn (☎ 912-635-2531, 888-333-5055; N Beachview Dr; d $100-200; P X R X) On the beach at the north end of the island, this hotel – the largest on the island – spans 15 acres. There are 188 rooms, a large outdoor pool, and 75 one- and two-bedroom villas. A restaurant, bar and game room round it all out. The higher-priced rooms have ocean views.

Beachview Club (☎ 912-635-2256, 800-299-2228; www.beachviewclub; N Beachview Dr; d $140-180; P X R X) Located on the beach, this is the newest hotel on the island. The Beachview has 38 spacious, recently remodeled rooms, all with an efficiency kitchen. All rooms have ocean views and a balcony or patio. Suites with hot tubs and gas fireplaces are also available. There's even a heated pool and hot tub outside.

Georgia Coast Inn (☎ 912-635-2111, 800-835-2110; www.georgiacoastinn.com; S Beachview Dr; d $60-215; P X R X) The largest hotel pool (shaped like the state of Georgia – go figure!) on the island, a playground, beach games, a restaurant, a popular sports bar and complimentary continental breakfast are the big attractions at this 110-room facility. All rooms have an ocean view.

Also recommended are **Clarion** (☎ 912-235-2261, 888-412-7770; www.motelproperties.com; S Beachview Dr; d $100-190; P X R X), **Comfort Inn** (☎ 912-635-2211, 888-412-7770; www.motelproperties.com; S Beachview Dr; d $120-200; P X R X), **Days Inn** (☎ 912-635-9800, 888-635-3003; www.daysinnjekyll.com; d $105-240; P X R X) and **Holiday Inn** (☎ 912-635-3311, 800-753-5955; d $110-150; P X R X). All have midsized beachfront properties.

Jekyll Island Club Hotel (☎ 912-635-2600, 800-535-9547; www.jekyllclub.com; Historic District; d $140-290; P X R X) What a great place for a romantic getaway – it looks like a castle. Once the exclusive domain of the island's vacationing millionaires, this elegant, turreted hotel is now accessible to the rest of us. Set in the midst of the Historic District on the opposite side of the island from the beach, the Club Hotel still draws the rich and famous with old-school amenities, service (the professional bellmen and waiters aren't to be believed) and ambiance. Matt Damon and Will Smith stayed here while making *The Legend of Bagger Vance*, and you can follow in their footsteps if you choose one of the king suites in the Main Club House. The rooms in the Annex, with their private porches and easy access to the pool, are memorable. There are also rooms in Crane Cottage and Cherokee Cottage, two of the historic mansions. The hotel has two killer restaurants and a private beach club on the ocean side of the island.

Eating

Most of the island hotels have restaurants. The following are island eateries with uncommon temptations.

Huddle House (☎ 912-635-3755; Fortson Pkwy; breakfast $2-5; X X) Yes, it's a chain, and it looks like a fast-food joint from the '50s, but dang if they don't serve fresh coffee and filling omelets (with grits, toast and jelly) 24 hours a day. If you like service with a smile and waitresses who call you 'hon,' you gotta catch this scene.

Courtyard at Crane (☎ 912-635-2600, 800-535-9547; www.jekyllclub.com; Riverview Dr; lunch $10-14) Just treat yourself, darlin'! You don't want to miss the Courtyard at Crane, located at Crane Cottage in the Historic District. Originally built in 1917 and featuring grand, Italianate villa architecture, the mansion is now the site of intimate, alfresco dining in the Cottage's luxurious, landscaped courtyard (which serves lunch Monday to Saturday, weather permitting). The menu features salads and entrees with a Northern California wine-country flair. People go back again and again for the mussels San Remo, which are sautéed with scallions, rosemary, artichokes, sun-dried tomatoes and garlic, and served atop fettuccine.

Seajay's Waterfront Cafe & Pub (☎ 912-635-2300; 1 Harbor Rd; mains $6-14; 🏃) Hey there, Jimmy Buffett fans, this one's for you. This neat little seafood shack hidden on the property of the Jekyll Harbor Marina is home to a Famous Lowcountry Boil Buffet Dinner ($14): all-you-can-eat steamed shrimp, sausage and corn on the cob. Bob and Lynn, who work the bar and small dining-room deck, are a couple of good old folks ready to make you feel at home with a mug of ice cold suds, a basket of popcorn and some crispy crab balls ($6). Come for the breathtaking sunsets over the Lowcountry marshes and to hear the Wharf Rats play 'new grass' on Thursday, Friday and Saturday after 7pm.

Latitude 31° (☎ 912-635-3800; Jekyll Wharf; mains $15-18; 🏃 ✗) Set in the Historic District on the wharf opposite the Jekyll Island Club Hotel, Latitude 31° is the place local islanders recommend most often for fresh seafood. Specialties include the catch of the day, such as grouper, and also shellfish, steak, pasta and chicken. Don't miss the seafood crepes ($17). Bands rock the deck Sunday afternoon and evening.

Zachry's Seafood Restaurant (☎ 912-635-3128; Jekyll Island Shopping Center; mains $10-17; 🏃 ✗) Check out this family-owned bistro, which conjures up an intimate and urbane ambiance with its Tiffany lamps and white tablecloths. Fresh local seafood and a delicious salad bar are the main attractions, but the grilled or blackened chicken breast with salad, veggies and rolls ($10) is a popular choice for both kids and adults.

Blackbeard's Restaurant (☎ 912-635-3522; N Beachview Dr; mains $15-19; 🏃 ✗) Folks favor Blackbeard's for upscale dining overlooking the ocean. The menu is heavy on fresh local seafood, like the deviled crab platter ($16). Come and sip Pinot Grigio, graze on scallops Jekyll (sautéed in garlic), and watch the moon rise over the Atlantic from the outdoor deck.

Jekyll Island Club Hotel Grand Dining Room (☎ 912-635-2600; Historic District; mains $19-27; 🏃 ✗) This is the place to come for classic haute resort dining amid scents of sweet basil and the tinkle of crystal and silver. Impeccable service is provided by waiters in cutaway jackets and bowties. The chef serves omelets ($9) for breakfast; and seafood, salads, soups and sandwiches ($9) for lunch; and seafood and steak for dinner. We recommend the almond-crusted grouper ($22). Dinners and Sunday brunch unfold with Cole Porter riffs on a grand piano. Men wear a jacket for the evening meal.

Entertainment

Some would say that 'Jekyll Island nightlife' is an oxymoron and that true party hounds beat it over to St Simons to work on their night moves. This perception is largely true during the colder months, when the tourist scene on Jekyll is low key. But when the weather heats up and vacationers flock to the beaches, you can ring in the midnight hour with like-minded folks without crossing the off-island bridge.

Riptide Lounge (☎ 912-635-2521; Villas by the Sea Resort, N Beachview Dr) This is the most happening night spot on the island – by far! And it's a great venue. Consider the possibilities for stirring up the juices in a room that looks like a Hawaiian tiki hut decorated with surfboards, bathed in cool light and furnished with comfortable lounge chairs and couches. The clientele is mostly a mix of locals and resort workers (lots) from ages 22 to 62. Tourists haven't quite found this place yet. There's karaoke midweek and live dance music Thursday to Saturday. The bands favor classic rock and Top 40.

Vincent's Pub If you're looking for a quaint, old English-style pub that looks a lot like the place where legendary golfers Bobby Jones and Bagger Vance tossed back some bourbon, you'll find it on the garden level of the Jekyll Island Club Hotel (p104).

Seajay's Waterfront Cafe & Pub (see previous column) Dog, there is just no better place to sit by the dock of the bay, get a good buzz on, talk to boat folks drifting through on the Intracoastal Waterway and watch the tide slip away.

Some hotels have live entertainment and theme nights during the busy summer season. **Remington's** is at the Holiday Inn (p104) and **Mr Hyde's Sports Bar** is at the Georgia Coast Inn (p104).

Getting There & Away

AIR
There are currently three flights (from $140) a day to/from Atlanta on **Delta Connection** (☎ 800-221-1212). **Brunswick-Golden Isles Airport** (☎ 912-265-2070) is on Glynco Pkwy, 2 miles off I-95 at exit 38.

CAR & MOTORCYCLE
The turnoff for Jekyll Island is 4 miles south of Brunswick on US Hwy 17, then you drive another 6 miles on Hwy 520 to the island. As you cross the causeway, you'll need to pay a $3 daily parking fee; multiday permits are also available.

BRUNSWICK
Pop 16,953
Mainly used as a jumping-off point for nearby St Simons Island and Jekyll Island, Brunswick is worth a stop. With its large shrimp-boat fleet and downtown Historic District shaded beneath lush live oaks – including the 900-year-old **Lovers Oak** (cnr Prince & Albany Sts) – this town dates from 1733 and has charms you might miss when sailing by on I-95 or the Golden Isle Parkway (US Hwy 17). During WWII, Brunswick shipyards constructed 99 Liberty transport ships for the Navy. Today, a new 23-foot scale model at **Mary Ross Waterfront Park**, on Bay St, stands as a memorial to those ships and their builders.

Information & Orientation
Brunswick-Golden Isles Visitors Bureau (☎ 912-265-0620; www.bgivb.com; US Hwy 17 & FJ Torras Causeway; � 8:30am-5pm Mon-Fri). You can get current information on all the Golden Isles, accommodations and dining at this well-stocked and welcoming site. Another good source of information is www.brunswickexperience.com.

The **Old Town** lies about a half mile south of the visitors center. Bound by H St to the north, First Ave to the south, Martin Luther King Jr Blvd to the east and Bay St to west, Old Town is a collection of restored homes and commercial buildings featuring an eclectic mix of turn-of-the-century architecture. Shops and restaurants pepper the area, especially around the intersection of Gloucester St and New Castle St. Bay St, with the **Mary Ross Waterfront Park** and shrimp-boat wharves, lies just to the west.

Sleeping
Because it is not seaside, Brunswick offers some exceptional accommodations values, particularly in the B&B category. For a complete list of Brunswick area lodgings, you can check out www.bgivb.com. Here are a few of our favorites.

Brunswick Manor (☎ 912-265-6889; 825 Egmont St; d $80-105; P ⬚ ⊠) What a gem! Built in 1886 and set in the heart of Old Town, this manor with four guest rooms faces one of the Brunswick's original 18th-century squares. The exterior look is all about white columns, broad porches, tall palms and plantations of wisteria. Inside you get high ceilings, baronial furnishings, plush luxurious towels, cozy robes, fragrant nosegays, chilled fruit and cheese, chocolate mints, sherry and juice, a refrigerator, a hot tub and a gourmet breakfast.

At Waters Hill (☎ 912-264-4262; www.watershill.com; 728 Union St; d $85-120; P ⬚ ⊠) Southern hospitality is part of everyday life in this white clapboard Victorian manse. The innkeepers pride themselves on providing guests with a peaceful setting surrounded by lawns and flower gardens. Rooms feature an array of period antiques from America and England. Rich fabrics and gilded objets d'art accent public rooms and guest quarters.

McKinnon House (☎ 921-261-9100; 1001 Egmont St; d $90-130; P ⬚ ⊠) Located in the heart of the Old Town, this century-old home is perfect for those who desire the opulence of a Queen Anne mansion decorated with fine furnishings from Charleston and New Orleans. Amenities include three luxurious guest rooms, two grand parlors, four porches, fireplaces and footed tubs.

Many chains, like **Comfort Inn** (☎ 912-264-6540, 800-551-7591; www.comfortinn.com; I-95 exit 36B; d $65-110; P ⬚ ⬚ ⊠), **Ramada Inn** (☎ 912-264-3621, 800-272-6232; www.ramada.com; I-95 exit 36A; d $60-90; P ⬚ ⬚ ⊠) and **Best Western** (☎ 912-264-0144, 800-528-1234; www.bestwestern.com; I-95 exit 36B; d $60-70; P ⬚ ⬚ ⊠), cluster around the I-95 exits, especially exit 36 (US Hwy 341). They can be quite a bit cheaper than accommodations on the islands, but be forewarned: these motels often fill up with the hordes heading to/from Florida during the fall/spring migration of snowbirds.

CAMPING

There are a couple of camping options.

Hostel in the Forest (☎ 912-264-9738; www
.foresthostel.com; US Hwy 82; s $15; **P**) For free
spirits who appreciate communal living, this
is a brilliant place to stay. The hostel is set
on 105 acres in the middle of the forest and
has been here for more than 25 years. Private
accommodations are provided in nine rustic
tree houses with double beds, electricity,
fans and lights, but no air-conditioning.
The owners have created a natural retreat:
Amenities include a duck pond, bushes
full of blueberries in June/July, boardwalks
through the forest, outside showers, a sweat
lodge every full moon, free-range chickens, a
pool table, laundry and – everyone's favorite
– composting sawdust toilets. You'll need
insect repellent and flashlights. To reach the
hostel, head 9 miles west of town (2 miles
west of I-95) on US Hwy 82.

Blythe Island Regional Park & Campground
(☎ 912-261-3805, 800-343-7855; Hwy 303 S; tent/RV
$21/23; **P**) This park has a lake for
swimming, fishing pier, boat ramp, beach,
laundry, full hookups and 40 wooded sites
screened with palmettos.

Eating

Cargo Portside Grill (☎ 912-267-7330; 1423 Newcastle
St; mains $12-25; 🍴 ✖) Owner and chef Alix
Kenagy has a penchant for rehabilitating
100-year-old buildings and turning them
into award-winning eateries. In recent
years, Cargo has been picked for the Top
10 'Best of the Best' rating by *Georgia
Trend* magazine. 'Best crab cakes I've
ever eaten,' gushes a reviewer in Atlanta's
Knife & Fork. Don't miss the Tuscan free-
range chicken ($18). Reservations are
recommended.

PG Archibald's (☎ 912-262-1402; 1618 Newcastle
St; mains $8-17; 🍴 ✖) Here's the brainchild
of former NFL star Pete Archibald. The
eclectic menu includes huge salads, grilled
pork chops, chicken and seafood. This is a
great place to try Brunswick Stew (p60).

Georgia Pig (☎ 912-264-6664; I-95 exit 29 at
US Hwy 17; mains $7-18) This log cabin reeks
of pork BBQ. There is an old-time sign
saying near the door that says 'Salesmen
recommend it.' For good reason!

Willie's Wee-Nee Wagon (☎ 912-264-1146; 3599
Altama Ave; mains $5-11; 🍴 ✖) Dogs, burgers
and Polish sausage rule the menu, but

PIT STOPS ON THE COAST ROAD

Travelers looking to do a little highway adventuring will want to follow US Hwy 17 and its
tributaries as they meander the length of the Georgia Coast from Brunswick to Savannah, skirting
the fringe of Lowcountry marshes, traversing coastal plains and snaking through shady forests.

If you are heading north from the Golden Isles, consider stopping at **Mudcat Charlie's** (☎ 912-
261-0055), located between Darien and Brunswick, to tie on a feedbag of Lowcountry boil.

A little further north, you can visit **Fort King George State Historic Site** (☎ 912-437-4770),
with its fortifications and a museum.

Just before reaching Darien, you'll see signs for the **Hofwyl-Broadfield Plantation State
Historic Site** (☎ 912-264-7333), which features the remnants of one of the rice plantations that
once dominated this section of the Lowcountry.

The waterfront of **Darien** is definitely worth a stop, especially when the shrimp boats are
unloading their savory catch. Sometimes you can negotiate with one of the shrimpers for a
pound or two of their fresh catch to use in your own shrimp boil.

North of Darien, look for the sign and turnoff for the **Harris Neck National Wildlife Refuge**,
a vast retreat among the salt marshes and a great place for bird-watching and gaining a cosmic
perspective on life and planet Earth.

At **Fort Morris State Historic Site** (☎ 912-884-5999), you can view earthworks used against
the British in the War of 1812. Near here, **Seabrook Village** (☎ 912-884-7008), open mainly for
school groups, is a living-history museum portraying African American culture.

Just before you reach Savannah, **Fort McAllister State Historical Park** (☎ 912-727-2339) has
Confederate earthworks on the banks of the Ogeechee River, as well as live oaks, salt marshes,
a museum, hiking trails and camping.

local diners claim this little bistro has the best pork-chop sandwiches ($6) in South Georgia. The family-run business has a loyal following.

Getting There & Away

AIR
There are currently three flights (starting at $140) a day to/from Atlanta on **Delta Connection** (☎ 800-221-1212). **Brunswick-Golden Isles Airport** (☎ 912-265-2070) is on Glynco Pkwy, 2 miles off I-95 at exit 38.

BUS
The old standby **Greyhound** (☎ 912-265-2800) connects Brunswick with Savannah ($15, 1½ hours, six daily) and Jacksonville, Florida ($16, 1½ hours, four daily).

CAR & MOTORCYCLE
Contemporary Brunswick is a sprawling place. The easiest way to access the Historic District is to take I-95 exit 29, which takes you to US Hwy 17. From US Hwy 17, take the Gloucester St exit and head west.

SAPELO ISLAND
Pop 70

If you want to feel like you've stepped into another dimension, where the tides and seasons of the marshes rule the lives of an independent black community of sea islanders, check out Sapelo. Some folks say that Sapelo is the prototype for the island of Willow Springs in Gloria Naylor's blockbuster novel *Mama Day*.

About 55 miles south of Savannah, Sapelo is a rare combination of history and nature. The fourth-largest barrier island along the Georgia coast, it's home to the **Sapelo Island National Estuarine Research Reserve** (www.cr.nps.gov/goldcres/sites/sapelo.htm), which focuses on scientific research and education. In the midst of an estuary, the reserve consists of 2100 acres of coastal upland and 4000 acres of tidal salt marsh.

The mix of ecosystems includes maritime forest, salt marsh, beaches and dunes. Visitors might sight wild turkey, deer, armadillos and feral cows. The maritime forest is dominated by live oaks and their accompanying Spanish moss.

Planter Thomas Spalding purchased land here in 1802 and converted it into a productive antebellum plantation – with the help of 400 slaves. When the Civil War ended slavery, ex-slaves established five communities around the island. RJ Reynolds, the tobacco magnate, owned the island from 1934 until 1964.

Reynolds forced these five communities into one – Hog Hammock, which still exists today. Its 70 permanent residents are descendents of the Saltwater Geechee peoples (often grouped with the Gullah culture, along the South Carolina coast). Due to generations of isolation in the small island communities, the Geechee were able to preserve many customs handed down from their tribal ancestors in West Africa. Today, the island is owned by the state of Georgia, except for the community of Hog Hammock.

Note that access to the island is limited to people on the state tour and guests of residents. See the Getting There & Around section (p109) for details.

Information
The **Sapelo Island Visitors Center** (☎ 912-437-3224; sapelovc@darientel.net; 7:30am-5:30pm Tue-Fri, 8am-5:30pm Sat, 1:30-5pm Sun), near the dock in the mainland village of Meridian (which is a district of Darien, the main town on this section of the coast), has exhibits and books on the island's history. Facilities on the island include private lodging facilities, campgrounds, restrooms, a small convenience store, a gift shop, and drinking fountains.

A great website for information on the island is www.sapelonerr.org.

Organized Tours
The only ways to visit Sapelo Island itself are by taking a regularly scheduled state tour, arranging overnight accommodations at a local home or B&B in Hog Hammock, or through an overnight group tour. The ranger-led **state tours** (☎ 912-437-3224; adult/child $10/6) involve a 30-minute ferry ride across Hudson Creek Sound (leaving from the mainland visitors center) and a ride in an old yellow school bus around the sandy island tracks, stopping at sites such as the Reynolds Mansion (called 'the Big House' by locals), ruins of a tabby sugar mill and (on some tours) a lighthouse. There are different stops on different days.

The half-day tours start only at 8:30am Wednesday and 9am Saturday. In the summer (June through Labor Day), an additional tour runs at 8:30am Friday. You can take an extended tour on the last Tuesday of the month from March to October. Reservations are required.

The state bus tours only scratch the surface of the local culture. For more information about the island's history and fading Geechee culture, visit the island on a tour with **Cornelia Walker Bailey** (☎ 912-485-2206; tour $20), who likes to say, 'When you come to Sapelo you see birds and bees, flowers and trees, and me – and that's the way God intend it to be.' For more on Ms Bailey, see the boxed text 'I Am Sapelo' (below).

Southeast Adventure Outfitters (☎ 912-638-6732; www.gacoast.com/navigator/sea.html; 313 Mallery St, St Simons Island; 10am-6pm) offers overnight kayaking tours here. See p97 for more information on the company.

By the way, insect repellent is a wonderful thing – bring it!

Sleeping & Eating

Sapelo author Cornelia Walker Bailey is a welcoming guide and hostess at the **Wallow** (☎ 912-485-2206; d $75-95), a guest house located in historic Hog Hammock. The lodge-like B&B has a long front porch for chillin' and six bedrooms with air-conditioning and private bath. The great room features a comfortable living-room area and color TV. A long family-style dining table separates the living room from the spacious kitchen, where you do your own cooking unless pre-arranged meals are scheduled with the Baileys.

Two more of Hog Hammock's gregarious residents, Lulu and George Walker, have a small restaurant/inn, **Lulu's Kitchen & Mobile Homes** (☎ 912-485-2270; d $80-90). You pay $15 for Lulu's BBQ chicken, ribs and Lowcountry seafood boil. You can also rent a car from them for about $35 a day.

Groups of 16 to 29 people can arrange overnight lodging and camping at the **Reynolds Mansion** (☎ 912-485-2299; s $135). **Cabrita Campground** (sites $12), on the same property, takes groups of 15 to 25 people. Both accommodations have a two-night minimum.

Getting There & Around

To reach the visitors center and the Sapelo ferry dock, take US Hwy 17 north to Darien. Turn right on US 99, at the courthouse. Drive 8 miles and follow the signs.

The *Sapelo Queen* leaves the dock at Meridian every day at 8:30am, 3:30pm and 5:30pm. Passage to Sapelo costs $1. Note: Sapelo calls itself a limited-access island, which means you cannot go to the island on a whim. You must be a guest (either overnight or on a day tour) of the park service or of an island resident, who will put your name on the ferry manifest. If the captain does not have your name, you cannot sail.

If you are an overnight guest on the island, you can rent a car for about $35 a day from Lulu and George Walker at Lulu's Kitchen & Mobile Homes.

ST MARYS

Pop 14,000

For most travelers, this sleepy little town is just a place to catch the ferry to Cumberland

I AM SAPELO

One of the matriarchs of the Geechee community on Sapelo, author Cornelia Walker Bailey was born some 50 years ago in the Belle Marsh community of Sapelo Island as the daughter of a cast-net weaver. Bailey's family are direct descendents of the slaves of Thomas Spalding, the scientific agriculturalist who ran a plantation on the island from 1802 until the beginning of the Civil War.

Like her parents and the other older members of the community, Cornelia still speaks Geechee, the native dialect, although she writes her books in English.

Like the African *griot* (musical storyteller), Cornelia Walker Bailey has taken on the duty of keeping her culture alive through vivid remembrances. To read her reflection 'I Am Sapelo,' go to www.gacoast.com/navigator/iamsapelo.html. Her book *God, Dr Buzzard, and the Bolito Man* (Doubleday, 2000) is a Lowcountry staple.

Island. However, it does have a pleasant but small downtown historic area, with a couple of blocks of shops, restaurants, several B&Bs, outfitters and **Orange Hall** (1829), a fine example of Greek Revival architecture.

Before or after visiting Cumberland Island, you may want to stop by the new **Cumberland Island Museum** (☎ 912-882-4335; Osborne Rd; admission free; ☽ 1-4pm). The museum features a collection of Native American relics, as well as artifacts from African American residents, the Carnegie family and other inhabitants of the island.

The **St Marys Submarine Museum** (☎ 912-882-2782; 102 St Mary St; adult/child $3/1; ☽ 10am-4pm Tue-Sat, 1-5pm Sun) pays homage to subs, crews and support personnel at nearby Naval Submarine Base Kings Bay and the Trident Training Facility, which is home to 10 of the largest nuclear submarines in the world. The museum has a significant display of models, uniforms, memorabilia, patrol reports and movies. There is an actual sub steering station and a working modern periscope that affords views of the St Marys River.

Up the Creek Xpeditions (☎ 912-882-0911; 111 Osborne St; ☽ 10am-5pm Mon-Thu, 10am-6pm Fri & Sat) is an outfitter offering kayak rental and instruction as part of guided tours ($25 to $75) to Cumberland Island, St Marys River and Crooked River. They also rent bicycles ($15 per day).

Sleeping & Eating

You'll find a string of chain hotels and fast-food chains 10 miles west of the St Marys dock at the GA Route 40 exit on I-95 (exit 2).

For tasty home-style food in a family-run restaurant, locals recommend **Greek Mediterranean Grill** (☎ 912-576-2000; 122 Osborne St; mains $6-12; ☒). Moussaka runs $8 at lunch, $11 at dinner. The Greek pizza on pita bread ($5) is a slice of paradise, and the service sets high standards.

The **Riverview Hotel** (☎ 912-882-3242, 888-882-1807; 105 Osborne St; s/d $45/55; P ☒ ☒) Located right across from the Cumberland Island dock, this somewhat neglected, historic (1916) hotel has lots of character and a great 2nd-story balcony overlooking downtown St Marys. Rooms do not have phones. Ask for a room overlooking the dock.

Cumberland Island Inn & Suites (☎ 912-882-6250, 800-768-6250; www.cumberlandislandinn.com; s/d $40/50, suite $75; P ☒ ☒ ☒) Here's a modest but modern motel at the intersection of Route 40 and Spur 40, 4 miles from downtown St Marys. Rates include a continental breakfast; suites are available.

Camping

Those looking for a full-service campground should check out St Marys.

Crooked River State Park (☎ 912-882-5256, 800-864-7275; tents/RVs $14/16; P ☒) Located about 10 miles north of downtown St Marys on Spur 40; this 500-acre park is bordered by large areas of salt marsh. It provides boat access to Crooked River, on which saltwater fishing is popular. Many of the 60 camping sites are in an open area under pine trees, but there are also sites set back among the palmettos. Cottages cost $75/85/90 for one/two/three bedrooms, $10 more on weekends. There's also a swimming pool. It's possible to park a car here and kayak to Cumberland Island. Entrance to the park requires a $2 ParkPass.

Getting There & Away

To reach St Marys, take exit 2 off I-95 and head east for 10 miles on Route 40.

CUMBERLAND ISLAND

With lanes shaded by mammoth mossy live oaks, wild horses on the beaches and the ruins of an enormous chateau, this isle is a must-see and is a place to engender all manner of romantic fantasies.

The **Cumberland Island National Seashore** (☎ 912-882-4335; www.nps.gov/cuis) occupies most of the southernmost barrier island in Georgia. Almost half of the total 36,415 acres are marshland, mud flats and tidal creeks. The island is 17.5 miles long and 3 miles wide. Some private owners still live here; a one-lane dirt road runs almost the entire length of the island.

On the ocean side are 16 miles of wide sandy beach that you might well have all to yourself. There are shorebirds such as sandpipers, gulls and ospreys, as well as nesting loggerhead turtles. Heading inland, delicate sand dunes protect interdune meadows and shrub thickets.

The interior of the island is characterized by a maritime forest, consisting of mossy live oaks and dense palmetto stands. These shelter a variety of birds, including painted buntings and pileated woodpeckers. On the western side are saltwater marshes containing tall grasses, fiddler crabs and wading birds such as egrets and herons.

Animals include deer, raccoons, feral pigs and armadillos (a recent arrival). Freshwater ponds harbor alligators. Wild horses roam the island and are a common sight around the mansion ruins, in the interdune meadows and occasionally on the beach. There are plenty of sand gnats too, and they bite!

Sights & Activities

Indians, Spanish soldiers, missionaries, and British forts have given the island a rich human history. Nathanael Green (a Revolutionary War hero) and his wife built a home, called Dungeness, here in the late 18th century.

In 1884, Thomas and Lucy Carnegie built a mansion on the ruins of the original Dungeness. Their mansion was eventually set afire by vandals, buts its **ruins** are still visible today. **Plum Orchard** is an 1898 Georgian Revival-style mansion built for their son George Carnegie.

This is the perfect place to spend a day walking – meandering around the crumbling walls of mansions, along the beach and marshes, and through maritime forests and interdune meadows. Visitation to the island is limited to 300 people per day, ensuring a peaceful experience.

Most of the day-use areas are on the southern end of the island. The **Ice House Museum**, **Dungeness ruins** and **Cemetery** are all worth visiting. The live oaks around **Sea Camp Beach** are worth seeing, even if you aren't camping. If time permits, walk north to the end of Old House Rd, where there's a dock overlooking **Old House Creek.** Here, thousands of fiddler crabs scurry through the mud and grasses at low tide, while wading birds hunt for dinner.

Be aware that unless you're a guest of the Greyfield Inn there are no food or other supplies available on Cumberland Island. Pack your lunch.

You'll need sunscreen and insect repellent too. Ticks here may carry Lyme disease, so check yourself often, and know what to do when you find a tick (see the Health chapter p211). Restrooms and water are available at four locations on the southern side of the island.

Sleeping

The only private accommodations on the island are at the **Greyfield Inn** (☎ 904-261-6408; www.greyfieldinn.com; d $250-395 meals included; 🔌 ✖), a grand and graceful mansion built in 1900 as a home for Lucy and Thomas Carnegie's daughter, Margaret Ricketson. Sometimes called 'Tara on the Beach' by travel writers, this place lives up to its name, with both the public and private rooms furnished in baronial splendor. Three-day midweek packages run only $250.

Camping is available at **Sea Camp Beach** (☎ 912-882-4335; $4 per person), a pristine developed campground set among magnificent live oaks. Each of the campsites is surrounded by palmetto stands and comes with a raccoon box (to store your food, not your raccoons). Facilities include flush toilets, cold showers and drinking water. It's a short walk to the beach or the ferry from here, and there are a few carts you can borrow to help move your equipment.

Four **backcountry campgrounds** are located in the middle of the island, far from civilization. Sulfur water is available from wells for drinking, but should be treated. Campfires are not permitted in the backcountry, so bring a campstove.

Reservations are required for both developed and backcountry camping; call Sea Camp Beach between 10am and 4pm weekdays.

Getting There & Away

The only public access to the island is via the ferry, *Cumberland Queen*, which leaves from the St Marys dock. **Reservations** (☎ 912-882-4335; 🕙 10am-4pm Mon-Fri) are strongly recommended. The 45-minute ride is part of the whole experience. The ferry leaves the St Marys dock daily at 9am and 11:45am and returns from the island at 9:45am and 4:45pm.

During the spring and summer (March 1 through September 30), there is an additional departure from the island at 2:45pm Wednesday through Saturday. During fall and winter (October 1 through February 28), the ferry does not operate on Tuesday or on Wednesday. Rates are adult/child $12/7. An additional $4 user fee is charged to go on the island. Bicycles are not allowed on the ferry.

OKEFENOKEE NATIONAL WILDLIFE REFUGE & WILDERNESS AREA

The Okefenokee Swamp (www.okefenokee .fws.gov) is a national gem. Less than an hour's drive west from the Brunswick-Golden Isles area, the swamp is actually a huge bog trapped within a depression that was once – along with the rest of southern Georgia – part of the ocean floor.

The swamp area encompasses about 650 square miles and is home to 234 species of reptiles, including an estimated 9000 to 15,000 alligators; 234 species of birds, such as egrets, ibises, herons, the Florida sandhill crane and the endangered red cockaded woodpecker; 49 types of mammals, from the common raccoon to the less common black bear; and 60 species of amphibians. Wildlife viewing (from rental canoes, boats and cars) is a major attraction.

The term 'Okefenokee' is a variant of a Seminole word meaning 'land of the trembling earth.' Peat deposits that build up on the swamp floor are so mushy that you can cause nearby trees to tremble by stomping on the peat. The swamp water – about two feet deep – is the color of tea as a result of tannic acid released by decaying plants; the swamp has the acidity of a soda. The Suwannee River and St Marys River drain the swamp. A variety of swamp habitats (including islands, lakes, moss-laced cypress forests, scrub-shrub areas and wet prairies) support ample wildlife.

The area was inhabited as early as 2500 BC. Israel Barber was the first white settler here, establishing his homestead in 1807. Other settlers followed, farming and logging in the swamp. In the late 19th century, the Suwannee Canal Company attempted to drain the swamp to allow more extensive logging and agriculture; fortunately, they went bankrupt in the process. A railroad was built into the western part of the swamp, and cypress trees were logged for almost 30 years. Since becoming a wildlife refuge in 1937, the swamp has been mostly protected from such manmade momentous changes.

The Okefenokee Swamp has three main entrances, each managed by a different entity. Each entrance has its own activities and charms; the eastern entrance is closest to the coast.

Be warned that biting yellow flies can be excruciating in May or June. Mosquitoes can be a problem after dark.

Greyhound buses serve the towns around the Okefenokee Swamp, including Fargo, Homerville, Waycross and Folkston. To see the swamp, however, you will need a car, a bicycle, a tour or a lift to the water.

Eastern Entrance

At the eastern entrance, the **Suwannee Canal Recreation Area** (☎ 912-496-7836; ☽ half-hour before sunrise-5:30pm Nov-Feb, half-hour before sunrise-7:30pm Mar-Oct), 11 miles southwest of Folkston, is the most convenient for visitors who are also exploring the Georgia coast. It has some of the most comprehensive facilities and is the main US Fish & Wildlife Service entrance. The lakes and gator holes dotting the prairies offer promising sportfishing. Gator sightings are a near certainty.

The entrance contains a visitors center with exhibits of basic information on swamp culture and wildlife. The 9-mile **Swamp Island Drive** is suitable for exploration by car or bike and leads to Chesser Island, where the reconstructed homestead of the Chesser family demonstrates how pioneer families lived in the 19th and early 20th centuries. From the island, a boardwalk leads ¾ mile to an observation tower overlooking a classic swamp prairie and lake.

Much of the canoeing is along the wide Suwannee Canal and is shared with motorboats. For a quieter experience, take the side trails to Mizell Prairie and Cooter Lake if the water level permits. There are a couple of chemical pit toilets on the route.

The private concession **Okefenokee Adventures** (☎ 912-496-7156; ☽ 8am-5pm) rents canoes, motorboats and single-speed bicycles and also sells sandwiches and snacks. Access is available here by water to the swamp lakes and marshlike prairies. One- or two-hour guided boat tours are offered; for a sense of true swamp mystery, try the night tours. You can bring your own canoe or kayak, but you must register with the concessionaire.

Entrance to the park costs $5 per vehicle for a seven-day pass (also good at the

PACKING FOR A CANOE TRIP

Heading out on a canoe in the Okefenokee Swamp? Here's a handy packing list from the US Fish & Wildlife Service.

For your safety, the following items are required for each party:

- Coast Guard–approved flotation device for each person
- Portable toilet with disposable bags
- Compass and map
- Flashlight

To make your wilderness canoe experience a positive one, the following items are strongly suggested:

- Extra flashlights and batteries
- Trash bags
- Rope for pulling canoe
- First-aid kit
- Food (plus enough for one extra day)
- Foul weather gear
- Sleeping bag or blanket
- Map of canoe trail
- Stove and fuel
- Insect repellent
- Duct tape for emergency repairs
- Spare paddle
- Waterproof bags
- Paddling gloves
- Free-standing tent
- Bailer
- Sun protection (SPF 15+, wide brimmed hat, long sleeved shirt and pants)
- Drinking water (two to six quarts per person each day, depending on weather). Drinking swamp water is *not* recommended. Because of suspended organic matter, filtering is difficult.

Courtesy of the US Fish & Wildlife Service

western entrance). There are no accommodations or camping here; see the Around the Swamp section (p114) for some nearby possibilities.

Western Entrance

The entrance to the western side of the swamp is at **Stephen C Foster State Park** (☎ 912-637-5274; www.gastateparks.org), an 18-mile drive from the tiny town of Fargo along state Hwy 177. The park is named after the composer of 'Way Down upon the Suwannee River.'

By far the best activity here is to get out on the water in a rented canoe or motorized boat. Twenty-five miles of day-use waterways are accessible from here. Alligator sightings are almost certain if you keep alert. There's also a 90-minute guided boat tour, which leaves daily at 10am, 1pm and 3pm. Visitors can also canoe to 3140-acre Billy's Island and explore rusting fragments of the area's logging history. Rent boats and catch the tour from near the entrance, at the parks office.

A small **interpretive center** has an introduction to the area's ecology and history. A 1½-mile nature walk leads over a boardwalk into the swamp. There's no food here, so bring your own.

The park's 66 pleasant **campsites** are individually enclosed by palms, shrubs, pine and hardwood trees. Rates are $18/20 for tents/RVs from March 1 through May 31, and $15/17 the rest of the year. Cabin rentals are $76/86 weekdays/weekends from March 1 through May 31, and $66/77 at other times; there's a $15 surcharge for one-night-only stays. Campsites and cabins can be reserved through a **central reservations line** (☎ 800-864-7275).

Entrance to the state park costs $5 per vehicle for a seven-day pass (this is also good at the eastern entrance). It's open 7am to 7pm in winter, longer in summer; the park office closes at 5pm in winter, 6pm in summer.

Northern Entrance

Northern access to the swamp is at the **Okefenokee Swamp Park** (☎ 912-283-0583; www .okeswamp.com), a private concession and wildlife park eight miles south of Waycross. The park's main attraction is a zoo of live swamp creatures, including alligators (many unfenced), black bears, otters, turtles and deer. Exhibits include a natural history center, a snake display, an educational live reptile show (snakes and gators) and a corny animatronics show for the kids. A railroad runs through the park and provides the only access to Pioneer Island, a collection of buildings and artifacts from the pioneer days. A short boardwalk provides direct access to the swamp.

Once again, a visit to the swamp is hardly complete without a ride on the water. Guided boat tours are a good way to learn about the history, culture and wildlife of the swamp. If you'd like to strike out on your own, canoe rentals are also available.

The park is open 9am to 5:30pm; admission is $12/11 for adult/child and includes all exhibits and the railroad tour. The guided boat tours are an additional $16/20/30 for 30 minutes/one hour/two hours. Canoe rental costs an additional $18 per person.

A concession in the park provides food, but it may be closed in the off-season.

Wilderness Canoeing

The ultimate Okefenokee experience is a multi-day trip on the 120 miles of waterways through the swamp. On these trips, canoeists (no motors are allowed) paddle through the swamp all day and camp on platforms over the water at night. Trips can range from two to five days, although they are limited to two nights' length in March and April.

Trips are allowed via permit only by calling Okefenokee National Refuge **canoe reservation line** (☎ 912-496-3331; ☷ 7-10am Mon-Fri). Permits can be reserved up to two months before your trip, and you must register, send in a nonrefundable fee of $10 per person per night and receive your permit before you can get out on the water. There are only seven platforms in the swamp, so only seven groups per night can register; available space can fill up quickly. Be sure to get the US Fish & Wildlife Service's **Okefenokee National Wildlife Refuge Wilderness Canoe Guide** (☎ 912-496-7836; http://okefenokee.fws.gov) if you are considering a trip. Canoeists are expected to comply with a number of requirements: no pets or other potential alligator food; no fires in most locations; portable toilets are required (available for rent at the eastern entrance); and you must carry enough drinking water for the entire trip.

For trips that do not begin and end at the same entrance, Okefenokee Adventures (p112), at the eastern entrance, can provide shuttles.

Around the Swamp

You'll find accommodations, places to eat and some interesting things to do in the towns around the Okefenokee.

In Waycross, the **Okefenokee Heritage Center Museum** (☎ 912-285-4260; adult/child $3/2; ☷ Tue-Sat 10am-4:30pm) displays a train depot, a 1912 steam locomotive, local art and exhibits on swamp pioneers. **Obediah's Okefenok** (☎ 912-287-0090; adult/child $4.50/3) honors Obediah Barber, one of the first white settlers on the swamp's northern border. Exhibits include Barber's homestead and cabin, animal displays, boardwalks over the swamp and nature trails.

Camping is available at the 626-acre **Laura S Walker State Park** (☎ 912-287-4900, reservations 800-864-7275 or 770-389-7275), nine miles southeast of Waycross on Route 177. Recreational activities include waterskiing, boating, fishing and a swimming pool. The 44 tent and RV sites are set among pine trees at the edge of a 120-acre lake, providing a pretty setting but little privacy. The park also has laundry facilities, a nature trail and a golf course.

Plenty of motels and chain hotels are located on the eastern side of Waycross, near the intersection of US Hwys 82 and 23. The **Waycross Tourism and Conference Bureau** (☎ 912-283-3744, www.okefenokeetourism.com) can provide more information on area accommodations and attractions.

Nearer the eastern entrance, private campgrounds are available near **Kingfisher Wilderness Campground** (☎ 912-496-2186), on US Hwy 1, 13 miles north of Folkston; at **Okefenokee Pastimes** (☎ 912-496-4472, www.okefenokee .com), on state Hwy 121/23 at the Suwannee Canal Recreation Area turnoff; and at **Traders Hill Recreation Area** (☎ 912-496-7037), a county park seven miles south of Folkston on state Hwy 23. Hotels can be found in Folkston or at the I-95 Kingsland exit, 22 miles east of Folkston, on state Hwy 40.

Southeast Adventure Outfitters (☎ 912-638-6732; www.southeastadventure.com; 313 Mallery St, St Simons Island; 🕙 10am-6pm), on St Simons Island, offers guided tours to the swamp.

Hilton Head

HILTON HEAD

At 12 miles long and 5 miles wide, Hilton Head is South Carolina's largest barrier island, the focal point of a Lowcountry estuary that includes Daufuskie Island, Beaufort and Historic Bluffton. The entire area is a veritable temple to the worship of leisure time and the game of golf. There are dozens of courses enclosed in private communities of condominiums and vacation homes (called 'plantations'), and the island's great cultural events are the annual golf tournaments.

Hilton Head is one of the few places where the prized word 'heritage' can be used in conjunction with 'golf.' The island's golf heritage dates back to 1961, when Sea Pines Plantation, the first exclusive resort, opened. Ten others have followed, since golf is a year-round business in this subtropical climate. Once, Hilton Head had the ambiance of a place far beyond the reaches of Main Street America; today, real estate development has given the island the look and feel of an upscale suburb comprised of gated communities.

The island prides itself on being designed in concert with the natural environment, but summer traffic and miles of stoplights make it hard to see the forest (or a tree) along US Hwy 278. There are, however, some very lush nature preserves. The beaches are wide, white and so hard-packed that you can ride a bike on them for miles.

HILTON HEAD

HIGHLIGHTS

- **Wining**
  The bars and clubs of the Barmuda Triangle (p130)
- **Dining**
  Two Eleven Park (p128), a wine bar bistro with the feel of Hollywood
- **Sporting Event**
  The Worldcom Classic Heritage of Golf tournament (p125) in April
- **Wildlife Encounter**
  Dolphin-watching on Broad Creek (p124)
- **Offbeat Experience**
  Checking out the Gullah culture of Daufuskie Island (p133)

■ TELEPHONE CODE: **843**   ■ POPULATION: **33,862**   ■ AREA: **60 SQ MI**

ORIENTATION

Hilton Head Island is shaped like a sneaker, with the ankle at the north end and the toe at the south. Calibogue (*cal-uh-boh*-gee) Sound, Port Royal Sound and Skull Creek (all part of the Intra-coastal Waterway) separate Hilton Head from the mainland and the rest of Lowcountry.

US Hwy 278 (William Hilton Pkwy) is the main commercial artery, as well as the access road to the island. The high-way is the direct route from I-95 to the Hilton Head bridge. From here the US Hwy 278 Business Route bisects the island from north to south, ending at the com-mercial heart of the island, Sea Pines Circle (a traffic circle where Palmetto Bay Rd, Pope Ave, Greenwood Dr and the high-way meet).

If your island destination lies some-where in the vicinity of Sea Pines Circle, you can take the Cross Island Pkwy toll road ($1) from the north end of the island to the circle to avoid the stoplights and traffic on US Hwy 278. Sea Pines Plantation, the first and the largest of the resort plantations, covers the entire toe area of the island.

There is no 'town' to speak of. For shopping, restaurants and nightlife, you must either take advantage of the offerings available within the individual plantations or visit one of the shopping plazas or malls lining the main arteries, like the William Hilton Pkwy (US Hwy 278). The largest collection of shopping plazas is around Sea Pines Circle. One of the shopping areas, **Harbour Town**, in Sea Pines Plantation, has the feel of a small Mediterranean port, with shops, restaurants, cafes, a marina and a lighthouse.

Note: street addresses are almost useless in helping you find island businesses, since most are hidden within a plantation or in a maze of shops and restaurants within a plaza. Islanders always give directions in terms of the landmark plantations and shopping plazas. This guide does the same.

Maps

While you will find a plethora of free-map offerings at hotels, shops and restaurants, most of these items are extremely vague. The visitors center has maps of the island ($1) showing the private communities, public golf and tennis courts, shopping malls and beach access.

In addition to the map in this book (pp120–1), you may want to get AAA's *Savannah* map, which includes very detailed coverage of Hilton Head.

HILTON HEAD IN...

Two Days

Catch a sun-dappled breakfast at an outdoor café at **Coligny Plaza**. Then head down to the **beach** for a walk (or rent a bike) and a lazy morning of exploration and toe-dabbling at the water's edge. Take lunch at a harborside restaurant, such as the **Salty Dog**, and watch the comings and goings of pleasure boats and yachts. Then get out on the water yourself for a **dolphin tour**, a sailing adventure or a fishing trip. Resist the temptation to 'dine in' and head off to one of the **shopping** plazas like Coligny Plaza and Park Plaza, where you will find an abundance of restaurants vying for your attention. After dinner you may well want to catch the bar/club scene in the **Barmuda Triangle** and neighboring **Park Plaza**.

Plan a golf, tennis, bike or water-sport outing for your second morning. Chill by a pool or beach for the afternoon, or join one of the **historic or nature tours** sponsored by the Coastal Discovery Museum. By night head out to dinner in a romantic corner of the island that you haven't visited yet, such as Harbor Town, South Seaport, Shelter Cove or the Fort Mitchel area.

Three Days

Follow the two-day itinerary, but spread your activities over three days so you have time for more of a favorite activity, such as golf. Allow some time for wandering through a plaza or two in search of pretty things to buy. Take a trip off-island to explore **Bluffton**, **Beaufort** or the Gullah community on **Daufuskie Island**.

INFORMATION
Bookstores
Authors Café & Bookstore (☎ 843-686-5020; 1000 William Hilton Pkwy, in the Village at Wexford Plaza)

Barnes & Noble (☎ 843-342-6690; 20 Hatton Pl, in the Main St Village mall, on the north end of the island)

Waldenbooks (☎ 843-785-4301; Mall at Shelter Cove, located midisland)

Island Bookseller (☎ 843-671-3773; Sea Pines Center, Sea Pines Plantation)

Gullah Bookstore (☎ 843-342-2002; 148 William Hilton Hwy) You'll find this bookstore on the right side of US Hwy 278 shortly after passing the visitors center as you enter the island.

Emergency
Emergency numbers (☎ 911) Police, ambulance, firefighters.

Beauford County Sheriff's Department (☎ 843-689-4300) Nonemergencies only.

AAA Roadside Service (☎ 800-222-4357)

Internet Access
You can get online at many of the city's inns and hotels. You can also go surfing on the library's computers (see below) for around $3 for 30 minutes.

Internet Resources
www.hiltonheadisland.org Hotels, restaurants and activities.

www.hiltonhead.com Restaurants, activities, calendar of events and hotels.

www.islandpacket.com News, weather and sports.

Libraries
Beaufort County Public Library (☎ 843-342-9200; Beach City Rd at US Hwy 278, near the airport on the north end of the island)

Medical Services
Hilton Head Regional Medical Center & Clinics (☎ 843-681-6122; Hospital Center Blvd at Beach City Rd, just off US Hwy 278, near the airport)

Burke's Pharmacy (☎ 843-681-2622; Main St Village)

Hilton Head Pharmacy (☎ 843-681-4002; Coligny Plaza)

Media
Island Packet The island's daily paper.

Money
Banks and ATMs are plentiful on Hilton Head. Every shopping plaza and mall has an ATM, a bank or both. Bank hours are generally 9am to 5pm, Monday to Friday.

Post
Main post office (☎ 800-275-8777; Palmetto Bay Plaza, cnr Palmetto Bay Rd and Bow Circle, ¼ mile west of Sea Pines Circle)

Tourist Offices
Hilton Head-Bluffton Visitors Center (☎ 800-523-3373; www.hiltonheadchamber.org; US Hwy 278; ☒ 9:30am-5pm) On your right just after you cross the bridge onto the island; it is run by the chamber of commerce and doubles as the Coastal Discovery Museum (p120).

DANGERS & ANNOYANCES
Biting insects, especially mosquitoes and no-see-ums, are ubiquitous from mid-March to November. Don't go anywhere on a windless day without lathering up with repellents.

With 33,000 residents and about 2.5 million visitors a year, Hilton Head has significant traffic problems during the busy spring and summer seasons. There is talk about installing 'smart' traffic lights to improve the back-ups at lights along US Hwy 278, but it hasn't happened yet. Traffic is worst at traditional morning and late-afternoon rush hours, when island workers are on the move. Use the Cross Island Pkwy to avoid the snags if you need to get from one end of the island to the other quickly.

SIGHTS
Harbour Town
Set at the southwest end of Sea Pines Plantation (and the island), this little seaport is Hilton Head's most popular attraction. Although there is absolutely nothing historic here, Harbour Town does a good job of recreating the look of a Mediterranean anchorage, complete with its signature red-and-white striped lighthouse, boutiques, inns, galleries, shops and eateries, like **CQ's Restaurant** (p130). The place is definitely touristy, but it is also a fine place for strolling, people-watching or calling a time-out during a biking adventure. The village rocks out with crowds during the Heritage Golf Classic, played on the Harbour Town course in April.

HILTON HEAD

The guards at the gated entrances to Sea Pines Plantation will charge you a $5 entrance fee if you are not a plantation guest (just to tour the plantation or to visit Harbour Town). But check the back pages of the various tourist tabloids, which are available at hotels and restaurants throughout the island, for coupons offering free admission.

Coastal Discovery Museum

For an introduction to the nonsuburban aspects of Hilton Head, stop by this **museum** (☎ 843-689-6767; www.coastaldiscovery.org; 100 William Hilton Pkwy; $2 donation; ☇ 9:30am-5pm), on the 2nd floor of the visitors center, to see exhibits on coastal history, archaeology and ecology. You can arrange nature and history tours, sea-turtle watches during the summer nesting season (see boxed text p46), and dolphin and kayak trips through the museum.

Hilton Head has a few historic sites, but the truth is that these sites are visually underwhelming. Because the stories behind the sites are much richer than the surviving remnants, you may want to visit these places on a tour through the museum. Land-based tours usually cost adult/child $10/5; the boat and bus tours run $15/10.

Historic Sites

Located in the northwest corner of the island's ankle, **Fort Mitchel Historical Site** is an earthen fort built in 1862 by Federal soldiers to protect Skull Creek (now the Intracoastal Waterway) from a Confederate assault. To get there, take Squire Pope Rd off US Hwy 278. Squire Pope Rd turns into Seabrook, then make a left on Skull Creek Rd.

You will find **Fort Howell**, another Civil War–era earthworks, off the north end of the airport runway on Beach City Rd.

The **Baynard Ruins**, off Plantation Dr at the south end of Sea Pines Plantation, has a few surviving walls from a plantation house, foundations from slave quarters and a free-standing chimney, all dating from early 19th century, when sea-island cotton was king. The mortar walls are made of tabby, a mix of oyster shells, sand, water and lime from burned shells.

The **Shell Ring** is a collection of Indian shell middens in the **Sea Pines Forest Preserve**.

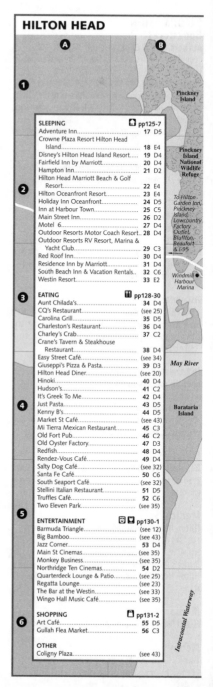

HILTON HEAD

HILTON HEAD

Archeologists believe that Native American occupation of Hilton Head may date back 4000 years.

Baynard Mausoleum and **Zion Chapel Cemetery**, at the corner of US Hwy 278 and Mathews Dr, mark the site of a 1780s chapel (now gone) erected for local Episcopal worshipers. The mausoleum dates to 1846. The remains of many of the island's gentry were buried here before the Civil War.

Nature Preserves

Protected wilderness areas on the island give effective snapshots of what early explorers and Native Americans might have encountered. On the trails you will find a slowly undulating forest floor of former sand dunes now covered in short palmettos, tall palms, ferns, entangled vines and pools of standing water.

Covering 50 acres, the **Audubon Newhall Preserve** was set aside during the first invasion of golf courses in the 1960s. A sharp contrast to the nearby traffic circles and manicured lawns, the preserve is on Palmetto Bay Rd, west of Sea Pines Circle.

Pinckney Island National Wildlife Refuge protects the small slivers of land that have developed between Hilton Head and the mainland. The main island, Pinckney, is 8 miles long and can be hiked or biked; trails lead through canopied forests and expansive salt marshes. The park entrance is on Hwy 278 just before you reach Hilton Head.

ACTIVITIES

It's hard to be bored here. From surf to turf, Hilton Head has enough activities to make your head spin.

Beaches

There are almost 12 miles of nearly flat Atlantic beach on Hilton Head. The beach is particularly broad at low tide and is an excellent place for walking, jogging and biking. But most people swim in resort pools. Beach bathing is not particularly popular, as the water is often a turgid gray and there can be a lot of seagrass underfoot. Sharks are also known to patrol the shallows, and there are sometimes riptides at the north end of the island.

Because private homes, condo developments and hotels line the island beaches, finding a public-access right-of-way to the beach is a bit difficult unless you are staying in a beachfront property, such as Sea Pines Plantation, Shipyard Plantation, Palmetto Dunes or Port Royal Plantation. **Coligny Beach**, just off Pope Ave (which has a pavilion and restrooms), is the most popular public beach on the island. Parking runs $4 a day in the lot across the street.

Additional public beach access is available at the midisland **Folly Field Beach, Driessen Beach** and **Bradley Beach**. Folly Field Beach also has toilets, changing facilities and parking.

Golf

With courses designed by Robert Trent Jones, Jack Nicklaus, and the Fazio brothers,

---

NOT JUST PRETTY FAIRWAYS

William Hilton, an English sea captain, stumbled upon Hilton Head in 1633 in search of good land to promote to prospective buyers. Two hundred years later, the island supported 12 plantations raising the famed sea-island cotton. During the Civil War, the Union Navy sailed into Port Royal Sound, set their sites on Hilton Head and made an amphibious landing of 13,000 troops – a force so large that it would not be duplicated until the invasion of Normandy in 1944. The Union used Hilton Head as a headquarters for launching attacks on nearby islands and plantations.

Many of the freed slaves remained on the island, bought pieces of their former owners' land and lived a quiet life of farming and fishing. Gullah communities still exist on Hilton Head, tucked behind the neatly landscaped strip malls and gated communities. Many of the Gullah people are immigrants from nearby islands, such as Daufuskie and St Helena. During the last 10 years, resort work has drawn many Latinos to the island as well. Today, Hilton Head may well have the largest Latino population of any city in South Carolina, and in 2003, the community launched its own Spanish-language newspaper, *La Patina*.

Hilton Head may well lead the world in famous resort courses. Although all of these courses are semiprivate and within the bounds of the island's gated plantations, visiting golfers are welcome at most courses. And there is more good news: except on exclusive and famous courses, the greens fees can run under $80. Of course, you will pay double that for a prime tee time on a celebrity course designed by Robert Trent Jones. To find out about golf packages, call ☎ 888-445-8664.

All courses have a dress code (if you have to ask for details, you're probably not ready for the Hilton Head golf scene) and require reservations (which you should make months in advance if you want the course and tee time of your choice).

Close to a million rounds of golf get played on Hilton Head annually, so the competition for tee times is fierce. Many visitors make reservations more than a month ahead of time. You can golf the links with the rich and famous (President Clinton loved these courses). Unfortunately, the water holes that challenged Bobby Jones and company in the film *The Legend of Bagger Vance* are part of a private club in neighboring Bluffton that is not open to the public.

Among the don't-miss courses are the following:

George Fazio Course (☎ 843-785-1130; Palmetto Dunes; ☽ 8am-5pm) The island's premier test; often ranked among the top 50 resort courses in the USA; known for its extremely tight fairways on the back nine.

Harbour Town Golf Links (☎ 843-842-1806; Sea Pines Plantation; ☽ 8am-5pm) Site of the Heritage Golf Classic every April.

Hilton Head National (☎ 843-842-5900; ☽ 8am-5pm) On the mainland, just across the US Hwy 278 bridge from Hilton Head. Exceptional rates for junior (under 14) and senior (over 60) players; off-season rates under $20.

Island West Golf Club (☎ 843-689-6660; ☽ 8am-5pm) In Bluffton, 8.8 miles west of the Hilton Head bridge on US Hwy 278. The area's newest course, known for rolling fairways and high trees; lowest greens fees around.

Ocean Course (☎ 843-842-1806; Sea Pines Plantation; ☽ 8am-5pm) Known as an extremely playable course for golfers of varying abilities.

Robert Trent Jones Golf Course (☎ 843-785-1136; Palmetto Dunes; ☽ 8am-5pm) Challenges with an intricate lagoon system, complete with gators.

Sea Marsh Course (☎ 843-842-1806; Sea Pines; ☽ 8am-5pm) Greens have significant traps and often slope away from the fairways.

Shipyard Golf Club (☎ 843-686-8802; Shipyard Plantation; ☽ 7am-5:30pm) A favorite of the Senior PGA tour.

Tennis

The 300 hundred courts on the island speak for this sport's popularity. Of the 19 clubs on the island, seven are open to the public.

Expect to pay $15 to $25 for courts fees, although you will get lower rates if you are using plantation courts and are a guest.

Palmetto Dunes Tennis Center (☎ 843-786-1152; Palmetto Dunes; ☽ 8am-5pm) 23 clay courts and two hard courts.

Port Royal Racquet Club (☎ 843-686-8803; Port Royal Plantation; ☽ 7am-5:30pm) A mix of clay, hard and grass surfaces, 16 courts in all.

Sea Pines Racquet Club (☎ 843-363-4495; Sea Pines Plantation; ☽ 8am-5pm) 24 clay courts.

South Beach Racquet Club (☎ 843-671-2215; Sea Pines Plantation; ☽ 8am-5pm) 11 clay courts, near South Beach Village.

Van der Meer Tennis Center (☎ 843-785-8388; 19 DeAllyon Rd; ☽ 8am-5pm) Near Sea Pines Circle, the premier 'outside the gate' facility on the island, with three clay and 25 hard courts; four are covered, eight are lighted.

Van der Meer Tennis University (☎ 843-686-8804; Shipyard Plantation; ☽ 8am-6pm) Clinics and competitions for pros and amateurs throughout the year; 20 courts, 11 clay, eight with lights.

Biking

What a joy! Hilton Head has some 25 miles of flat bike paths on the island for your recreation. But it doesn't stop here. The unusually hard sand on the beach makes for exhilarating peddling.

Renting a bike is easy. Most lodgings have rentals for guests. Plus, about a half dozen 'outside the gate' rental shops will deliver a bike to your doorstep and pick it up later.

Really, if you don't go cycling while you're on the island, you've missed one of the quintessential island experiences.

Give a call to one of the tried-and-true shops listed here. They have everything from mountain/touring bikes to tandems. Expect to pay $12 to $17 a day, with better rates for longer rentals. All rentals include locks, and almost all island accommodations have racks or places to lock up your bike.

Following are some recommended companies; they will deliver and pick-up bikes at your door.

AAA Riding Tigers Bike Rentals/Palmetto Bike
Barn (☎ 843-686-5833; 🕒 8am-4pm)
Bubba's Bike Rental (☎ 843-785-3971; 🕒 9am-5pm)
Hilton Head Bicycle Company (☎ 843-686-6888; 🕒 9am-5pm)
Pedals (☎ 843-842-5522; 🕒 9am-5pm)

Kayaking
With lots of protected backwater creeks, marshes, light breezes and warm weather, kayaking can be a great way to see Hilton Head's abundant maritime wildlife, including dolphins and brown pelicans, with their aerial acrobatics.

Try one of the following companies. They run out of various rendezvous points like Broad Creek, Shelter Cove and Pinckney Island. Expect to pay $25 to $35 per person for a two-hour guided tour, or about $35 to rent a two-person kayak for two hours.

The following operators have a reputation for professionalism and experience. They will meet you with the kayaks at a rendezvous point that is appropriate for weather conditions and the length of your tour.

Coastal Kayaking (☎ 843-842-4194; 🕒 9am-5pm)
Cool Breeze Kayaking (☎ 843-683-4040; 🕒 9am-5pm)
Outside Hilton Head (☎ 843-686-6996; 🕒 7am-10pm)

Boat Tours
Harbour Town, Broad Creek and the Shelter Cove Marina (on the shores of Broad Creek) are the places to head for boat tours of Calibogue Sound, the Intracoastal Waterway and Hilton Head's rural sister island, Daufuskie, which is still home to a small Gullah community.

Scott's Low Country Nature Tours (☎ 843-683-0187; 🕒 8am-7pm) Get up-close and personal with the dolphins. Captain Scott Henry's six-passenger open boat departs Shelter Cove Marina for a two-hour private tour. Rates run adult/child $30/20. Tuesday-night fireworks trips run $40/30; beachcombing trips to Daufuskie to look for petrified shark teeth run $40/30.

Calibogue Cruises (☎ 843-342-8687; Broad Creek Marina; 🕒 9am-5pm) This company also does tours to Daufuskie ($40).

Adventure Cruises (843-785-4558; 9 Shelter Cove Lane; 🕒 9am-5pm) Adventure Cruises runs a large passenger vessel that does tours to Daufuskie ($40) and two-hour dolphin-watching tours (adult/child $19/9).

Spirit of Harbour Town (☎ 843-842-7179; Harbour Town; 🕒 9am-5pm) This is a large party boat carrying passengers from right in front of the lighthouse at Harbour Town through the Intracoastal Waterway and down the Savannah River to Savannah (adult/child $39/29). There are both daytime and nighttime trips; both last five hours.

Other Activities
There's gobs more than golf here.

Chartering a fishing trip is no problem in Hilton Head. **Harbour Town** (☎ 843-671-4534; Harbour Town; 🕒 9am-5pm) is a booking agent for a half-dozen sport-fishing boats; charges are $375 for a half-day trip, $750 for a full day. **Captain Hook Party Fishing Boat** (☎ 843-785-1700; Shelter Cover Marina; 🕒 8am-5pm) does 5½-hour bottom-fishing trips for adult/child $45/35.

There's nothing like a good night's sleep after a day spent aboard a boat plying gentle waves. There are several places that can make this happen for you. **Schooner Welcome** (☎ 843-785-5566; Shelter Cove Harbour; 🕒 9am-5pm) has a 62ft wooden yacht that carries up to 30 guests out of Shelter Cove Harbour, which is a separate landing, located next to the marina. The trips last for three hours, leave in the morning and afternoon and cost adult/child $35/25. **Stars & Stripes** (☎ 843-842-7933; Harbour Town boat basin; 🕒 9am-6pm) offers 90-minute day sails and a two-hour sunset cruise aboard a former America's Cup sloop. The cost is adult/child $25/20.

If you've got a little girl in tow, or in your heart, an afternoon spent horseback riding is a real treat. **Lawton Stables** (☎ 843-671-2586; 190 Greenwood Dr; Sea Pines Plantation; 🕒 8am-6pm) is the premier stable and has wilderness trails throughout Sea Pines Forest Preserve. The cost is $30 an hour. Lessons costs $35 for 30 minutes. **Sea Horse Farms** (☎ 843-681-7746; 34 Mitchellville Rd; 🕒 9am-5pm) offers one-hour trips four times a day on north end of the island; the cost is $35.

HILTON HEAD

HILTON HEAD FOR CHILDREN

With a plethora of outdoor activities, warm weather, broad beaches, green spaces, bike trails and organized kids programs at most plantations, Hilton Head is a mecca for children. In addition, some attractions appeal specifically to youthful visitors.

Adventure Cove Family Fun Center (☎ 843-842-9990; Hwy 278 at Folly Field Rd) Two miniature golf courses, a driving range, batting cages, an indoor playworld, a video arcade, bumper cars, laser tag and restaurants.
Legendary Golf (☎ 843-785-9214; Hwy 278 at Pope Ave)
Pirate's Island Adventure Golf (☎ 843-686-4001; Hwy 278) Next to the Hilton Head Diner and Fairfield Inn by Marriott.

FESTIVALS & EVENTS

Hilton Head and neighboring Bluffton have a special event for just about every week of the year. But a few events have true cultural significance and/or create quite a spectacle.

JANUARY
Hilton Head Orchestra Concert Season

FEBRUARY
Native Gullah Celebration Most of the month, at various venues, like the Arts Center of Coastal Carolina and the Mall at Shelter Cove; gospel music, drama, cooking, artists, basket makers, storytellers.

MARCH
Wine Fest Tasting, food, silent auction.

APRIL
Worldcom Classic, The Heritage of Golf Celebrity watching; paaaarty time!

MAY
Bluffton Village Festival Food, entertainment, vendors in the streets of Historic Bluffton.
Family Fiesta Latina Latin American food, music and dancing.

JUNE
Turtle Talk & Walk Your chance to watch the magnificent loggerhead sea turtles come ashore and lay their eggs; reserve a tour with the Coastal Discovery Museum (p120).

JULY
Let's Go Crabbing On Tuesday and Thursday; kids gather at the Sea Pines Recreation Department (☎ 843-363-4530) to experience the art of catching blue crabs.

DETOUR: HISTORIC MITCHELVILLE

If you are interested in going to the roots of Hilton Head's indigenous Gullah culture, head to the corner of Fish Haul and Mitchelville Rds, at the north end of the island. Here you'll find the site of the African American community that developed after plantation workers were freed from slavery by the Federal invasion at the beginning of the Civil War and the Emancipation Proclamation.

Many of the island's older Gullah residents still live in the area, and there are plans to list Mitchelville on the national Registry of Historic Places and to restore/reconstruct some of the traditional Gullah homes to commemorate what may well be the first community of freed slaves in the South.

Currently, there is not much to see, but you will learn a lot if you take a tour here with one of the guides from the Coastal Discovery Museum (p120).

For more information on Hilton Head's Gullah culture, you can browse for books at the Gullah Bookstore (p119).

AUGUST
Dance under the Oaks at Pepper's Porch Weekend dance parties to soul and beach music at Bluffton's favorite juke joint.

SEPTEMBER
Annual Celebrity Golf Tournament Movie stars and politicos play for the crowds and cameras on the courses of Indigo Run, Palmetto Dunes and Harbour Town.

OCTOBER
Halloween at Coligny Plaza Everyone comes in costume for ghoulish music and treats.

NOVEMBER
Hilton Head Concours d'Elegance Great collection of classic cars at Shelter Cove Commons.

DECEMBER
Christmas at Harbour Town Shops, restaurants and boats are decorated for the holidays.

SLEEPING

With 3000 hotel rooms, 6000 villas/condos and 1000 time-share units, Hilton Head has space for a lot of travelers.

Staying at a resort plantation is the most popular and convenient lodging option on the island. The resorts offer golf courses, tennis courts, pools, shopping and dining.

In addition to the accommodations listed here, you will find a listing of lodgings at www.hiltonheadisland.com. Travelers looking for a capable reservation service should check out the **Visitors Bureau** (☎ 800-523-3373; www.hiltonheadisland.org) or the **Signature Group** (☎ 843-851-2922; www.accesssouthcarolina.com).

You can often get significant discounts through **hotels.com** (☎ 800-246-8357) and other online booking services.

Villas, townhouses and time-shares are available at the **Plantations of Hilton Head** (☎ 800-475-2631), **Palmetto Dunes Plantation** (☎ 800-845-6130) and **Sea Pines Plantation** (☎ 800-732-7463). Rates vary widely and are cheaper during the off-season and for non-beachfront property, but expect to pay $700 to $3500 a week.

Try a rental agency, such as **Hilton Head Oceanfront Rentals** (☎ 800-845-6132) or the **Vacation Company** (☎ 843-686-6100, 800-545-3303), if the other options seem overwhelming.

Budget

Simply put, the prices of the waterfront resort hotels on Hilton Head are not for the budget traveler, except in January and February, when the resorts may offer rates under $100. The rest of the year, resort rack rates can exceed $275 a night. To limit the strain on your budget, use an online booking service or ask the resorts about five- or seven-day package rates that can bring the cost down to $150 to $200 a night. Note: the range of rates given below indicate low- to high-season prices (the low price being the low-season cost, and the high price being the high-season cost).

If those numbers don't work for you, take heart. You will find a collection of modern, clean, motor-inn chains (generally with swimming pools and a free continental breakfast) along US Hwy 278 on the island, and across the bridge in Bluffton.

Hilton Garden Inn (☎ 843-837-8111, 800-444-8667; www.hiltongardeninn.com; 1575 Fording Island Rd; d $50-100; P 🍴 🐾 🗙) Located on the Intracoastal Waterway, this new property makes a great hub for Lowcountry touring. It has an outdoor pool and hot tub, a

fitness center and a business center. There is a microwave, refrigerator and coffee-maker in every room and a full-service restaurant on the property.

RV PARKS

Outdoor Resorts Motor Coach Resort (☎ 843-785-7699, 800-722-2365; www.hiltonheadmotorcoachresort.com; 133 Arrow Rd; full hook-up $31-37; P 🐾) Located near Sea Pines Circle, this motorcoach-only (minimum length 18 feet) resort boasts a large pool, Jacuzzi, six tennis courts, health club with sauna, fishing lake, shuffleboard, golf driving cage and playground. You'll find over 400 privately owned and landscaped campsites set among towering pines and live oaks, all with full hook-ups, including cable. Lots of friendly folk here.

Outdoor Resorts RV Resort, Marina & Yacht Club (☎ 843-681-3256, 800 845-9560; 43 Jenkins Rd; full hook-up $31-37; P 🐾) Located at the north end of Hilton Head, this landscaped RV resort overlooks its own marina on the Intracoastal Waterway. There are pools, tennis, a playground and a restaurant on-site.

Mid-range

Holiday Inn Oceanfront (☎ 843-785-5126, 800-423-9897; www.hihiltonhead.com; 1 S Forest Beach Dr; d $75-210; P 🍴 🐾 🗙) Set on Coligny Beach, the Holiday Inn is good choice and a great value if you want to stay 'outside the gates' and be within walking distance of the 60 shops and restaurants of Coligny Plaza. The five-story motor inn offers large rooms that are brightly decorated in tropical fabrics, but you don't really get a sea view from the small balconies unless you are on the top two floors. There's a pool, oceanfront restaurant and beachside Tiki Hut bar for chilling.

South Beach Inn & Vacation Rentals (☎ 843-671-6498, 800-367-3909; www.southbeachvillage.com; 232 South Sea Pines Dr; d $75-160; P 🍴 🗙) This B&B-style lodge on Sea Pines Plantation is built over the complex of shops and restaurants on the toe of the island. There are only 17 units here. Rooms have kitchenettes and are furnished like a country B&B, with hooked rugs and reproduction 19th-century furniture. The beach is a two-minute walk, and the legendary Salty Dog Café (p128) is virtually downstairs.

Adventure Inn (☎ 843-785-5151, 800-845-9500; www.advinn.com; 41 S Forest Beach Dr; d $70-120;

P X Z X) The price is right at this seaside property less than a half mile south of Coligny Beach. In addition to poolside and oceanside studios with kitchenettes, the inn offers two- and three-bedroom condo units, mostly in three-story modern concrete buildings that give the place the look and feel of a Florida resort. The single pool is not particularly large, given the number of guests, but there are 12 miles of broad beach just a few steps away if you want private sunbathing.

Main Street Inn (☎ 843 681-3001, 800 471-3001; www.mainstreetinn.com; 2200 Main St, d $120-170; P X Z X) Named one of America's top 10 hotels by *Country Inns* magazine, this 33-room gem is on the edge of the Main St Village shopping complex, at the north end of the island. The look and feel of this place is pure 'English Manor House' – complete with fireplaces, Windsor chairs and shuttered windows. Rooms open onto formal gardens rich in flora and bird songs. You'll find the small garden pool great for private evening dips. The tariff includes a hearty gourmet breakfast.

Inn at Harbour Town (☎ 843-363-8100, 800-732-7463; www.seapines.com; d $130-230; X X) If you are looking for a romantic retreat with the elegance and charm of an intimate five-star European hotel, check out this inn. The 60-room establishment in the heart of the Mediterranean-style village of Harbour Town offers private butler service and views of Harbour Town Golf Links and Sea Pines Racquet Club. The library has matchless serenity, but there is no pool.

Disney's Hilton Head Island Resort (☎ 843-341-4130, 800-453-4911; www.dvcresorts.com; 22 Harbourside Lane; d $110-310; P X Z X) Set on 15 acres near Shelter Cove in Broad Creek, the resort offers guests villa-style vacation homes with all the amenities and lots of kids activities with Disney themes.

For inexpensive offerings off the water, midisland along US Hwy 278, you can't go wrong with the following:

Fairfield Inn by Marriott (☎ 843-842-4800; www.fairfieldinn.com; 9 Marina Side Dr; d $ 80; P X Z X)

Hampton Inn (☎ 843 681-7900; www.hamptoninn.com; 1 Dillon Rd; d $75; P X Z X)

Motel 6 (☎ 843-785-2700; www.motel6.com; 830 William Hilton Pkwy; d $75; P X Z X)

Red Roof Inn (☎ 843-686-6808; www.redroofinn.com; 5 Regency Pkwy; d $75; P X Z X)

Residence Inn by Marriott (☎ 877-247-3431; www.residenceinnhhi.com; 12 Park Lane; d $75; P X Z X)

Top End

Crowne Plaza Resort Hilton Head Island (☎ 843-842-2400, 800-334-1881; www.crowneplazaresort.com; 130 Shipyard Dr; d $185-300; P X Z X) Here's a great place for a family with young kids! Tucked amid towering live oaks, the oceanfront Crowne Plaza Resort offers the Van Der Meer Shipyard Racquet Club, 27 holes of championship golf, diverse dining options, a 24-hour fitness center, and indoor/outdoor pools. Kids' services include Camp Castaway, Evening Adventures, and Kids Play Free Golf programs during high season.

Westin Resort (☎ 843-681-4000, 800-937-8461; www.westinhiltonhead.com; 2 Grasslawn Ave; d $185-400; P X Z X) If you have always admired the Moorish architecture and lavishness of the famous Breakers Hotel in Palm Beach, Florida, then the Westin may be your fantasy come true on Hilton Head. Set on a pristine strand of beach in the Port Royal Resort at the north end of the island, this mammoth property has 412 large and luxurious rooms, three swimming pools (two are heated) and a staffed fitness center. Once thought of as a place that was off-limits for kids, the hotel now markets itself as family-friendly and offers daily Kids Club activities for the children of guests.

Hilton Oceanfront Resort (☎ 843-842-8000, 800 845-8001; www.hilton.com; 23 Ocean Lane; d $185-265; P X Z X) Secreted among the dunes of the Palmetto Dunes Plantation, the low-rise hotel has about 300 rooms. Each room comes with a kitchenette, living and dining area and balcony with ocean or island views. With two pools, the beach, babysitting services and a Pizza Hut on-site, the Hilton is another good choice for families.

Hilton Head Marriott Beach & Golf Resort (☎ 843-686-8400, 800-295-5998; www.marriotthiltonhead.com; One Hotel Circle; d $185-295; P X Z X) There are 550 large rooms and suites (mostly with ocean views) in this 10-story palace in the Palmetto Dunes Plantation. You also get three on-property golf courses, indoor and outdoor pools, a fitness center, tennis, oceanfront dining and about $20 million worth of big-time renovations.

EATING

With more than 200 restaurants on Hilton Head, you've got to wonder if anybody cooks or eats at home here. Every plantation has its own award-winning restaurant, but for the uniformed, eating in Hilton Head feels a lot like an outing to the mall, because so many restaurants have set up camp in the roadside shopping plazas. Because of the host of traffic lights on US Hwy 278, going out to eat on Hilton Head can be an ordeal unless you stay within a mile-or-two radius of your lodging.

In addition to some of our personal favorites listed below, you can access an extensive list of eateries and an interactive map at www.hiltonheadisland.com. Also look around at hotels and at the visitors center to see if you can get your hands on annual the 170-page book of island menus, called *Hilton Head Restaurants*. Most restaurants are open for lunch and dinner, 11:30am to 10pm. Quite a few of the upscale dinner places are closed on Monday.

Budget

Hilton Head Diner (☎ 843-686-2400; 6 Marina Side Dr; dishes $3-10; 🍴 ✗) Just south of Palmetto Dunes on Hwy 278, you'll find the one and only all-night diner on the island. Popular with the Sunday-brunch crowd, the diner also serves liquor and beer all day, every day, 24/7. Go for the western omelet ($5).

Kenny B's (☎ 843-785-3315; Circle BiLo Center; mains $6-14; 🍴 ✗) If you can find your way behind Wild Wings on Pope Ave to this hot little Cajun bistro, it will knock your socks off. This is the kind of place that's festooned with hand-painted murals on the wall. You order at the counter and then the wait staff delivers to your table. The kitchen also does a big take-out business. The Frogmore Creole (shrimp, potatoes, onion and smoked sausage smothered in

AUTHOR'S CHOICES

Two Eleven Park (☎ 843-686-5212; Park Plaza; mains $11-20; 🍴 ✗) This wine bar and bistro by the cinemas in Park Plaza (near Sea Pines Circle) flaunts Melrose-style chic, with lots of brushed steel, candlelight, 75 different wines by the glass and jazz filtered in from the sound system. It's a great date restaurant and upscale couples and quads pack this place after 7pm. The smoked-salmon pizza ($10) makes for a great appetizer while you're sipping vino at the bar and waiting for a table. Consider the grilled eggplant topped with portobello ($12).

Redfish (☎ 843-686-3388; 8 Archer Rd; mains $16-25; 🍴 ✗), near Sea Pines Circle, is a hot newcomer to the fusion/seafood scene. The menu is eclectic, featuring entrees like 'spicy latina ribs' ($20) and 'naked salmon' ($18). The attached Collins & James Provisions store is a great place to get a take-out picnic lunch to carry to the beach.

Salty Dog Cafe (☎ 843-671-2233; South Beach Marina Village; mains $7-10; 🍴 ✗) Yep, it's an island institution. Folks love to come for the cheeseburger ($9) and stand in front of the live webcam that sends out their images over the Internet to all the poor slobs stuck back home dreaming of an endless summer. With its associated T-shirt shop and iconic Salty Dog logo that turns up on the backs of the leisure class worldwide, the Dog is – without a doubt – a mecca for tourists. But you can't beat the chill on the Heineken ($3.50) or a table on the deck when the sun is settling toward the marsh.

Old Fort Pub (☎ 843-681-2386; 65 Skull Creek Dr; $19-30; 🍴 ✗) Located near the airport, this pub serves Lowcountry and American cuisine in a charming setting overlooking the water and surrounded by live oaks draped in Spanish moss. This is the one place on the island where you can count on seeing a fabulous sunset (either from the deck or the through the picture windows). And if you have to wait for a table, you can get a drink and explore the earthworks of nearby Fort Mitchel (p120). The baked grouper with a three-cheese fondue ($26) is major league.

Old Oyster Factory (☎ 803-681-6040; 101 Marshland Rd; $13-24; 🍴 ✗) Set in a rebuilt oyster cannery on a wharf overlooking Broad Creek, this midisland restaurant starts you salivating with six different oyster dishes and goes on from there. Ask for a table near the large glass windows or on one of the outdoor decks, then strap on your bib and dive into a chargrilled garlic peppered salmon salad ($18) or the seafood medley ($18).

creole sauce, $9) is as good as it gets. Come for the bountiful Sunday brunch (8am to 1pm, $7). Don't miss the beignets (hot French donuts).

Giuseppi's Pizza & Pasta (☎ 843-785-4144; 32B Shelter Cove Lane; pies $8-17; 😵 ✖) is the place to call for take-out. Locals rave about the pizza here for good reason. The chicken and roasted red-pepper pie basted with olive oil and minced garlic (no sauce) rules.

Mi Tierra Mexican Restaurant (☎ 843-342-3409; 160 William Hilton Pkwy; mains $6-12; 😵 ✖) If its authentic Mexican cooking and conversations in Spanish that you seek, Mi Tierra is home base. But finding this hole-in-the-wall can be a challenge, as it is tucked behind two buildings and a parking lot just east of the visitors center (p119) and Gullah Flea Market (p132) as you enter the island on US Hwy 278. Hilton Head's significant Spanish-speaking community cherishes the food (and prices) here, and so will you. Don't miss the ceviche ($7).

Mid-range

Santa Fe Café (☎ 843-785-3838; 700 Plantation Center; mains $12-22; 😵 ✖) Here's a spot right out of New Mexico, and everybody loves it. Now with a new outdoor dining deck, the café features an upscale Tex-Mex menu. Lots of diners swear by the shrimp dishes.

South Seaport Café (☎ 803-671-7327; South Beach Marina Village; mains $19-23; 😵 ✖) Often overlooked by the tourists swarming toward Harbour Town's eateries and the nearby Salty Dog Café (p128), the South Seaport Café offers great water views of Braddock Cove from its deck and fresh crab dip ($6) that melts in your mouth. The seafood casserole ($19) is delicious too.

Truffles Café (☎ 803-671-6136; Sea Pines Center; mains $10-24; 😵 ✖) This hip California bistro is right in the middle of Sea Pines Plantation. Do not miss the grilled salmon with mango chutney sauce ($12) for lunch. Surprisingly, this place does a good job serving kids as well.

Just Pasta (☎ 843-686-3900; Coligny Plaza; pastas $12-18; 😵 ✖) You might think the price of pasta dishes here is a little on the steep side, but the portions are large, the entrees are creative, and the ambiance of this place will transport you into Billy Joel's song 'Our Italian Restaurant,' if not to a side street in Rome. Picture candlelight, walls

of wine racks, seating for fewer than 30 and concertina music. Don't miss the pappardelle alla vodka ($19), wide ribbon pasta tossed with tomato-vodka cream sauce, green peas and crumbed Italian sausage.

Rendez-Vous Café (☎ 843-785-5070; 14 Greenwood Dr; mains $14-20; 😵 ✖) With this French bistro among the Gallery of Shops near Sea Pines Circle, chef/owner Serge Pratt has earned a regional reputation by constantly coming up with creative new French fusion dishes, like pan-seared tilapia niçoise ($19). You can make a meal of his corn and crabmeat soup ($5).

Stellini Italian Restaurant (☎ 843-785-7006; 15 Pope Ave; pastas $12-15; 😵 ✖) With the scent of basil and burgundy decor, Stellini's has earned a reputation by consistently good Northern Italian entrees. Try the capellini marinara ($12).

It's Greek to Me (☎ 843-341-3556; 1 New Orleans Rd; mains $8-22; 😵 ✖) While this place near Sea Pines Circle may look a bit like your neighborhood sub shop, the food will transport you to Athens or Corfu.

Hinoki (☎ 843-785-9800; 37 New Orleans Rd; sushi $7-15; mains $11-24; 😵 ✖) This rather large and formal restaurant is a lot of people's favorite sushi bar. The deluxe sushi ($15) is a popular choice. Also good is the *yosenabe* (seafood, veggies, tofu, shiitake mushrooms and scallions in a hot seaweed broth).

Charley's Crab (☎ 843-342-9066; 2 Hudson Rd; mains $18-22; 😵 ✖) Located on the sound in a old wooden building, Charlie's temps you with delights like she-crab soup ($6) and pistachio-encrusted mahi mahi ($18). The crab cakes have won culinary awards.

Hudson's (☎ 843-681-2772; 1 Hudson Rd; mains $14-20; 😵 ✖) When you're feeling in a Forrest Gump kind of mood for Lowcountry fried seafood, head for the northwest corner of the island. Down by the shrimp-boat wharf, you'll find this remodeled shack serving killer hush puppies (free with entrees). The fried oysters (about $15 in season) melt in your mouth.

Aunt Chilada's/Easy Street Café (☎ 843-785-7700; 69 Pope Ave; mains $9-20; 😵 ✖) Here's a place where young, single locals and travelers mix at happy hour and stay for the enchiladas. The chimichangas ($10) rock. While the cuisine is not really authentic Mexican, it is tasty, and the crowd of attractive hard-bodies makes everything go down easy. Possibly the most popular happy hour on the island starts here at 4:30pm daily. Domestic beer runs under $2.

Market St Café (☎ 843-686-4976; Coligny Plaza; mains $7-15; 🍴 ✖) The outdoor patio of this little Greek spot makes a great place to kick back for a light lunch or dinner after a shopping trip to Coligny Plaza or after a few hours of catching rays across the street at Coligny Beach. You can get most common Greek entrees here and some that just popped out of the chef's head. At lunch we favor the Greek grilled cheese ($5), melted feta and provolone in a hot pita fold with lettuce, tomato, onions and *tzatziki* (yogurt-cucumber sauce).

Top End

Charleston's Restaurant (☎ 843-785-5008; 8 New Orleans Rd; mains $19-34; 🍴 ✖) Located near Sea Pines Circle, this place has the feel of a Lowcountry manor and has built its reputation on offering guests the total experience of Southern dining. There's plenty of seafood on the menu and some creative pasta dishes, like salmon lasagna and lobster ravioli ($24). But if you want to eat like Southern gentry, you will try the applewood-smoked pork rack with fried cheese-grits cake, sautéed spinach and hopping John ($20).

CQ's Restaurant (☎ 843-671-2779; mains $14-30; 🍴 ✖), in Harbour Town, is one of the island's most popular restaurants. The setting is a reproduction of a 19th-century rice barn, overlooking the water. The cuisine is upscale Lowcountry fare. The sea bass, served with Jerusalem artichoke hazelnut puree and butternut squash flan ($23) is out of sight.

Carolina Grill (☎ 843-785-3000; 215 Park Plaza; dinner $16-24; 🍴 ✖) Upscale and classy, as well as down-home and warm, the décor of Greg Blatt's hip new spot in Park Plaza gives the feeling of the historic Lowcountry with plantation shutters, Charleston brick and mahogany bar. The menu features traditional American, with Southern specialties like shrimp creole ($16). Come early or call for reservations – legions of diners descend on this place from nearby Sea Pines Plantation.

Crane's Tavern & Steakhouse Restaurant (☎ 843-341-2333; 26 New Orleans Rd; mains $16-35; 🍴 ✖) Among the clutch of popular restaurants on New Orleans Rd near Sea Pine Circle, this one stands out for its prime rib ($19 for 12oz) and English-pub atmosphere.

ENTERTAINMENT

Arts Center of Coastal Carolina (☎ 843-842-2787; 14 Shelter Cove Lane; tickets $12-35) This is a gem of a theater. It hosts plays and musical performances, including shows with the Hallelujah Singers, who perform Gullah songs and storytelling. They appeared in the movie *Forrest Gump*, and the group's founder, Marlena Smalls, played Bubba's mother (see 'Hallelujah!' p139). In addition to showcasing local talent, the center mounts major Broadway productions, like *42nd St* and *Mame*, with New York talent (not road companies), and draws concert musicians like well-known pianist Michael Feinstein.

Bars & Clubs

Given Hilton Head's sprawling and complicated system of roads and gated plantations, you might think that trying to find a nightspot would be a challenge for even veteran pub crawlers. But there's good news here. Many of the liveliest spots are in the vicinity of Sea Pines Circle.

BARMUDA TRIANGLE

The young and the restless often spend their weekends lost in a place known locally as the Barmuda Triangle. This is a collection of pubs (just steps apart, south of Sea Pines Circle in Hilton Head Plaza) that snare legions of the beautiful people (and their admirers) especially during the high season. Most of these places serve pub food.

Hilton Head Brewing Company (☎ 843-785-2739; 7B Greenwood Dr) Twelve different microbrews are offered here during the year. Consider the Calibogue Amber ($3.50). This is also a popular burger-and-pizza ($7–16) dinner venue for families with children

Jump & Phil's (☎ 843-785-9070; 7B Greenwood Dr) Right next door to the Hilton Head Brewing Company, J&P's is the spot to hang with the local hard-bodies.

Reilley's (☎ 843-842-4414; Port Royal Plaza) This place is a total sports-bar scene, decorated with autographed jerseys of famous hockey players and patrons like Ray Bourque.

The Lodge (☎ 843-842-8966; Hilton Head Plaza) This cigar bar–cum–pool hall is right in the middle of the Triangle. The young and beautiful like to come here.

BEYOND THE TRIANGLE

Even those bars outside the boundaries of the Barmuda Triangle aren't too far from Sea Pines Circle.

Wingo Hall Music Café (☎ 843-686-4343; Unit 11 Park Plaza; no cover) Here's the newest hot spot on the island. It draws baby boomers, their second wives and their younger siblings. You will find a hip dance scene with folks rocking out to the DJ, who spins classics like Cool & the Gang's 'Celebrate.' But the big attraction is Dave Wingo's band, Wingo & Friends. While you get plenty of couples here, Wingo's also draws quite a lot of single men and women traveling in trios, ripe to meet their opposites.

Monkey Business (☎ 843-686-3545; Unit 25 Park Plaza; cover $5 after 10pm) This is probably the best pick-up scene on the island. The under-40 crowd romps here to either DJs or bands playing classics like Gladys Knight's 'Midnight Train to Georgia,' Top 40 and dance tunes. The club brings in national acts like the Wailers, the Drifters and the Basstones. There are local acts that rock as well, like Tim O'Gorman's band from Bluffton.

Jazz Corner (☎ 843-842-8826; Village at Wexford Plaza) This is the island's first-rate jazz cave, luring aficionados with the sounds of Bob Alberti and the Howard Paul Group. There's swing dancing on Tuesday night, and all sorts of taste thrills for the table, like artichoke and spinach dips ($6).

Regatta Lounge (☎ 843-842-8500; 23 Ocean Lane) Come to this place to dance the Carolina shag if you are a baby boomer (or if you just love the '60s). The long-standing band Target gets high marks from the dancin' fools who cram this place on weekends.

Quarterdeck Lounge & Patio (☎ 843-671-2222; 149 Lighthouse Rd, Harbour Town) Every April, Hilton Head's annual rite of spring (the Worldcom Classic, Heritage of Golf) unfolds its after-hours splendor at this pub. The deck packs in with golf fans, superstar athletes (like Greg Norman) and everyone else on the island looking for action.

Big Bamboo (☎ 843-686-34430; upstairs at Coligny Plaza) The pub draws an after-beach crowd with its two–for–one margaritas and Bamboo Brews. This is a 1940s theme bar with the look of something out of the classic Air Force flick *Twelve O'Clock High*. You won't find pin-up girl Betty Grable here, but her granddaughter might be on-scene. There's live music most nights. A lot of folks like to hang around after happy hour for the live bluegrass during dinner (ribs/chicken/pasta) on Saturday.

Bar at the Westin (☎ 843-681-4000; Port Royal Resort Plantation) Check out this place when you've had enough of noise, crowds and smoke. It's the place to go for a romantic tryst. You can sip martinis in your cocktail dress while listening to soft jazz and staring out at the waves. Then you can kick off your shoes and stroll the beach (just feet away) with the love of your life.

Cinemas

Main St Cinemas (☎ 843-785-5001; Park Plaza; tickets $7)
Northridge Ten Cinemas (☎ 843-342-3800; 435 William Hilton Pkwy; tickets $7)

SHOPPING

You probably didn't come here to shop, but sometimes it's too hot for golf or too cloudy for the beach. So when the moment calls for a shopping fix, Hilton Head offers a bazaar of over 20 boutique malls, full-scale malls and shopping plazas. Each is loaded with clothiers, galleries, antique dealers and specialty shops.

Here are some places to begin. Most shops are open 9am to 9pm in the high season (March to December).

Harbour Town (☎ 843-363-5355; Sea Pines Plantation) Yes, Toto, it is the most popular tourist destination on the island. The Mediterranean-like village has an upscale collection of boutiques like Knickers (featuring Tommy Bahama sportswear), galleries (with the respected maritime art of John Stobart) and restaurants. You'll pay a $5 entrance fee per car to get into Sea Pines Plantation.

The Art Café (☎ 843-785-5525; 10 Heritage Plaza) If you want to make your own art and indulge in one of Winnie the Pooh's favorite pastimes, 'elevenses,' don't miss this spot. You can get take-out beverages (margaritas are popular with adults) or a turkey sandwich ($6 from the Frosty Frog next door). Then come in here and select an unglazed bowl, plate or mug to decorate with help and tools from the staff. Design your own objet d'art, and eat while the glaze bakes in the kiln. This place is a blast for kids and adults alike.

Coligny Plaza Shopping Center (☎ 843-842-6050; 125 Cordillo Pkwy) With 60 shops and restaurants right near the main public beach, the plaza makes it easy to mix fun and sun.

Main Street Village (☎ 843-689-6200; 1405 Main St) This attractive plaza is at the north end of the island has a bank, pharmacy, grocery, liquor store and gift shops.

Shelter Cove Mall (☎ 843-686-3090; Highway 278) Located midisland, this is a full-scale indoor mall complete with Saks Fifth Avenue, Belk and Talbots.

Lowcountry Factory Outlet Village (☎ 843-837-4339; US Hwy 278) You'll see this mall just before you cross the bridge onto Hilton Head. The place recently added a second village, and it has more than 50 shops, including J Crew and Ralph Lauren.

Gullah Flea Market (103 William Hilton Pkwy; 10am-6pm Mon-Sat) Here's an excellent place to pick up locally grown produce, eavesdrop on the locals or browse for books and other junk. This is also a good spot to pick up one of the traditional Gullah sweetgrass baskets (see 'Gullah Culture' p32) and possibly watch some basket weavers at work.

GETTING THERE & AROUND

US Airways (☎ 800-428-4322) offers direct flights from Charlotte to **Hilton Head Island Airport** (☎ 843-689-5400), on Dillon Rd, for about $240. **Savannah International Airport** (☎ 912-964-0514) is only 45 miles away and has more frequent and cheaper service (see p85).

If you are driving to Hilton Head, take I-95 to exit 8 (US Hwy 278), which will lead directly to Hilton Head. Hwy 170 to Beaufort is a scenic drive, full of water views.

You'll need a car to get to the island, but once you're here, there are bike paths connecting most major attractions and shopping areas. Resorts and a host of vendors offer bike rentals (see p123). The Hilton Head airport has a number of rental car agencies, including **Budget** (☎ 843-689-4040; 9am-7pm) and **Enterprise** (☎ 843-689-9910; 9am-7pm).

Yellow Cab (☎ 843-686-6666) can meet your short-term transportation needs.

AROUND HILTON HEAD

HISTORIC BLUFFTON
Pop 300

If you want to see a place time forgot; if you want to get the feel of traditional Lowcountry life, you've got to pay a visit to Historic Bluffton.

No, this isn't the Bluffton of strip malls and chain hotels you see as you pass along US Hwy 278 to or from Hilton Head. Historic Bluffton is about seven square blocks of Civil War–era homes. But don't expect spit-and-polish restoration in the style of Williamsburg, Savannah or Charleston. Historic Bluffton is a true backwater port (on the May River) gone dormant with the

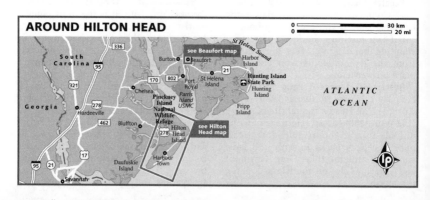

advent of better roads for shipping goods overland.

In recent years the village has sprouted a few small shops and galleries selling pretty things for your home, like antiques, art and glassware. The town has an informative historic center and a walking-tour brochure, but most of the time that you are ambling down the shady lanes beneath the magnificent live oaks, the only signs of life will be a couple of boys heading to the town dock with their fishing poles and a stray black dog that follows you like you are his long-lost friend. People come here for the solitude and for the fecund smell of salt marshes, sweetgrass and Spanish moss.

Someday somebody will open a B&B here, but at the moment, you can only enjoy the history and serenity as a daytripper.

Sights & Activities

The **Heyward House Historic Center** (☎ 843-757-6293; 52 Boundary St; admission free; ☼ 10am-3pm Wed-Sun) is the place to start your visit. The summer home of rice planter James Cole dates from 1840 and includes remnants of the original outdoor summer kitchen and a slave cabin. The center is still in the process of building its collection of photos, manuscripts and artifacts, so don't expect extensive and slick exhibits yet. But the docents are welcoming and will give you guided tour of the house/museum. You can also pick up the a very informative map and walking-tour guide to Historic Bluffton here.

If there is one eatery not to miss in Bluffton, it is **Pepper's Porch** (☎ 843-757-2295; 1255 May River Hwy; mains $11-20). This is a tin-roofed shack near the May River where inspired oyster roasts, Friday seafood buffet, Sunday brunches and live country music have drawn so many fans that Pepper's added an outdoor pavilion to handle the overflow. Don't miss the Brunswick stew for only $5.

Getting There & Away

Historic Bluffton lies on Hwy 46, a mile south of its intersection with four-lane US Hwy 278, the main artery to Hilton Head.

DAUFUSKIE ISLAND

Pop 200

In 1969, when Pat Conroy published *The Water Is Wide* (the film version was *Conrac*), a memoir of his life as the first white and male schoolteacher on Daufuskie, the island was an outpost of Gullah culture. It was a place reminiscent of the film *Daughters of the Dust*, where Gullah islanders lived their lives according to the tides, the fishing seasons, the moon and spirits (called 'haints'). Just a mile south of Hilton Head, Daufuskie is 5 miles long and 2 miles wide, and takes its name from an Indian word meaning 'sharp feather.'

HILTON HEAD

ANATOMY OF A BACKWATER

The first settlement of Historic Bluffton dates to the early 19th century, when inland planters built summer retreats here. The attraction was a high, south-facing bluff above the river, which caught the summer breezes, staving off the infestations of mosquitoes and yellow fever. Planners laid out the grid of the town in 1830, and Bluffton soon thrived as both a miniscule summer resort for gentry and as a port for the trans-shipment of rice and cotton from nearby plantations. During the 1840s the village became a locus for debates on Southern secession. Shortly after the outbreak of the Civil War and the occupation of Hilton Head by Union troops, southern families abandoned Bluffton, leaving it to be pillaged and burned by the North. Fifteen houses and two churches survived, and the town was rebuilt.

The building of the local highway and bridge to Savannah, in 1926, ended Bluffton's claims as a commercial port, and for the next 80 years or so it remained a sanctuary beloved by a few locals and overlooked by tourists rushing past, a mile away on US Hwy 278, to Hilton Head. In recent years Hilton Head development has spread to the mainland, and modern Bluffton, along US Hwy 278, has become a boomtown of malls, condo developments and all the associated commercialism. Little of that has spilled over into Historic Bluffton yet, but with its funky charm, the town is ripe for gentrification, if not exploitation.

As recently as the mid 1980s, little had changed on Daufuskie. It was still a place where the only way to eat out was to get take-out from the general store at the state dock. Music came in the form of gospel singers, and the sounds of frogs and warblers. You bought liquor from an old Gullah lady in a head scarf who hid her still back in the woods. Prehistoric shark teeth turned up regularly on the beaches at the south end of the island.

Those days are not quite gone. The southern half of the island still remains in control of the islands' Gullah families. But the northern end has been developed into the exclusive Daufuskie Island Club & Resort (p134), with its golf courses and vacation homes. Most of the young Gullah islanders have moved to Hilton Head or Savannah for work. At church services, white transplants to the island outnumber native blacks.

Still, Daufuskie seems like a bit of the 'long ago and far away' when compared to Hilton Head's modern development. While it is no longer the best place to sample Gullah culture on the Carolina–Georgia Coast (Sapelo Island, in Georgia, is better), Daufuskie is worth a visit or a stay if you are looking for a low-key retreat that blends old and new, rich and poor, manicured and wild, white and Gullah. On Daufuskie you will be welcomed for Sunday church services and for brunch in the Melrose Clubhouse, no matter the color of your skin or the size of your wallet.

Sights & Activities

The beauty of Daufuskie lies along its dirt roads on the south end of the island, beneath its moss-dripping oaks, on the edge of its marshes and along its driftwood-strewn, eroding beaches. Along the way you will see the Mt Carmel and First Union African Baptist Churches, the lighthouse, the old winery and cemeteries dating back more than 150 years. To get to all of these places, you need wheels or a horse. So one way to see the island is to stay at the Daufuskie Island Club & Resort (p134) and hire one of their horses ($30 per hour) for a trail ride.

These days, most visitors come to Daufuskie on a tour from Hilton Head, usually with one of two companies. **Calibogue Cruises** (☎ 843-342-8687; adult/child $40/20;

 9am-5pm) has tours that start midday and last about three hours. **Outside Hilton Head** (☎ 843-686-6996; adult/child $40/20; 9am-5pm) allows you to either tour the island on a bus with a gang of folks or to get a golf cart with a roof and a map to tour on your own.

Sleeping & Eating

Freeport Marina (☎ 843-342-8687; www.freeport marina.com; cabins $100) On the north end, Wick Scurry's Marina, at mile marker 35 on the Intracoastal Waterway, offers what he calls 'crab shacks' for overnighting. Placed on the actual site of the Freeport Plantation, the four cottages have water views, a bunk bed with full-size mattresses (for four good friends or a family), a refrigerator, microwave, television and VCR. They offer tours, weekly cookouts with entertainment (April to November) and a restaurant called the Daufuskie Island Crab Company that sometimes brings in Marlena Small and the Hallelujah Singers (see p139).

Daufuskie Island Club & Resort (☎ 843-842-8000, 800-960-9089; www.daufuskieresort.com; d $175-350;) The resort features 190 rooms, including elegant ones in the Melrose Inn, as well as two- and four-bedroom cottages with views of the marsh or ocean. There are four restaurants and lounges, two championship golf courses, three swimming pools and a beach club. To top it off, there are extensive water-sport activities, three miles of white-sand, pristine beach, an equestrian center, a tennis center and supervised children's programs.

Marshside Mama's (mains $7-16;) You'll find this combination restaurant, bar, general store and US post office on the south end of the island (Intracoastal Waterway, marker 39), at the Beaufort County Public Dock. The complex is one building, and it's operated by the gregarious Beth and Bryan Shipman. Fried chicken ($8) is the way to go.

Getting There & Away

If you don't have your own boat, the only way to get to Daufuskie currently is to take one of the tours mentioned in Sights & Activities (p134). The **Calibogue Cruises** (☎ 843-342-8687) tour ferry departs Hilton Head at 7:15am and 12:15pm, and departs Daufuskie at 11:45am, 3:30pm and 5:30pm.

The ferry dock on Hilton Head is at the Broad Creek Marina. Your ferry lands at Freeport Marina on Daufuskie.

BEAUFORT

Pop 9516

Never to be confused with North Carolina's Beaufort (*bow*-fort), South Carolina's Beaufort (*byoo*-fert) is an elegant small town with magnificent antebellum homes, a sleepy downtown and shady lanes where life moves a bit more slowly. Beaufort River laps at the main streets, sparkling like a million diamonds in the bright sunlight and glowing like tiny fireflies in the pale moonlight. Locals conjecture that the area's high phosphate level is responsible for the water's uncommon reflections.

This little gem by the sea is named after Henry Somerset, the second Duke of Beaufort. Somerset left England to come to this chunk of high ground at the mouth of an unnamed river in 1711 – making Beaufort the state's second-oldest town after Charleston.

With a naval hospital, an Air Force base and a Marine recruit center, the military provides the town's main industry, but the movie business and tourism are upcoming rivals. Smaller than Savannah and Charleston, and with fewer tourist-related attractions, Beaufort often gets overlooked

HILTON HEAD

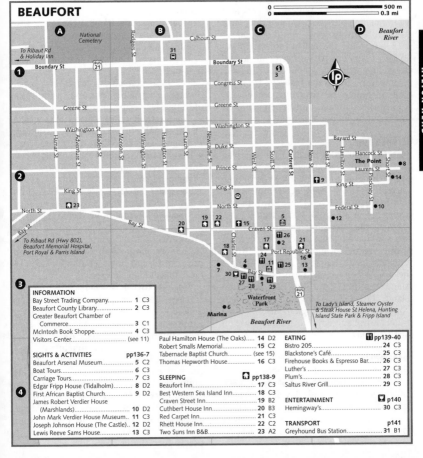

BEAUFORT

0 —————— 500 m
0 —————— 0.3 mi

INFORMATION	
Bay Street Trading Company	**1** C3
Beaufort County Library	**2** C3
Greater Beaufort Chamber of Commerce	**3** C1
McIntosh Book Shoppe	**4** C3
Visitors Center	(see 11)

SIGHTS & ACTIVITIES	pp136-7
Beaufort Arsenal Museum	**5** C2
Boat Tours	**6** C3
Carriage Tours	**7** C3
Edgar Fripp House (Tidalholm)	**8** D2
First African Baptist Church	**9** D2
James Robert Verdier House (Marshlands)	**10** D2
John Mark Verdier House Museum	**11** C3
Joseph Johnson House (The Castle)	**12** D2
Lewis Reeve Sams House	**13** C3

Paul Hamilton House (The Oaks)	**14** D2
Robert Smalls Memorial	**15** C2
Tabernacle Baptist Church	(see 15)
Thomas Hepworth House	**16** C3

SLEEPING	pp138-9
Beaufort Inn	**17** C2
Best Western Sea Island Inn	**18** C3
Craven Street Inn	**19** B2
Cuthbert House Inn	**20** B3
Red Carpet Inn	**21** C2
Rhett House Inn	**22** C2
Two Suns Inn B&B	**23** A2

EATING	pp139-40
Bistro 205	**24** C3
Blackstone's Café	**25** C3
Firehouse Books & Espresso Bar	**26** C3
Luther's	**27** C3
Plum's	**28** C3
Saltus River Grill	**29** C3

ENTERTAINMENT	p140
Hemingway's	**30** C3

TRANSPORT	p141
Greyhound Bus Station	**31** B1

A STAR IS BORN

Many filmmakers agree that Beaufort's pretty streets and antebellum homes make excellent backdrops for everything from Vietnam to Mississippi. Numerous films have been shot in Beaufort and its surrounding areas, including *The Big Chill*, *Forrest Gump* and *Rules of Engagement*. Beaufort's favorite literary son, Pat Conroy, who lives in the area, once said that all of his novels (which are mostly based on his experiences in South Carolina) were love letters to the city of Beaufort. Filmmakers took those letters to the big screen, bringing much adulation to the town through the scenic gems in *The Great Santini* and *The Prince of Tides*. Though locals are beginning to doubt it'll ever happen, the adaptation of Conroy's *Beach Music* is slated for filming in Beaufort, starring (rumor has it) Brad Pitt. You might see some familiar scenes while wandering around town. For more about movie locations, contact the **South Carolina Film Office** (☎ 803-737-0490; www.scfilmoffice.com).

on travelers' itineraries: but don't make that grievous mistake! Even an hour spent sitting on a bench along the Waterfront Park seawall, watching the tide rise above the marsh grass, will do your soul a world of good.

In late May, the **Gullah Festival** (☎ 843-525-0628) celebrates African arts, music and storytelling – and lots of good Gullah food. In mid-July, the **Water Festival** (☎ 843-524-0600) celebrates the river and sea bounty with music, dancing, tournaments and air shows put on by the Marines.

Orientation

Beaufort is 30 miles north of Hilton Head on Route 170. Hwy 21 comes in from the north, becoming Boundary St and then Carteret St as it approaches downtown and the Beaufort River. Downtown sits in a compact 4 sq miles along the river.

It's an easy town to walk around – you can see it all in just a few hours. Most businesses are located on Bay St, which intersects with Carteret St. just before the bridge connecting Beaufort to Lady's Island, Hunting Island State Park and Fripp Island. Ribaut Rd (Hwy 802) heads south from Boundary St through the fishing town of Port Royal and onto the military base on Parris Island.

Information

There are a couple of good bookstores in town, namely **McIntosh Book Shoppe** (☎ 843-524-1119; 917 Bay St) and **Bay Street Trading Company** (☎ 843-524-2000; 808 Bay St), which is the heart of the town's active literary community. You can find signed books by favorite son Pat Conroy here.

Beaufort County Library (☎ 843-525-4000; 311 Scott St) offers computers with free Internet access.

Beaufort Memorial Hospital (☎ 843-522-5200; 955 Ribaut Rd) is a full-service hospital located 3 miles west of downtown off Ribaut Rd.

The *Beaufort Gazette* is the town's daily newspaper.

The local **post office** (☎ 843-524-4746; 501 Charles St) is a few blocks north of the thick of things, between King and North Sts.

The **Greater Beaufort Chamber of Commerce** (☎ 843-986-5400, 800-638-3525; www.beaufortsc.org; 1106 Carteret St; ☺ 9am-5:30pm) distributes maps of the historic downtown area and organizes boat, carriage and walking tours. The chamber of commerce also runs a satellite **visitors center** (☎ 843-986-5400, 800-638-3525; cnr Bay & Scott Sts; ☺ 10am-5:30pm) in the basement of the historic John Mark Verdier House.

Museums

If you visit both of these museums, you can save $2 and buy a combo pass for $6 (available at either museum).

Beaufort Arsenal Museum (☎ 843-525-7077; 713 Craven St; admission $3; ☺ 11am-4pm Mon-Sat) is housed in the 1798 arsenal built for storing gunpowder and experimenting with explosives. Interesting exhibits cover the city's early Native American inhabitants and the extinct industries of sea-island cotton, commercial oystering and phosphate mining, as well as the antebellum past.

John Mark Verdier House Museum (☎ 843-379-6335; 801 Bay St; admission $5; ☺ 10:30am-3:30pm Mon-Sat) is an 1805 Federal-style home lovingly restored to its original glory, with period furnishings and a nice garden.

The Point

A high bluff in the eastern corner of Beaufort became the fashionable residential neighborhood during the height of the cotton boom. Some brochures call this the 'Old Point,' but locals are tender-yet-firm in pointing out that 'The Point' is the correct term. These old homes all face south to catch the ocean breezes, and have wide porches, raised basements and old trees lending a little shade. All of the homes in The Point are private residences, but a leisurely stroll for a bit of guarded voyeurism is a fun pastime.

WALKING TOUR OF THE POINT

Start at Bay St east of Carteret St. At 601 Bay St, the 1852 **Lewis Reeve Sams House** was used as a hospital by Union troops during the Civil War; afterwards, unlike most families, the original owners were able to reacquire their home. The house is a good example of the Beaufort style (raised basements in case of flooding).

Turn left onto New St, and you'll see the 1717 **Thomas Hepworth House** (214 New St), the oldest residence in Beaufort. The house has musket slits cut into the foundation, for protection against Indian attacks.

Go another block and turn right on to Craven St to find the **Joseph Johnson House** (411 Craven St), an 1850s solid-brick home known as **'The Castle'** because of its imposing Doric columns and stuccoed facade. It was featured on a 1960s promotional US travel poster, and the owners once hosted annual Christmas parties open to the entire town.

Turn left onto East St, then right on Federal St to Pinckney St. There, the 1814 **James Robert Verdier** mansion (501 Pinckney St), called **'Marshlands'** is a combination Barbados plantation house and formal Adams-style. The grandest part of the house faces the marsh, which would have been the entrance point for most visitors.

Take a left onto Pinckney St, a right onto King St, and left onto Short St to Laurens St. There, you'll find the **Paul Hamilton House** (100 Laurens St), called **'The Oaks.'** It is an Italianate house with a wide porch running along three sides. While pretending to look for your lost cat, sneak a peak at the **Edgar Fripp House** (1 Laurens St), better known as **Tidalholm.** This house hosted hosted the reunion of friends in the movie *The Big Chill.* Actor Tom Berenger got married on the lawn during the filming. Edgar Fripp built this summer home in 1856, then promptly lost it when Union troops occupied the town. When it was placed on the auction block, a generous Frenchman bought it and unexpectedly signed the deed back over to Fripp.

Wander along back the side streets and admire the pretty houses. If you take New St south, you'll get back to where you started.

Robert Smalls Memorial

In the yard of the **Tabernacle Baptist Church** (907 Craven St) is a bust of Civil War hero Robert Smalls. Smalls never rode beside General Robert E Lee or wore Confederate gray, though he was a slave in Beaufort at the time of the war and worked as a crewman for the Confederate Army on the steamer the *Planter.* Having some prior knowledge of the harbor, Smalls sneaked aboard the Confederate ship and piloted it into the hands of Union forces. Celebrated by some and vilified by others, Smalls joined the Union as part of the 1st South Carolina Volunteers, a regiment of freed slaves. After the war, Smalls invested the money that the Union had paid him for the *Planter* and became quite wealthy. He served in the Reconstruction-era government and in the US Congress for five terms. The wife of Smalls' former owner was elderly and penniless at the end of the war, and Smalls gave her a room in his own house until her death.

National Cemetery

Just outside the historic district, the **National Cemetery** (1601 Boundary St) is one of 12 such sites authorized for the burial of Civil War dead by President Abraham Lincoln in 1863. Live oaks and magnolias make this a serene resting place for Confederate and Union soldiers, including members of the African American Massachusetts 55th and 54th Infantry who were killed in the battle at Folly Beach. Memorial Day services are held in May, when graves are decorated with US flags. The cemetery is open daily during daylight hours.

Tours

A variety of tours are available. Ask at a visitors center for details about fishing, walking and bus tours.

HILTON HEAD

CARRIAGE TOURS

Horse-drawn carriage tours are available from the downtown marina parking lot. **Carolina Buggy Tours** (☎ 843-525-1300) and **Southern Rose Buggy Tours** (☎ 843-524-2900) offer comparable 45-minute tours that depart often throughout the day. Both charge adult/child $16/7.

BOAT TOURS

The best way to embrace the charm of Beaufort and the surrounding area is by getting on the water. Experienced tour operators who live and breathe the ebbing tides and saltwater air make excellent guides to the area. A variety of boat tours leave from the city marina, beside Waterfront Park.

Lowcountry Rafting Adventures (☎ 843-986-1051, 877-722-7238; www.lowcountryraftingadventures.com) offers fun and informative tours of the ACE Basin and surrounding barrier islands in a motorized raft, leaving from the downtown marina. Two-hour tours cost adult/child $25/20 and leave daily at 12:30pm and 3pm; four-hour tours are $75/70 (includes lunch) and leave at 8am Monday, Wednesday and Friday.

ACE Basin Tours (☎ 843-521-3099, 888-814-3129; Coosaw Island) takes a 38ft pontoon through the rivers and estuaries of the ACE Basin. The boat leaves from Coosaw Island, 9 miles northeast of Beaufort, via Hwy 802. Three-hour tours cost adult/child $30/15 and leave at 10am Wednesday and Saturday, or by appointment.

Island Steamship Company (☎ 843-524-4000; www.islandercruises.com) offers 1¾-hour tours aboard the *Islander* steamship, leaving from the downtown marina. The cost is adult/child $20/12, and departure is at 2pm Tuesday, Thursday, Saturday and Sunday.

Sleeping

Grand architectural gems turned into gentle B&Bs confirm Beaufort's air of authentic history and gentility. You've got many choices of charming lodging, most of which come with a delicious breakfast and friendly hosts. Staying in the historic district can be expensive, however, and you'll do well to reserve ahead. Rates given are for high season (spring and summer). All B&Bs are nonsmoking, but you can

usually smoke on the outside verandas. A 10% room tax is added to the bill.

Red Carpet Inn (☎ 843-521-1121, 800-251-1962; 301 Carteret St; s/d $65/75; P ⊠ ⊠) All rooms at this inexpensive motel are basic, but each one comes equipped with a fridge and microwave or stove. Though lacking in charm, it is a good value and is the cheapest place in the historic district.

Best Western Sea Island Inn (☎ 843-522-2090, 800-528-1234; www.sea-island-inn.com; 1015 Bay St; d $115-125; P ⊠ ⊠) No ordinary Best Western, this lovely lodge-style hotel sits right on Bay St, across from the waterfront. The 43 rooms offer comfortable accommodations, and the price includes breakfast.

Craven Street Inn (☎ 843-522-1668, 888-522-0250; www.thecravenstreetinn.com; 1103 Craven St; d $125-195; P ⊠ ⊠) Housed in an 1870 Victorian home with original fireplaces and pine floors, this B&B has rooms in the main house, in the carriage house and in the cottage on the pretty property.

Two Suns Inn B&B (☎ 843-522-1122, 800-532-4244; www.twosunsinn.com; 1705 Bay St; d $130-170; P ⊠ ⊠) With just six guest rooms, this cozy inn has excellent views of the bay. You'll want to claim the porch swing and watch the sun go down as you enjoy a sip of complimentary evening sherry. Rooms are uniquely designed, and innkeepers Henri and Patricia are full of good area information.

Beaufort Inn (☎ 843-521-9000; www.beaufortinn.com; 809 Port Republic St; d $145-245; P ⊠ ⊠) This large, pink dollhouse-like abode was built in 1897. Completely renovated in the '90s, it has every ounce of 19th-century charm, but with full modern amenities, like spacious rooms, luxurious bathtubs, super comfortable beds and nice touches (lavender soap, bathrobes and rich linens). In addition to the inn, small cottages on the property offer privacy, hardwood floors, poster beds and similar amenities. A full gourmet breakfast is served. The formal restaurant (p140) is among the best in the Lowcountry.

Rhett House Inn (☎ 843-524-9030; www.rhetthouseinn.com; 1009 Craven St; d $165-235; P ⊠ ⊠) Barbra Streisand stayed here while location scouting for *The Prince of Tides*. Obviously she liked what she saw, and we do too. In a picture-perfect 1820s plantation house, with luxurious rooms and special touches like afternoon tea and evening hors d'oeuvres, this place will make you swoon. Soon, you won't give a damn about anything, except relaxing with a good book on the double piazza. Breakfast is included.

Cuthbert House Inn (☎ 843-521-1315, 800-327-9275; www.cuthberthouseinn.com; 1203 Bay St; d $195-225; P ❄ ✕) On a prestigious perch overlooking the waterfront, this B&B is listed on the National Register of Historic Places. Rooms are outfitted with period furniture, and all have TVs, phones and refrigerators.

On Hwy 21 outside of town are several chain hotels and motels ranging from new and clean to tired and worn. The nicest of them is the **Holiday Inn** (☎ 843-524-2144, 2001 Boundary St/Hwy 21; d $70-90), at the junction of Hwy 802.

Eating

When locals are asked where to find a good meal, most recommend catching it and cooking it yourself. Every Beaufortonian is a well-heeled angler, crabber and clammer. This makes for charming conversation but rarely leads to a dinner invitation. For the tourists, however, there are a handful of fine restaurants serving the fruits of the sea. Most downtown restaurants are closed on Sunday.

Firehouse Books & Espresso Bar (☎ 843-522-2665; 706 Craven St; wraps $6.75; ☺ 7:30am-7pm Mon-Sat, 9am-3pm Sun) Sit surrounded by books in this old firehouse turned coffeehouse/restaurant/bookstore. Java, homemade desserts, delicious wraps and deli sandwiches, plus outdoor seating, make it a nice place to linger.

Blackstone's Café (☎ 843-524-4330; 205 Scott St; breakfast & lunch $5-8) Perhaps the best place in town for a full breakfast, Blackstone's has local favorites like corned beef hash or shrimp 'n' grits topped with cheese. It's also a great place for soups and sandwiches at lunch.

Plums (☎ 843-525-1946; 904½ Bay St; lunch $5-9, dinner $12-24) Tucked behind the storefronts of Bay St, and with outside tables overlooking the water, Plum's is a must-visit for its casual atmosphere, great value and gourmet versions of seafood classics, such as blue crab cake with wasabi slaw and Thai pepper sauce, or ginger-crusted grouper. Be sure to ask the ultrafriendly staff about the daily specials. It's a 'jeans and flip-flops' kind of place – and a favorite of Hollywood refugee Tom Berenger.

HILTON HEAD

HALLELUJAH!

West Africans first came to the South Carolina sea islands via the Caribbean as slaves. They toiled on plantations and moved among the islands, developing new dialects, new cuisines and new stories. After the Civil War, emancipated slaves remained on the islands and began to carve out their futures and identities as free Americans. While they fostered new traditions in everything from spirituality to industry, they also fought to preserve the old traditions that were, it seemed, slowly disappearing.

A Gullah woman named Marlena Smalls decided to do something about it. In 1985 she started the Gullah Festival in Beaufort, a hugely popular annual celebration of music and culture. Then, in 1990, concerned that the folklore and oral history of the Gullah people would one day just simply vanish, Smalls created the Hallelujah Singers. The musical group gave sweet voice to the hymns and rhythms of Africa; they resurrected the plantation melodies and the stories that the slaves had held onto tight as hope.

Since 1990, the group has played all over the world, to international acclaim. They sang for the Queen of England, starred in TV documentaries and even hit the big screen (the group sang – and Marlena Smalls played Bubba's mother – in *Forrest Gump*). Through song, the Hallelujah Singers continue to pass on the cultural history and musical heritage of the Gullah people.

Despite a busy touring schedule, the Hallelujah Singers perform regularly at festivals and special concerts in Beaufort and at the Penn Center in St Helena (p141). The group also performs at the Arts Center of Coastal Carolina in Hilton Head (p130). For more information, call ☎ 843-379-3594.

Luther's (☎ 843-521-1888; 910 Bay St; lunch $6-9, dinner $15-20) In an old pharmacy building, Luther's will cure your hankering for a big juicy burger or steak. Casual outdoor seating overlooks the waterfront park.

Saltus River Grill (☎ 843-379-3474; 802 Bay St; dinner $18-25) Saltus is in a great location and has funky modern décor, a nice patio, and a menu that features fish, steak and a raw bar. It attracts the beautiful people, but it's something of a new kid on the block, and our verdict's still out. Both the service and food can be hit or miss here – but when it's a hit, it's all good.

Bistro 205 (☎ 843-524-4994; 205 West St; dinner $18-25; ⊙ Tue-Sat only) Reservations are essential at this fashionable bistro whose menu is devoted to adding sophisticated twists to the freshest Lowcountry ingredients. Like a spa for seafood, shrimp and fish come here to get a total makeover before going out to party. Try the macadamia-encrusted mahi mahi, or the crab cakes with peach Dijon sauce.

Beaufort Inn (☎ 843-521-9000; 809 Port Republic St; dishes $18-30; ⊙ 6-10pm, plus brunch 11am-2pm Sun) Highly regarded as one of the best restaurants in the Lowcountry, the inn's restaurant offers excellent regional dishes and a wine list as long and complete as a Carolina summer. Try the tasty Lowcountry

bouillabaisse, or the shrimp 'n' grits, which just ooze with garlic and basil flavors.

Across the bridge on Lady's Island, **Steamer Oyster & Steak House** (☎ 843-522-0210; 168 Sea Island Pkwy; lunch $5-9, dinner $8-22; ⊙ Mon-Sat) is an essential stop-off for any traveler. Once you've sucked out the juicy seafood, a big bucket in the middle of the table fills up with all your oyster shells and empty crab legs. Steamers serves giant platters of fresh local seafood, steaks and the legendary Frogmore stew (p56), a famed local dish of shrimp, sausage, corn and seasonings. There's also a kid's menu.

Entertainment

Though Beaufort's not exactly a rockin' town, a few places liven up in the evenings. Try **Hemingway's** (☎ 843-521-4480; 920 Bay St), a fun pub with good snacks and live music on the weekends. A bar scene often forms on weekend evenings at **Plums** (p139), and **Steamer's Pub**, part of the Steamer Oyster & Steak House (above) on Lady's Island, has karaoke Wednesday and weekend live music.

Getting There & Away

The nearest major airports are in Savannah (45 miles away) and Charleston (65 miles away). There's also a small regional airport

---

DETOUR: SCENIC DRIVE TO THE CLAY HILLS

This drive takes you on two-lane country roads from the salt marshes of the coast to the fragrant pine forests of the Midlands.

From **Beaufort**, take Hwy 21 N to Old Sheldon Church Rd; follow signs to **Yemassee**, which hosts an annual shrimp festival in September. At Yemassee the road turns into Hwy 68 and follows the railroad tracks past abandoned country stores, one-intersection downtowns and clapboard churches within tippling distance of squat, concrete liquor stores. Soon you'll reach **Hampton**, which hosts an annual midsummer watermelon festival. Tune your radio to 92.1FM for a local morning chat show. Hwy 68 will turn into Hwy 278 near **Allendale**, which hosts an annual spring cooter fest (a cooter is a turtle).

As the Spanish moss begins to disappear, you are approaching **Barnwell**, the birthplace of James Brown. The town has yet to erect a memorial to the Godfather of Soul, but he was honored on James Brown Day a few years ago. Brown was reportedly so impressed with the school band that he donated money for uniforms.

In Barnwell, take Hwy 3 to get to **Blackville** and its famous healing springs, just north of town. The former owner deeded the springs to God so private interests couldn't bottle the fine-tasting water.

Follow Hwy 78 to **Aiken** and tune your radio to 94.7FM for a mix of Latin, funk and James Brown tunes. About halfway there, you'll see on the right the **Williston Gin**, which gins cotton from October through January.

on Hilton Head Island (p132). By car, Beaufort is 25 miles from I-95; take I-95 to Hwy 17/21 to Garden's Corner, then take Hwy 21 to Beaufort.

Greyhound (☎ 843-524-4646; 1307 Boundary St), near the National Cemetery, runs daily buses to Savannah ($13.50, one hour), Charleston ($26, two hours) and Myrtle Beach ($45, 4½ hours).

AROUND BEAUFORT

The string of islands off the coast of Beaufort are crisscrossed by ribbons of sandy roads, shaded by swaying palmetto trees and decorated by produce-laden pickup trucks and veggie stands. Development is creeping in: Strip malls have blossomed along Hwy 21 on Lady's Island, and long lines of cars idle at the Beaufort bridge, waiting for sailboats to pass. But the last stoplight is always within sight, and beyond is a bold, blue sky merging with the tongues and fingers of the Atlantic Ocean.

St Helena Island

pop 9486

The largest of Beaufort's sea islands, St Helena (sint hell-*een*-uh) is an Anglicization of the original Spanish name 'Punta de Santa Elenas,' so named during a Spanish exploration of the area in 1521. The island's planters were said to have protested the French government's decision to exile Napoleon to St Helena in 1815, only to discover that there is more than one St Helena in the world.

After the Civil War, freed slaves lived in relative isolation and were able to preserve their strong Gullah culture – the language, food, music and folk tales. St Helena's Penn School became first school for newly emancipated slaves. During the Civil War, five Gullah regiments from the area fought alongside the Massachusetts 54th, the regiment made famous by the film *Glory*.

At the island's only major crossroads is the small town of Frogmore, more commonly known as the Four Corners Community, centered around Hwy 21 and Martin Luther King Jr Blvd. One or two modest storefronts define the downtown. Farther east, small dirt roads sport street signs that read 'Joe Polite Rd' or 'Clarence Mitchell Rd' – when the emergency

telephone service system was put in place and emergency vehicles needed to located specific streets, the roads were christened after their longtime residents.

SIGHTS & ACTIVITIES

Right at the Four Corners is **Red Piano Too** (☎ 843-838-2241; 780 Sea Island Pkwy; ☻ 10am-6pm), an excellent gallery with the works of local artists and craftspeople who live steeped in Lowcountry traditions. It also sells maps of historic St Helena ($5). Also near the crossroads and not to be missed, **Ms Natalie's Workshop** (☎ 843-838-4446; 802 Sea Island Pkwy) is the whimsical shop of Natalie and Ron Daise, creators of the popular children's TV series *Gullah Gullah Island*. A craft room and periodic classes bring people from all ages and walks of life.

Turn right at Martin Luther King Jr Rd to reach **Penn Center** (☎ 843-838-2432; www.penncenter .com), the first school for freed slaves in the US. Opened in 1862 by missionaries from Pennsylvania, Penn Center began in a single room on the former Oaks Plantation and quickly expanded to the complex seen today. By 1900, the school adopted the Tuskegee University curriculum and gave training in agricultural and technical skills. The state assumed responsibility for educating the island's African American population in 1948, but Penn Center's facilities were used as a school until 1953.

In the '60s, Dr Martin Luther King, Jr and members of the Southern Christian Leadership came here to plan strategies and train leaders during the Civil Rights movement.

The 50-acre, 19-building campus provides after-school learning programs to sea-island children, promotes environmental issues and conducts lectures and courses on the history of the Gullah people. Rocked by financial strain, the center struggles to continue its important work.

On the campus, the **York W Bailey Museum** (☎ 843-838-2432; admission $4; ☻ 11am-4pm Mon-Sat), named after a Penn school graduate and the island's first black doctor, covers the school's history and cultural aspects of the sea islanders. You can pick up a self-guided walking-tour map of the campus here.

At the **Ibile Indigo House** (☎ 843-838-3884), you can witness the once viable, age-old art of organic indigo processing. You can dye your own clothing, or take a workshop.

HILTON HEAD

Hours and schedules are sporadic, so call to find out what's happening ahead of time. Penn Center celebrates Heritage Days in early November, with parades, Gullah crafts and gospel performances.

SLEEPING & EATING
Only one bare-bones hotel caters to guests on St Helena, but a few restaurants offer authentic Gullah cuisine.

Royal Frogmore Inn (☎ 843-838-5400; 863 Sea Island Pkwy; d $60; P ☒ ☒) Bland and eeking its way into disrepair, the only place to stay on St Helena isn't so royal, but it offers a cheap place to stay in lovely downtown Frogmore. Rumor has it the inn is for sale for $1,250,000.

Ultimate Eating (☎ 843-838-1314; 859 Sea Island Pkwy; mains $5-10; ☺ 6am-9pm) Next door to the Royal Frogmore Inn, this local spot serves honest-to-goodness Gullah food, including ribs, sweet-potato chips, crabs straight from the marsh and Frogmore stew (see p56). Try the mouthwatering lunch buffet.

Just before the bridge to Harbor Island, on the east side of St Helena and about 6 miles past the Four Corners, is the **Shrimp Shack** (☎ 843-838-2962; 1929 Sea Island Pkwy; shrimp burger $6). Sitting in a little sandlot, the simple, blue shack is like a fast-food joint specializing in – you guessed it – shrimp! Try the shrimp burger (essentially a crab cake on a bun). Something of a regional icon, Shrimp Shack draws people en route to Hunting Island (below) for a leisurely lunch on the screened-in porch.

Hunting Island State Park
The only public beach in the area, **Hunting Island** (☎ 843-838-2011; 2555 Sea Island Pkwy; day pass $3 ; ☺ 6am-6pm, til 9pm summer), 16 miles east of Beaufort, is straight out of a conquistador's diary. The island wasn't settled until the late 1930s, and it still retains its wild appearance. A narrow blacktop road winds through a thick canopy of palm and live oak trees that fracture the sunlight into golden bands – not a house or human in sight. Local planters used the island as hunting grounds for deer and raccoons in the 19th century, hence its name.

This 4-mile-long, 1-mile-wide island also exemplifies the dynamic nature of barrier islands. The islands lying off the coast of

South Carolina were formed about 4000 years ago by a buildup of sediment from as far away as the Appalachian Mountains. Tides, hurricanes and storms toss loose sand from one end of an island to another – and from one island to another.

Because of its front-row seat on the Atlantic Ocean, Hunting Island is more vulnerable to erosion than less seaward islands. It's estimated that the island loses 10ft of shore a year. The missing beach is evident during high tides, when the water rushes into the maritime forest and swallows once high-ground boardwalks. The receding sea leaves behind carcasses of trees, steals the sand dunes and dumps shells and shark teeth for the beachcombers, who can walk for miles and not see a soul.

The lighthouse in the center of the island is like an erosion measuring stick. It used to be 1¼ miles from the highest tide; now it's less than 400ft. You can climb the 175 recently renovated lighthouse steps (10am to 5pm) to get sweeping views of the beautiful coastline.

At the southern end of the island are 18 **cabins** (mostly $190/540 weekend/weekdays), many bordering the ocean or the lagoon. At the north end is the 190-site **campground** (sites $23). The park headquarters handles reservations for both the cabins and the campground. Public beach access is available at South Beach and North Beach. The park's headquarters features displays on the island's tidal erosion, as well as on its flora and fauna. A nature center at the fishing pier before the bridge to Fripp Island displays shells, plants and animals commonly seen on the beach, as well as exhibits on the loggerhead turtle (see boxed text p46), which nests on the island.

Fripp Island
This **private resort** (☎ 843-838-3535, 800-845-4100; www.frippislandresort.com; 1 Tarpon Blvd) sits on 3000 acres 19 miles east of Beaufort. A residential community with tennis, golf and kids' activities programs, Fripp attracts families who usually rent private houses for a week or two at a time. More than 300 properties are for rent, making the year-round population almost nonexistent. Renting a house will cost about $1200 to

$2600 per week, depending on size, location and time of year. Check the website to see what's available.

Parris Island

All new Marine recruits from east of the Mississippi River (and all female recruits nationwide) come here for basic training. The summers are hot, the sand fleas bite, and the 13-week regimen is grueling. Still, some 18,000 men and 1500 women complete the training every year.

Visitors used to be able to wander around freely, but increased security over the past few years has changed all that. Visitors are welcome to tour the **museum** (☎ 843-228-2951; admission free; ✆ 10am-4pm) in the War Memorial Building, which covers the military history of the Marines and Parris Island, as well as an archaeological display on the area's early Spanish outpost. From downtown Beaufort, take Ribaut Rd (Hwy 280) south and follow the signs. They'll give you directions at the main gate.

Charleston

CONTENTS

Overflowing with charming streets and historic districts, Charleston is one of the oldest and most appealing urban areas in America. Its history is peppered with defining moments in US history – Charleston fueled American patriotism in the Revolutionary War; its Confederate soldiers fired the first shots of the Civil War; and the Civil Rights era rocked the cultural landscape, one whose success had grown on the backs of slavery and segregation. This is a city where rampant fires, ignited during the Revolutionary and Civil Wars, torched homes and left Charleston simmering in a charred state of ruin. Tropical hurricanes continually test the city's resolve, storming in and blowing away dreams. But despite its heated political history and glut of natural disasters, Charleston managed, miraculously, to keep her head held high. Unlike many cities in the US, Charleston embraced her history instead of shopping around for a new one. It never recreated itself, it simply opened its heart to what it already had.

Today, this birthplace of Southern hospitality oozes with charm, elegance and a whole lot of whimsy. Blooming gardenias, magnolias, lavender and jasmine send intoxicating scents meandering through the streets. Grand pillars of early American architecture abound alongside formal and wild gardens. You can shuck oysters dockside or dine on haute cuisine, sip vintage *vino* on an open-air deck or swill a beer on a shrimping boat. The friendly people will happily share the city's history and secrets. Whether you choose to wander on your own or to join one of many cultural tours, Charleston will leave its sultry, saltwater kiss lingering on your skin.

HIGHLIGHTS

- **Wining**
  The encyclopedic wine list at Vintage (p166)
- **Dining**
  Spooning up the city's best she-crab soup at Anson (p166)
- **Green Haven**
  The gardens at Middleton Place and Magnolia Plantation (p154)
- **Wildlife Encounter**
  Indigenous creatures at the South Carolina Aquarium (p152)
- **Offbeat Experience**
  A nighttime Charleston Ghost Tour (p161), leaving from Waterfront Park

CHARLESTON

| ▪ TELEPHONE CODE: **843** | ▪ POPULATION: **96,650** | ▪ AREA: **88 SQ MI** |

ORIENTATION

The Charleston metropolitan area sprawls over a broad stretch of coastal plains and islands, but the historic heart is very compact – it consists of about 4 sq miles at the southern tip of a peninsula between the Cooper and Ashley Rivers. I-26 goes to North Charleston and the airport. Hwy 17, the main coastal road, cuts across the Charleston peninsula as the Crosstown Expressway, with soaring bridges connecting west to James Island and West Ashley, and east over the Cooper River to Mount Pleasant.

Charleston's main north–south streets are Meeting, Church and King Sts; Market and Broad Sts are the main streets running east–west.

INFORMATION
Bookshops

Boomer's Books (☎ 843-722-2666; 420 King St) Stocks room after room of used books.
Waldenbooks (☎ 843-853-1736; 120 Market St) Has a good selection of fiction and nonfiction, including regional titles.

Emergency

Emergency numbers (☎ 911) Police, ambulance, firefighters.
AAA Roadside Service (☎ 800-222-4357)

Internet Access

Charleston has not embraced the Internet café concept, but you can use the computers at the public library (below).

Internet Resources

www.charlestoncvb.com The official Convention & Visitors Bureau website, full of good information on dining, hotels and attractions.
www.charleston.com Coupons, attractions and real estate information.
www.charlestonloop.com Gay and lesbian online newsletter.
www.discoversouthcarolina.com Information on the whole state.

Libraries

Charleston Public Library (☎ 843-805-6930; 68 Calhoun St) Offers free Internet access.
Charleston Preservation Society (☎ 843-722-4630; 147 King St) Has a bookshop and upstairs resource room full of historical documents.
Historic Charleston Foundation Preservation Center (☎ 843-723-1623, 40 E Bay St) Has a resource library, by appointment only.

Media
PUBLICATIONS

Post & Courier Charleston's daily newspaper
Charleston City Paper An alternative weekly, published on Wednesday. Good entertainment and restaurant listings.

CHARLESTON IN...

Two Days

Start your visit in Charleston by sipping a coffee on a bench in **Waterfront Park** or on the **Battery** overlooking Charleston Harbor. Before the sun gets too hot, take the Charleston Walking Tour (p158) to see the best of the city's historic sites. By then you'll be ready for lunch at **Hyman's** or **Sticky Fingers**. Afterward, take a stroll or shop for souvenirs in shops and stalls of the **Old City Market**. Head up to the **Pavilion Bar** in the Market Pavilion Hotel for sunset and pre-dinner cocktails. Have a Lowcountry seafood dinner at **Hank's** or **Magnolia**.

Day two, get up at a leisurely pace and head down to Aquarium Wharf for a visit to the **South Carolina Aquarium**. Afterward, head next door to the **Fort Sumter Visitor Education Center** and sign up for a boat tour over to the historic fort. Bring along a picnic lunch from the **E Bay Deli**. Take an afternoon and then go for a special dinner at **Il Cortile Dei Re**, followed by a romantic nighttime **carriage ride** through the streets.

Three Days

Follow the two-day itinerary and take advantage of the third day by making a trip out to the Ashley River Rd Plantations. Take in **Middleton Place** in the morning, followed by **Magnolia Plantation** or **Drayton Hall** in the afternoon. In the evening, watch the fishing boats unload their catch of the day at one of the waterside restaurants at **Shem Creek Marina**, in Mount Pleasant.

Barfly A monthly magazine telling the local secrets of the bar scene.

RADIO
MPAL 100.9FM Urban Contemporary
WAVF 96.1FM Alternative
WEZL 103.5FM Country/classic rock/talk radio
WSCI 89.3FM NPR
WTMA 1250AM Talk radio and news

Medical Services
Charleston Memorial Hospital (☎ 843-577-0600; 326 Calhoun St)
Eckerd Pharmacy (☎ 843-723-0263; 334 E Bay St)

Money
Charleston levies a 6% tax on accommodations, along with the 6% state tax. You'll find ATMs throughout the city. There are several full-service banks along Meeting St. A couple of banks are on the map.

Post
Main post office (☎ 843-577-0690; 83 Broad St) In the federal building at the corner of Meeting and Broad Sts.

Tourist Offices
Charleston Visitors Center (☎ 843-853-8000, 800-774-0006; 375 Meeting St; ☽ 8am-5pm Mon-Sat) Well-stocked and helpful; can help with accommodations and tours. Its 23-minute *Charleston Forever* video is worth seeing ($2). You can also pick up coupons here for various sights and restaurants.
Convention & Visitors Bureau (www.charlestoncvb.com; 81 Mary St; ☽ 9am-5pm Mon-Fri)

DANGERS & ANNOYANCES
Charleston is a safe place, especially on the peninsula, where the downtown and historic districts are, and where tourists spend most of their time. The economic prosperity of the peninsula contrasts greatly with the poverty north of Mary St. Here, shotgun shacks stand like beacons of disparity compared with the grand homes of the historic district. Though it's fine to wander around during the day, travelers will feel safer staying within the tourist areas at night.

Though insects are prevalent in many US cities, Charleston gets an astounding number of palmetto bugs – essentially a genteel term for giant, flying cockroaches. Though exterminators work overtime to keep the bugs away, they thrive in the heat and humidity and are simply a fact of life here. They are harmless – the worst thing a palmetto can do is scare you. Mosquitoes, especially along the rivers and away from the coast, can do more harm that a monster cockroach. Bring bug spray.

SIGHTS
The main attraction is the city itself, especially the quarter south of Beaufain St and east of King St, where you can wander along elegant thoroughfares and quaint, bending backstreets. There are maps with walking tours, but an aimless stroll is just as good – Tradd, Meeting and Church Sts have some of the best buildings.

The **Old City Market**, on Market St between Meeting and E Bay Sts, is a bustling stretch of tourist shops, craft stalls, restaurants and bars. This is a great place to see Gullah women weaving sweetgrass baskets. Look for benne (sesame seed) wafers, sold by vendors at the market.

Overlooking the Cooper River near the tip of the peninsula, **Waterfront Park** is a shady retreat with spouting fountains that are usually teeming with kids or anyone looking for a cool splash. **White Point Park & Gardens**, at the tip of the peninsula, is superb at sunset, when the S Battery St mansions are beautifully illuminated. **Marion Square**, on Calhoun St between Meeting and King Sts, is a good spot for a picnic. **King St** is full of upscale shops and eateries. West of King St are residential blocks with colorfully painted houses that are less grand but still appealing. Farther north, around the **College of Charleston**, many smaller timber houses are somewhat timeworn, but the humble, tree-lined streets are a nice contrast to the posh neighborhoods.

Combination tickets for various historic attractions are available from the visitors center. The Charleston Heritage Passport (adult/child $34/23) is a good deal and includes the Nathaniel Russell House, Aiken-Rhett House, Edmonston-Alston House, Gibbes Museum of Art, and the plantation homes of Drayton Hall and Middleton Place.

Historic Houses
Quite a few fine historic houses are open to visitors. Discounted combination tickets may tempt you to see more, but one or

CHARLESTON

CHARLESTON

CHARLESTON

A

INFORMATION
Bank of America.................................. 1 G4
Boomer's Books.................................. 2 F3
Charleston Public Library.................... 3 G3
Charleston Visitors Center................... 4 F2
Convention & Visitors Bureau.............. 5 F2
Eckerd Pharmacy................................ 6 G3
Preservation Society of Charleston....... 7 G5
Wachovia Bank................................... 8 H5
Walden Books..................................... 9 G4

SIGHTS & ACTIVITIES   pp147-57
Aiken-Rhett House............................. 10 F2
Avery Research Center........................ 11 E4
Bicycle Shoppe.................................. 12 G3
Charleston Museum............................ 13 F2
Circular Congregational Church........... 14 G4
Denmark Vesey House......................... 15 E4
Edmonston-Alston House..................... 16 G6
Emanuel African Methodist Episcopal
  Church.. 17 F3
First Baptist Church........................... 18 G5
Fort Sumter Visitor & Education
  Center... 19 H2
French Huguenot Church..................... 20 G5
Gibbes Museum of Art........................ 21 G4
Halsey Gallery & Simon Center for
  the Arts... 22 F3
Harp of David Gate............................ 23 G2
Hazel Parker Playground..................... 24 H5
Heyward-Washington House................. 25 G5
John Rivers Communications
  Museum... 26 F3
Joseph Manigault House..................... 27 F3
Kahal Kadosh Beth Elochim................ 28 G4
Market Hall...................................... 29 G4
Mt Zion AME Church.......................... 30 F4
Nathaniel Russell House..................... 31 G5
Old Exchange & Provost Dungeon....... 32 H5
Old Slave Mart.................................. 33 G5
Olde Town Carriage Co...................... 34 G4
Palmetto Carriage Tours.............. (see 34)
Powder Magazine............................... 35 G4
South Carolina Aquarium.................... 36 H2
St John's Reformed Episcopal
  Church.................................... (see 17)
St Mary's Roman Catholic Church...... 37 G4
St Michael's Episcopal Church............ 38 G5
St Philip's Episcopal Church............... 39 G4

SLEEPING   pp162-5
1837 Bed & Breakfast........................ 40 F4
Andrew Pinckney Inn.......................... 41 G4
Ansonborough Inn.............................. 42 H4
Barksdale House Inn........................... 43 F3
Bed, No Breakfast.............................. 44 D4
Best Western King Charles Inn............ 45 G4
Charleston Place................................ 46 G4
Charleston's Historic Hostel & Inn....... 47 E2
Charleston's Not So Hostel................. 48 D2
Days Inn Downtown........................... 49 G4
Elliott House Inn............................... 50 G5
Hayne House..................................... 51 G6
Historic Charleston Bed & Breakfast.... 52 G5
Holiday Inn...................................... 53 F3
Indigo Inn....................................... 54 G4
Jasmine House.................................. 55 G4
Maison du Pré.................................. 56 G3
Market Pavilion Hotel........................ 57 H4
Meeting Street Inn............................ 58 G4
Meeting Street Suites........................ 59 G4
Mills House Hotel.............................. 60 G5
Planters Inn..................................... 61 G4
Two Meeting St Inn........................... 62 G6
Westin Francis Marion Hotel............... 63 F3

EATING   pp165-7
39 Rue de Jean................................. 64 F3
AW Shucks....................................... 65 G4

Andolini's Pizza................................ 66 F4
Anson... 67 G4
Basil... 68 F2
Bocci's.. 69 G4
Charleston Grill......................... (see 46)
East Bay Deli................................... 70 G3
Gaulart & Maliclet............................ 71 G5
Hank's Seafood Restaurant................. 72 G4
Hominy... 73 D3
Hyman's.. 74 G4
Il Cortile Del Re............................... 75 G4
Jestine's Kitchen.............................. 76 G3
Joseph's Restaurant.......................... 77 G5
Juanita Greenberg's Nacho Royale...... 78 F3
Magnolias.. 79 H4
Pinckney Café & Espresso................... 80 H4
Sermet's Corner................................ 81 F4
Slightly North of Broad...................... 82 H4
Southend Brewery & Smokehouse........ 83 H5
Sticky Fingers.......................... (see 59)
T-Bonz.. 84 G4
The Boathouse on East Bay................. 85 G2
The Terrace..................................... 86 F3
Vintage Restaurant & Wine Bar........... 87 H4
Wild Wing Café................................. 88 H4

ENTERTAINMENT   pp167-9
Big John's Tavern............................. 89 G4
Blind Tiger....................................... 90 G5
Charleston Ballet Theater................... 91 F3

Charlie's Little Bar............................ 92 H5
City Bar... 93 H4
Club Pantheon.................................. 94 F2
Cumberlands.................................... 95 G4
Dock St Theater................................ 96 G5
Dudley's.. 97 F2
Footlight Players Theater................... 98 G5
Gaillard Auditorium........................... 99 G3
Griffon Pub..................................... 100 H4
IMAX Theater.................................. 101 H2
Meritage... 102 G4
Mezzané................................... (see 81)
Momma's Blues Palace...................... 103 F3
Music Farm..................................... 104 F2
Pavilion Bar.............................. (see 57)
Vendu Rooftop Bar........................... 105 H5
Vickery's.. 106 F4

SHOPPING   pp169-70
Eighty-Two Church........................... 107 G5
George C Birland & Co...................... 108 G4
Historic Charleston Foundation
  Museum Shop................................ 109 G5
Historic Charleston Reproductions.... 110 G5
King St Antique Mall........................ 111 E2
Old Charleston Joggling Board Co....112 E1

Hampton
Park

The
Citadel

Macy Murray Dr
Moultrie St
President St
Elmwood Ave
Parkwood Ave
Sutherland Ave
Huger St
Ashley Ave
Rutledge Ave
Race St
King St
78
Tracy St
Sumter St
Percy St
Congress St
Sumter St
Fishburne St
President St
17
Bogard St
Rose Lane
Ashe St
Percy St
Hagood Ave
Norman St
Kracke St
48
Spring St
Ashley Ave
71
73
Ashton St
Cannon St
17
Rutledge Ave
Bee St
17
MUSC
Medical
Complex
Lockwood Blvd
To West Ashley, Drayton
Hall, Magnolia Plantation,
Middleton Place, Kiawah
Island, Edisto Island,
Beaufort & Savannah (GA)
Courtenay Dr
Doughty St
Mill St
Charleston
Memorial
Hospital
44
Ashley River
Bridge
James
Island
Connector
30
To James Island
& Folly Beach
Alberta
Long Lake
Cadden St
Barre St
Halsey Blvd
Lockwood Dr
City
Marina

Joseph
P Riley
Jr Park

CHARLESTON

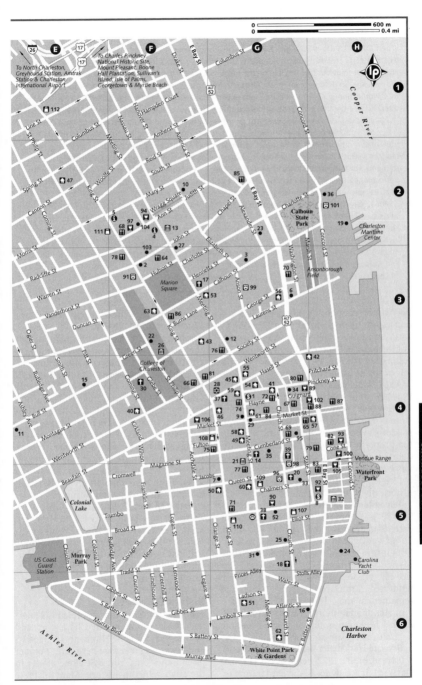

SPOLETO USA

When Pulitzer Prize–winning composer Gian Carlo Menotti founded the *Festival dei Due Mondi* (Festival of Two Worlds) in Spoleto, Italy, he said he wanted to prove that art was 'not only an after-dinner mint but that it could be the main meal itself.' It was with that same sentiment that he brought the Spoleto Festival to Charleston in 1977. He wanted to create an American celebration that would honor all forms of art, from experimental dance to classical ballet, heart-wrenching opera to live theater, abstract painting to pretty poetry, solo acoustics to symphonies of sound.

He checked out several cities in the Southeast – Richmond, Charlotte, Atlanta, New Orleans, Houston and Miami. Charleston won out, because for a festival of such artistic magnitude, the chosen city needed to be an art form in itself. With Charleston's architectural bounty, its glorious gardens and its dedication to historical preservation, it seemed the perfect place (not to mention Charleston has a longstanding history of cultural appreciation). The city had the first performance theater in the US (the Dock St Theater), the first museum, the first ballet, and the first real population of cultural patrons and connoisseurs.

For 17 days in May and June, **Spoleto USA** (☎ 843-722-2764; www.spoletousa.com) trumpets, dances, sings and colors its way across the city. More than 130 performances take place in theaters, churches, on plantations, and in parks and gardens. National and international audiences so loved Spoleto that they augmented it with **Piccolo Spoleto**, another explosion of the arts that follows on the heels of Spoleto. Culture creatures of every persuasion delight in the air of arts and musical melodies that overcome the city.

There are no after-dinner mints here – indeed, Spoleto USA is a full-meal deal.

two will be enough for most people. Most houses are open 10am to 5pm Monday to Saturday and 1pm to 5pm Sunday, and guided tours are run every half hour or so. Admission is $7 to $9. The following are a few of the most interesting.

Aiken-Rhett House (☎ 843-723-1159; 48 Elizabeth St) is the only surviving urban plantation and gives a good look at antebellum life – and more than a cursory look at the role of slaves. Along with the 1818 home, the property includes well-preserved slave quarters and other outbuildings. The house has been preserved but will never receive a face-lift, resulting in a less pretty but historically interesting tour.

Edmonston-Alston House (☎ 843-722-7171; 21 E Bay St) is wonderfully located along the battery in front of the harbor. The 1828 home was built in the late Federal style by Edmonston, a Scottish shipping merchant. In 1838, the house was purchased by rice-plantation mogul Charles Alston and renovated in the Greek Revival style. It has remained in the Alston family ever since – in fact, the family still resides on the 3rd floor. The home is full of original period portraits, porcelain and furniture.

Heyward-Washington House (☎ 843-722-0354; 87 Church St), built c 1772, belonged to Thomas Heyward, Jr – a signer of the Declaration of Independence. When George Washington visited in 1791, he rented the house. Though the outside isn't much to look at, the interior contains some fine examples of Charleston-made mahogany furniture.

Joseph Manigault House (☎ 843-723-2926; 350 Meeting St) was the showpiece of a French Huguenot family who made their fortune trading rum, sugar and rice. Built on the edge of town in 1803, in a newly expanding subdivision, this Adams-style house was designed by the owner's brother Gabriel, who is credited for introducing the architectural style to the city. The house was saved from near demolition in the 1920s and now displays period furniture.

Nathaniel Russell House (☎ 843-724-8481; 51 Meeting St) was built by a Rhode Islander, known in Charleston as 'the king of the Yankees.' His 1808 Federal-style townhouse is noted especially for its spectacular, self-supporting spiral staircase and lovely formal garden.

Historic Churches

From the city's beginnings, religious tolerance was fashionable in Charleston, and persecuted French Huguenots, Baptists and Jews sought refuge here. The number of churches on Church St alone attests to the city's religious history. Many of these congregations are the oldest of their faiths in the US. Visitors are welcome to attend religious services (call the churches for times).

French Huguenot Church (☎ 843-722-4385; 136 Church St) was founded in 1681 by French Protestant refugees. Congregants living on the Cooper River plantations came in boats, coming in on the ebb tide and leaving on the flood tide, which sometimes meant they'd be in church a long time. The 1845 pipe organ is considered one of the nation's most treasured musical relics.

St Michael's Episcopal Church (☎ 843-744-1334; 78 Meeting St), built in 1752, is the oldest church building in Charleston. George Washington and Robert E Lee sat in pew No 43 when they visited. In the church's graveyard, James L Petigru, the state's most outspoken Unionist, is buried. A talented and well-respected lawyer, he described South Carolina during the midst of the secession debates as being 'too small for a republic and too large for an insane asylum.' He was never dissuaded from this opinion and was described as the only person in South Carolina who did not secede. When a friend told him that Louisiana had joined the Confederacy, he replied 'Good God, I thought we had bought Louisiana.' The yard is open to visitors 9am to 4pm.

St Philip's Episcopal Church (☎ 834-722-7734; 146 Church St) has the oldest congregation in Charleston, dating from 1680. Statesman John C Calhoun and the author of *Porgy & Bess*, DuBose Heyward, are buried in the adjoining cemetery.

First Baptist Church (☎ 843-722-3896; 61 Church St) is the oldest Baptist church in the South and was established in 1699. The present structure was designed by Robert Mills, the first Federal architect, in 1822.

Emanuel African Methodist Episcopal Church (☎ 843-722-2561; 110 Calhoun St) is the oldest African Methodist Episcopal (AME) church in the South and the second oldest in the US. During slavery times, free blacks and slaves who had formerly worshiped at white Methodist churches left to join the AME movement.

Emanuel's congregation expanded into **Mt Zion AME Church** in 1882. Members of the 54th and 55th Massachusetts regiments, which were composed of black infantrymen, worshiped here. Sunday services feature six choirs ranging from classical to early spirituals.

St Mary's Roman Catholic Church (☎ 843-722-7696; 95 Hasell St) is the mother church for Catholics in the Carolinas and Georgia.

Kahal Kadosh Beth Elohim (☎ 843-723-1090; 90 Hasell St) is the oldest continuously used synagogue in the country (the oldest temple is in Savannah). Sephardic Orthodox Jews came to Charleston in the late 17th century. Fire burned the original synagogue, which was rebuilt in 1838. Along with the new

---

SYMBOL OF HOSPITALITY

Throughout Charleston, you'll see pineapple motifs everywhere – on doors, on iron gates, in the fountain at Waterfront Park, in stained-glass windows, even on wallpaper. This goes back to colonial days, when a pineapple was as sweet and rare as a summertime breeze.

In the Caribbean, the pineapple has long been a symbol of hospitality, and in colonial Charleston, the expensive and cherished fruit also symbolized wealth. Visitors gasped with delight when a pineapple appeared as a centerpiece at a dinner table; the presence of the fruit symbolized the height of generosity. When special guests spent the night, they'd be given rooms with pineapples carved into the doorframes or bedposts.

If a pineapple was placed at the entrance to a Caribbean village, explorers came to know that that meant they were welcome. This tradition became custom in colonial Charleston – returning seafaring captains would impale fresh pineapples on gateposts or piazzas, sending the message to friends that they'd made it home safely and that visitors were welcome.

Columns carved with pineapples showed up in doorways and at the entrance to plantations. Pineapples were stitched into needlework and formed into iron or brass door handles.

Look closely as you tour through Charleston. It won't take you long to realize you're welcome almost everywhere you turn.

ST MIKE'S BELLS

The impressive church bells at St Michael's Episcopal Church have traveled so much, they could write a trans-Atlantic travel guide. Charleston's precious bells were first imported from England in 1764. During the American Revolution, the British gave Charleston a slap in the face by hauling the bells back as a war prize. After the war, the bells returned. During the Civil War, having experienced what war can do, Charlestonians cleverly sent the bells to Columbia for safekeeping. It was a good idea gone sour – fire in Columbia damaged the bells, so they went back to England to be recast. They once again returned to Charleston, only to be damaged by Hurricane Hugo in 1989. Back for another recasting they went, until finally returning to the St Michael's in 1993. May they ring in peace.

---

building came new ideas, and the temple became home to the nation's first Reform congregation. Tours are available weekdays 10am to noon.

Museums

Charleston Museum (☎ 843-722-2996; www.charlestonmuseum.org; 360 Meeting St; adult/child $9/4; 9am-5pm Mon-Sat, 1-5pm Sun), opposite the visitors center, offers some excellent exhibits on the state's history. It's in a modern building but claims to be the country's oldest museum, founded in 1773. The permanent collection includes everything from Charleston's early silver collection to slave tags, natural history and important documents of American history. For $14, you can get a combination ticket to visit the museum and either the Joseph Manigault House or the Heyward-Washington House. For $18, you can visit all three. Once conservation work is completed, the Confederate submarine CSS *HL Hunley* will be displayed at the museum. Until then, the museum shows a model, the history of early submarine technology and coverage of the ship's recent discovery. Real submarine buffs can tour the 65,000lb *Hunley* as it's being restored ($10). Contact **Friends of the Hunley** (☎ 843-722-2333; www.hunley.org) for reservations or more information.

Gibbes Museum of Art (☎ 843-722-2706; www.gibbes.com; 135 Meeting St; adult/child $7/4; 10am-5pm Tue-Sat, 1-5pm Sun), established in 1905, is an American fine arts museum with an excellent collection of early Charleston depictions, along with portraits and miniatures of South Carolina's aristocracy.

Old Exchange & Provost Dungeon (☎ 843-727-2165; www.oldexchange.com; 122 E Bay St; adult/child $7/3.50; 9am-5pm) is a Palladian structure that was built in 1771 as an exchange and customs house for the busy port. As resentment toward England began to boil, Charlestonians met here to protest the controversial Tea Act in 1773 and to elect delegates to the Continental Congress in 1774. The city had more wind in its sails than ammunition in its reserves, and it was easily occupied by English troops near the start of the Revolutionary War. Prominent patriots were thrown into the building's dungeon, where outlaws and pirates were once imprisoned. Stede Bonnet, 'the gentleman pirate' (see boxed text opposite) was one of the dungeon's famous occupants.

The **Powder Magazine** (☎ 843-805-6730; 79 Cumberland St; admission free; 10am-5pm Mon-Sat, 2-5pm Sun mid-Mar–mid-Oct), the oldest building in Charleston, was built in 1712 just inside the fortified walls that protected the early city from Spanish, pirate and Indian attacks. Its supply of ammunition and gunpowder was crucial to the defense of the city. This low-slung building is constructed of tabby, a brick-like material made from crushed oyster shells.

Aquarium Wharf

The Aquarium Wharf surrounds pretty Liberty Square and is a great place to stroll around and watch the tugboats guiding ships into port. Charleston is the seventh largest container port in the US. The wharf is home to the South Carolina Aquarium (hence the name) and is the embarkation point for tours to Fort Sumter. Boat tours of the harbor depart from the Harbor Tour Dock and nearby Charleston Maritime Center. Also here is the IMAX Theater (p167).

South Carolina Aquarium (☎ 843-720-1990; www.scaquarium.com; 100 Aquarium Wharf; adult/child $14/7; 9am-6pm, till 5pm Aug-Jun) covers 69,000 sq ft, almost all of which are devoted to South Carolina habitats, flora and fauna. You'll see river otters, freshwater fish and lush flora in the cool mist of the *Mountains* exhibit. You'll follow the foothills through the Piedmont as it slopes into the swamps of the *Coastal Plain* exhibit, where you'll see snakes and alligators and a re-created blackwater swamp. In the *Saltwater Marsh*, you'll see turtles and herons, seahorses and flounder. The best part of the aquarium is the 330,000-gallon Great Ocean Tank, where sharks, massive fish and a giant loggerhead turtle swim behind a 27ft-tall window. The window is the tallest in North America, and the glass (actually acrylic) is 18 inches thick, so don't worry, a leak is unlikely! When you enter or exit the aquarium, which is designed to resemble a Charleston **single house**, look up at the 180ft mobile, 'Birds in Flight.' Look down and you'll see the South Carolina topography depicted in a mosaic on the floor. Most of the birds and animals acquired by the aquarium were rescued. Many rehabilitated animals are later returned to the wild.

Fort Sumter is the pentagon-shaped island in the center of the harbor. It was here where the first shots of 'the War Between the States'

were fired. Union troops that had been stationed in Charleston retreated to Fort Sumter when the Ordinances of Secession were signed. Confederate troops lined the harbor and waited for orders to fire upon the strategic fort. The bombardment began April 12, 1861, and the Union contingent surrendered 30 hours later. A Confederate stronghold, Fort Sumter was shelled by Union forces from 1863 to 1865. By the end of the war, it was a pile of rubble, and some very forbidding concrete defenses were later added. A few original guns and fortifications, and the obviously strategic location, give a sense of the momentous history here. The only way to get here is by boat tour.

Tours leave from the excellent **National Park Service's Fort Sumter Visitor & Education Center**, at Aquarium Wharf, or from Patriot's Point in Mount Pleasant. **Fort Sumter Tours** (☎ 843-881-7337, 800-789-3678; adult/child $12/6) offers three to five tours daily, depending on the season. Even if you're not a Civil War buff, you'll enjoy the trip. Tours last 2¼ hours and include a colorful tour of the fort and a scenic cruise around the harbor.

THE GENTLEMAN PIRATE

Piracy and an 18th-century midlife crisis immortalized the story of Stede Bonnet, 'the gentleman pirate.' On the little island of Barbados, Bonnet was a member of the landed gentry; he received a classical education, dressed in the finest English fashions and married a respectable woman. Active in civic affairs, Bonnet was a justice of the peace and a major in the island's militia.

In 1716, he made arrangements for what appeared to be an extended business trip. This trip was actually Bonnet's escape route: He had bought himself a sloop (the *Revenge*), outfitted her with armaments of war and hired a crew of 70 men for a new life of piracy.

The Atlantic Ocean was filled with ships carrying valuable cargo to and from Europe, North America and the Caribbean, and piracy had long been a profitable but despised profession that usually attracted destitute sailors. The only pirate in history to buy his own ship, Bonnet knew little about robbing vessels and even less about sailing. That's when he met Blackbeard, who took the novice pirate under his wing for a spree of looting and commandeering. Their most outrageous stunt occurred in Charleston in 1718. With five vessels, Blackbeard blocked the entrance to the port for a week and seized every ship that stumbled into them. One ship carried prominent Charlestonians (including a member of the colonial council), and they were taken hostage. Blackbeard demanded medical supplies, allegedly for syphilis, from the Charleston governor in exchange for the hostages. At the mercy of the pirates, the governor complied.

Bonnet's apprenticeship soon ended when Blackbeard made off with all the booty, and Bonnet followed him, hoping to take back his share. Bonnet was finally captured in the Cape Fear River by Colonel William Rhett, a Charleston planter turned pirate vigilante. The Charleston courts charged Bonnet with taking more than 28 vessels, committing other acts of piracy and murdering 18 law-abiding men. Stede Bonnet was hanged at White Point Gardens on December 10, 1718. Friends from his previous life as a Barbadian aristocrat whispered that it was his nagging wife who drove him to a life of crime.

THE SINGLE HOUSE

At one stage in its long history, Charleston based its property taxes on the length of street frontage. As a result, many houses were built just a single room wide, with a 'piazza' (porch) running down the side of the building instead of across the front. The porch is a traditional feature of Southern architecture, offering a shady, cool and private place to sit. The typical 'single house' is a smallish timber home rather than a grand mansion, and what appears from the street to be a front door actually opens to the end of the piazza. Often there's a narrow garden alongside, with azaleas, wisteria and a shade tree overhanging the street – an essential ingredient of Charleston's unique charm.

The Citadel

North of downtown, along the banks of the Ashley River, the **Citadel** (☎ 843-953-5000; www .citadel.edu; 171 Moultrie St) is South Carolina's state-sponsored military college. Founded in 1842, the young men receiving military training at the Citadel – originally located in downtown Charleston at Francis Marion Square – also acted as guards in case of a slave revolt. Citadel cadets technically fired the first shots of the Civil War in January 1861, when they shot at a Union military ship bringing supplies to Fort Sumter; no retaliation followed, so this event has become an obscure factoid.

The school moved to its present location in 1922. It was forced by the US Supreme Court to accept women in 1996 after a high-profile case in which an applicant, who erased gender references from her high-school transcript, was accepted and then immediately barred from full enrollment after the school realized the new cadet was a woman.

Famous graduates include US Senator Ernest Hollings and author Pat Conroy, whose book *The Lords of Discipline* is not so loosely based on his experience here.

You can wander around the campus from 8am to 6pm daily. Stop by the admissions office in Bond Hall for a walking-tour map. Visitors are also welcome to watch the Military Dress Parade, starting at 3:45pm every Friday during the school year.

Citadel Museum (☎ 843-953-6846; admission free; 2-5pm Sun-Fri, noon-5pm Sat), on the 3rd floor of the Daniel Library, chronicles cadet life and has exhibits on South Carolina's military history.

College of Charleston

This liberal arts **college** (☎ 843-953-5507), approximately between St Philip and Coming Sts, opened in the 1770s and later became an extension of the city's school system, free to city residents. An interesting mix of Charleston debutantes and artsy out-of-towners now attend. The college green, referred to as 'the Cistern,' is decorated by imposing Greek Revival structures and gnarled live oaks dripping with Spanish moss.

Halsey Gallery (☎ 843-953-5680; 54 St Philip St; admission free; 11am-4pm Mon-Sat), in the Simons Center for the Arts on St Philip St, displays modern works by international and national artists.

John Rivers Communications Museum (☎ 843-953-5810; 58 George St; donation suggested; noon-4pm Mon-Fri) covers the history of broadcasting, with early animated movies and historical radio speeches.

To the west of the college, the **Avery Research Center** (☎ 843-953-7608; 125 Bull St; donation suggested; noon-5pm Mon-Sat) contains genealogical records, documents and a small museum dedicated to the African Americans of Charleston. The center is housed in the former Avery Normal Institute, which was a secondary school for African Americans from 1868 to 1954.

Near the college, the **Denmark Vesey House** (56 Bull St), now a private residence, was the home of Denmark Vesey, the alleged leader of a slave uprising. He was a West Indian slave who came to Charleston with his master. In 1800, he bought his freedom with $1500 he won in a public lottery. Supporting himself as a carpenter, Vesey was active in the AME church and began to talk openly about leading other blacks out of bondage. Inspired by the slave uprising in Haiti, Vesey and four close conspirators planned to unite 6000 slaves, rob banks, burn the city, kill the whites and escape via ships to Haiti. The white authorities found out about the conspiracy, and Vesey, along with 34 associates, was sentenced to death in 1822. There is much disagreement over whether a plot really existed or whether the scheme was concocted by whites to deter possible uprisings and tighten slave laws.

Hwy 61 & the Ashley River Plantations

Only a 20-minute veer away from Charleston, three spectacular plantations are worthy of the detour. Though you'll be hard-pressed for time to visit all three in one outing, you could squeeze in two, but you'll want to allot at least a couple of hours for each. If you've only got time to visit one, choose Magnolia Plantation (a better bet with kids) or Middleton Place (a delight for the sheer mastery of its gardens).

DRAYTON HALL

A fine brick mansion (c 1738) and the only remaining colonial structure on the Ashley River to survive the Revolutionary and Civil War, **Drayton Hall** (☎ 843-769-2600; 3380 Ashley River Rd; adult/child $12/6; �) 9:30am-3pm, till 4pm in summer) is the oldest example of Georgian Palladian architecture in the South. This National Historic Landmark, still without water or electricity, remains in nearly original condition and gives a compelling history. The house is preserved, not restored. This authenticity, with the help of knowledgeable staff and exhibits, lends a hand in studying the paradoxes of early plantation life.

Admission includes a 50-minute guided tour, during which you'll learn about architecture, historic preservation and the lives of the Draytons and their slaves. You'll also want to roam around along the river or under the property's giant oaks.

MAGNOLIA PLANTATION

This lush, expansive **home and gardens** (☎ 843-571-1266; www.magnoliaplantation.com; 3550 Ashley River Rd; adult/child $13/7; ☉ 8am-5:50pm) sits on 500 acres that have been owned by the Drayton family since Thomas Drayton came from Barbados and bought the land in 1676. Through its long history, the plantation crops included everything from indigo and rice to cotton, sugar cane, corn and potatoes, all tended by hundreds of slaves who lived on the plantation. After the Civil War, when cash crops were no longer profitable but freed slaves still needed work, Magnolia turned to phosphate mining. The phosphate rock contained a valuable component that

was used in fertilizer, but the strip mining proved devastating to the land.

The plantation gardens, which first mimicked formal English gardens, developed into a delightful informal design. Today, the land explodes with azaleas and camellias. A variety of garden styles grow here, including a tropical garden filled with plants indigenous to Barbados, an herb garden, a topiary garden and a horticultural maze. Especially neat is the **Audubon Swamp Garden** (an additional $5/4), filled with water oak, cypress and tupelo trees. Wildlife abounds – you're virtually guaranteed to see alligators. More than 200 species of birds live or migrate through, including egrets, herons and cormorants.

Though the first plantation house was destroyed after the Revolution, and the second burned in the Civil War, you can visit the current pre-Revolutionary home (which was barged in from nearby Summerville, South Carolina). There is also a petting zoo and snack shop. A great way to see the plantation is by taking the nature train (adult/child $7/5), which toots around the property. You can also take a boat tour ($7/5).

MIDDLETON PLACE

Sprawling and delightful, **Middleton Place** (☎ 843-556-6020; www.middletonplace.org; 4300 Ashley River Rd; adult/child $30/15 for gardens, house & stables; ☉ 9am-5pm), designed in 1741, is the oldest landscaped gardens in the US. For 125 years, the property belonged to a succession of the illustrious Middletons: Henry was president of the first Congressional Congress; Arthur later signed the Declaration of Independence; another Henry was the state governor and minister to Russia; and finally, there was Williams, who signed the Ordinance of Secession. Just five years later, Civil War flames torched Middleton Place. The gardens were overgrown and neglected until JJ Pringle Smith, a Middleton descendent, began restoring the grounds. In the 1970s, the plantation was declared a National Historic Landmark, and it is now governed and lovingly maintained by a nonprofit foundation.

The grounds – a mix of classic formal French gardens and romantic wooded settings – are truly formidable. Azaleas and camellias burst open, while gardenia, freesia and roses flood the air with scent. A flooded rice field demonstrates rice cultivation, the giant Middleton Oak seems too incredible to be real, and marble statues studded around the grounds seem to grow out of the earth. Plantation animals munch grass in the paddocks and working stables. You can visit the 1755 mansion, in whose terraced backyard Cornwallis said 'I should be in Virginia, but I'm stuck here at Middleton Place,' during the British ball in *The Patriot*.

There are various ways to tour Middleton. Admission for the whole thing (gardens, house, stables and a horse-drawn carriage tour) is adult/child $39/28. If you've already toured homes in Charleston, you could easily forgo the house tour and carriage ride, which drops the admission to $20/15. Middleton also offers kayak rentals ($20 per person) and guided kayak tours ($25 per person). The **Middleton Inn Restaurant** (☎ 843-556-6020; lunch $6-11, dinner $15-21) serves Lowcountry cuisine and is open for lunch and dinner.

The outdoorsy swank of the **Inn at Middleton Place** (☎ 843-556-0500, 800-543-4774; 4290 Ashley River Rd; d $190-500; P 🏋 🛋 ✕) makes it a great place to stay for those wishing to tour the plantation in depth. The inn's 55 rooms have fireplaces, floor-to-ceiling windows and rich cypress paneling. Guests get unlimited access to the plantation.

GETTING THERE & AWAY

Transportation to the plantations is limited, and most people take their own cars. Driving from Charleston, take Hwy 17 S across the Ashley River Bridge (stay in the right lane). Take Hwy 61 N (Ashley River Rd) for about 10 miles. Drayton Hall is first, followed by Magnolia Plantation and Middleton Place.

Greyhound (☎ 843-722-444; adult/child $31.50/22.50) offers summertime bus tours that take in Drayton Hall and Magnolia Plantation.

Folly Beach

Surf's up, dude. Only a 15-minute drive from downtown, **Folly Beach** is a pretty barrier island and fun day trip for beachgoers. Ira Gershwin came to this narrow island in the 1920s to write the music for the folk opera *Porgy & Bess*. Today the island attracts dropout hippie

types, boardwalk cruisers, fisherfolk and surfers. The area called 'the Wash Out,' on E Ashley Rd, gets a steady run of rideable waves and hosts surfing tournaments throughout the year. At the far east end of the island, the Morris Island Lighthouse is all that remains of a Confederate fort. The boardwalk maintains a Coney Island–style air of festival, with food, music and lots of good people watching.

Follow E Ashley road to find streetside public parking; east of E 8th St, the beach no longer has groins (concrete structures built into the ocean perpendicular to the shore to keep sand from eroding). Short-term rentals are available; contact the **Charleston Visitors Center** (☎ 843-853-8000, 800-774-0006) for more information.

From Charleston, Follow Calhoun St west, which becomes Hwy 17 over the James Island Connector. Take Folly Rd (Hwy 171) south to Folly Beach.

Just before the causeway leading to Folly is a sign for **Bowen's Island Oyster Bar** (☎ 843-795-2757; mains $8-16; 🕔 5-10pm Tue-Sat), on the right. This rundown shack sits on an isolated pitch of land overlooking the marsh and serves incomparable shrimp, crab cakes and regional tastes like Frogmore stew (p56) and shrimp 'n' grits. Stop by the **Ocean Deck Tiki Bar** (☎ 843-588-6464; 1 Center St), in the Holiday Inn – it has a great outdoor deck for sunset drinks.

Charles Towne Landing

In 1670, a group of English colonists sailed through what would later become Charleston Harbor and up the Ashley River. They landed on the first high ground they encountered and set up a home. This was the original site of the Charles Town settlement (p22), which would later move south to the peninsula between the Ashley and Cooper Rivers.

Today the site is a wooded park that does a great job recreating 17th-century life. A fun trip for kids of all ages, the site features the Adventure, a reproduction trading ship like the vessels that plied the river carrying rice and indigo. A natural-habitat zoo features animals once native to the Carolina coast. A theater shows a 30-minute film of the town's history, and the 'Settlers Life Area' depicts what life was like during that time.

DETOUR: HISTORIC SUMMERVILLE & FRANCIS BEIDLER FOREST

Just 24 miles northwest of Charleston, historic **Summerville** is a great place to spend an afternoon. Sit and watch the world go by in the pretty, 12-acre Azalea Park in the heart of town. Wander into the shops and restaurants or check into one of the many B&Bs and inns, including the 5-star **Woodlands Resort & Inn** (☎ 843-875-2600, 800-774-9900; 125 Parsons Rd) on a 1906 Greek Revival mansion on 42 wooded acres. The fancy **restaurant** (breakfast & lunch $10-20, 4-course prix fixe dinner $64) at the inn has been hailed as one of the best restaurants in the country. Stop by the Summerville **visitors center** (☎ 843-873-8535; www.summervilletourism.com; 402 N Main St) for information and maps. From Charleston, take I-26 W to Hwy 17A, and follow it into town.

About 10 miles past Summerville, in the heart of Four Holes Swamp, is the **Francis Beidler Forest & Audubon Sanctuary** (☎ 843-462-2150; 336 Sanctuary Rd; www.beidlerforest.com; adult/child $6/3; ☷ 9am-5pm Tue-Sun). Here you'll find the area's largest remaining stand of ancient cypress-tupelo forest (40,000 acres). There are 1½ miles of boardwalk trails, blackwater streams and more than 300 species of wildlife. Canoe trips ($20) are available on weekends in summer. Take I-26 W to exit 187, then go left onto Hwy 27. At the end of the road, take a right onto Hwy 78, then veer right onto Hwy 178. Francis Beidler Forest is on the right. The route is well signed.

You can take guided history tours, meander along miles of walking trails, take a tram tour or rent a bike and cruise along bike paths. There's a restaurant and picnic area, and strollers for the little ones are available to rent.

The **site** (☎ 843-852-4200; www.southcarolinaparks .com; 1500 Old Towne Rd; adult/child $5/3; ☷ 8:30am-5pm, till 6pm in summer) is 3 miles north of Charleston; take Hwy 17 to West Ashley and turn right onto Hwy 171.

ACTIVITIES

If your feet are tired from walking, try cycling around the city's sights. Charleston, is flat and easy to ride around, and you'll see many residents and students rolling by on cruisers. The **Bicycle Shoppe** (☎ 843-722-8168; 280 Meeting St) rents single-speed bikes for a starting price of $5/20 per hour/day.

Charleston Tennis Center (☎ 843-724-7402; 19 Farmfield Ave; hard/clay courts $3.50/7 per hr) is a city-run club just 2 miles west of Charleston, off Hwy 17 in West Ashley. It has 15 hard and clay lit courts. **Family Circle Tennis Center** (☎ 843-856-7900; 161 Seven Farms Dr; hard/clay courts $10/15 per hr) opened in 2001 and is a swanky public facility with 17 clay, hard and lit courts. In April, it hosts the Family Circle Cup, bringing in the top guns in women's tennis. Private lessons cost $55 per hour. To get here, take I-26 west to the Mark Clark Expressway (I-526) and go east toward Mount Pleasant. Take the Daniel Island exit and follow signs. **Hazel Parker Playground**, near the Carolina Yacht Club on E Bay St,

has free public tennis courts available on a first-come, first-served basis.

Throw a golf ball in the air and you might just get it in a hole – that's how many **golf courses** surround Charleston. The city's Harleston Green, established in 1786 on the corner of St Philip and Coming Sts, where the College of Charleston sits today, was home to the South Carolina Golf Club, the country's first golf club. The course, which was essentially just an uncultivated patch of green, is said to have given birth to the term 'greens fee,' a membership sum early golfers had to pay to help maintain the greens. For information on all area courses, contact **Charleston Golf Inc** (☎ 800-774-4444; www.charlestongolfinc.com), a nonprofit organization that produces the *Charleston Area Golf Guide* and helps travelers make golf arrangements.

Within 20 miles of the city, you'll find pristine **beaches** on Sullivan's Island (p173) and the Isle of Palms (p172), east of the Cooper River. Closer to town is Folly Beach (p156).

Though the waters of the Cooper River are slightly murky, **divers** can find fossilized shark teeth and see the wonders of the inshore habitat. Those wishing to venture farther will be rewarded with some excellent coral-encrusted wrecks. **Charleston Scuba** (☎ 843-763-3483; www.charlestonscuba.com; 335 Savannah Hwy/Hwy 17), on the west side of the Ashley River Bridge, is a reputable dive shop offering PADI training courses and a variety of trips for certified divers. Dives, including transportation and rentals, cost $75 to $100.

Slipping along the coastal marshes and estuaries in a **kayak** is an excellent way to discover the natural side of the city. Kayak tours and rentals are available at Shem Creek in Mount Pleasant. See p72 for details.

CHARLESTON WALKING TOUR

The great thing about Charleston is that the entire city is a walking tour. You can wander along elegant thoroughfares, sneak through winding backstreets and never see the same thing twice. The following tour takes about 90 minutes and follows a straightforward loop that points out some of Charleston's architecturally and historically poignant sights. If you want to venture on your own, you'll find pretty residential areas on lower King, Tradd, Lomboll and Legare Sts.

Start your tour at **Market Hall (1)** (188 Meeting St). This building held the meat market – look up at the frieze decorated with sheep and bull skulls over the market archway. Swooping buzzards used to feed on scraps, which kept the market clean. It was illegal to kill the birds because their cleaning services were deemed so necessary.

Walk south down Meeting St. The **Circular Congregational Church (2)** (150 Meeting St) was the city's first meeting place, which gave Meeting St its name. The original church was built in 1806 but was later destroyed by fire and earthquake. This Romanesque Revival structure was built in 1861. It's suggested that the building's three circles are meant to represent the Holy Trinity.

Past the church, on your right, the Beaux Arts–style **Gibbes Museum of Art (3)** was built in 1905. Continue south past the Italianate **Mills House Hotel (4)** to the Greek Revival **Hibernian Society Hall (5)** (105 Meeting St), home to an Irish benevolent organization that was founded in 1801. Each year a new president is elected, alternating between a Protestant and Roman Catholic. Take note of the pretty Irish harp above the doorway.

Keep walking south. On your left is **Washington Square (6)**, a great spot to take a book on a nonsightseeing day. At Meeting and Broad Sts is the intersection nicknamed the **Four Corners of Law** – or as one local called it, 'hail, mail, bail and jail.' On the northwest corner, the **Charleston County Courthouse (7)**

protects state law, **City Hall (8)** handles civil law, the **US Federal Courthouse (9)** manages federal law and **St Michael's Episcopal Church (10)** upholds the law of the lord. The church steeple was painted a less conspicuous black during the Revolutionary War, but the British found the black only made the steeple more obvious.

Continue on Meeting St across Broad St. You are now crossing into the colonial and most prestigious part of the city, known as 'South of Broad,' most of which is landfill sitting atop marshland.

The **Andrew Hasell House (11)** (64 Meeting St) is a good example of the Charleston single house. The **Branford-Horry House (12)** (59 Meeting St) is an example of both Georgian architecture and what Charlestonians call a 'double house' (a variation on the single house, but with a street frontage that's two rooms wide).

Continue on Meeting St and cross Tradd St to the **First (Scots) Presbyterian Church (13)** (37 Meeting St). Its Scottish roots are identified by the seal of the Church of Scotland in the window above the main entrance. Just past it, the **Nathaniel Russell House (14)** is one of the more popular house museums.

The pink, brown and yellow houses known as the **'Three Sisters' (15)** (Nos 23, 25 and 27 Meeting St) were built between 1750 and 1788 and reflect the three distinct looks of the single house (see boxed text p154).

George W Williams, a financier of blockade runners, was the only person in post–Civil War Charleston who could afford a new home. His slap in the face to the blueblood society was the 1876 **Calhoun Mansion (16)** (16 Meeting St). With 24,000 sq ft and some 25 rooms, it is the largest single residence in the city.

At Meeting and S Battery St, **Two Meeting Street Inn (17)** is one of the city's finest B&Bs. Cross Battery St to **White Point Park & Gardens (18)**, named for the piles of oyster shells that covered the point. The park is also known as 'The Battery' for its early role as a strategic fortification.

Cross Murray Blvd at the far end of the park, and walk up the steps to the bend in the promenade. Below you is the **Charleston Harbor**, where the Cooper and Ashley Rivers meet before pouring into the Atlantic. Look to the far left and you'll see Patriot's Point and the USS *Yorktown*. Look straight ahead

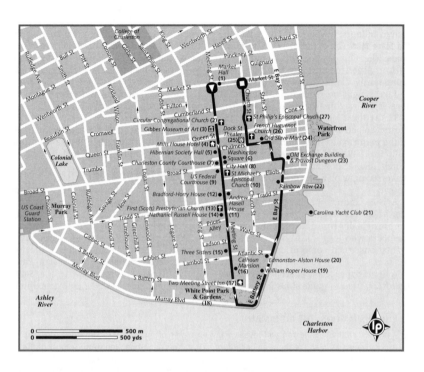

Map labels:
College of Charleston · King St · Wentworth St · Hasell St · Pritchard St · Rutledge Ave · Bull St · Pitt St · Coming St · Glebe St · Saint Philip St · Meeting St · Pinckney St · Guignard · Concord St · Montague St · Smith St · Kinloch Wilson · Archdale St · Market Hall (1) · Market St · E Bay St · Cooper River · Wentworth · Beaufain St · Cromwell · Franklin St · Fulton · Cumberland St · Church St · State St · Cone St · St Philip's Episcopal Chuch (27) · Colonial Lake · Queen St · Circular Congregational Church (2) · Gibbes Museum of Art (3) · Dock St Theater (25) · French Huguenot Church (26) · Waterfront Park · Mills House Hotel (4) · Old Slave Mart (24) · Trumbo · Hibernian Society Hall (5) · Chalmers · Washington Square (6) · Old Exchange Building & Provost Dungeon (23) · Charleston County Courthouse (7) · City Hall (8) · Broad St · Elliots · US Coast Guard Station · Murray Park · Logan St · Rutledge Ave · Colonial St · Savage St · New St · US Federal Courthouse (9) · St Michael's Episcopal Church (10) · Rainbow Row (22) · Bradford-Horry House (12) · Andrew Hasell House (11) · Tradd St · First (Scots) Presbyterian Church (13) · Nathaniel Russell House (14) · King St · Carolina Yacht Club (21) · Greenhill St · Limehouse St · Council St · Gibbes St · Tradd St · Elinwood St · Legare St · Prices Alley · Water St · Meeting St · S Battery St · Gibbes St · Ladson St · Three Sisters (15) · Atlantic St · Lamboll St · Calhoun Mansion (16) · Edmonston-Alston House (20) · S Battery St · Two Meeting Street Inn (17) · William Roper House (19) · Murray Blvd · White Point Park & Gardens (18) · E Battery St · Ashley River · Charleston Harbor · 0 500 m · 0 500 yds

and you'll see Fort Sumter, marked by the big American flag. To the left is Fort Moultrie, and to the right is Fort Johnson, where Confederate soldiers fired the first shot of the Civil War at Federally occupied Fort Sumter.

Head north up E Battery, and you'll see the row of majestic homes that grow even more beautiful at sunset. The **William Roper House (19)** (9 E Battery St) is a Greek Revival mansion built in 1838. People say the 'rope' molding around the front door was a pun on the owner's name, but you'll notice other homes have it too. The complex molding became something of a status symbol.

The 1825 **Edmondston-Alston House (20)** is open to the public and is worth a visit for the display of original furniture. It's carefully preserved by the Alston family, some members of which still live on the 3rd floor.

Continue along E Battery, which becomes E Bay St along this stretch. On your right you'll see the private **Carolina Yacht Club (21)**. The bright houses of **Rainbow Row (22)** (Nos 79-107 E Bay St) were built as merchant houses, with shops on the 1st floor and residences

above. Before landfill was added, these homes fronted the water, which is why the intersecting streets are named after wharves. This was a seedy stretch until the 1930s, when a slow but dramatic restoration endeavor transformed it into a pretty and valuable area.

At the top of Broad St where it meets E Bay, the **Old Exchange Building & Provost Dungeon (23)** has seen its share of history. From here, take a left onto Broad St, a right on State St and a left on Chalmers St. The big cobblestones on Chalmers St were used as ballast to weigh down empty ships coming from European ports. Once here, the ships dumped the stones and filled their holds with rice, indigo and furs. No stone like this was found anywhere near Charleston, so the rocks were mixed with sand and used to pave the streets.

Before 1856 slaves were openly traded on the streets in Charleston. Owners were required to register their slaves, who wore copper tags stamped with an individual number, so the city could keep track and collect fees. After 1856, slave trading

CHARLESTON

moved indoors, to special markets like the **Old Slave Mart (24)** (6 Chalmers St). For many years, the Old Slave Mart served as an African American museum, but it has been 'temporarily' closed for many years.

Take a right on Church St. The **Dock St Theater (25)** was first built on Queen St in 1735. At the time, a creek flowed by the theater, so patrons could hop from the boat to the performance. The present structure, built in 1809, was the original Planter's Hotel. Take a look at what's playing, and make seeing a play or concert here a top priority.

Across Church St, the **French Huguenot Church (26)** was organized in 1861. Services were originally timed so that the church members who lived on Cooper River rice plantations could come in and leave with the tide.

A light in the steeple at **St Philip's Episcopal Church (27)** used to guide ships into port. St Philip's has the oldest congregation in Charleston, first organized in 1680. The graveyard beside the church was *the* place to be buried, but resting rights were only given to people considered to be from Charleston. 'Strangers and other transient whites' were buried across Church St, in the Western Graveyard.

At Market St, take a left and you'll get back to where you started, or take your time and stroll around the market stalls.

CHARLESTON FOR CHILDREN

With lots of restaurants and activities catering to families, Charleston is a great place to brings kids. A few activities are especially kid-focused.

When the sun's shining, your little ones will spend delightful hours playing in the **Vendu Fountain** at Waterfront Park, at the foot of Vendu St. At the **South Carolina Aquarium** (p152), most exhibits

---

PHILIP SIMMONS: THE IRON MAN

Any walk around Charleston will reveal many examples of intricate wrought-iron gates and decorative works. Many of these are a century old, and it's mind-boggling to think most of the work was done by hand. For centuries blacksmithing was a common profession for the city's middle-class freed blacks, and the skill of forming iron into decorative swirls and shapes was passed down from master to apprentice.

Philip Simmons (b 1912 on nearby Daniel Island), now in his nineties, is one of the city's only remaining practitioners of this fading tradition. Simmons started learning the art of metalworking in a blacksmith's shop, where he began making horseshoes in 1920, at the ripe old age of 13. He learned from his elders and grew into his tremendous natural gifts. Today, more than 500 pieces of his work grace homes, gardens, schools and churches throughout Charleston. In 1982, he was awarded the National Endowment for the Arts' prestigious National Heritage Fellowship. He's been honored at the state legislature and was awarded a lifetime achievement award, and he is something of a deity in the craft of ornamental ironworks.

Any walk through Charleston will reveal Simmons' work; for example, take a look at the **Harp of David Gate** (67 Alexander St) and the **Egret Gate** on Stolls Alley, just off Church St.

At the **St John's Reformed Episcopal Church** (George & Anson Sts), a garden commemorates Simmons' work – a particularly touching tribute, as Simmons is a longtime church member. Check out the fence along Anson and George Sts, along with the **Heart Gate**, at the entrance to the walkway on Anson St. The **Double Heart Gate**, which leads to the topiary garden, was designed by Simmons and crafted by his nephew (Carleton Simmons) and cousin (Joseph Pringle). In middle of the Bell Garden hangs an **iron bell** that Simmons had in his blacksmith shop for 50 years.

Simmons work can also be viewed at the National Museum of American History at the Smithsonian Institute in Washington, DC; at the National Museum of American Folk Art, in Santa Fe, New Mexico; and at the state museum in Columbia, South Carolina – to name a few. Simmons' work and designs are in such demand that he informs the customer when to expect the completed project, and Charlestonians are willing to wait. Now advanced in his years, Simmons is training his nephew to carry on the tradition. To find out more about Simmons work, contact the **Philip Simmons Foundation** (☎ 843-723-8018; www.philipsimmons.org).

are at children's eye level, and there are interactive displays designed especially for toddlers. A 1700-gallon touch tank delights kids, as they can discover the bumpy ridges of starfish or the sliminess of seaweed.

Exhibits in the **Provost Dungeon** (p152), in the Old Exchange, are especially entertaining for children. Animated figures tell the stories of grizzled pirates and brave patriots, and kids can pick up scavenger hunts in the gift shop. The boat tour to **Fort Sumter** (p153) is fun for kids, as is touring the USS Yorktown at **Patriot's Point** (p171).

Charles Towne Landing (p156) has many fun and educational activities just for kids. **Magnolia Plantation** (p155) has a petting zoo and an open-air train that circles the property, skirting by the Audubon Swamp Garden (p152) and wildlife such as alligators, snakes and cormorants.

ORGANIZED TOURS

We could fill an entire book describing the variety of tours available in Charleston. Tours are a great way to see the city from another point of view – from the water or from the road, through the eyes of a carriage driver or a walking-tour guide. The following is a sampling of recommended tours.

Walking Tours

Whether you take a thematic tour, a history tour, an architectural tour, or the walking tour in this book (p158), getting some feet time on the streets is a Charleston must. The city's pool of excellent tour guides make a walk seem like a ride. Schedules and availability vary, so it's best to call ahead.

Charleston Stroll (☎ 843-766-2080; www.charleston strolls.com; tours $16.50) A slow-paced meander that focuses on Charleston history. Departures are at 9:30am from Charleston Place (p165), 9:40am from Days Inn Downtown (p164) and 10am from Mills House Hotel (p163).
Civil War Walking Tour (☎ 843-722-7033; www.civilwartours.com; tours $17, children under 12 free) Tailored for Civil War buffs interested in Charleston's Confederate history. Tours depart at 9am from Mills House Hotel (p163).
Ghosts of Charleston (☎ 843-723-1670, 800-854-1670; adult/child $15/10) A fun nighttime tour exploring the deep dark haunts of Charleston's ghosts. Tours depart from Waterfront Park at 5pm, 7:30pm and 9:30pm.

The company also runs the Ghosts of Charleston II (in a different part of the city), the Pirates of Charleston and the Story of Charleston walking tours.
Original Charleston Walks (☎ 843-577-3800, 800-729-3420; www.charlestonwalks.com; 58½ Broad St; adult/child $15/8) Offers a variety of two-hour thematic tours, including ghost, pirate, Civil War and slavery tours. Tours take place all day; call ahead for a current schedule.

Carriage Tours

A horse- or mule-drawn carriage tour is a great way to see the city and get some tidbits of quirky information. Most tours leave from the Old City Market, where they have to check in at a tiny hut to ensure that no more than 20 carriages are touring the city at the same time. Tickets cost adult/child $18/8, but discount coupons are available in tourist publications. The following take good care of the animals and offer colorful commentary.

Olde Town Carriage Company (☎ 843-722-1315; 20 Anson St)
Palmetto Carriage Tours (☎ 843-723-8145; 40 N Market St)

Bus Tours

Weary of walking? Longing to sit in an air-conditioned bus? Hop on one of the motorized tours, all of which leave from the visitors center (p147), though they'll also pick you up at area hotels.

Gray Line (☎ 843-722-4444; 90min tour adult/child $18/11, 2hr tour $24/16) Offers a variety of in-city tours, plus trips to Middleton Place and Magnolia Plantations (p155).
Doin' the Charleston (☎ 843-763-1233, 800-674-4487; www.do9inthecharlestontours.com; adult/child $17/10) Offers 90-minute narrated tours of the historic homes, accompanied by video footage of the home interiors.
Gullah Tours (☎ 843-763-7551; www.gullahtours.com; 9 Trachelle Lane; tours $15) Led by owner Alphonso Brown, who takes you through the city's African American history. Tours take place 11am and 1pm Monday to Friday; there's an additional 3pm departure on weekends.
Talk of the Town (☎ 843-795-8199; www.talkofthetown.com; 75min tour adult/child $13/8, 2hr tour $21/14) A fully narrated, jam-packed tour in a minibus. The two-hour tour includes a visit (including admission) to either the Nathaniel Russell House (p150) or the Edmonston-Alston House (p150).

Boat Tours

A great way to see the watery side of Charleston is by taking a harbor tour.

CHARLESTON

SpritLine Harbour Tours (☎ 843-722-2628; www.spiritlinecruises.com; adult/child $10.50/5.50) Offers 90-minute tours departing from the dock behind the IMAX Theater at Aquarium Wharf. Call ahead for the current schedule.

Charleston Harbor Tours (☎ 843-722-1112; Charleston Maritime Center; adult/child $13/8 ; ⏱ 11:30am, 1:30pm & 3:30pm) Offers a colorful two-hour tour aboard a paddlewheeler.

Schooner Pride (☎ 843-559-9686; www.schoonerpride.com; adult/child $20/15; ⏱ 2pm, 4:30pm & 7pm) Departs from the IMAX dock at Aquarium Wharf and runs two-hour sailing tours aboard a Class C tall ship. Call ahead to reserve.

FESTIVALS & EVENTS

JANUARY
Lowcounty Oyster Festival At the end of the month at Boone Hall Plantation (p171). Features oyster-shucking contests, kids' events and good eatin'.

FEBRUARY
Lowcountry Blues Bash Features national and local blues acts.
Southeastern Wildlife Exposition An art festival devoted to the celebration and preservation of indigenous wildlife.

MARCH
Festival of Houses & Gardens Opens more than 150 of Charleston's private homes to the public.

APRIL
Cooper River Bridge Run This extremely popular 10K run is followed up by music and fun. Participants must preregister.
Family Circle Cup One of the oldest tournaments in tennis (formerly played on Hilton Head). This event attracts the best players in professional women's tennis.

MAY–JUNE
Spoleto USA This is Charleston's internationally renowned cultural festival, celebrating opera, chamber music, theater and dance. It's followed up by **Piccolo Spoleto**, an offshoot festival with street performances, free concerts and other popular artforms.

SEPTEMBER–OCTOBER
MOJA Arts Festival African American and Caribbean culture are honored through dance, theater and films.
Fall Candlelight Tour of Homes & Gardens People can tour historic homes by candlelight for six weeks in September and October.
Taste of Charleston Restaurateurs share their feasts at Boone Hall Plantation (p171) in mid-October.

DECEMBER
Christmas in Charleston The city celebrates the holiday with tree lightings, a parade of boats, house tours and choral performances.

SLEEPING

Staying in the historic downtown is the most attractive option, but it can get downright expensive, especially on weekends and during special events. All of the chain hotels operate on the nearby highways. Rates in town fluctuate all over the place – a $70 room in winter could be $200 in summer – so call ahead to see if you can get a better deal.

The rates below are for high season (roughly mid-February to mid-June and September to mid-November). Expect to pay much less in the low season (roughly mid-June to September and mid-November to mid-February). Pay attention to parking fees, which can add up if you stay for a few days.

Budget
HOSTELS
Charleston's two hostels both opened in late 2002 and are a bit of a trek from the historic district, though both sit on Carta bus lines (p170) and offer a good deal if you just need a place to crash for the night.

Charleston's Historic Hostel (☎ 843-478-1446; www.charlestonhostel.com; 194 St Philip St; dm/private $19/40; ⚙ 💻 ✕) Owner Heather Lombard opened up this hostel after traveling around herself. It's a laid-back and friendly place with very simple but clean accommodations, free Internet access and laundry, plus a shared living room, kitchen and piazza.

Charleston's Not So Hostel (☎ 843-722-8383; www.notsohostel.com; 156 Spring St; dm/private $19/35-50; Ⓟ ⚙ 💻 ✕) In a sort of sketchy but up-and-coming neighborhood, this eco-friendly hostel is housed in two old rambling houses. There's a vegetable garden, plenty of parking and free Internet access, as well as cruiser bicycles, lockers and common areas. There's even a raised platform for anyone wishing to pitch a tent.

CAMPING
Three campgrounds southwest of Charleston offer shuttle services to downtown. Most campgrounds charge around $20 or more for RVs. These include **Oak Plantation Campground**

(☎ 843-766-5936; 3540 Savannah Hwy/Hwy 17) and **Lake Aire RV Park & Campground** (☎ 843-571-1271), at Hwy 17 and Hwy 162. The nicest is the campground at **James Island County Park** (☎ 843-795-9884, 800-743-7275; 871 Riverland Dr). From downtown, follow Calhoun St west over the James Island Connector. Take a right onto Folly Rd, a left onto Central Park Rd and another left onto Riverland Dr. The park is on the right.

Mid-range

B&BS

Perhaps the greatest way to enjoy Charleston charm is to stay at one of the city's many B&Bs. **Historic Charleston Bed & Breakfast** (☎ 843-722-6606, 800-743-3583; www.historiccharlestonbedandbreakfast.com; 57 Broad St) has additional listings of B&Bs, plus photos of the different houses. Note that most B&Bs are nonsmoking only, and some do not allow children.

Bed, No Breakfast (☎ 843-723-4450; 16 Halsey St; d $80-100, cash or check only; P 🞬 🞬) Though only a B, not a B&B, this small, pensione-style place, with just two rooms and a shared bathroom, is friendly. It's a great option, if they have rooms available.

1837 Bed & Breakfast (☎ 843-723-7166, 877-723-1837; www.1837bb.com; 126 Wentworth St; d $120-165; P 🞬 🞬) This 1837 single house has nine rooms, all with unique period furnishings and canopy beds. The afternoon tea service is a nice touch. The piazza is a great place to read a book and capture the breeze.

INNS

Larger than a B&B but not as big as a hotel, inns typically have garden piazzas, antique reproductions and Southern or continental breakfasts. They are usually friendly places that focus on personalized and excellent service.

Maison du Pré (☎ 843-723-8691, 800-844-4667; www.maisondupre.com; 317 E Bay St; s & d $95-195; P 🞬 🞬) At first glance, this inn just looks like an old house north of the market, but look a little further and you'll see it's a true diamond in the rough. The inn is composed of three single houses and two carriage houses that surround a lovely courtyard, where flowers intoxicate the air. Each room features unique period furnishings and paintings by owner Lucille Mulholland. Highlights include a

continental breakfast and afternoon tea. Parking is $8 per day.

Andrew Pinckney Inn (☎ 843-937-8800, 800-505-8983; www.andrewpinckneyinn.com; 40 Pinckney St; d $130-280; P 🞬 🞬) With a great location near the market, a courtyard, rooftop garden and 32 rooms, the inn's design gives a nod to the West Indies style. A continental breakfast is served on the rooftop terrace. Parking is $12 per day

Indigo Inn (☎ 800-845-7639, 843-577-5900; 1 Maiden Ln; d $120-165; P 🞬 🞬) Housed in an old indigo warehouse that was nicely restored, this inn has special touches, like afternoon wine and cheese. The Indigo also runs the Greek Revival **Jasmine House** (☎ 800-845-7639, 843-577-5900; 64 Hasell St; d $130-170; P 🞬 🞬), which has broad front verandahs and 10 spacious rooms with high ceilings. Rates here are slightly higher. Parking is $6 per day.

Other recommendations include the well-priced **Barksdale House Inn** (☎ 843-577-4800; 27 George St; $120-180; P 🞬 🞬), near the College of Charleston, and the **Elliott House Inn** (☎ 800-729-1855, 843-723-1855; 78 Queen St; $130-160; P 🞬 🞬), tucked behind a narrow courtyard in a great location near King St's antique row.

HOTELS

The nice thing about Charleston hotels is that most of them have pools. A refreshing splash does the soul good after a day of strolling and eating.

Mills House Hotel (☎ 843-577-2400, 800-874-9600; 115 Meeting St; d start at $150; P 🞬 🞬 🞬) In a great location, the Mills House is a beautiful hotel whose rooms are filled with antiques. The hotel has a restaurant and lounge. The outdoor pool is in a private courtyard on the 2nd floor. Parking is $16 per day.

Westin Francis Marion Hotel (☎ 843-722-0600; 387 King St; d start at $140; P 🞬 🞬) Charleston's only high-rise hotel (a giant at 12 stories!) overlooks the Old Citadel and Marion Square and has 226 rooms that range widely in size and price range. Because it has so many rooms, the hotel gives good discounts during lulls. Parking is $10 per day.

Holiday Inn (☎ 843-805-7900, 877-805-7900; www.charlestonhotel.com; 125 Calhoun St; d $120-200; P 🞬 🞬 🞬) Rooms come with standard amenities, but the real bonuses include a courtyard pool, fitness center and restaurant. Parking is $10 per day.

Best Western King Charles Inn (☎ 843-723-7451; www.kingcharlesinn.com; 237 Meeting St; d $130-180; P ✖ ✖ ✖) With few frills except a great location, tidy rooms and free parking, this standard hotel underwent dramatic renovations and is a pleasant place to stay. It sometimes offers heavy discounts.

Days Inn Downtown (☎ 843-722-8411; 155 Meeting St; d $160-180; P ✖ ✖) Although way overpriced in high season, this a good option for people with cars, as the motel style grants easy access and free parking. Rooms are very basic and can get noisy from traffic passing by.

Top End
B&BS

There are a couple of good high-end B&B options in town.

Two Meeting St Inn (☎ 843-723-7322; www .twomeetingstreetinn.com; 2 Meeting St; d $165-325; P ✖ ✖) Housed in a stunning Queen Anne mansion on the Battery, this beautiful home could give you the best stay you've ever had. The nine rooms are uniquely decorated, with private baths and period furnishings. The story goes that George W Williams left his daughter Martha $75,000 on a satin pillow to celebrate her marriage to Waring P Carrington. They used the cash to build this house in 1892. Check out the oak paneling and Tiffany stained glass in the den – the glass was supposedly crafted and installed by Tiffany himself.

Hayne House (☎ 843-577-2633; www.haynehouse .com; 30 King St; d $150-275; P ✖ ✖) The owner of this B&B, Brian McGreevy, is a Charleston native and can bestow great information on the city's history. He and his wife Jane serve afternoon sherry in a Victorian drawing room to guests staying in one of their six rooms.

INNS

Charleston has some very memorable top-end inns.

Ansonborough Inn (☎ 843-723-1655, 800-522-2073; www.ansonboroughinn.com; 21 Hasell St; d $130-230; P ✖ ✖) Housed in an old paper warehouse, this lovely inn has exposed pine beams, antique furnishings and suites designed with a Lowcountry or nautical

theme. Each of the 37 suites has a kitchenette, a full seating area and a separate bedroom, making it a great value. A good continental breakfast is included. Parking is $8 per day.

Meeting Street Suites (☎ 843-720-5915, 800-280-1849; www.meetingstreetsuites.com; 233 Meeting St; d $190-210; P ✖ ✖) Stay in one of these four luxury suites and you'll feel like you live in your very own apartment in the heart of Charleston. On the 3rd floor, above the Sticky Fingers restaurant (p165), this is likely Charleston's best-kept secret. The space was drastically refurbished in 2001 and now has gleaming hardwood floors, exposed brick walls and modern amenities like high-speed Internet connections, gas fireplaces and Jacuzzis. Each suite has a kitchen, and pets are welcome. There is no lobby, so you'll have to make prior arrangements to get your key and free parking pass.

Meeting Street Inn (☎ 843-723-1882, 800-842-8022; www.meetingstreetinn.com; 173 Meeting St; d $170-250; P ✖ ✖) All of this hotel's 56 small rooms open onto their own patio overlooking a courtyard, which has a hot tub. The rooms are furnished with 19th-century antiques. A complimentary continental breakfast is served in the morning. Parking is $12 per day.

Planters Inn (☎ 843-722-2345, 800-845-7082; www.plantersinn.com; 112 N Market St; d $170-250; P ✖ ✖) All of the 62 spacious rooms here have a canopy bed and a 10ft ceiling. Some rooms have fireplaces, Whirlpools and verandahs. There's also an excellent restaurant and lounge. Rates fluctuate, so call to see if you can get a better deal. Parking is $14 per day.

HOTELS

Make sure to keep the price of parking in mind for these places.

Market Pavilion Hotel (☎ 843-723-0500, 877-440-2250; www.marketpavilion.com; 225 E Bay St; d start at $275; P ✖ ▢ ✖ ✖) Very swanky, baby. This luxury boutique hotel is new to Charleston, but the designers did such a fine job recreating the historic veneer and ambiance that you'd never know the difference. Where you can tell is in the ultramodern amenities, mahogany furniture and sumptuous linens. Even if you don't stay here, you must have cocktails at the rooftop **Pavilion Bar** (p167). Parking is $15 per day

Charleston Place (☎ 843-722-4900, 800-611-5545; www.charlestonplacehotel.com; d $290-460; P ⊠ 🖳 ⊠ 🕭) This ultra posh hotel in the heart of the city has 440 gorgeously decorated and spacious rooms, a bar, a spa, an excellent fitness center and a pool with a retractable roof. Its restaurants include the ritzy **Charleston Grill** (p166). Even if you don't stay here, walking around the lobby and window-shopping in the hotel's boutiques is a nice way to kill an hour or two. Parking is $25 per day.

EATING

In many ways, Charleston is a small town, but you'd never think it by the vast selection of excellent restaurants. So much good eatin' is goin' on that you just have to indulge and enjoy. As one local waiter said, 'Diets are for people who think life lasts forever.' So roll up your sleeves and enjoy the Lowcountry cuisine – often featuring seafood caught just hours before your arrival. In addition to the catch of the day, you can get a great steak, authentic Italian, finger-lickin' ribs and tantalizing Thai, just to name a few. On Saturdays in summer, stop by the **farmer's market**, which sets up in Marion Square from 8am to 1pm from April to October.

All restaurants have air-conditioning, are open for lunch and dinner and have nonsmoking sections (unless otherwise noted).

Around Market & Meeting Sts

Many tourists hang out around Market St, and a host of restaurants cater to their every whim. While some of these can draw huge line-ups of people, fear not: you rarely have to wait long, and if your hunger won't hold on, rest assured that another good restaurant is right around the corner.

Joseph's Restaurant (☎ 843-958-8500; 129 Meeting St; breakfast $5-9; 🕑 8am-3pm Mon-Sat, 9am-2pm Sun) Try the delicious crab omelet served with potatoes or grits at this excellent breakfast spot, where the friendly staff keeps the coffee flowing.

Jestine's Kitchen (☎ 843-722-7224; 251 Meeting St; mains $6-10) They're not shy about fryin' here at this good home-style kitchen a few

blocks north of Market St. Here you'll get Southern favorites like fried oysters, hush puppies, grits and fried green tomatoes. There are also great pies.

Sticky Fingers (☎ 843-853-7427; 235 Meeting St; mains $6-11) They don't call it Sticky Fingers for nothing. Memphis-style ribs fall off the bone and taste like a party in your mouth, whether you chose wet, dry, sweet or tangy. This place stays hopping all day and offers good value in a lively atmosphere; it's especially good for families.

Hyman's (☎ 843-723-6000; 215 Meeting St; mains $8-20) Talk about line-ups! For lunch or dinner, this immensely popular seafood restaurant is famous the world over for its giant po'boy sandwiches, as well as for its fresh scallops, oysters, shrimp, mussels and soft-shell crab. If waiting around in the heat's not your thing, come for lunch, when the lines are more reasonable. This is a fun place for kids.

Wild Wing Café (☎ 843-556-3737; 36 N Market St; mains $6-10) Their Chernobyl wings threaten meltdown. With 25 different wing flavors and burgers, quesadillas and other big portions, you get bang for your buck here.

T-Bonz (☎ 843-577-2511; 80 N Market St; meals $10-15) Often winning accolades for having the best steaks in town, the menu here also features ribs, chicken, seafood and a selection of good salads.

Pinckney Café & Espresso (☎ 843-577-0961; 18 Pinckney St; mains $7-12) With a nice outdoor porch, this restaurant housed in a yellow cottage serves up fresh variations on Southern cuisine. You can get excellent desserts here and good coffee, and the Sunday brunch is an excellent way to start the day.

Bocci's (☎ 843-720-2121; 158 Church St; lunch $7-10, mains $12-18) A longtime favorite with both locals and tourists, this jovial place serves up affordable authentic Italian dishes and is a great choice for families.

AW Shucks (☎ 873-723-1151; 35 S Market St; mains $9-14) This gets major promo around town, and your tourist-trap alarm might ring, but fear not – it's just a splendid oyster-shucking place that welcomes everyone for affordable seafood, such as she-crab soup, seafood casserole and fresh crab.

Hank's Seafood Restaurant (☎ 843-723-3474; 10 Hayne St; mains $15-24; 🕑 dinner only) Ah, Hank, how we love thee. Just a shell's toss from the bustle of Market St, Hank's is a trusty

A ROOM WITH A VIEW

Charleston has a great selection of places with outdoor patios. The top three such establishments are the **Pavilion Bar**, **The Terrace** and the **Vendu Rooftop Bar** (all on p167). All three offer revealing views of the city, as well as delicious snacks and friendly bar staff.

oasis where locals come for Lowcountry bouillabaisse, crab soup and other fresh fish dishes.

Anson (☎ 803-577-0551; 12 Anson St; mains $13-22; ☽ dinner only) Mel Gibson ate here often when he was in town filming *The Patriot,* and there's just something nice about knowing his butt sat on these chairs. With a reputation for having the city's best she-crab soup and for using only the finest and freshest local ingredients, Anson tops many a local's list of best restaurants. Free-range meat and fowl and super-fresh seafood make this a great dinner option.

Charleston Grill (☎ 843-577-4522; 224 King St; mains start at $30; ☽ dinner only) Inside the Charleston Place hotel, the décor at this upscale dining room is so delicious you'll want to lick the walls. But please don't – you'll get kicked out, and if you blame Lonely Planet, we'll get in trouble. The food is fantastic – Chef Bob Waggoner has a flare for mixing fresh Lowcountry ingredients with more traditional, 'Northern' flavors. Even if you don't eat here, stop by the bar for a cocktail and soak up the ambiance.

Around E Bay St

East Bay Deli (☎ 843-723-1234; 334 E Bay St; sandwiches $4-7) With a great variety of healthy soups, salads and hearty sandwiches and wraps, this deli near the Aquarium is a great place to pick up a packed lunch, or you can eat inside.

Southend Brewery & Smokehouse (☎ 843-853-0956; 161 E Bay St; mains $7-14) The wall-to-ceiling windows at this fun microbrewery open up, giving the impression you're outside but without all the pollen and sticky air. The menu serves up brick-oven pizza, pasta, seafood and smoked meats.

Slightly North of Broad (☎ 843-723-3424; 192 E Bay St; mains $8-15; ☽ lunch Mon-Fri, dinner daily)

Casual dining and 'maverick' Southern cuisine can be found here at SNOB, whose name takes a jab at the uppercrust society that lives 'south of Broad.' In a converted warehouse, SNOB's menu offers crab cakes, fish and beef dishes, many of which come in smaller sizes for lighter eaters. It can be hit-or-miss here, and seems best at slower times or early in the evening.

Magnolias (☎ 843-577-7771; 185 E Bay St; mains $7-18) Offering Lowcountry, 'Down South dishes with uptown presentation,' this long-standing truly Southern spot has interesting traditional dishes dressed up with modern touches. Try the salads at lunch and the meat dishes at dinner.

Boathouse on East Bay (☎ 843-577-7171; 549 E Bay St; mains $12-18; ☽ dinner only) A lively place housed in an old boat warehouse, the Boathouse is great for catch-of-the-day oysters, mussels, clams and shrimp – although you can also get steaks and pasta. The awning bar is the place to share a plate of raw oysters and soak up the upscale casual scene.

Vintage Restaurant & Wine Bar (☎ 843-577-0900; 14 N Market St; mains $16-26; ☽ dinner only) Vintage owner Kevin Kelley might be the most knowledgeable wine guy in Charleston. His intimate bistro is a great stop for a meal of carefully prepared meat and seafood. Or stop by the bar and enjoy an appetizer or cheese plate, along with a selection off the encyclopedic wine list.

Around King St

Juanita Greenberg's Nacho Royale (☎ 843-723-6224; 439 King St; burritos $6-8) Come for the friendly atmosphere and the fat yummy burritos, piled-high nachos and margaritas.

Andolini's Pizza (☎ 834-722-7437; 82 Wentworth St; slice $3; ☽ till 11pm Mon-Fri, midnight Sat & Sun) Near the college, this revered pizza joint is a favorite with students and anyone looking for good pizza, by the slice or pie, day or night.

Hominy (☎ 843-937-0930; 207 Rutledge Ave; mains $5-15; ☽ breakfast daily, lunch Mon-Fri, dinner Mon-Sat) Near the MUSC Medical Complex, this wonderful spot is worth the walk off the beaten path, with good options for vegetarians. Breakfast features homemade granola and delicious omelets; lunch offers delicious salads and sandwiches. Dinner blends seafood with fresh veggies, all with an interesting, wholesome twist. The weekend brunch is fantastic.

Gaulart & Maliclet (☎ 843-577-9797; 98 Broad St; mains $6-14) Known mostly by its nickname 'Fast & French,' this tiny bistro has a groovy mixed clientele who know to come for the wine and bargain meals. Nightly specials ($14) include a main dish, soup and wine. Also try the Thursday-night fondue ($13) or veggie lunches ($6).

Sermet's Corner (☎ 843-853-7775; 276 King St; mains $7-12) Sermet, the owner, whose art decorates the walls in this cool bistro, cooks up delicious grub, like crab burgers served with sweet-potato fries. Upstairs has couches and a loungelike atmosphere; it's a great place to go for drinks.

Basil (☎ 843-724-3490; 460 King St; mains $6-9; ⏱ lunch Mon-Fri, dinner daily) Ever since opening in late 2002, Basil has been filled to the gills with locals who can't get enough of the terrific Thai dishes at outrageously good prices. Full of fresh ingredients, these Thai standards are prepared on the spot in an exposed kitchen.

39 Rue de Jean (☎ 843-722-8881; 39 John St; lunch $7-10, dinner $9-20) With the lively ambiance of a French bistro, this is a wonderful place for coq au vin and fresh seafood prepared with a French twist.

The Terrace (☎ 843-937-0314; 145 Calhoun St; lunch $6-10, dinner $8-13) The best things about this open-air patio restaurant are the excellent views of Marion Square and the breeze you can catch being up this high. The menu offers decent pizzas, sandwiches, burgers and salads. Service can be a little sluggish, but the view and great bar make up for it.

Il Cortile Del Re (☎ 843-853-1888; 193 King St; pasta $12-15, meat $18-24; ⏱ 6-10pm Tue-Sat) This wonderful little Italian bistro tucked in an alley off King St is almost as good as transporting to Rome. With a dozen tables in a plant-filled courtyard and another handful of tables inside, the atmosphere stays as authentic as the food. The Roman owners offer finger-kissing pasta, wines, cheeses, fish and meat.

ENTERTAINMENT

The balmy evenings are conducive to latenight dining, drinking and dancing at the various venues around Market and E Bay Sts. *Barfly*, an excellent source for bar listings, is a CD-sized monthly magazine written by the most discernable drinkers in town. For live music and theater listings, check out the weekly Charleston *City Paper* (published every Thursday) and the Preview section of Friday's *Post & Courier*.

IMAX Theater (☎ 843-725-4629; www.charleston imax.com; 360 Concord St; adult/child $8/7; call for times) Right behind the Aquarium, this swanky theater runs numerous shows on its basketball court–sized screen, where some 12,000 watts power the explosive surround-sound.

Bars & Clubs

All bars listed here also serve food but are better for sipping a frosty beer, sharing shots with friends or for cocktailing with strangers. Bars often offer live music on weekends. By South Carolina law, all bars must close at 2am, some slightly earlier due to noise ordinances.

Griffon Pub (☎ 843-723-1700; 18 Vendue Range) This is a popular English-style place with good bar food and a friendly, welcoming crowd.

Vendue Rooftop Bar (☎ 843-723-0486; 23 Vendue Range) Until condos sprang up to block the view, this friendly bar in the Vendu Inn used to be the best place in town to sip drinks while overlooking the sea. Though newer bars have better views, the Vendu is still a great spot for an open-air cocktail.

Vickery's (☎ 843-577-5300; 15 Beaufain St) The locals' watering hole of choice, Vick's has big diner-style booths, ice-cold mugs of beer, greasy burgers and a fun crowd. The barstools are always packed. It's smoky, but there's also an outdoor patio for those seeking cleaner air.

AUTHOR'S CHOICE

Pavilion Bar (☎ 843-723-0500; 225 E Bay St) This fun and casual rooftop bar on the upper reaches of the Market Pavilion Hotel offers luscious views over the Cooper River and downtown Charleston. High enough to catch the warm breeze, with friendly bartenders and a mixed, casual crowd, the Pavilion is a must-visit whether you drink Coke or cocktails.

Charlie's Little Bar (☎ 843-723-6242; 141 E Bay St) With comfortable couches and a friendly, loungelike vibe, Charlie's is a great local secret. Look for the wrought-iron entrance off the Wachovia Bank parking lot off E Bay St, upstairs from Saracen restaurant.

Meritage (☎ 843-723-8181; 235 E Bay St) With interesting tapas ($6 to $8), a great happy hour for beer drinkers, and two outdoor patios, Meritage is a great stop for an early evening drink and snack.

Other recommendations include the super-seedy, funky **Big John's Tavern** (251 E Bay St) and the **Blind Tiger** (38 Broad St), where the cool outdoor patio draws students and yuppies alike.

City Bar (☎ 843-577-7383; 5 Faber St) The city's hottest dance club has a hot tub and a lot of beautiful people grooving to DJ tunes. Also check out **Club Pantheon** (p160).

Live Music

Momma's Blues Palace (☎ 843-853-2221; 46 John St) The fine, bluesy sound of Momma & the Misfitz is a must for any blues fan. Momma headlines here on Friday and Saturday nights starting at 10pm. Other nights, stop by for other live local blues bands.

Music Farm (☎ 843-722-8904; 32 Ann St) Both big-time national and smaller regional bands headline here. The crowd varies depending on who's playing, though the college set packs the house on weekends. Call to find out who's playing while you're in town.

Cumberlands (☎ 843-577-9469, 26 Cumberland St) The music menu here has traditionally served local blues, but you can also hear local alternative and grunge rock.

Mezzané (☎ 843-853-7775; 276 King St) Above Sermet's Corner restaurant, this jewel of a jazz venue is all about the mellow scene. Park your butt on comfortable couches and slurp up the excellent live jazz Tuesday to Saturday nights.

Gay and Lesbian Venues

Charleston's gay scene is still pretty low-key, and you'll find fewer gay-friendly venues here than you'll find in Savannah. Two places, right next to each other, are exceptions.

Dudley's (☎ 843-577-6779; 42 Ann St) Almost as artsy as a gallery, Dudley's is a drinking spot mostly for gay men, young and old. Stop by for drink specials during happy hour Monday to Saturday 4pm to 8pm.

Club Pantheon (☎ 843-577-2582; 28 Ann St) Open Friday to Sunday, this super-fun dance club caters to both gay and lesbian clientele, but straight folks are welcome too. Check out the drag-queen cabaret on Friday and Sunday, or boogie to the state's only Billboard DJ.

Performing Arts

Dock St Theater (☎ 843-965-4032; www.charlestonstage.com; 135 Church St) Reconstructed in 1936 from original 1736 blueprints, Dock Street is America's oldest live-performance theater. The busy venue hosts an array of community and professional music and theater groups.

Footlight Players Theater (☎ 843-722-4487; 20 Queen St) The community Footlight Players produces six main-stage productions in its intimate 240-seat theater from August to May.

Theater 99 (☎ 843-853-6687; www.thehavenots.com; 30 Cumberland St) This small theater is home base for The Have Nots!, a comedy improv troupe that performs regularly. Check the website for schedule and tickets.

CHARLESTON JOGGLING BOARD

While walking through Charleston, you might notice a warped-looking bench on the occasional piazza. No, this warping wasn't caused by the sun; this is a joggling board, a Charleston staple since the early 19th century. The board was the brainchild of Mrs Huger, who suffered from severe rheumatism. She wrote to relatives in Scotland and mentioned that she'd outfitted her carriage with a chair so that she could get at least mild exercise by the jostling of the carriage. Her family sent over an early-model joggling board – a long, springy bench she could bounce on to get more exercise. Well, the board was a hit and soon became as popular as a porch swing. Joggling boards faded out with the timber shortage after WWII, but something of a resurgence has happened since the 1970s. Today, you can purchase the bouncy benches at the **Old Charleston Joggling Board Co** (☎ 843-723-4331; 652 King St; ☽ 8am-5pm Mon-Fri).

THE BASKET LADIES

The Gullah women weaving grasses on the street corners are doing more than creating intricate baskets; they are protecting an integral part of Charleston's history. Sweetgrass basketry is a unique skill brought by slaves from West Africa. Carrying everything from food to clothing, the strong baskets were used extensively on plantations and in homes. Today, sweetgrass basketry is one of the oldest art forms of African origin in the US.

Baskets are woven together through a series of coils using bulrush, palmetto leaves, long-leaf pine needles and sweet-smelling sweetgrass. Each basket is different, full of character and created with the blood, sweat, tears and joy of many generations. The skill is passed down from grandmother to granddaughter, and with it comes a sense of history, pride and unique artistry. A basic basket could take an experienced weaver 12 hours. Something bigger and more intricate could take months. The tighter the weave, the better the basket.

The art of basket-making faces many threats: private development and associated land erosion has caused a decline in sweetgrass materials; suburban growth has displaced basket weavers farther north; and younger family members are less eager to learn. But like any art form, sweetgrass basket-making will ebb and flow. Today's artists hold firm that the skill is as important to identity and cultural preservation as language or written history.

Extensive collections are exhibited at the **Charleston Museum** (p152) and in collections around the world, including the Smithsonian Institute in Washington, DC. The best place to buy them in Charleston is at the **Marion Square Old Farmer's Market** (p165), or on the street at Meeting and Broad Sts. Roadside stands on Hwy 17 on the north side of **Mount Pleasant** (p171) are also good for high-quality pieces.

Charleston Ballet Theater (☎ 843-723-7334; www .charlestonballet.com; 477 King St) The ballet puts on an eclectic and exciting mix of traditional and contemporary shows.

Charleston Symphony Orchestra (☎ 843-723-7528; www.charlestonsymphony.com) Nearing its 70th season, the symphony, led by David Stahl, performs in the **Gaillard Auditorium** (☎ 843-577-7400; 77 Calhoun St).

Spectator Sports

The **Charleston RiverDogs** (☎ 843-723-7241; www .riverdogs.com) is an A-league farm team of the major league baseball Tampa Bay Devil Rays. The Dogs, which put on a lively show, play at 'The Joe' – officially, Joseph P Riley Jr Park.

SHOPPING

Most of the notable art galleries and antique shops are situated on Broad St between E Bay and Meeting Sts. Fans of antique-shopping will definitely also want to wander along King St south of Market St. On King St north of market, upscale shops and chains mix with local clothiers and shoe shops. Anyone wishing to purchase some Charleston souvenirs will have fun perusing the stalls and shops at the Old City Market.

Antiques

George C Birland & Co (☎ 843-722-3842; 191 King St; ⓨ 9am-5pm Mon-Sat) is an antique in itself, selling silver, brass, crystal and English antiques. The pride and joy here, however, is the Charleston 'Battery Bench,' like the iron and cypress benches found all along the Battery.

Historic Charleston Reproductions (☎ 843-723-5699; 105 Broad St; ⓨ 10am-5pm Mon-Sat, 1-5pm Sun), at the corner of King and Broad Sts, sells authentic adaptations of 18th- and 19th-century Charleston furniture, ironwork and garden accessories.

King St Antique Mall (☎ 843-723-2211; 495 King St; ⓨ 10am-6pm) is near the visitors center and is a giant antique mall filled with china, silver, jewelry and a vast collection of estate items.

Gifts

The Old City Market is the best place to buy souvenirs, including Charleston sweetgrass baskets, traditional benne (sesame seed) crackers and Lowcountry cookbooks. The shops surrounding the market sell everything from T-shirts to seashells.

Charleston Crafts (☎ 843-723-2938; 87 Hasell St; ⓨ 10am-5:30pm Mon-Sat) A cooperative made up of local artists, including weavers, sculptors, photographers and painters sell their creations here.

Eighty-Two Church (☎ 843-723-7511; 108 Church St; ✆ 10am-6pm Mon-Sat) The ladies here have been crafting the famous, frilly Charleston bonnets for more than 60 years. If you're looking for a classic gift for a child, the hats and dresses here are definitely unique.

Historic Charleston Foundation Museum Shop (☎ 843-724-8484; 108 Meeting St; ✆ 10am-5pm Mon-Sat, 2-5pm Sun) Here you'll find exhibits on Charleston architecture, along with a gift shop that carries an extensive collection of books on local history, culture and architecture.

Preservation Society of Charleston (☎ 843-722-4360; 147 King St; ✆ 10am-5pm Mon-Sat) An excellent stock of Southern literature, books on Charleston history and architecture, and Gullah recordings can be found here.

GETTING THERE & AWAY
Air

The **Charleston International Airport** (☎ 843-767-7009; 5500 International Blvd) is 12 miles outside of town, in North Charleston. Continental, Continental Express, Delta, Northwest, United Airways and United Express serve Charleston with direct flights to and from Atlanta, Charlotte, Chicago, Cincinnati, Dallas, Detroit, Houston, Philadelphia, Raleigh, New York, Newark and Washington.

Bus

The **Greyhound station** (☎ 843-744-4247; www .greyhound.com; 3610 Dorchester Rd) is about 7 miles north of downtown. Carta (p170) bus No 5 runs between downtown and the station. Following is information for some sample destinations.

Destination	Cost	Duration	Frequency
Atlanta, GA	$64	8 hrs	3 daily
Beaufort, SC	$26	2 hrs	2 daily
Columbia, SC	$24	2¼ hrs	2 daily
Macon, GA	$59	7½ hrs	2 daily
Myrtle Beach	$26	2¼ hrs	2 daily
Savannah, GA	$27.50	3 hrs	2 daily
Jacksonville, FL	$53	6 hrs	3 daily

Car & Motorcycle

To reach Charleston from points along the north or south coast, including Savannah, Beaufort and Myrtle Beach, use the coastal Hwy 17, also called the Savannah Hwy. From I-95, take I-26 for about an hour. I-26 is also the fastest route from Charleston to Columbia.

Train

The **Amtrak train station** (☎ 843-744-8264; 4565 Gaynor Ave) is 8 miles north of downtown. The *Silver Meteor* and *Silver Palm* travel the coast; fares to New York are $155 (11 hours); to Savannah, $16 (1½ hours). Carta (p170) bus No 17 goes into town from near the train station.

GETTING AROUND
To/From the Airport

Shuttle buses operate between the airport and downtown for $10 per person (one way).

Taxi fare from the airport is $22. Cab companies include **Yellow Cab** (☎ 843-577-6565) or **North Area Taxi** (☎ 843-554-7575), in North Charleston.

To drive to the airport, take I-26 west to exit 212B and follow the signs.

Avis, Budget, Hertz and National have offices at the airport.

Car & Motorcycle

You'll want to park your car if you're staying in the downtown area, as most sights are accessible by foot, or by the Dash (see below). Many hotels offer secure parking, but you'll pay $10 to $25 per day. You can find meter-free parking on side streets away from the main drag. Parking lots around town charge $8 to $10 per day.

Bus

Charleston Area Regional Transportation Authority (Carta; ☎ 843-747-0922; www.ridecarta.com) runs city buses, as well as the Downtown Area Shuttle (Dash), which has faux streetcars doing five loop routes from the visitors center. All Carta buses are wheelchair accessible. Pick up route maps at the visitors center (p147). The fare is $1.25, or $4 for an all-day pass (for the Dash and all Carta buses).

AROUND CHARLESTON

Across the narrow Cooper River Bridge, Hwy 17 leads to the residential community of Mount Pleasant, which was originally a summer retreat for early Charlestonians.

Today, it's a busy suburban hub. Off the mainland from Mount Pleasant and connected by bridges, the slender barrier islands of Isle of Palms and Sullivan's Island have lovely windswept beaches, small year-round communities and a handful of beachside hotels, resorts and restaurants.

MOUNT PLEASANT
Pop 47,610

Across the narrow Cooper River Bridge is the residential community of Mount Pleasant (originally a summer retreat for early Charlestonians), along with the slim barrier islands of Isle of Palms and Sullivan's Island. A recent boom has brought a glut of strip malls that serve Mount Pleasant's new subdivisions and burgeoning population, but the city's pretty charm still exists, especially in the historic downtown, called the **Old Village**. Along Shem Creek, some of the area's best seafood restaurants sit overlooking the water, and it's fun to dine creekside at sunset while the incoming fishing-boat crews unload their catch.

Stop by the **Mount Pleasant/Isle of Palms Visitors Center** (☎ 843-849-9172; 311 Johnnie Dodds Blvd/Hwy 17); ☽ 9am-5pm Mon-Fri) for information and maps.

Patriot's Point Naval & Maritime Museum

On the east side of the Cooper River, this **maritime museum** (☎ 843-884-2727; 40 Patriots Point Rd; adult/child $13/6; ☽ 9am-5pm, till 6pm in summer) features the USS *Yorktown*, a giant aircraft carrier used extensively in WWII. This 'Fighting Lady' was also deployed in the Vietnam War. You can tour the ship's flight deck, bridge and ready rooms, and learn what life was like for its sailors. Also open for tours are the Medal of Honor Museum, a submarine, a naval destroyer, a Coast Guard cutter and a re-created fire base from Vietnam. Give yourself a good two or three hours to see it all. To get here from Charleston, take Ashley Ave north to the Hwy 17 Crosstown Expressway, which goes north to Mount Pleasant. Follow the sign to your right immediately after the bridge.

From Patriot's Point, you can also catch the Fort Sumter Boat Tour (p153).

Boone Hall Plantation

On the north side of town, 7 miles from Charleston on Hwy 17 N, this former **cotton plantation** (☎ 843-884-4371; www.boonehallplantation .com; 1235 Long Point Rd; adult/child $13/6; ☽ 8:30am-6:30pm Mon-Sat, 1-5pm Sun Apr-Sep; 9am-5pm Mon-Sat, 1-4pm Sun Oct-Mar) is famous for its Avenue of Oaks, a long, magical row of moss-dripping oak trees planted by Thomas Boone in 1743. The plantation home is a 1936 Colonial Revival–style reconstruction filled with period furniture. Costumed guides give glorified history tours of the house and outbuildings, including the former slave cabins. Boone Hall is still a working plantation, though strawberries, tomatoes, peaches and Christmas trees long ago replaced cotton as the primary crop.

About a mile past the plantation, **Palmetto Islands County Park** (☎ 843-884-0832; 444 Needlerush Pkwy; admission $1; ☽ 8am-6pm, till 8pm in summer) has a 943-acre tropical-themed park, with family picnic areas, paddleboat rentals

---

DETOUR: CYPRESS GARDENS

Tour an alligator-infested blackwater swamp in a flat-bottom boat at this cool **attraction** (☎ 843-553-0515; www.cypressgardens.org; 3030 Cypress Gardens Rd; adult/child $9/3; ☽ 9am-5pm), 24 miles north of Charleston. Marvel at the knobby-kneed cypress trees, whose root acids turn the water black. Walk along paths lined with blooming azaleas, tea olives, camellias and daffodils. Watch metamorphosis take place in the butterfly house, stop and smell the roses at the Antique Rose Garden, or discover what lives below at the freshwater aquarium.

Originally part of the Dean Hall Plantation, today's swamp gardens used to be an old reservoir used in rice cultivation. The plantation was purchased as a hunting preserve in 1909, and in 1927 its owner cleared trails through the swamp and began planting thousands of flowering plants. Cypress Gardens opened to the public in 1932. Today, it is a fantastic place to learn about Lowcountry flora and fauna and to get a glimpse of the fascinating swamp ecology.

To get here, take I-26 W to exit 208 and follow Hwy 52 W towards Moncks Corner. Turn right on Cypress Gardens Rd and follow it to the end.

and the Splash Island Water Park ($7). An observation deck offers great views of the salt marshes and tidal creeks.

Charles Pinckney National Historic Site

Near Boone Hall, this **historic site** (☎ 843-881-5516; 1254 Long Point Rd; admission free; ☺ 9am-5pm) sits on the remaining 28 acres of Snee Farm – once an expansive plantation of Charles Pinckney, a famous South Carolinian states-man who helped frame the US Constitution. Exhibits cover archaeological findings on the site, as well as historical descriptions of the slaves and the farming techniques they employed on the plantation. The present house, built after Pinckney sold the property to settle his debts, is a good example of an 1820s coastal cottage. The site is 6 miles north of Charleston, off Hwy 17 on Long Point Rd.

Shem Creek

In addition to waterside restaurants and bars that provide great views at sunset, the Shem Creek Marina has a few outfitters that offer organized boat tours and kayak rentals – a great way to explore the Lowcountry estuaries.

Coastal Expeditions (☎ 843-884-7684; www.coastalexpeditions.com) offers tours of the barrier islands, cypress swamps and along the Shem Creek salt marshes. Half-day tours cost $55 per person, or $85 for a full day. You can also rent kayaks and cruise around on your own for $45/55 for a full day's use of a single/double kayak. **Barefoot Island Sports** (☎ 843-568-3222; www.barefootislandsports.com) has similar offerings, plus shorter trips, such as a two-hour sunset trip in Charleston Harbor ($40 per person).

Shem Creek attracts a lot of visitors for its seafood restaurants. Many locals are critical of the restaurants' prices (which tend to be high) and quality (which suffers sometimes), though you'll still find plenty of 'em sipping beer while watching the sun set on the creek waters. Visitors come for the fresh-though-often-fried seafood and great atmosphere.

Old standbys with good outdoor seating include the **Trawler** (☎ 843-884-2560; 100 Church St; lunch $8-10, dinner $12-25) and the festive **Shem Creek Bar & Grill** (☎ 843-884-8102; 508 Mill St; lunch $8-10, dinner $12-20). More hidden is **The Wreck** (☎ 843-884-0052; dinner $15-18; ☺ 5:15-8:15pm Sun-Thu, till 9:15pm Fri & Sat), a

no-nonsense seafood restaurant in an old icehouse, which the owners bought with the insurance money they received after Hurricane Hugo smashed their boat.

ISLE OF PALMS

Pop 4600

Though primarily residential, the slender barrier islands of Isle of Palms and Sullivan's Island (next) offer up pretty, windswept beaches, with hard-packed white sand and excellent sunsets. Isle of Palms is bigger and more accessible than Sullivan's Island, with 7 miles of unbroken beach, low-key hamburger and T-shirt stands, and a beachside county park (at 14th Ave). Locals and visitors come to windsurf, sail and chill on the beach, or to drop a fishing line in one of the creeks. Isle of Palms is 12 miles from Charleston via Hwy 17 N to Hwy 517 (the Isle of Palms Connector).

Sleeping & Eating

Wild Dunes Resort (☎ 843-886-2260, 888-845-8926; www.wilddunes.com; 5757 Palm Blvd; d $110-220, villas $250-1200) Dominating 1600 acres on the northeastern end of the island is this family resort and golfing paradise (with two courses designed by Tom Fazio). Pro-grams for kids, a top-notch tennis facility, a private beach and a pool are just a few of the amenities. You can rent boats and join fishing charters at the resort marina. Many families come for their two-week vacation and enjoy the full services. Accommodations range from one-room villas to beachside condos to full houses. Most accommodations have kitchen and laundry facilities. Rates vary dramatically, so call ahead or check online to see what's available.

On the main part of the island, there are lots of beach rentals; contact the **Mount Pleasant/Isle of Palms Visitors Center** (☎ 843-849-9172) for a list of realty agencies.

Sea Biscuit Café (☎ 843-886-4079, 21 JC Long Blvd; mains $6-9; ☺ 6:30am-2:30pm Tue-Fri, 7:30am-1pm Sat & Sun) This is the place to go for breakfast or lunch. It's a laid-back local place with great Lowcountry breakfasts and yummy soups and sandwiches.

Boathouse at Breach Inlet (☎ 843-886-8000; 101 Palm Blvd; mains $10-22; ☺ dinner only) Right on the Intracoastal Waterway, the Boathouse serves Lowcountry dishes and plenty of seafood. The sunset view from the upstairs deck is magnificent, and you can often see dolphins playing in the marshy water.

Windjammer (☎ 843-886-8596; 1000 Ocean Blvd; pub grub $6-12) Though burgers and fried seafood dishes are available, most people hit the Windjammer to gaze at the frolicking bikinis and flexing hard-bodies. With sand on the floor, volleyball out back and live music, this is a fun place to relax after a hard day on the beach.

SULLIVAN'S ISLAND
Pop 1910

Edgar Allen Poe used Sullivan's Island as the backdrop for his tale of buried treasure in 'The Gold Bug.' Perhaps not as wild and eerie as Poe painted it, Sullivan's Island is noncommercial, with elegant early 20th-century beach houses and abandoned military fortifications now covered in moss and weeds. Public beach access is available on certain parts of the island; observe all parking and swimming signs posted or face heavy fines. Even if you don't like books, check out the **library** (1921 I'on Ave), which is housed in an old battery fortification.

Poe was actually stationed on the south end of the island at Fort Moultrie for 13 months. The first European settlement on the island, **Fort Moultrie** (☎ 843-883-3123; 1214 Middle St; adult/child $2/1; ☽ 9am-5pm) was built in the 1770s to protect Charleston from a sea invasion. Made of spongy palmetto logs, the fort's walls were able to absorb, without fracture, shells from the British navy in one of the first American victories of the Revolutionary War. A good example of the now defunct coastal defense system, Fort Moultrie was modernized and manned until 1947, when new military technologies made such forts obsolete.

To soak up the true ambiance of the island, stop by for a meal or drink at **Dunleavy's Pub** (☎ 843-883-9646; 2213 Middle St), which has pub grub and excellent outdoor seating overlooking the beach. You'll see it if you continue straight after the bridge.

Sullivan's Island is about 10 miles from Charleston. Take Hwy 17 N Business to Mount Pleasant and turn right on Hwy 703. To get to Fort Moultrie, turn right onto Middle St and follow it for a mile.

CHARLESTON'S SOUTH ISLANDS

Beachcombers, sun worshipers, body surfers, golfers and anyone fond of casting a line will find plenty to do on the slim, sandy beaches of Charleston's south islands. Family-friendly resorts with pools and vast activity programs share luscious beaches with the loggerhead turtles, which nest by the light of the moon. Endangered birds swoop through the tide marshes, porpoises play in the sheltered bays, and gators lurk in the sweetgrass. Whether you stay for a weekend or rent a beach house for a month, you'll leave relaxed, with sun-kissed skin and soft sand in your shoes.

KIAWAH ISLAND
Pop 1165

With 10 miles of some of the east coast's most beautiful beaches, it's no surprise vacationers have been coming to Kiawah (kee-a-wah) in ever-increasing droves. The island was owned for much of its modern history by the illustrious Vanderhorst family, which grew cotton here until after the Civil War. Descendents sold the mostly wild island for $125,000 in 1951. Just 23 years later, developers purchased it for $18.2 million.

When you come to Kiawah Island Resort, you enter through a security gate. In order to get through the gate, you must

---

HONOR THE ANCIENT

On the way to Kiawah, stop at by the ancient **Angel Oak** on John's Island. This gigantic *Quercus virginiana*, or live oak, is believed to be more than 1400 years old and probably sprouted a thousand years before Columbus made his way to the New World. Surviving numerous hurricanes, centuries of development, war and disease, this tree is said to be the oldest living thing east of the Mississippi. It would take a team of people to hug this gorgeous oak, whose circumference measures 25ft. Though only 65ft high, its gnarly arms provide 17,000 sq ft of shade. Its largest limb is 11ft around and 89ft long.

CHARLESTON

be staying at the resort, using (and paying for) its facilities, or staying on one of the nearby properties. This air of exclusivity can be off-putting at first, but once you're settled in, you'll get used to it. I f you are not staying with the resort, you'll need to buy a $50 'amenity pass,' which is valid for a week and lets you use the resort programs and facilities (most of which also cost extra).

Activities

The island's white-sand beaches are accessible by walkways from the resort, or from public entry points along the way. The Kiawah Island Inn has two beachside pools; one for families and one for adults only. The 21-acre Night Heron Park also has a pool, mostly used by families with young kids. If you are not staying with Kiawah Island Resort, you have to pay $12 per day or $45 per week to use the pools. The resort also offers excellent kids programs, special events and outdoor excursions, including cookouts, fishing and kayak trips.

Kiawah has 30 miles of paved **bicycle** paths, making the two-wheel express the best way to get around. The following rent bikes.

Kiawah Island Resort (☎ 800-576-1570; Kiawah Island Inn; $12/half-day, $18/day, $42/week)
Seaside Cycles (☎ 843-768-5080; Bohicket Marina Village; $3/hr, $7/half-day, $10/day, $30/week)

With five of the country's best public **golf courses** on one small island, Kiawah attracts amateurs and pros alike. To book tee times at any of the courses, call ☎ 843-768-2121. Green fees are lower in summer, higher in the spring and fall. In the following list, the prices are given as low/high season.

Ocean Course ($160/230) Designed by Pete Dye; amid 2½ miles of oceanfront dunes.
Turtle Point ($110/150) Designed by Jack Nicklaus; has a 1st-class instructional facility.
Osprey Point ($110/150) Designed by Tom Fazio; check out the clubhouse for drinks along the fairway.

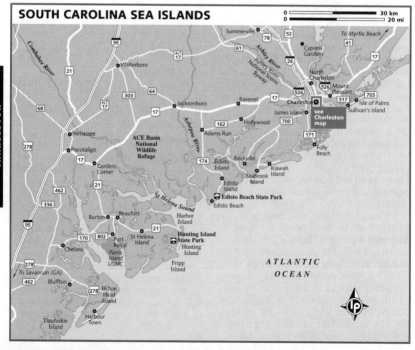

Cougar Point ($90/135) Designed by Gary Player; challenging but wide fairways.

Oak Point ($60/80) Designed by Clyde Johnston; on an old indigo plantation; probably the best bet for novices.

Kiawah's two premier **tennis** facilities offer hard and clay courts, excellent private instruction, and tennis clinics for players of all ages and abilities. Courts cost $20 per hour, most hour-long clinics cost $18, and private instruction is $57 per hour. Call ☎ 800-576-1570 for reservations and information.

The **Bohicket Marina**, between the entrances to Kiawah and Seabrook Islands, has shops, restaurants and the **Bohicket Boat Adventure & Tour Company** (☎ 843-768-7294; www.bohicketboat.com), which offers fishing, boating, kayaking, and sailing trips, as well as boat and kayak rentals. The Sea Island Excursion (adult/child $32/24) is a three-hour trip to shell-filled beaches; the two-hour Dolphin Watching trip ($24/16) follows the playful bottle-nosed dolphins; the two-hour Learn to Fish ($25, adults only) will teach you how to tie, bait, hook and catch fish. Kayak rentals cost single/double $15/25 per hour, or $80/95 per day.

Sleeping & Eating

Several companies own rental properties – houses, villas and condos – on Kiawah Island. Rates vary dramatically, depending on proximity to the beach and time of year. Summer is high season, with spring and fall as shoulder seasons and the low season being winter.

Renting a one-bedroom beachfront condo for a week ranges about $1200 to $1900 in the height of summer. A four-bedroom beachside house in summer would start at $3000. Contact **Great Beach Vacations** (☎ 843-768-2300, 800-845-3911; explorekiawah.com) or **Beachwalker Rentals** (☎ 843-768-1777, 800-334-6308; www.beachwalker.com).

Kiawah Island Resort (☎ 843-768-2121, 800-654-2924; www.kiawahresort.com; 12 Kiawah Beach Dr) Spread out along the island and composed of an inn, plus some 600 rental homes and villas, this resort sits in a natural setting, with two nationally ranked tennis centers and five world-class golf courses scattered within a few miles of each other. The Kiawah Island Inn sits at the heart of the resort, with a few shops, pools and beach access.

The resort offers daily and weekly rates in a variety of accommodations. Rooms in the Kiawah Island Inn run $160 to $360. One-bedroom villas cost $160 to $200 a night, or $980 to $2300 a week. Rates for larger villas and homes (with as many as six bedrooms) are $350 to $2400 a night, or $2140 to $9900 a week. Several **restaurants** are on-site; call ☎ 843-768-2768 for information.

Sidi's Cookhouse (☎ 404-768-4239; 4430 Bohicket Rd; lunch $6-9, dinner $12-14) Popular with locals and visitors, Sidi's offers big bang for your buck by serving up weighty portions of seafood barbecue (grilled shrimp, yum!), deli-sandwiches, pizzas and subs.

Past the turnoff to Kiawah en route to Seabrook Island, the **Bohicket Marina** offers the best nonresort dining options. The following are all located there.

Rosebank Farms Café (☎ 843-768-1807; Bohicket Marina; lunch $5-9, dinner $17-22) Deliciously fresh local ingredients are the order of the day at this friendly spot. At lunch try the fried shrimp and oyster po'boy sandwich, or a crisp salad. For dinner, try the fresh fish 'n' grits or the Carolina carpetbagger (filet mignon with corn-fried oysters).

Privateer (☎ 843-768-1290; mains $18-22; ☺ dinner only) Overlooking the marina, the Privateer serves up pasta dishes, crab cakes and Lowcountry surf 'n' turf. A special kids' menu offers good choices for $6. Head upstairs to the Sunset Lounge to sip after-dinner drinks while looking over the water.

Café St Tropez (☎ 843-768-1500; mains $20-30; ☺ dinner only) This 4½-star bistro serves excellent seasonal specials with a provençal flare. Reservations are recommended.

Getting There & Away

Kiawah Island is 21 miles south of Charleston. To drive there from Charleston, take Hwy 17 S over the Ashley River Bridge, then follow Hwy 171 (Folly Rd) to Maybank Hwy (Hwy 700). Take Maybank south to Bohicket Rd, turn left and follow it to the end. Kiawah Island is on the left, Seabrook Island (next) is on the right. That's the short route, but you can also take Hwy 20 S off Hwy 17 S.

SEABROOK ISLAND

Pop 1250

Almost entirely residential, Seabrook is a private, gated island resort, just a couple miles from Kiawah. It has 3 miles of

---

THE SANCTUARY

After 10 years, a lot of dreaming and some $125 million, the **Sanctuary** (☎ 800-576-1585) finally opened for business in early 2004. The 255-room luxury hotel may be the hottest thing to hit the beach since the invention of the bikini. Perched on edge of the island, overlooking the ocean and with just a miniskirt of sand and dunes between the hotel and the Atlantic, the Sanctuary is a beacon of indulgence. No expense was spared in her construction, which was designed to mimic an elegant four-story beach home. Because the coast is too shallow for ships or barges, most of the building materials came by truck. Some 185,000 cubic yards of dirt were hauled in and used to raise the land, so that wherever you stand – in the lobby or in your room, in the cigar bar, the martini bar or the grand dining room – you'll see sweeping views of the ocean. A million bricks also came in by truck, as did slate and copper for the roof. Service vehicles use a tunnel beneath the hotel. To keep the integrity of the landscape, a special team from Texas came in to transplant 169 ancient oak trees, using the world's largest mechanical spade.

Two outdoor pools, an indoor pool, two restaurants and a full-service spa are just a few of the amenities. The Southern-influenced décor offers both formality and beach appeal, so you'll feel as comfortable in flip-flops as you would in glass slippers. Reclaimed antique walnut floors were designed to give, so they creak a little, just like in an old beach house. All guest rooms have balconies and ample views of the ocean – you can even see the water while soaking in your bathtub! Custom-made Italian furniture fills the rooms, all of which have wireless high-speed Internet access, just in case you needed to check email from your beach chair or in between rounds of golf. A team of folks went around to the best hotels in the world to find the most comfortable beds (Omaha Bed Company won out), all of which are covered with rich linens and down duvets.

The cost to stay here, you ask? Like everywhere else in Kiawah, rates will vary by season and availability, but the starting rate for a standard room is $275. Prices go way up from there; you could stay in the 3100-sq-ft presidential suite for a mere $4500 per night. The Sanctuary is located behind the Kiawah Island Resort's East Village. Get there by taking Kiawah Beach Pkwy to Sanctuary Beach Dr. Reservations are booked through the **Kiawah Island Resort** (see p175).

---

coastline and a full-service **equestrian center** (☎ 843-768-7541) that offers beach and trail rides. You can arrange rental properties through **Great Beach Rentals** (☎ 843-768-5056, 800-845-2233; www.seabrook.com). The Seabrook Island gate is just two miles past the turnoff to Kiawah.

EDISTO ISLAND

Mainly visited by South Carolinians, Edisto (*ed*-iss-toh) is as homespun as big Sunday dinners. Families come here for annual beach trips, weddings and reunions. Row upon row of unassuming cottages line the oceanfront and marsh. Relatively little commercial development has occurred, and the island's preservation society works to keep it that way. Many of the full-time residents live on parcels of land that were originally part of plantations that their ancestors once farmed. The Edisto Indians first lived on the island, followed by plantations that were famous for sea-island cotton and the long thread it produced. The boll weevil and the Civil War permanently ended that phase of the island's history, which has been quiet ever since.

For area information, stop by the **Edisto Beach Welcome Center** (☎ 843-869-4528; 101 Jungle Rd; ☼ 9am-5pm Mon-Sat).

Edisto is 45 miles south of Charleston. From Charleston, take US 17 S, go left on Hwy 174 and follow it to the coast.

Sights

You'll find a remnant of the island's Indian culture at **Edisto Beach State Park** (☎ 843-869-2756; 8377 State Cabin Rd; ☼ 6am-10pm during daylight saving time, then 8am-6pm). The Spanish Mount is a large shell mound dating to 2000 BC. A 3½-mile trail winds through the maritime forest to the mound and back. Look for deer, osprey and alligators, and be sure to bring mosquito repellent.

Find out more about Edisto and coastal history at the small but surprisingly interesting **Edisto Island Museum** (☎ 843-869-

1954; www.edistomuseum.com; 2343 Hwy 174; admission $2; ☽ 1-4pm Tue, Thu & Sat).

Other attractions include the **Edisto Island Serpentarium** (☎ 843-869-1171; www .edistoserpentarium.com; 1374 Hwy 174; ☽ 10am-6pm Mon-Sat May-Sep), where a giant collection of turtles, alligators, lizards and snakes are lovingly cared for in their natural habitats. Exhibits and educational programs offered throughout the day help convince even the most dubious that serpents get a bad rap – some of 'em are even cute!

Sleeping & Eating

Edisto Beach State Park (☎ 843-869-2756; campsites/ cabins $25/80) The park rents two-bedroom marsh-front cabins (sleeping up to six people) that are furnished and air-conditioned, with kitchens, running water and screened-in porches. The campground has oceanfront or marsh-front campsites with water and power. The restrooms are clean.

Short- and long-term rentals are available through **Edisto Sales & Rentals** (☎ 843-869-2527, 800-868-5398; www.edistorealty.com). Rental properties here range from about $500 to $1300 per week in peak season.

Po-Pigs BBQ Restaurant (☎ 843-869-9003; 2410 Hwy 174; adult/child $7.50/3.50; ☽ 11:30am-9pm Wed-Sat) A must-stop for the finger-lickin' good, all-you-can-eat barbecue buffet. You can get other Southern faves, like fried chicken, collards and dirty rice.

Pavilion Restaurant (☎ 843-869-3061; 102 Palmetto Blvd; lunch $6-9, dinner $10-20; ☽ 11:30am-3pm & 5-9pm) With a great location overlooking the ocean, this is a great bet for seafood and sunsets. The chef takes fresh Lowcountry ingredients and adds unique and delicious flavors. Crab cakes: yummy.

EXPLORE THE ACE BASIN

While it's no wonder more Americans are migrating to the lush Carolina coast than ever before, the cost of development has left an already fragile ecosystem fighting for survival.

The **ACE Basin Preserve** was established in 1990 as part of a joint effort among federal and state governments, private conservation groups and local landowners. The area, mostly an undeveloped combination of maritime forests, estuarine rivers, tidal marshes and barrier islands, stretches for 350,000 acres. The preserve is named for the Ashepoo, Combahee, and Edisto Rivers, which combine to create one of the largest undeveloped estuaries on the Atlantic Coast.

With its rich diversity of landscapes, the ACE Basin protects a host of endangered and threatened species, including the bald eagle, wood stork, osprey, loggerhead sea turtle and shortnose sturgeon. Some 250 species of migrating birds traveling along the Atlantic Flyway stop by to eat, breed and nest in the basin.

The best way to see the ACE Basin is by boat and, given its position at the confluence of the north and south Edisto Rivers, Edisto Beach is a good place to launch. **Edisto Watersports & Tackle** (☎ 843-869-0663; 3731 Docksite Rd) offers tours. Boat operators in Beaufort (p138) also run tours of the basin.

You can also walk through part of the preserve. Rough trails wind through the refuge from the Grove Plantation, which houses the office of the **ACE Basin National Wildlife Refuge** (☎ 843-889-3084; acebasin.fws.gov; 8675 Willtown Rd, Hollywood, SC; ☽ 7:30am-4pm Mon-Fri). Here, you can pick up maps and get information on tours.

To get here from Hwy 17, take Hwy 174 through Adams Run. Take a right at the flashing light (Willtown Rd). The entrance is 2 miles down on your left.

Myrtle Beach & the Grand Strand

Attracting some 14 million visitors a year, the South Carolina Grand Strand takes the No 2 position as the most visited family or beach destination in the US (next to Florida). The Grand Strand is a 60-mile stretch of coastline beginning just inside the northern border of South Carolina and extending south to Georgetown. Though bridges and roadways make it seem otherwise, the Strand is actually an island flanked by the Intracoastal Waterway and the Waccamaw River on the west side, and the Atlantic Ocean on the other.

Myrtle Beach is one of the fastest-growing communities in the US, and as a result, surrounding communities are sprawling to catch the overflow. Environmentalists shudder at the effects of development; fragile ecosystems along the dunes and coastal waterways are at serious risk; and the beach – the thing that brought everyone here in the first place – can only handle so many people, construction and boat traffic before it starts to erode. Places like Huntington Beach State Park preserve the environment; here you can see what the wild, windswept coast was like just a couple decades ago.

While some fear growth, others embrace it. New hotels, restaurants and souvenir shops crop up every year. The good thing is that most developers realize that in order to sustain the growth, they need to protect the main attraction. If you want customers to keep coming to the circus, you need to protect the tiger.

For now, fun and easy livin' is the name of the game. The beachy vibe along the Strand is ample, and whether you spend time in a behemoth resort or in beach rental, or tucked in a tent at a state park, you'll likely get very intimate with your tank tops and flip-flops.

HIGHLIGHTS

- **Wining**
  Swill a cold beer while watching the sunset at Bummz Beach Café (p187), in Myrtle Beach

- **Dining**
  Slurp fresh oysters on the tidal creek in Murrells Inlet (p189)

- **Green Haven**
  Get tingles from the sculptures and pure beauty of Brookgreen Gardens (p183)

- **Wildlife Encounter**
  Get close with alligators at Huntington Beach State Park (p191)

- **Offbeat Experience**
  Take a shag-dancing lesson in North Myrtle Beach (p188)

- TELEPHONE CODE: **843**
- POPULATION: **25,500**
- AREA: **22 SQ MI**

MYRTLE BEACH

Myrtle Beach proper is the central area in a 25-mile strip of the Grand Strand, which stretches from North Myrtle Beach to Pawleys Island. Though the long stretches of sandy beaches promise natural bliss, the town is not exactly the place for nature lovers: if you were to relocate Las Vegas (minus the gambling) to the Carolina coast, you would have a close approximation to Myrtle Beach. The beach is beautiful, but it's a minor attraction compared to the huge outdoor malls, 120 golf courses, water parks, country music shows, hot dog stands and T-shirt shops.

One of the most popular resorts along the Eastern Seaboard, Myrtle Beach is successful because it's strangely democratic. Fancy upscale condos reside beside smaller and cheaper family-owned motels, and the beach's carnival attractions are diverse enough to entertain toddlers, teenagers and grandparents alike. Restaurants cater to the masses, offering inexpensive buffets and usually a special menu for children.

Visitors – from college students on Spring Break to European tour groups and from RV retirees to young families – come for the true taste of Americana, and while they're here, they soak up the sun, stroll along the sandy beaches and partake in the festival of beachside living.

Just a couple of decades ago, Myrtle Beach was a one-traffic-light town. According to one local, you could drive down Ocean Blvd at night and not see a soul. Now, several dozen traffic lights try to control the flow of cars, and in spring, summer and fall, the crowds flow in like the tide, not ebbing again until the depth of winter.

ORIENTATION

Myrtle Beach sits on a long stretch between the Intracoastal Waterway and the Atlantic Ocean. Hwy 17 runs roughly north–south and diverges at Murrells Inlet. Hwy 17 Business (Kings Hwy) goes into the heart of Myrtle Beach, and Hwy 17 Bypass skirts the city's west side, just east of the Intracoastal Waterway. Confused? Don't be. If you need to get to the communities north and south of the city, Hwy 17 Bypass is your friend. Take it north to get to Barefoot Landing and

North Myrtle Beach, or south to Murrells Inlet and Pawleys Island. If you need to drive through the heart of Myrtle Beach, you'll use Hwy 17 Business, trafficky as it is.

Ocean Blvd runs along the beach, which is flanked by a near-continuous row of 10- to 20-story concrete high-rises on the beachside, and on the other side are parking lots, neon signs, tourist shops, bars and restaurants. Kings Hwy (Hwy 17 Business) runs parallel to Ocean Blvd.

Just getting into Myrtle Beach will be difficult because of traffic; finding your hotel should be a little easier if you understand the oceanfront's simple grid system. The blocks on Ocean Blvd run by hundreds and are designated north or south depending on whether the streets are north or south of the 2nd Ave pier. If your hotel's address is 2700 N Ocean Blvd, it will be north of the 2nd Ave pier and near the intersection of Ocean Blvd and 27th Ave N.

INFORMATION
Bookshops

Barnes & Noble (☎ 843-444-4046; 1145 Seaboard St) In the Seaboard Commons shopping center on Hwy 17 Bypass, near 21st Ave N.

Living Room (☎ 843-626-8363; Hwy 17 Bypass near 38th Ave N) A groovy espresso bar with a good selection of used books. It also has DSL Internet access. There are occasional poetry readings and other literary events.

Emergency

Emergency numbers (☎ 911) Police, ambulance and firefighters.
AAA Roadside Service (☎ 800-222-4357)

Library

Chapin Memorial Library (☎ 843-918-1275; 400 14th Ave N) Has Internet access and offers temporary library cards to visitors.

Media

Sun News Myrtle Beach's daily newspaper.

Medical Services

Grand Strand Regional Medical Center (☎ 843-692-1000; 809 82nd Pkwy)
South Shore Ambulatory Care Center (☎ 843-692-1000; 5050 Hwy 17 Bypass)
CVS Pharmacy (☎ 843-448-1684; 6th Ave N & Kings Hwy)

Post

Myrtle Beach post office (☎ 843-626-9533; 505 N Kings Hwy)

MYRTLE BEACH
& THE GRAND STRAND

Tourist Offices

The Myrtle Beach Area Chamber of Commerce operates three visitors centers. All are well stocked with maps and information. Be sure to pick up the weighty *Stay & Play* guide, which lists area hotels and attractions. Coupons and modestly discounted tickets are available in booklets like the *Monster Coupon Book*; these are distributed in restaurants, hotels and at the visitors centers.

Myrtle Beach Visitors Center (☎ 843-626-7444, 800-356-3016; www.myrtlebeachinfo.com; 1200 N Oak

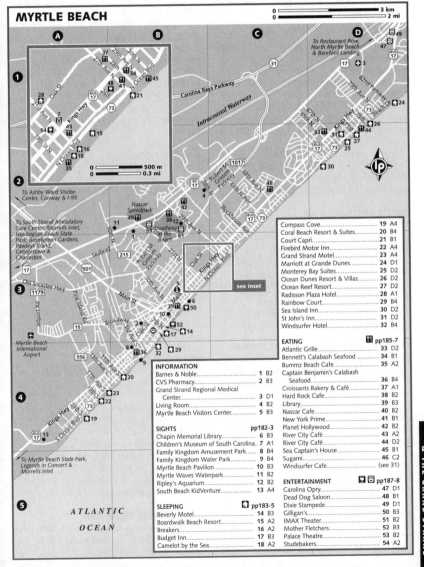

MYRTLE BEACH

INFORMATION	
Barnes & Noble.................................. 1	B2
CVS Pharmacy.................................... 2	B3
Grand Strand Regional Medical	
Center... 3	D1
Living Room....................................... 4	B2
Myrtle Beach Visitors Center........... 5	B3

SIGHTS	pp182-3
Chapin Memorial Library................... 6	B3
Children's Museum of South Carolina.. 7	A1
Family Kingdom Amusement Park..... 8	B4
Family Kingdom Water Park.............. 9	B4
Myrtle Beach Pavilion...................... 10	B3
Myrtle Waves Waterpark.................. 11	B2
Ripley's Aquarium............................ 12	B2
South Beach KidVenture................... 13	A4

SLEEPING	pp183-5
Beverly Motel................................... 14	B3
Boardwalk Beach Resort.................. 15	A2
Breakers.. 16	A2
Budget Inn....................................... 17	B3
Camelot by the Sea......................... 18	A2
Compass Cove.................................. 19	A4
Coral Beach Resort & Suites............. 20	B4
Court Capri...................................... 21	B1
Firebird Motor Inn............................ 22	A4
Grand Strand Motel.......................... 23	A4
Marriott at Grande Dunes................. 24	D1
Monterey Bay Suites......................... 25	D2
Ocean Dunes Resort & Villas............ 26	D2
Ocean Reef Resort........................... 27	D2
Radisson Plaza Hotel........................ 28	A1
Rainbow Court.................................. 29	B4
Sea Island Inn.................................. 30	D2
St John's Inn.................................... 31	D2
Windsurfer Hotel.............................. 32	B4

EATING	pp185-7
Atlantic Grille.................................. 33	D2
Bennett's Calabash Seafood............. 34	B1
Bummz Beach Cafe.......................... 35	A2
Captain Benjamin's Calabash	
Seafood.. 36	B4
Croissants Bakery & Café................. 37	A1
Hard Rock Cafe................................ 38	B2
Library.. 39	B3
Nascar Cafe..................................... 40	B2
New York Prime................................ 41	B1
Planet Hollywood............................ 42	B2
River City Café................................. 43	A2
River City Café................................. 44	B1
Sea Captain's House........................ 45	B1
Sugami.. 46	C2
Windsurfer Cafe.......................... (see 31)

ENTERTAINMENT	pp187-8
Carolina Opry.................................. 47	D1
Dead Dog Saloon............................. 48	B1
Dixie Stampede................................ 49	D1
Gilligan's... 50	B3
IMAX Theater................................... 51	B2
Mother Fletchers.............................. 52	B3
Palace Theatre................................. 53	B2
Studebakers..................................... 54	A2

St; 8:30am-5pm Mon-Fri year-round, weekend hours 9am-5pm Mar-Sep, 9am-noon Oct-Feb) The main visitors center and home to the chamber of commerce.

South Strand Visitors Center (☎ 843-651-1010; 3401 Hwy 17 Business; 8:30am-5pm Mon-Fri year-round, weekend hours 9am-5pm Mar-Sep, 9am-noon Oct-Feb) In Murrells Inlet, where Hwy 17 divides.

Ashby Ward Visitors Center (☎ 843-626-7444; 1800 Hwy 501 W; 8:30am-6pm Apr-Sep) On the way into town if you're coming east from I-95.

SIGHTS

Even though much of Myrtle Beach is an amusement park in itself, there are two humongous family-oriented parks that compete for attention along Ocean Blvd. This is also where youth on Spring Break cruise down the street in muscle cars or hang around in bikinis and boardshorts, getting fake tattoos and checking out the scene.

At the south end of the strip, the South Beach KidVenture caters to younger kids. Open and closing times vary, depending on the season. In winter, the parks shut down.

Myrtle Beach Pavilion

The heart of the resort, historically and geographically, the **Pavilion** (☎ 843-448-6456; www.mbpavilion.com; all-day pass adult/child $24/15; call for hours) fills the space between 8th and 9th Aves and Kings Hwy and N Ocean Blvd. It has 11 acres of amusement park rides and a Coney Island–style boardwalk. Teenagers dig the **Attic**, an under-21 nightclub with DJs and Top 40 tunes.

FAMILY KINGDOM AMUSEMENT PARK & WATER PARK

Just south of 3rd Ave S and Ocean Blvd, **Family Kingdom** (☎ 843-626-3447; www.family-kingdom.com; all-day ride pass $19.50, all-day water-park pass adult/child $16/15, combo pass $25; call for hours) might be a better value than the Pavilion. Both parks claim to have the biggest, baddest roller coaster, but Family Kingdom can claim Myrtle Beach's only oceanfront water park.

SOUTH BEACH KIDVENTURE

At the south end of Ocean Blvd, where it turns to become S Kings Hwy, this **amusement park** (☎ 843-913-5300; all-day pass $6 for under 3, $13 ages 3-6, $15 ages 7 & up; 1pm-8pm in summer) has many rides geared toward little kids who might not make the height

requirement at other amusement parks. KidVenture is also quieter than the others.

Broadway at the Beach

Built around an artificial and fish-filled lake and set as three thematic villages (Caribbean, New England Fishing, and Charleston Boardwalk), this lively **outdoor mall** (☎ 843-444-3200; www.broadwayatthebeach.com; 21st Ave N & Hwy 17 Bypass; 10am-9pm in summer, till 6pm in winter) has more than 100 specialty shops, 20 restaurants, six nightclubs, two minigolf courses, an **IMAX** (☎ 843-448-4629; adult/child $7.25/6.25; call for showtimes) and multiplex theater, and an aquarium. It might be more accurately called 'Broadway on the Bypass,' since it is on Hwy 17, between 21st and 29th Aves N – not near the beach.

RIPLEY'S AQUARIUM

You'll be pleasantly surprised by this **aquarium** (☎ 843-916-0888, 800-734-8888; www.ripleysaquarium.com; 110 Celebrity Circle; $15/9; 9am-11pm), which really isn't as cheesy as you might expect. Glass-encased tunnels travel through the tanks for an up-close view of 10ft sharks (it's a little unnerving to stand underneath a shark's belly!). There are also hourly dive presentations and marine-education shows, as well as a stingray petting tank. The aquarium claims to be the No 1 attraction in the state; to avoid those massive shark-loving crowds, come early in the morning or after 7pm.

NASCAR SPEEDPARK

Southerners love their Nascar, and at this **go-cart track** (☎ 843-918-8725; www.nascarspeedpark.com; 1820 21st Ave N; adult/child $25/15; 10am-10pm, till 8pm in winter) on steroids, speed-lovers can zip around on seven different tracks. Real-life race-car drivers occasionally drop in for special demonstrations. In addition to the tracks (you must be 40 inches tall to ride), there are kiddie go-carts, a climbing wall and the ubiquitous minigolf.

Myrtle Waves Water Park

About 10 blocks southwest of Broadway at the Beach, this **water world** (☎ 843-448-1026; www.myrtlewaves.com; Hwy 17 Bypass & 10th

---

DETOUR: BROOKGREEN GARDENS

Unbelievable, beautiful and altogether stunning, the **Brookgreen Gardens** (☎ 843-235-6000, 800-849-1931; www.brookgreen.org; 7-day pass adult/student & senior $12/10, children under 12 free; ☽ 9:30am-5pm) will likely be one of the most magical places you'll ever visit. Blooming on the site of four former rice plantations, these spectacular gardens were the vision of Virginia shipbuilder Archer Huntington and his wife, sculptor Anna Hyatt Huntington. The Huntingtons developed this site as a nature preserve and as an outdoor canvas to exhibit Anna's renowned artwork. The gardens opened to the public in 1932.

Today, the grounds hold the largest collection of American sculpture on the continent. More than 500 stone, marble and metal works from almost every sculptor of note in the past 130 years are displayed so naturally that it's as though they bloomed here along with the flora. One walk down the majestic Avenue of Oaks leaves your hair standing on end. A visit to the Children's Garden evokes fairytales and reminders of childhood whimsy. The new Lowcountry Center presents captivating exhibits of the cultural and natural history of the Carolina Lowcountry. Bunnies hop around, and birds chirp in the trees. It would take several days to explore the entire 9000-acre preserve, which is why the admission ticket is good for seven days. Special events take place on summer evenings; call to find out what's going on during your visit.

Brookgreen is 16 miles south of Myrtle Beach on Hwy 17 S, just across from Huntington Beach State Park.

Ave N; all-day pass $23/14, afternoon pass $15/11; ☽ 10am-6pm spring & summer only) has loads of fun features. Kids will love the 10-story-high Turbo Twister (claiming to be the world's tallest tubular slide) and the enormous wave pool, while adults can kick back on an inner tube as the lazy river floats them around the park. There's a special toddler pool and a fun bubble zone for kids.

Children's Museum of South Carolina

Afraid your tot is getting dumbed-down from excessive amounts of cotton candy and miniature golf? Stop by this **museum** (☎ 843-946-9469; 2501 N Kings Hwy; admission $5; ☽ 10am-4pm Mon-Sat, shorter hours off season) to jumpstart the old gray matter. Created for kids ages 1 to 11, the interactive, hands-on displays cover magnets and electricity – there's even a kiddie ATM. The museum is in the parking lot of the Myrtle Square Mall, across the street from the Radisson and convention center.

SLEEPING

Myrtle Beach used to be just a summer resort, and the locals had it to themselves the rest of the year. Thanks to the game of golf, the tourist season now extends into October and November, and March and April. The super high season is from June through August, when most kids are on summer holiday. The prices quoted below are high-season rates only.

Camping

Most campgrounds are veritable parking lots and cater to families with RVs, but the best camping is at **Myrtle Beach State Park** (p189), 3 miles south of central Myrtle Beach. Even better camping can be found at **Huntington Beach State Park** (p191), but it's a little further away – about 3 miles south of **Murrells Inlet** (p189).

Budget

The strip is loaded with budget hotels, especially south of the Myrtle Beach Pavilion. These lack frills and the resort-style amenities of the big hotels, but they are great for people who are using the hotel as a place to crash, not to hang out and soak up the ambiance.

Firebird Motor Inn (☎ 843-448-7032, 800-852-7032; www.firebirdinn.com; 2007 S Ocean Blvd; d $95-120; P ☽ ⓢ ✕) Lacking in frills, this friendly, family-oriented hotel is a great value for its beachfront location. Children's activities are available. The pool and lazy river overlook a parking lot, but the ocean is just on the other side.

Grand Strand Motel (☎ 843-448-1461, 800-433-1461; www.grandstrandmotel.com; 1804 S Ocean Blvd; d $80-90; P ☽ ⓢ ✕) It's across the street from the beach, but this motel has a great

---

GAGA FOR GOLF

With more than 120 golf courses in the Myrtle Beach area, hard-core golfers will have no problem getting their fill. Courses range from pricey private clubs – designed by the likes of Jack Nicklaus, Tom Fazio, Pete Dye and Arnold Palmer – to easy par 3s and everything in between.

One of South Carolina's top-rated golf clubs, **Wild Wing Plantation** (☎ 843-347-9464, 800-344-5590; 9 miles west on Hwy 501; greens fee $36-108, depending on course and season) has 72 holes on four separate courses, offering something for golfers of all levels. In addition, there's a driving range, wide practice green, restaurant and pub. South of Myrtle Beach, **Pawleys Plantation** (☎ 843-237-6200; www.pawleysplantation.com; 70 Tanglewood Dr, Pawleys Island; greens fee $100-125) was designed by Jack Nicklaus. Its golf school is one of the best in the country.

Myrtle Beach Golf Holiday (☎ 800-845-4653; www.golfholiday.com) publishes a self-titled comprehensive guide to area golf and can arrange golf packages or instruction, no matter what level you play at. You can order the publication online. Another excellent resource is **Myrtle Beach Golf** (☎ 888-633-6102; www.myrtlebeachgolf.com), which tailors golf/accommodations packages for visitors. Their website gives overviews and in-depth descriptions of area courses.

---

pool and nice rooms, making it the best value if you want to be close to the action.

Court Capri (☎ 843-448-6119, 800-533-1338; www.courtcapri.com; 2610 N Ocean Blvd; r $80-110; P ✦ ✦ ✦) Though the décor is somewhat dated, this hotel is a great value, with many rooms overlooking the water. Check out the perfectly kitschy heart-shaped rooftop pool.

St John's Inn (☎ 843-449-5251, 877-326-8669; www.stjohnsinn.com; 6803 N Ocean Blvd; d $90-100; P ✦ ✦ ✦) This old favorite toward the north end of the strip is not right on the water (the ocean's across the street), so the rates are lower than those of the beachside motels. A big, clean pool and outdoor hot tub help make this friendly spot a great value.

Other inexpensive hotels include the following; rates at these are about $80 in high season.

Budget Inn (☎ 800-968-1671; 504 N Ocean Blvd; P ✦ ✦)

Rainbow Court (☎ 800-951-2323; 405 N Ocean Blvd; P ✦ ✦)

Beverly Motel (☎ 843-448-9496; 703 N Ocean Blvd; P ✦ ✦ ✦) One of the few motels that will rent to people under 25.

Mid-range

A number of resorts are geared toward families on a budget and can offer some excellent amenities at very affordable rates.

Windsurfer Hotel (☎ 843-448-3475, 800-789-3123; www.windsurferhotel.com; 210 N Ocean Blvd; d $120-160; P ✦ ✦) In the thick of the action right between the Pavilion and Family Kingdom, the Windsurfer has a bunch of different room configurations, many of which have balconies overlooking the ocean. There's also a nice indoor/outdoor pool, a kiddie pool and an on-site restaurant.

Coral Beach Resort & Suites (☎ 843-448-8421, 800-843-2684; www.coral-beach.com; 1105 S Ocean Blvd; d $80-230; P ✦ ✦ ✦) Near the south end of the strip and boasting 301 rooms, indoor and outdoor pools, and a bowling alley and comedy club, this resort has something for everyone. A special kids' activity room is good for the little ones, and the poolside bar and British pub are a hit with the adults.

Compass Cove (☎ 843-448-8373, 800-228-9894; www.compasscove.com; 2311 S Ocean Blvd; d $100-280; P ✦ ✦ ✦) This sprawling oceanfront resort has many amenities, including 21 different pools. There's also a restaurant, a lounge, a games room and a fitness center. Rooms in three different buildings – the Pinnacle, Mariner and Schooner – range widely in price and size. Call ahead to see what deals are being offered.

Ocean Reef Resort (☎ 843-449-4441, 800-542-0048; www.oceanreefmyrtlebeach.com; d $120-200; P ✦ ✦ ✦) Up on the north end of the strip, at 71st Ave N, this hotel is right up against the beach, and all of its rooms overlook the ocean. There's an oceanfront pool, a kiddie pool and a covered lazy river, plus a fitness center and guest laundry.

Monterey Bay Suites (☎ 843-449-4833, 888-255-4763; www.montereybaysuites.com; 6804 N Ocean

Blvd; d $130-150; ⓟ ⓧ ⓡ ⓧ) At the north
end of the strip, this is a high-rise hotel;
every room is a suite and has a view of
the beach and a balcony. Colorful, clean
rooms, a nice pool and free breakfast are
bonuses.

Ocean Dunes Resort & Villas (☎ 843-449-7441,
888-999-8192; www.sandsresort.com; 201 75th Ave N; r
$135-280; ⓟ ⓧ ⓧ ⓡ) On the north end of
the strip, this 400-room Sands resort has
all the frills – bars, restaurants, eight pools,
a games room, kids' programs and even
an ice-cream shop. A variety of rooms are
available, from standard oceanview rooms
to two-bedroom villas.

Boardwalk Beach Resort (☎ 843-626-8772,
800-535-2297; 2301 N Ocean Blvd; r $130-300;
www.boardwalkresort.com; ⓟ ⓧ ⓡ ⓧ) With a
variety of rooms in three different high-
rise buildings, this resort has everything
from standard rooms to three-bedroom
Jacuzzi suites, many of which overlook the
ocean. All the rooms have at least two beds,
making this a good bet for families. The
resort has more than a dozen pools, plus a
250ft lazy river.

Breakers (☎ 843-444-444, 800-952-4503; www
.breakers.com; r $130-345; ⓟ ⓧ ⓡ ⓧ) With
three buildings (including the Paradise
Tower), the Breakers has a huge array of
room offerings, from standard rooms to
oceanfront four-bedroom suites. The resort
boasts a 418ft lazy river, numerous pools
and a nice rooftop lounge.

Sea Island Inn (☎ 843-449-6406, 800-883-8248;
www.seaislandinn.com; 6000 N Ocean Blvd; r $130-460;
ⓟ ⓧ ⓡ ⓧ) Situated in the middle of a
residential area toward the north end of
the strip, this resort and corresponding
beachfront stays quieter and less crowded
than resorts in the thick of it all. Its 113
rooms range from standard to penthouse
suite, with everything in between. You can
also get package deals that include meals in
the hotel's restaurant.

Top End
Swanky, swishy and filled with amenities,
more and more top hotels are cropping up
around Myrtle Beach to satiate those on
the higher end of the spending spectrum.
All relatively new, the following hotels
offer guests everything from plush gyms
and 5-star restaurants to golf outings and
luxury spas.

Radisson Plaza Hotel (☎ 843-918-5000, 800-333-
3333; 2101 N Oak St; d $150 and up; ⓟ ⓧ ⓡ ⓧ ⓓ)
Attached to the Myrtle Beach Convention
Center and two miles from the beach, this
high-rise hotel has 402 rooms and 20 suites
geared toward the convention set, with
bonuses like high-speed Internet access.
Amenities include an indoor pool and
fitness center, free happy-hour snacks in
the swanky M Bar and rooms stocked with
Starbucks coffee. Give the hotel restaurant
(Vidalia's) a pass – the recently opened
room is still working out the kinks.

Camelot by the Sea (☎ 843-916-4700, 800-
895-3721; www.camelot-resort.com; 2000 N Ocean Blvd;
r $180-330; ⓟ ⓧ ⓡ ⓧ) Though King
Arthur isn't hanging around, he'd likely
enjoy the accommodations in this newly
renovated big yellow building overlooking
the ocean. This hotel has four room
configurations, all of which face the
water. Rooms are narrow, so the sleeping
area is dark, but the sitting areas are
bright and sunny. Amenities include an
indoor and outdoor pool, a games room
and a fitness center.

Marriott at Grande Dunes (☎ 843-449-8880,
800-228-9290; 8400 Costa Verde Dr; d $220/250 garden/
ocean view; ⓟ ⓧ ⓡ ⓧ ⓓ) This new, fully
loaded hotel opened in January 2004 in
the heart of Grande Dunes, a private
residential and leisure community at the
very northern stretch of the strip. Geared
partially toward the business traveler and
partially toward golfers, tennis fiends and
beachgoers, the 400-room hotel has a ton
of amenities, including a spa, a beachfront
lounge, indoor and outdoor pools and
childcare services.

EATING
The 1700 or so restaurants are mostly mid-
range and high volume, but competition
keeps prices reasonable. For Americana
ambiance, hit the burger joints on Ocean
Blvd near the amusement parks. Seafood,
ironically, is not Myrtle Beach's specialty;
it tends to be mass-produced and deep-
fried in the 'calabash' style – that is, lightly
breaded with cornmeal and flour, then
flash fried in peanut oil. According to one
local, 'the only good fish is a fried one.' The
small fishing village of Murrells Inlet (p189)
is where locals go for oysters, fresh shrimp
and Lowcountry dishes.

SAVVY SLEEPING

With hundreds of hotels vying for the mighty tourist dollar, hotel rates fluctuate like crazy and can be downright fickle. Rates can vary by the season and the day – a room might cost $25 in January and more than $100 in July. If a summer weekend is slow, prices can plummet. Likewise, if a weekend is busy, rates can skyrocket. You'll do well to call around before arriving (all hotels listed have toll-free numbers) in order to see what kind of deal you can get. It's also worthwhile noting that most resorts will arrange a discount if you stay four nights or more. In the low season, you'd do just as well to drive along and around Ocean Blvd, looking at the signs for special prices – the big beachfront hotels may be no more expensive than a cheap-looking motel.

High season is usually June through August, with shoulder seasons in May and September. From October through April, rates drop drastically, and some hotels close down for the winter. Keep in mind that accommodations get tight during Harley Week (in May), golf tournaments and national holidays.

Knowing the hotel lingo can be helpful, as many resorts have multiple room configurations, and the terms they throw at you can leave you scratching your head. The term 'efficiency' means the room has a refrigerator and partial kitchen; 'suites' are either one or two bedrooms and have a kitchen and a sitting room. Regarding the view: 'oceanview' means you can see the ocean somewhere out your window. 'Oceanfront view' means you're overlooking the ocean, but you might be across the street from it, while 'oceanfront' means you're as close to the water as you can get. Note that 'standard,' 'courtside' and 'poolside' rooms do not have views of the ocean. Most resorts have in-room minifridges, coin-laundry facilities (for all those sandy towels) and outdoor pools. In an attempt to deter rowdy Spring Breakers, many hotels won't rent to those under 25, so call first to confirm.

The chamber of commerce can help find short-term accommodations, month-long condo and cabin rentals, and golfotels (lodging–golfing packages). The thick *Stay & Play* guide, available at the visitors centers or by mail, has full listings for hotels that are chamber members.

You'll have an endless choice of chain and theme restaurants in the area of Broadway on the Beach, including the following.

Hard Rock Cafe (☎ 843-946-0007; 1322 Celebrity Circle; meals $8-20; P ❄ ✕)
Planet Hollywood (☎ 843-448-7827; 2915 Hollywood Dr; meals $8-15; P ❄ ✕)
Nascar Cafe (☎ 843-946-7223; 1808 21st Ave N; meals $7-12; P ❄ ✕)

The area north of Myrtle Beach where Kings Hwy and Hwy 17 Bypass rejoin is referred to as 'Restaurant Row,' a name suggesting something different than the endless expanse of strip malls. In these cookie-cutter buildings, however, are some of the area's better restaurants. Serving up Australian favorites like meat pie, rack of lamb, steaks and seafood amid an impressive décor overlooking the moat at Barefoot Landing, **Greg Norman's Australian Grille** (☎ 843-316-0000; 4930 Hwy 17 S; dinner $15-30; P ❄ ✕), in North Myrtle Beach, gets top votes for originality and atmosphere.

Budget

With so many restaurants competing for your business, you'll find plenty that offer large portions at inexpensive prices.

Croissants Bakery & Café (☎ 843-448-2253; 504A 27th Ave N at Kings Hwy; dishes $3-9; ☺ 7am-4pm Mon-Fri, 8am-4pm Sat) Located off the strip, this great little spot serves good breakfasts and beautiful pies and desserts. At lunch, try a wrap or sandwich, like the chunky chicken salad or prosciutto and marinated artichoke hearts ($6).

Windsurfer Café (☎ 843-282-0226; 3rd Ave N & Ocean Blvd; dishes $4-6; ☺ 7am-4pm; ✕ P) Right in front of the Windsurfer Hotel, this little place serves delicious breakfasts and sandwiches, with lots of vegetarian options. Try the all-you-can-eat breakfast buffet ($6).

River City Café (☎ 843-448-1990; 404 21st Ave N; meals $5-12) This is a casual, beachy place with sunburnt bodies drinking beer and tossing peanut shells onto the floor. The menu features a wide selection of burgers and sandwiches. It's good fun and has a few locations, including another at the north end of the strip (☎ 843-449-8877; 208 73rd Ave N).

Bummz Beach Café (☎ 843-916-9111; 2002 N Ocean Blvd; dishes $6-10) Both a bar and restaurant, Bummz is a great place to stop for an after-beach bite, to watch the sunset on the outside deck and snack on a selection of pub grub and snacks. Look for it in a squat building between the Breakers and the Camelot Resorts.

Mid-range to Top End

You'll see a lot of signs advertising 'calabash' seafood. These places are plentiful and offer all-you-can-eat seafood buffets for about $20, featuring things like fried oysters, T-bone steaks, peel 'n' eat shrimp, soups and salads. **Bennett's Calabash Seafood** (☎ 843-448-2977; 2900 N Kings Hwy) claims to have originated the calabash seafood buffet idea; it offers the freshest seafood and has a few locations. **Captain Benjamin's Calabash Seafood** (☎ 843-626-9354; 401 S Kings Hwy) has similar fried-seafood offerings.

Sea Captain's House (☎ 843-448-8082; 3000 N Ocean Blvd; lunch $7-11, dinner $14-20; **P** **✗**) In a lovely old cabin overlooking the water, this old favorite is one of the few places in town where the seafood and Lowcountry dishes are superbly prepared. Try the oyster platter ($17.50), the crab cakes ($7) or the Lowcountry crab casserole ($15). Though oceanside, there isn't outdoor seating.

Sugami (☎ 843-692-7709; 4813 N Kings Hwy; mains $10-20; ☽ noon-1am; **P** **✗**) This is an excellent spot for hot Japanese dishes and superb sushi in a lively atmosphere.

Atlantic Grille (☎ 843-449-9596; 6507 N Kings Hwy; mains $16-25; ☽ dinner only) On the north end of town, at 65th Ave N, this is a great place for fresh seafood with interesting twists, like the calamari with curry dip, scallops in a pepper-jack sauce or blackened red snapper with cucumber-dill sauce. The raw bar shucks up a variety of oysters. Meat and chicken dishes are also available.

The **Library** (☎ 843-448-4527; 1212 N Kings Hwy; mains $18-34; ☽ 5:30-10:30pm Mon-Sat; **✗**) Here the walls are lined with books, and you'll find a formality not found elsewhere in Myrtle Beach. French-inspired continental cuisine is the name of the game, and the menu features beef, veal, chicken and seafood dishes prepared with fresh local ingredients and seasonal flair. Reservations are recommended.

Thoroughbred's Restaurant (☎ 843-497-2636; 9706 N Kings Hwy; mains $16-25; **P** **✗**) Run for the roses at this horseracing-themed restaurant along Restaurant Row. Dark leather and mahogany set the tone, and portions of the menu are named for the Triple Crown races. Try the Kentucky Derby's bronzed salmon zinfandel ($19), the Preakness chicken Dijon or one of the meaty Belmont steaks.

New York Prime (☎ 843-448-8081; 405 28th Ave N; mains $30-40; ☽ dinner only; **P** **✗**) If you want to splurge on perfect steaks, lamb chops or Maine lobster, New York Prime is an excellent choice. In the tradition of a slick, big-city steakhouse, this makes a pleasant and sophisticated detour from the usual ambiance of Myrtle Beach.

ENTERTAINMENT
Bars & Clubs

Hangouts catering to the college crowd include **Mother Fletchers** (☎ 843-626-7959; 710 N Ocean Blvd), on the boardwalk at the Pavilion, and **Studebakers** (☎ 843-448-9747; 2000 N Kings Hwy), which has swimsuit competitions on Friday nights. For laid-back beach ambiance, try **Dead Dog Saloon** (☎ 843-445-6700; 404 26th Ave N), where an outside deck hosts Saturday cookouts and live music. **Bummz Beach Café** (p187) has an ocean view, occasional karaoke and a fun-loving, swimsuit-clad crowd. **Gilligan's** (☎ 843-448-8438; 1206 N Ocean Blvd) is a bar and pool hall that offers happy-hour drink specials.

Variety Shows

Music variety shows are a Myrtle Beach standard, combining rock, country and bluegrass music with a dose of comedy, Christianity and patriotism. Even if this doesn't sound like your kind of thing, seeing at least one of these high-energy performances is definitely a worthwhile investment for the sheer novelty of it. Show times vary; call ahead to see what's playing when. Check out area publications for discount coupons.

Dixie Stampede (☎ 843-497-9700, 800-433-4401; www.dixiestampede.com; Hwy 17 N & Hwy 17 Bypass; adult/child $35/19 including dinner) This wild brainchild of the great Dolly Parton features a colorful, very Southern and super-patriotic show complete with four-course meal.

Carolina Opry (☎ 843-913-4000, 800-843-6779; www.thecarolinaopry.com; Hwy 17 N & Hwy 17 Bypass; adult/child $30/19) Music man Calvin Gilmore brought the Opry to Myrtle Beach in 1985, and the show has gotten rave reviews ever since. A mix of gospel music, comedy, drama, rock and Broadway, the Opry is a patriotic, Jesus-lovin' hoot.

Palace Theatre (☎ 843-448-0588; www.palace theatremyrtlebeach.com; 21st Ave N & Hwy 17 Bypass; admission $15 and up) At Broadway at the Beach, the Palace hosts a variety of lively song-and-dance performances, including the long-standing *Carolina Jubilee*, the *Spirit of the Dance* and *Broadway*.

Legends in Concert (☎ 843-238-1827, 800-960-7469; www.legendsinconcertsc.com; 301 Hwy 17 S; adult/child $30/16) So, you've never seen Elvis in concert? Well, here's your chance. Pro impersonators recreate the King, Cher, Michael Jackson, Garth Brooks and many others at this flashy show. The theater is 3 miles south of Myrtle Beach, in the Surfside Beach community. Show times vary, so call for times.

Alabama Theatre (☎ 843-272-1111, 800-342-2262; www.alabama-theatre.com; Barefoot Landing; adult/child $33/15) This live music and comedy theater – brought to you by the country-rock band Alabama – features 'One, the Show,' a funny and musically vibrant spectacle, at Barefoot Landing in North Myrtle Beach.

House of Blues (☎ 843-913-3740, tickets ☎ 843-272-3000; Barefoot Landing) This is the best place in town to see live local and national acts, from KC and the Sunshine Band to Ben Harper and the Wallflowers. Ticket prices vary. Stop by on Sundays for the Gospel Brunch ($17), which features an all-you-can-eat breakfast buffet accompanied by live gospel music.

GETTING THERE & AWAY

Myrtle Beach International Airport (☎ 843-448-1589) is within Myrtle Beach city limits and is undergoing a massive expansion that will give it a new terminal and concourse. The airport is served by most major US cities and by the following airlines: AirTran, Delta, Continental, Northwest, Spirit, US Airways and, most recently, Hooters Air.

Greyhound (☎ 843-448-2472; 511 7th Ave N) services New York ($92, from 16 hours); Atlanta ($46, from 9½ hours) and Charleston ($24, 2½ hours).

The nearest **Amtrak** station is in Florence, 70 miles west, with connecting bus service;

the Silver service connects to New York City ($140, 14 hours).

More than 90 percent of visitors to the Myrtle Beach arrive by car. From Charleston, Hwy 17 provides a pleasant, direct route up the coast. The fast route from cities north and south is I-95, from which you can pick up a number of direct routes that head east to the Grand Strand. Car rentals are available at the airport.

GETTING AROUND

When driving, the traffic coming and going on Hwy 17 Business (also called Kings Hwy) can be infuriating. To avoid the Strand altogether, stay on Hwy 17 Bypass. Two recently completed roads are also helping to alleviate traffic. Hwy 31 (Carolina Bays Pkwy), which parallels Hwy 17, is the fast route between Hwy 501 and Hwy 9. Mostly used by locals traveling between the town of Conway and North Myrtle Beach, Hwy 22 (Conway Bypass) connects Hwy 17 to Hwy 501 at Conway.

Coastal Rapid Public Transport (☎ 843-488-0865) has infrequent service up and down the resort area. Call **Anchor Taxi** (☎ 843-444-0101) if you need a cab. Taxis to and from the airport are about $5, but most hotels offer free shuttle service.

THE GRAND STRAND

NORTH MYRTLE BEACH
pop 11,000

North Myrtle Beach feels like a beach town – the pace is slow, the buildings are squat, and vacationers spend their days doing a lot of nothing. The crowd is older and has had a longer relationship with the Grand Strand than the average Myrtle Beach visitor. Way back when (in the '40s and '50s), they came as teenagers to the open-air pavilions and dance halls that dotted the oceanfront. With the sand-covered floors and the sweaty bodies packed in thick, they created the dance called 'shag,' which is the precursor to the British slang, as in Austin Power's 'Shag me, baby.'

Other than the shag dancing, the big attraction in North Myrtle Beach is the shopping and entertainment complex at Barefoot Landing. The North Myrtle Beach

Chamber of Commerce, which can help with area information and accommodations, operates a **visitors center** (☎ 843-281-2662, 877-332-2662; 270 Hwy 17 N).

Barefoot Landing
Built along the Intracoastal Waterway, **Barefoot Landing** (☎ 843-272-8349; 4898 Hwy 17 N; ⏰ open daily, hours vary by season) was once the hottest idea to hit the beach. Now displaced by the newer Broadway at the Beach, the Landing is beginning to show its age, although it still sports major attractions, such as the **Alabama Theatre** (p188) and **House of Blues** (p188). Its gimmick is to create the feeling of an old fishing village, with weathered wooden buildings surrounding a 27-acre lake.

At the Landing, take a walk down the marsh boardwalk. Songbirds perched on marsh grass sing in time with the highway noise, turtles sun themselves on nearly submerged logs, and the deep black mud emits its salty odors in the summer sun. At the end of the boardwalk is **Alligator**

Adventure (☎ 843-361-0789; adult/child $12/8; ⏰ 10am-6pm), a commercial zoo of more than 800 alligators, tropical birds and exotic reptiles.

MYRTLE BEACH STATE PARK
With boardwalks connecting a pristine beach, this **state park** (☎ 843-238-5325; 4401 Hwy 17 S; admission $3; ⏰ 6am-10pm), just 3 miles south of Myrtle Beach, is a great place to spend the day. Here you can see the abundant wax myrtle, the shrub after which Myrtle Beach was named. Fishermen cast a line from the pier, those seeking serenity walk for miles along the beach, and families gather in public picnic areas.

The park has cabins (sleeping four to eight) for $60 to $90 per night (weekly rates also available); there are also 350 campsites ($23) with varying levels of shade.

MURRELLS INLET
pop 5520
Laid-back, quiet and full of good seafood restaurants, Murrells (pronounced murlz)

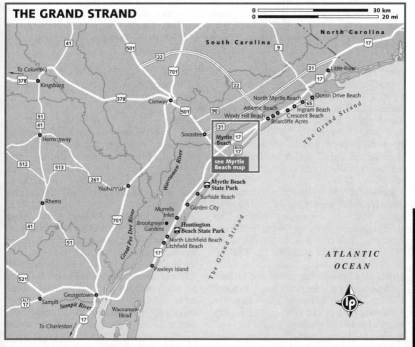

THE GRAND STRAND

SHAGGIN', BABY

Born in the 1940s and '50s in Myrtle Beach, the Shag continues as a local and ageless phenomenon. It doesn't matter whether you're young, old, a slickster or an uncoordinated hack, the very essence of the shag's laid-back, mellow moves is that as long as you're having a good time, you are welcome to shag along.

A close cousin of the 1930s craze called 'the Big Apple,' shag dancing is a much slower version of swing or jitterbug. Moving in an eight-count step with gentle twists and spins, the teenagers who danced the shag were rebelling against the region's dance-forbidding tradition. The music that inspired the steps was known as 'race music' (rhythm and blues) in the segregated South, and it was outlawed everywhere except the beach. At the same time, African American dancers adopted a slow, sexy jitterbug step, and they called their bumps and grinds 'the dirty shag.'

As times changed, such R&B classics as 'Under the Boardwalk' and 'Give Me Just a Little More Time' came to be known as 'beach music,' a name applied to any shaggable song. The nucleus of the shag culture was Ocean Drive (or 'OD'), the northernmost beaches of the Strand, which is now technically North Myrtle Beach. The shag peaked in the early '60s, and soon after its naughty reputation, it mellowed into respectability. The underground, teenage-rebel look, with bleached-out hair and tailored pants, transformed into full-blown preppy. By the late '60s, dancers donned khakis and crew cuts, or sock-hop dresses. The dance became so popular that it became the South Carolina state dance, and it is now performed at weddings, debutante parties and country-club events.

Die-hard dancers formed the **Society of Stranders** (SOS) in 1980 and stay devoted to the shaggin' culture. The group hosts a variety of events throughout the year, plus two major festivals: the Spring Safari and the Fall Migration. Shaggers travel from afar to take workshops, enter contests and, of course, shag the night away. To find out more, contact **SOS** (☎ 888-767-3113; www.shagdance.com).

To watch old-timers in action, or to take a lesson and try your feet at shaggin', head to **Fat Harold's** (☎ 843-249-5779; 212 Main St) or **Ducks and Ducks Too** (☎ 843-249-3858; 229 Main St). At the **Ocean Beach Resort** (☎ 843-249-1436; 98 North Ocean Blvd), shaggin's going on at the Beach Club and Spanish Galleon. While at the resort, be sure to check out the **Shaggers Hall of Fame**.

Inlet, 10 miles south of Myrtle Beach, is a small, quiet fishing village named after a pirate who would hide among the tidal marshes of Waccamaw Neck, a peninsula stretching from Murrells Inlet to Winyah Bay, near Georgetown. This is also a great place to get out on the water. The 'commercial strip,' which is delightfully not commercial, centers around the marina along Hwy 17.

Captain Dick's (☎ 843-651-3676; www.captdicks.com; Murrells Inlet Marina) is probably the best place to go for boat trips and fishing charters. The good captain rents out boats, including pontoons (half-/full-day $170/230), skiffs ($70/90) and kayaks ($25/40). The Cruisin' the Beach sightseeing cruise (adult/child $16/6) goes through the marsh and up past the beaches on the Strand. The educational and fun 2½-hour Saltwater Marsh Explorer Adventure (adult/child $19/11) is a boat trip led by a local marine biologist. Little kids and unadventurous types will enjoy the two-hour Gator Tours (adult/child $15/6), conducted in an amphibious vehicle. Deep-sea fishing trips are also available.

Eating

Since most seafood is harvested less than a mile away, restaurants in Murrells Inlet offer the freshest oysters, shrimp, crab and fish around. Restaurants here lack street addresses, but they are easy to find along the small strip that constitutes downtown.

Nance's Creekfront Restaurant and Oyster Roast (☎ 843-651-2696; 4583 Hwy 17; steamed oysters $15; ☾ dinner only) During the fall and winter months, oysters are at their sweetest; they get plucked from jet-black marsh mud and steamed over a hot grill. This is the place to get 'em fresh and delicious. At your table will be a large roll of paper towels and a hole in the middle for discarding the oyster shells. This will be a meal of physical exertion. Armed with an oyster knife, you pry into the gnarled shells and pluck out the tender morsels. Don't let the tight ones go unopened; usually they are the tastiest. Nance's sits right on the creek on the south end of the strip and features a wonderful sunset view.

Creek Ratz (☎ 843-357-2891; dishes $6-13; ☻ 11am-11pm) This casual place with a nice outside deck offers seafood baskets with goodies like steamed shrimp, crab cakes and catfish, as well as po'boy sandwiches and fried dill-pickle chips (really, they're good!). Salads and pizzas are also available.

Drunken Jack's (☎ 843-651-2044; dishes $15-23; ☻ 4-10pm) This is a fun, rollicking place that gives a nod to old Jack, who, as the story goes, was a member of Blackbeard's pirating crew in the 17th century. Jack got so drunk, he missed the boat and was left behind with a stockpile of hijacked rum. When Blackbeard came back to get him, all he found was some bleached-out bones (poor Jack) and 32 empty casks. The restaurant overlooks the water and serves up Lowcountry seafood, along with steaks and a kids' menu.

HUNTINGTON BEACH STATE PARK

One of the state's prettiest public beaches, **Huntington Beach State Park** (☎ 843-237-4440; 16148 Hwy 17; ☻ 6am-10pm, till 6pm in winter; day-use adult/child $5/3) is home to broad white-sand beaches, sloping dunes covered by bowing sea oats, and a tidal marsh fished by great blue heron, purple gallinules and snowy egrets. Located 3 miles south of Murrells Inlet, it is named after the land's former owners, the Huntingtons. In the 1930s, Archer Huntington, a wealthy shipper and philanthropist, and his wife, Anna Hyatt Huntington, a renowned animal sculptor, left the cold winters of New York City for this isolated preserve, which was once the land of the Waccamaw Neck's most prosperous rice plantations. While here, they developed the **Brookgreen Gardens** (p183), which is across the highway and well worth a visit.

The Huntington's home, Atalaya, was built in the style of a Moorish fort, with narrow passageways, meandering rooms and a guard tower, where bats were kept to eat malaria-carrying mosquitoes. A scholar of all things Spanish and ever the concerned

citizen, Archer Huntington insisted that only local labor be used in the home's construction. Built over three years during the height of the Great Depression, the construction jobs were a godsend – even if the house is a little odd.

Atalaya is empty now, but it can be self-toured during daylight hours. You can pick up a brochure about the house at the park headquarters.

This lovely, windswept, wildlife-filled park is by far the best place to **camp** near Myrtle Beach. Most sites ($26) are shaded and near the beach, with clean restrooms nearby.

PAWLEYS ISLAND

pop 140

Only 4 miles long and a quarter-mile wide, Pawleys Island is affectionately called 'arrogantly shabby,' because the island's swanky roots are combined with informal, noncommercial elegance. Once a summer resort for wealthy planter families, Pawleys retains its reputation as a getaway for the wealthy. Still, many of the huge rustic cottages, some predating the Civil War, lack air conditioning and manicured lawns. Sea breezes enter the sleeping porches, footwear is an accessory, and golf courses are strictly a mainland obsession. Visitors and locals alike might do a little fishing in the morning, read a skinny paperback before an afternoon nap or watch the sun go from one end of the island to another – following a worry-free schedule.

A salt marsh separates the tiny island from the mainland, and two causeways connect it. For a little excitement, pick up a map of historic homes at the **visitors center** (☎ 843-237-1921; Hwy 17 at Planter's Exchange; ☻ 9am-5pm Mon-Sat, 10am-2pm Sun).

Folks come from all over to watch demonstrations of the famous Pawleys Island handmade hammocks at the nearby **Original Hammock Shop** (☎ 843-237-9122, 800-332-3490; 10880 Ocean Hwy/Hwy 17; ☻ 9am-6pm Mon-Sat, noon-5pm Sun). Other indigenous crafts can be found at the **Gullah Ooman Shop** (☎ 843-235-0747; Waverly Rd at Petigru Dr). The shop sells quilts, dolls, sweetgrass baskets and books on the African American Gullah tradition. **Pawleys Island Chapel** is a nondenominational church precariously

GHOST STORIES OF SOUTH CAROLINA

Almost every corner of the state is filled with tales of the unrestrained dead. Featuring everything from mourning specters and disappearing hitchhikers to swamp creatures and alien sightings, these tales should be avoided if you're planning on driving alone down dark, country roads.

The ghost of Alice Flagg has haunted her family home for three generations. Her figure, clad in all white, glides through the hallway to her old room, or sits in the garden. Residents have spotted her combing the beach and or even standing on the breaking waves.

Who was Alice Flagg? She was from a wealthy family who lived in the Hermitage, a well-known plantation home between Murrells Inlet and Pawleys Island. While away at school in Charleston, Alice fell in love a man beneath her family status – a turpentine salesman. She pursued the relationship, despite her family's disapproval, sometimes wearing his ring to public functions in Charleston. While at school, she caught yellow fever and was sent home to the Hermitage. Her brother saw the ring and was so angry that he took it and threw it into the inlet. She died shortly thereafter but refuses to leave without her ring.

For more than a hundred years, the Gray Man has walked the beach at Pawleys Island, warning residents of impending storms. Dressed in tattered gray clothes, the Gray Man first appeared to a distraught young woman who had just lost her fiancé in a riding accident. Soon after the sighting, the family left the island to take her to a Charleston physician, because she insisted that the mysterious figure was the ghost of her lover. The infamous storm of 1822 hit shortly after they left, and most of the island residents were killed. The Gray Man appeared again in 1893 at the home of a prominent family, asking for bread. It was a tightly knit community, and since they did not recognize the man, the family remembered the original Gray Man story and left the island as a precaution. A disastrous tidal wave followed soon after their departure.

Modern weather prediction might have made the Gray Man redundant, but he changed with the times. People who have spotted or been approached by the Gray Man have suffered little to no damage to their property during storms. Before Hurricane Hazel, the Gray Man knocked on the door of a family that had come to spend the week at their beach house. Heeding the unknown man's warning, they left, and the hurricane swept through the island, destroying their neighbors' houses but leaving theirs untouched.

balanced on the creek bank; the 10am Sunday service is one of the island's few social functions.

Pawleys Island is 25 miles south of Myrtle Beach on Hwy 17, and 60 miles north of Charleston.

Sleeping & Eating

Most people vacationing at Pawleys rent beach cottages. Weekly rentals (sleeping eight to 12) run between $1500 and $3000 during the peak summer season. Contact one of the following rental companies for a brochure on rental properties.

Dieter Company (☎ 843-237-2813, 888-950-6232; www.dietercompany.com)

James W Smith Realty (☎ 843-237-4246, 800-476-5651; www.jwsmithrealestate.com)

Lachicotte Realty (☎ 843-237-2094, 800-422-4777; www.lachicotte.com)

Pawley's Island Realty Company (☎ 843-237-2431, 800-937-7352; www.pawleysislandvacations.com)

The closest commercial hotels are on the mainland, including **Holiday Inn Express** (☎ 843-235-0808, 800-830-0135; 11445 Ocean Hwy/Hwy17; low/high season d $60/110; P ⊠ ⊠).

Sea View Inn (☎ 843-237-4253; www.seaviewinn.net; daily/weekly d $250/1550; P ⊠) On the private end of the island, the Sea View is a rustic guesthouse (no air-conditioning). Ocean-view rooms are $50 to $100 cheaper. Rates include three meals daily.

Litchfield Plantation Inn (☎ 800-869-1410, 843-237-9121; fax 843-237-1041; d $190-550; P ⊠ ⊠ ⊠). For a much more pampered experience, make a reservation at this 1750s mansion in neighboring Litchfield. Framed by an alley of live oaks, it has spacious bedrooms and outlying cottages, with a range of accommodations and rates. Amenities include a health club, spa services, tennis and a pool.

Most restaurants are off the island on Ocean Hwy/Hwy 17. Local hangout **Pawley's Island Tavern & Restaurant** (☎ 843-

237-8465; lunch $5-10, dinner $10-15) is the self-proclaimed home for shrimp, beer and blues. It's on a little dirt road (marked by a tattered pizza sign) off Ocean Hwy (Hwy 17). Live bands play weekend nights.

For fine dining, **Frank's Restaurant** (☎ 843-237-3030; 10434 Ocean Hwy; mains $15-25; ☷ dinner only) offers an extensive menu of Low-country specialties, such as pan-fried grouper with shrimp ($23) and Frank's famous oyster pie ($8).

GEORGETOWN & AROUND

pop 9000

The Spanish tried to settle here in 1526, but they soon retreated to St Augustine, Florida. In colonial times, Georgetown became a center for rice plantations on the estuarine, where four rivers combine and pour into Winyah Bay before heading out to the Atlantic. A bustling shipping port in pre–Revolutionary War times, Georgetown was founded in 1729 and has more than 50 historic buildings, some dating back to the 1730s. During plantation times, West African slaves, who were experienced in rice cultivation, provided expertise and labor.

Georgetown rolls to a very slow pace. The old downtown, with quaint shops and restaurants, contrasts with the big steel and paper mills that generate revenue and boost the local economy.

The **visitors center** (☎ 843-546-8436, 800-777-7705; 1001 Front St; ☷ 9:30am-4:30pm Mon-Fri, 10am-3pm Sat) has brochures on the town's historic homes, including that of **Joseph Hayne Rainey** (909 Prince St), the first African American elected to the US House of Representatives (1871–79). An **annual tour** (☎ 843-545-8291) of privately owned plantations and historic houses occurs in April.

Georgetown sits on a nub of land at the confluence of the Sampit, Black, Great Pee Wee and Waccamaw Rivers. A few outfitters offer kayak rentals and trips up the rivers. **Black Water Adventures** (☎ 800-761-1850) and **Black River Expeditions** (☎ 843-546-4840) are reputable local outfitters that offer variety of interesting and affordable trips.

Kaminsky House Museum (☎ 843-546-7706, 888-233-0383; 1003 Front St; adult/child $5/2; ☷ 10am-4pm Mon-Sat), in a 1769 town home, is loaded with 18th- and 19th-century antiques. The home's yard overlooks the Sampit River.

Guided tours run hourly. A museum shop sells arts, crafts and books about Georgetown.

Rice Museum (☎ 843-546-7423; 633 Front St; adult/student $5/2; ☷ 10am-4:30pm Mon-Sat), in the Clock Tower building at Front and Screven Sts, has interesting models and maps that explain rice cultivation in the area.

Between Georgetown and Charleston, some old plantation homes show a glimpse of antebellum life. The privately owned **Hopsewee** (☎ 843-546-7891; 494 Hopsewee Rd; www .hopsewee.com; adult/child $8/5; ☷ 9am-6pm daily in summer, 10am-4pm Tue-Fri in winter), on US 17 and about 12 miles south of Georgetown, was a rice plantation from about 1740 to 1860 and was the birthplace of Thomas Lynch, Jr, a signer of the Declaration of Independence. The house has antique furnishings and atmospheric grounds. If you just want to drive around the grounds, admission is $5 per car.

From the same era, **Hampton Plantation State Historic Site** (☎ 843-546-9361; 1950 Rutledge Rd; ☷ 9am-6pm Thu-Mon), off US 17 and about 15 miles from Georgetown, in McClellanville, is an imposing white building but is unfurnished and unrestored, with overgrown surroundings and big old trees. George Washington visited this home on his Southern tour in 1791; he so admired a live oak that grew in front of the house that he persuaded the plantation owner never to cut it down. Guided tours of the mansion run 11am to 4pm on the hour.

Sleeping & Eating

Georgetown has a great selection of B&Bs. Call the visitors center (☎ 843-546-8436) for a full listing.

DuPre House B&B (☎ 843-546-0298, 877-519-9499; www.duprehouse.com; 921 Prince St; d $90-125; P ☒ ☒ ☒) In a 1740 house just a couple of blocks from the waterfront, this friendly place is a good choice for its superb breakfast and outdoor swimming pool.

1790 House B&B (☎ 843-546-4821, 800-890-7432; www.1790house.com; 630 Highmarket St; d $110-175; P ☒ ☒) Most rooms at this historic home have fireplaces and plenty nice details, like fresh flowers, a video library and antique-filled spacious rooms. A delicious breakfast is served in the dining room, and a formal English high tea is served in the Angel's Touch Tea Room.

CAROLINA GOLD

Named for the golden color of its husk, Carolina Gold rice first arrived in the Lowcountry in the early 18th century, coming in on ships from Madagascar. Soon after, and for more than a hundred years, the fragrant grain became the dominant crop and was grown on Lowcountry plantations that sat snuggled up next to riverbanks all up and down the coast. At its peak, half of the world's rice supply came from the Lowcountry.

Cultivating rice was no easy task. The work was very labor-intensive and exhausting. Because alluvial deposits rendered the Lowcountry soils so soft, it was difficult to use mules and makeshift tractors, because they would sink into the boggy soil. West African slaves, who were invaluable for their rice-growing knowledge, cleared the land and constructed dikes almost entirely by hand. Planting took place in the spring, and slaves planted the rice by digging holes with their toes, dropping the seeds into the holes, and then lightly tamping them with their heels.

An ingenious series of dikes and sluices were used to control the flooding. Throughout a season, flooding occurred three times, first to sprout the seeds and to allow them to germinate; second to kill invasive weeds and protect the sprouts from insects and birds. The third flooding supported the stalks as the grain matured. The water had to be just right. Given that Carolina plantations were working with a mix of fresh and saltwater, they had to be sure the water wasn't too salinated. A young slave would be sent out with some soap to determine the saline content. If his soap wouldn't lather, he knew there was too much saltwater. Once the soap started to produce suds, he'd know the water was right.

Harvesting took place in fall. First it was threshed to remove the grain from the stalk, then it was milled with a mortar and pestle to remove the outer husks. The rice would then be shipped to Britain and Europe.

Rice cultivation in these parts died out in the early 20th century. Hurricanes had wreaked havoc on the plantation lands, and new grains competed with the pricey Carolina Gold. The mechanization of growing rice was finding success elsewhere, where the soil wasn't so yielding. But probably the biggest cause of the fall of rice plantations in the Carolinas was the decline in labor. Once slaves were emancipated, they were free to find other, less grueling work.

Harbor House B&B (☎ 843-546-6532, 877-511-0101; www.harborhousebb.com; d $115-165; P ✗ ✗) Look for the red roof on this three-story Georgian house (c 1740) that sits right on the bank of the Sampit River. The four bedrooms have private baths, and the parlor and dining room overlook the water. The front porch is a perfect place to sit on a rocker and finish your Harlequin romance novel.

Inexpensive hotels geared toward out-of-towners coming to work at one of the mills include the basic **Days Inn** (☎ 843-546-8441; 210 Church St; d $50-60; P ✗ ✗) and the nicer **Clarion Carolinian Inn** (☎ 843-546-5191, 800-722-4667; 706 Church St; d $70-80; P ✗ ✗).

Thomas's Cafe (☎ 843-546-7776; 703 Front St; breakfast $4-6; ☾ 7am-2pm Mon-Sat, 11am-3pm Sun) That South Carolina accent seems stronger in this longtime favorite for Lowcountry breakfast. It's open for lunchtime sandwiches, fried fish and barbecue.

River Room (☎ 843-527-4110; 801 Front St; mains $10-20; ☾ 11am-2:30pm & 5-10pm Mon-Sat) In a lovely spot overlooking the boardwalk, this is an excellent place to enjoy Lowcountry seafood and a view of the water. Steaks and pasta dishes are offered, in addition to fish, crab and old favorites like tasty shrimp 'n' grits.

Rice Paddy (☎ 843-546-2021; 732 Front St; lunch $9-13, dinner $19-22; ☾ 11:30am-2:30pm & 6-10pm Mon-Sat) With a lovely outside deck overlooking the river and a kitchen that continually produces unique yet savory Lowcountry dishes, the Rice Paddy is Georgetown's best restaurant. Try the daily specials, which use the freshest ingredients – oftentimes, the seafood is caught just hours before.

Getting There & Away

Georgetown is 35 miles south of Myrtle Beach and 60 miles north of Charleston on Hwy 17.

Greyhound (☎ 843-546-4535; 2014 Highmarket St) has two daily scheduled trips to Myrtle Beach ($10, 45 minutes) and Charleston ($17, 90 minutes).

FRANCIS MARION NATIONAL FOREST

Twenty miles north of Charleston, this 250,000-acre forest, named in honor of Revolutionary War hero Francis Marion, contains more than 120 miles of recreational trails for hikers, mountain bikers or canoeists. Within the forest, moving west to east, you will find sand ridges and pine forests, then swamps, and finally the Atlantic Ocean. Along the sand ridges (which in ancient times were beaches) grow tall loblolly pines that shoot up for many feet before ever sprouting a branch. Nearer the ocean, blackwater swamps seep into the cypress and palmetto forests. The carnivorous trumpet pitcher plant grows here, and endangered species include the red-cockaded woodpecker, bald eagle and American alligator.

The first stop for outdoor enthusiasts should be the **Sewee Visitor & Environmental Education Center** (☎ 843-928-3368; 5821 Hwy 17 N; ☺ 9am-5pm Tue-Sun), where you can pick up trail maps and get information on Lowcountry ecosystems.

Also managed by the forest service and sharing the same visitors center is the neighboring **Cape Romain National Wildlife Refuge**, which encompasses 64,000 acres of wetlands, salt marshes and beaches along the Atlantic Coast. As a stop along the Atlantic Flyway, the refuge is essential to migratory bird species, as well as to recently introduced red wolves and massive loggerhead turtles (p46), which lay their eggs in the sand.

The most popular destination in the refuge is **Bull Island,** a wild island accessible via boat. Boneyard Beach is strewn with sun-bleached trees, marking where a forest succumbed to the sea. The island is for day-use only, and visitors should bring drinking water. **Coastal Expeditions** (☎ 843-881-4582; www.coastalexpeditions.com) runs a 30-minute private ferry from Garris Landing to Bull Island at 9am and 12:30pm on Tuesday, Thursday, Friday and Saturday (adult/child $30/15); call for directions to the landing.

DETOUR: NORTH CAROLINA'S CAPE FEAR COAST

Hwy 17 continues across the state border into North Carolina, turning inland until it reaches **Wilmington**, a busy little port town with factories, a university, film studios and a neat old downtown and waterfront area. Stop for lunch and stroll around its pretty historic district.

From Wilmington, take Hwy 421 south to explore the Cape Fear Coast, a string of barrier islands that extends down to the cape itself. Good stops along the way include Carolina Beach and Kure Beach.

Carolina Beach's specialty is pure, prepackaged nostalgia. There's an amusement park, boardwalk, merry-go-round and oodles of souvenir shops. **Kure Beach** is a bit quieter and has a 711ft fishing pier. On most days anglers line the rails to cast and chat, and the crabbing is great too.

Just to the north is **Carolina Beach State Park**, with nature trails that are home to the ferocious-looking Venus flytrap, an indigenous plant.

South of Kure Beach, the earthworks and exhibits of **Fort Fisher State Historic Site** (☎ 910-458-5538) explain its vital Civil War role. The two land-and-sea battles here were just about the fiercest in the whole war, with 40,000 projectiles fired on both sides. It's open daily (admission free). The **Fort Fisher State Recreation Area** (☎ 910-458-5798) is an oasis of calm after the hubbub of Carolina and Kure Beaches. The park office conducts nature hikes throughout the year. Several evenings a month in summer, the gates are closed to allow the loggerhead sea turtles to nest undisturbed.

The nearby **North Carolina Aquarium** (☎ 866-301-3476; www.ncaquariums.com) has elaborate biotopes with sharks, alligators, 6ft catfish, schools of glowing jellyfish and much more.

From here, catch a **ferry** (www.ncferry.org; $5 per car, $1 per pedestrian) across the mouth of Cape Fear River to the old fishing village of Southport, which, like lots of places around here, sees lots of movie-production activity. From Southport, there's a ferry to car-free **Bald Head Island**, which lies just south of Pleasure Island. Bald Head Island is mainly an upmarket resort and retirement community, and most residents get around on golf carts. **Cape Fear**, the bane of seamen for its tricky currents, lies at the tip.

DIRECTORY

Directory

CONTENTS

ACCOMMODATIONS

A variety of accommodations are available throughout the region, from inexpensive roadside motels to full-service resorts. One of the best ways to get a good night's sleep in this region is to stay at one of the many historic homes that have been turned into B&Bs. At these places, you'll usually find charming hosts who will feed you gorgeous Southern breakfasts and share all sorts of local secrets. Campgrounds range from lush wilderness areas to practical parking lots for RVs.

Rates vary like crazy. The peak season is mostly June through September, though there can be a lull in July and August, when the thermometer starts to rise and the humidity gets downright sweaty. In winter, rates can positively plummet. Most hotel owners will adjust rates according to other comparable places in the area, but you'd do well to call around and ask for discounts during a slow time. You'll usually pay less for rooms on weekdays and substantially more on weekends or during festivals and holidays. During peak season, you might find it difficult to find a room, so it's always best to call ahead to see what's available.

Hostels are few and far between, but budget travelers can find plenty of roadside chain motels for comfortable, if unexciting, accommodations. If you're willing to stay a little further outside of town, motels can get downright cheap. Beware that calling the toll-free 800 numbers of the chains will usually get you a higher quote than if you call the local numbers. These hotlines also can't guarantee a particular room (say, one with a balcony or a view, or one that's been remodeled).

In Charleston and Savannah, hotels often charge up to $20 a day for parking. Be sure to ask first; you can often find free (albeit less secure) parking on the street. Also be prepared to add room tax – usually 6% – in addition to sales and other local taxes. Children often stay free with their parents, but rules for this vary; inquire if traveling with a family.

In this book, we list accommodations in order of price range, followed by preference, and we usually give the high-season rate. Unless otherwise noted, the categories fall into the following price ranges: Budget ($75 or less), Mid-range ($75 to $150) and Top

---

PRACTICALITIES

- **Electricity** Electric current is 110–120 volts, 60-cycle. Appliances built to take 220–240 volt, 50-cycle current (as in Europe and Asia) will need a converter (transformer) and a US-style plug adapter with two flat pins.

- **Media** Find out what's going on in the Charleston Post & Courier, the Savannah Morning News or the Myrtle Beach Sun.

- **Video** Overseas visitors considering buying videotapes should note that the US uses the national television system committee (NTSC) color TV standard, which is incompatible with other standards, such as phase alternative line (PAL).

- **Weights & Measurements** Use the US imperial system for weights and measures.

End ($150 and up). In cities like Charleston and Savannah, those ranges go up by about $20 in each category.

ACTIVITIES

All along the coast, opportunities to get outside and enjoy the weather abound. You can cycle on trails around the barrier islands; kayak in the streams, rivers and protected bays; slither through swamps; play tennis or a round of golf – the activities are endless. Check out the Outdoors chapter (p50) for ideas.

BUSINESS HOURS

Standard US business hours prevail in the larger towns, but watch out for seasonal opening times in some of the resort communities. Public and private office hours are normally 9am to 5pm weekdays (Monday through Friday). Most stores are open Monday through Saturday, from 9am or 10am to around 6pm, or later in big cities or at shopping malls. Supermarkets are usually open until 8pm, though some, along with convenience stores and gas stations, may be open 24 hours; places with these hours are usually located along the interstates around larger cities. Post offices are open 8am to 4pm or 5:30pm on weekdays, and some are also open 8am to 3pm Saturday. Banks are generally open from 9am to 5pm Monday to Thursday, often extending to 6pm on Friday. Some banks offer limited hours on Saturday as well.

In the Southeast, many businesses are closed Sunday, though most tourist-oriented businesses and attractions usually stay open during peak season. Some tourist-oriented shops stay open weekends but then close Monday or Tuesday. Visitors centers are for the most part open from 9am to 5pm daily in summer, often closing on weekends in winter.

Restaurants are generally open until about 9pm or 10pm, later on Friday and Saturday and usually earlier on Sunday. In this book, we've noted when a restaurant is only open for lunch or dinner. Laws in both Georgia and South Carolina say that bars can stay open until 2am; some close earlier if business is slow.

Businesses, especially banks and federal and state offices, typically close on major holidays; in some instances, they might close on the nearest Monday instead, creating a three-day weekend.

Many museums, theaters and galleries are closed Monday.

CHILDREN

South Carolina and Georgia are very family-friendly destinations, with many discounts, services, facilities and attractions for kids, including such considerate touches as high chairs on wheels at cafeterias.

The definition of 'child' varies widely – some places will count anyone under the age of 18 eligible for children's discounts, although most places will only consider children under 12 for discounts.

For ideas on how to keep the little ones entertained, turn to *The Unofficial Guide to the Southeast with Kids,* by Menasha Ridge Press. Lonely Planet's *Travel with Children*, by Cathy Lanigan and Maureen Wheeler, offers advice and reassurance.

Practicalities

Many hotels and motels allow children to share a room with their parents for free or for a modest fee, though B&Bs rarely do, and some don't allow children at all. More expensive hotels and resorts will arrange baby-sitting services or organize 'kids' clubs' for younger children. Restaurants offer inexpensive children's menus with a limited selection of kid-friendly foods at cheap prices for patrons under 12 years of age. Car rental companies provide infant seats for their cars on request.

Most restaurants, family-oriented attractions and campgrounds have a baby-changing table in the restroom. While many people have a relaxed attitude about breastfeeding in public, others will frown on it – most Southern women are generally discreet about breastfeeding in public.

Sights & Activities

In **Myrtle Beach** (p180) there are more kid-oriented activities than there are things geared toward adults. Amusement parks, water slides, theme parks and arcades all vie for your child's attention. On Kiawah Island, many activities run by the **Kiawah Island Resort** (p176) are just for kids, including pools, camps and programs. Family-oriented resorts on Hilton Head and St Simons have lots of activities to amuse the tots while the adults' golf. Children rarely get bored in Charleston, where they can play in **water fountains** (p147), join boat tours to **Fort Sumter** (p153), visit the **aquarium** (p152) or check out the old **Provost Dungeon** (p152). Across the water in Mount Pleasant, the USS *Yorktown* is a must for older kids that are into old Navy ships. Savannah is filled with parks and features the kid-friendly **Savannah National Wildlife Refuge** (p90). Children also enjoy exploring **Fort Pulaski** (p90), taking the **Savannah Belles** ferry (p86) or playing on the beach at **Tybee Island** (p86).

CLIMATE CHARTS

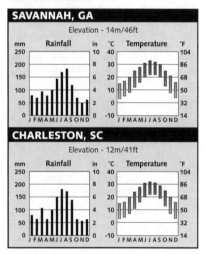

DANGERS & ANNOYANCES

Except for some parts of metro Charleston and Savannah, this entire region is relatively safe and experiences minimal crime. The biggest threat to travelers is petty theft, so always lock cars and put valuables out of sight, whether leaving the car for a few minutes or longer, and whether you are in a town or in the remote backcountry.

Be aware of your surroundings and who may be watching you. Avoid walking on dimly lit streets at night, particularly when alone. Walk purposefully. At night, it's best to use ATMs in well-trafficked areas.

It's also wise to not leave valuables lying around your hotel room. Use safety-deposit boxes, or at least place valuables in a locked bag. Don't open your door to strangers

– check the peephole or call the front desk if unexpected guests try to enter.

The most pervasive threat in this area is the major summer annoyance of mosquitoes and biting gnats called no-see-ums (cuz ya can't see 'em). These biting fools are mostly in marshy areas (like the Okefenokee Swamp) and along inland rivers, especially when the heat and humidity cocktail is at its strongest. Make sure you bring plenty of insect repellent with the active ingredient deet (some locals swear by an Avon product with repellent qualities called Skin So Soft, readily available locally).

DISABLED TRAVELERS

Travel within the US is becoming easier for people with disabilities. Public buildings are now required by law to be wheelchair accessible and to have accommodating restrooms, and transportation must be made accessible to all. Telephone companies are required to provide relay operators for the hearing impaired. Many banks now provide ATM instructions in braille.

Many hotels in the region have wheelchair-accessible rooms, although rooms often lack a comfortable amount of floor space once you're in. Often, historic B&Bs have cramped hallways and smaller rooms that aren't suitable for wheelchairs. Look to chain motels for the most modern accessible rooms and fully equipped suites. Wooden walkways that protect the dunes lead to beaches, making them wheelchair accessible.

Resources & Organizations

A number of organizations and tour providers specialize in the needs of disabled travelers.

Access-Able Travel Source (☎ 303-232-2979; www.access-able.com) This travel resource has an excellent website with links to international disability sites, travel newsletters, guidebooks and travel tips for US destinations, including lists of attractions that can be enjoyed by people with hearing, vision and/or mobility impairment.

Moss Rehabilitation Hospital's Travel Information Service (☎ 215-456-9600, TTY 215-456-9602; www .mossresourcenet.org)This rehabilitation center can provide hospital and doctor referrals for disabled travelers.

Society for the Advancement of Travel for the Handicapped (SATH; ☎ 212-447-7284; www.sath.org) This society provides information for disabled travelers and publishes a quarterly magazine.

Inn Seekers (☎ 888-466-7335; www.innseekers.com)
This is a great resource for finding wheelchair-accessible B&Bs.

DISCOUNT CARDS

Hotels, many attractions and some restaurants will give discounts to seniors who can verfiy age with identification. Students with student cards can often get a discount on activities and attractions.

AAA

For its members, **AAA** ('triple-A'; ☎ 800-922-8228; www.aaa.com) provides great travel information, distributes free road maps and guidebooks, and sells American Express traveler's checks without a commission fee. The AAA membership card will often get you discounts for accommodations, car rental and admission charges. If you plan to do a lot of driving – even in a rental car – it is usually worth joining AAA. It cost $59 for the first year and $39 for subsequent years. AAA also provides emergency roadside service to members in the event of an accident or breakdown, or if you lock your keys in the car. The nationwide toll-free roadside assistance number is ☎ 800-222-4357. All major cities and many smaller towns have a AAA office where you can start membership or get affiliate benefits.

Seniors

The Southeast is particularly gracious toward seniors. What's more, the mild climate, low prices, golf courses and extensive camping facilities for RVs also appeal to many older travelers. Senior travelers can often find discounts at hotels, campgrounds, restaurants, parks, museums and other attractions. The age at which senior discounts apply starts at 50, though it more commonly applies to those 65 or older. Be sure to inquire about discount rates when you make your reservation.

American Association of Retired Persons (AARP; ☎ 800-424-3410; www.aarp.org) is an advocacy group for Americans 50 years of age and older and is a good resource for travel bargains. US residents can get a one-year membership for $12.50. Citizens of other countries can get the same memberships for $15.

FESTIVALS & EVENTS

Numerous festivals throughout the region celebrate food, flowers, art, music and culture. See the regional chapters for details. For our Top 10 Festivals, see p11.

FOOD

Oh, my, there's so much good food in these parts. Excellent restaurants, creative chefs and good home-cookin' kitchens let you get your fill of seafood and regional specialties. Check out the Food & Drink chapter (p55) for details.

GAY & LESBIAN TRAVELERS

Many towns in the rural South are positively stone age when it comes to accepting and understanding alternative lifestyles, and while things are changing, this can be true in some coastal communities as well. While most people will keep comments to themselves, others will not hide their shock or disdain for a gay couple holding hands or kissing in public. This is not true in Savannah, the only city in this region that has accepted and even welcomed homosexuality (see 'Gay & Lesbian Savannah' p74). Charleston has a couple of gay-friendly bars and is starting to come around, but old-school Southerners are still slow to embrace the notion. As is usually the case, same-sex couples need to determine the 'temperature' of the current attitudes.

HOLIDAYS

On major holidays, expect celebrations, parades or observances, and be prepared for the closure of local businesses. See the destination chapters for more events and for complete information on those holidays mentioned here.

JANUARY

New Year's Day January 1 is a federal holiday.
Martin Luther King Jr Day Observed on the third Monday, this holiday celebrates the civil rights leader's birthday (January 15, 1929).
Robert E Lee's Birthday On January 19, more than a few Southerners remember the Confederate general with parades or celebrations. This is not an official holiday, so most businesses stay open.

FEBRUARY

Presidents' Day Held on the third Monday, this day commemorates the birthdays of Abraham Lincoln (February 12, 1809) and George Washington (February 22, 1732).

APRIL
Confederate Memorial Day Fallen Southern heroes, and to a certain extent, the fallen South, are remembered on April 26. Businesses stay open, but festivals are common on this unnofficial holiday.

MAY
Memorial Day On the last Monday in May, Americans honor the war dead.

JULY
Independence Day July 4 is a national holiday.

SEPTEMBER
Labor Day Observed on the first Monday, this holiday honors working people.

OCTOBER
Columbus Day The Italian-born explorer is remembered on the second Monday of the month.

NOVEMBER
Veterans Day On November 11, Americans honor their war veterans.
Thanksgiving On the fourth Thursday, Americans give thanks for divine goodness before stuffing themselves with turkey and pumpkin pie.

DECEMBER
Christmas This major holiday, where Christians celebrate the birth of Christ, falls on December 25. The night before (Christmas Eve), people attend church services, go caroling and cruise neighborhoods looking for the best light displays.

INSURANCE

A travel insurance policy to cover theft, lost tickets and medical problems is a good idea, especially in the US, where some hospitals will refuse care without evidence of insurance. There is a wide variety of policies, and your travel agent will have recommendations. International student travel policies handled by STA Travel and other student travel organizations are usually a good value. Some policies offer lower and higher medical expenses options, and the higher one is chiefly for countries with extremely high medical costs, such as the US. Within the US, **Access America** (☎ 800-729-6021; www.accessamerica.com) and **Travel Guard** (☎ 877-216-4885; www.travel-guard.com) are both quite reasonable and reliable insurers. For more information on insurance, see the Health chapter (p209).

Some policies specifically exclude 'dangerous activities' such as scuba diving, motorcycling and even trekking. If these activities are on your agenda, avoid this sort of policy. Check the fine print.

You may prefer a policy that pays doctors or hospitals directly, rather than one where you pay first and make a claim later. If you have to claim later, keep *all* documentation. Some policies ask you to call back (reverse charges) to a center in your home country for an immediate assessment of your problem.

Information on car insurance is given in the Transport chapter (p205).

INTERNET ACCESS

Campus or public libraries provide free or inexpensive Internet usage. Internet cafes have not made it to this part of the world, though occasionally a restaurant or coffee shop will have a computer or two available for patrons (for a fee). Also see Internet Resources in Getting Started (p9).

LEGAL MATTERS

Police in the South mean business and are especially firm with outsiders (anyone not from the South). If you are stopped by the police for any reason, bear in mind that there is no system of paying fines on the spot – try to bribe a cop and the circumstances could get much worse. For traffic offenses, the police officer will explain your options to you. Should the officer decide that you should pay up front, you may be taken directly to the magistrate instead of being allowed the usual 30-day period to pay the fine.

If you are arrested for more serious offenses, you have the right to remain silent. There is no legal reason to speak to a police officer if you don't wish, but never walk away from an officer until given permission. All persons who are arrested are legally allowed (and given) the right to make one phone call. If you're a foreigner and don't have a lawyer or family member to help you, call your embassy. The police will give you the number upon request.

See the Transport chapter (p205) for DUI and speed-limit laws.

MAPS

As for most of the US, you can find good state and city maps for both Georgia and South Carolina. Local visitors centers have good, useable maps that highlight the best sights and attractions in cities like Charleston, Savannah and Beaufort. The Myrtle Beach visitors centers give out a pretty rough map of the area.

If you plan to do a lot of driving between towns, you'll want a good map of Georgia and South Carolina. The American Automobile Association (AAA) issues the most comprehensive and dependable highway maps, which are free with AAA membership and available for a price to nonmembers. Rand McNally has up-to-date maps, as does Universal Maps.

SOLO TRAVELERS

You won't find a lot of other people traveling alone in this region, but it's a pleasant and easy place to do so. Most hotel rates are based on double occupancy, and you'll rarely get a break for flying solo.

Traveling alone is a great way to meet locals, who are genuinely curious about visitors from elsewhere. When dining or drinking alone, try sitting at the bar, and you'll likely have new friends in no time.

Women traveling alone will feel safe, though they should be aware that Southern male chivalry seems a little like a come-on if you're not used to it (see Culture p29). Men will hold doors open for women, pull out chairs, offer to carry heavy bags etc. It's a product of their upbringing, not necessarily a sign that they want something.

TOURIST INFORMATION

The following tourist offices distribute statewide guides, maps, events calendars and specialized guides such as B&B listings, African American heritage sites or Civil War sites – all free of charge.

Each state also operates welcome centers at its borders, usually at major interstate highways.

Georgia Department of Industry, Trade & Tourism (☎ 404-656-3590, 800-847-4842; www.georgia.org) Publishes the annual *Georgia on My Mind* travel guide, which you can order for free on their website.
South Carolina Department of Parks, Recreation & Tourism (☎ 803-734-1700; www.travelsc.com)

City and regional visitors centers along the coast are excellent. Most are well stocked with maps and brochures, and helpful staff

---

> **COMING OF AGE**
>
> **For the record:**
>
> ■ The legal driving age is 16, once you get a valid license.
>
> ■ Heterosexual sex is legal when you turn 16; consensual sodomy is illegal in South Carolina.
>
> ■ The legal drinking age is 21.

---

can help you book hotels, tours and tickets. Contact the visitors centers ahead of time, and they'll send you information to help you plan your trip.

Beaufort Visitors Center (☎ 843-986-5400, 800-638-3525; www.beaufortsc.org; 1106 Carteret St)
Brunswick-Golden Isles Visitors Bureau (☎ 912-265-0620; www.bgivb.com; US Hwy 17 at FJ Torras Causeway)
Charleston Visitors Center (☎ 843-853-8000; www.charlestoncvb.com; 375 Meeting St)
Hilton Head-Bluffton Visitors Center (☎ 800-523-3373; www.hiltonheadchamber.org; US Hwy 278)
Myrtle Beach Visitors Center (☎ 843-626-7444, 800-356-3016; www.myrtlebeachinfo.com; 1200 N Oak St)
Savannah Visitors Center (☎ 912-944-0455, 877-728-2662; www.savannahvisit.com; 301 Martin Luther King Jr Blvd)

WOMEN

The feminist movement never made much inroads in this area, and outright, if unintentional, sexism exists. Southern men (and most women) think nothing of calling a woman 'girl' or of commenting on her fragility or weakness. Men, out of deeply ingrained lessons of chivalry, can be condescending to women. In many homes, women still do all the cooking and cleaning (though many also work outside the home), and there's still an 'old boys' club' mentality in business.

Southern men are taught to revere women (and you could take a course on the psychological ramifications of this!) but they'll often get threatened by 'strong' or independent women. This is mostly a reaction akin to wonder or simple fascination. Women traveling alone will have no problem in this region if they understand something of the culture – see Solo Travelers (previous column) and Culture, (p29).

INTERNATIONAL VISITORS
ENTERING THE COUNTRY

To enter the USA, you must have a non-refundable, roundtrip ticket, except when entering overland from Canada or Mexico (in which case sufficient funds for the duration of your stay must be shown).

Thanks to heightened security measures, travelers can expect long waits at immigration and security checkpoints. The Department of Homeland Security is phasing in the US-VISIT program, which will track every single one of the 35 million visitors who come to the USA every year. Visitors may be photographed and fingerprinted, and in the future, may be subject to iris scanning and facial recognition technology. The program should be fully implemented by 2005; check www.dhs.gov for current procedures and requirements.

Public health, customs and agricultural inspections may be carried out separately or together with immigration clearance.

No immunizations are required to enter the USA, but you should have adequate health insurance before setting out.

For up-to-date information on passports, visas and travel advisories, go to www.lonelyplanet.com and click on Travel Ticker.

Passport

All foreign visitors to the US must have a valid passport, and many are also required to have a US visa. It's a good idea to keep photocopies of these documents; in case of theft, they'll be a lot easier to replace.

Your passport should be valid for at least six months longer than your intended stay in the US. Documents of financial stability and/or guarantees from a US resident are sometimes required, particularly for visitors from developing countries.

Visas

The USA is in the process of overhauling its entry requirements as it establishes new national security guidelines. It is imperative that travelers double check current regulations before coming to the USA, as changes will continue for several years. The best website for comprehensive visa information is www.unitedstatesvisas.gov.

Most foreign visitors need to obtain a visa from a US consulate or embassy. In most countries the process can be done by mail or through a travel agent. Canadians and those entering under the Visa Waiver Pilot Program may enter the country without a US visa for stays of 90 days or less. Currently, 27 countries are in the program, including most EU countries, Australia and New Zealand. All other travelers will need a visitor's visa. These can be obtained at most US consulates and embassies overseas; it is usually best to apply for a visa from an office in your home country.

The most common visa is a Non-Immigrant Visitor's Visa: B1 for business purposes, B2 for tourism or visiting friends and relatives. A visitor visa is good for one or five years with multiple entries, and it specifically prohibits the visitor from taking paid employment in the US. If you're coming to the US to work or study, you will probably need a different type of visa, and the company or institution you're connected with should make the arrangements. Allow six months in advance for processing the application.

Visa Extensions & Re-entry

If you want to stay in the US longer than the date stamped on your passport, call the **State Department's Visa Services' Public Inquiries Branch** at ☎ 202-663-1225, or check online at www.unitedstatesvisas.org for current instructions. Do this well before the stamped date to apply for an extension.

International Driving Permit

An International Driving Permit is a useful accessory for foreign visitors in the US. Local traffic police are more likely to accept it as valid identification than as an unfamiliar document from another country. Your national automobile association can provide one for a small fee. In the US, you can obtain one for a $10 fee from travel agencies such as STA Travel or AAA; bring along two passport photos and your home license. They're usually valid for one year.

CUSTOMS

US Customs allows each person older than the age of 21 to bring one liter of liquor and 200 cigarettes duty free into the US. US citizens are allowed to import duty free, $400 worth of gifts from abroad, while non-US citizens area allowed to bring in $100 worth. Forget bringing in fresh fruits, vegetables or plants – most of them can (and will) be confiscated.

US Embassies & Consulates

Other US embassies and consulates can be found on the government's website: http://usembassy.state.gov.

Australia ACT (☎ 02-6214-5600); 21 Moonah Place, Yarralumla ACT 2600); WA (☎ 08-9202-1224; 16 St George's Terrace, 13th Floor, Perth WA 6000); NWS (☎ 02-9373-9200; Level 59 MLC Center 19-29 Martin Place, Sydney NSW 2000); Victoria (☎ 03-9526-5900; 553 St Kilda Rd, Melbourne, Victoria)

Canada Ottawa (☎ 613-238-5335; 490 Sussex Dr, Ottawa, Ontario K1N 1G8); Toronto (☎ 416-595-1700; 360 University Ave, Toronto, Ontario, M5G 154); British Columbia (☎ 604-685-4311; 1095 W Pender St, Vancouver, BC V6E 2M6); Quebec (☎ 514-398-9695; 1155 rue St-Alexandre, Montreal, Quebec H2Z 1Z2)

France (☎ 1 43 12 22 22; 2 ave Gabriel, 75008 Paris)

Germany (☎ 030-8305-0; Neustädtische Kirschstr 4-5, 10117 Berlin; Clayallee 170, 14195 Berlin)

Ireland (☎ 1-6688777; 42 Elgin Rd, Ballsbridge, Dublin 4, Ireland)

Japan (☎ 03-3224-5000; 1-10-5 Akasaka 1-Chome, Minato-ku, Tokyo 107-8420)

UK England (☎ 20-7499-9000; 24 Grosvenor Square, London W1A 1AE); Scotland (☎ 131 556-8315; 3 Regent Terrace, Edinburgh EH7 5BW); Northern Ireland (☎ 28-9032-8239; Queens House, 14 Queen St, Belfast BT1 6EQ)

Embassies & Consulates in the South

Most embassies are in Washington, DC, though it's possible that your country maintains a diplomatic mission in Atlanta. See the list below, or check the yellow pages telephone directory under 'Consulates.' All of the following are in Atlanta.

Australia (☎ 404-760-3400; Buckhead Plaza NW)
Austria (☎ 404-264-9858; 4200 Northside Pkwy NW)
Belgium (☎ 404-521-1079; 235 Peachtree St SW)

Canada (☎ 404-532-2000; 100 Colony Sq, 1175 Peachtree St NE)
France (☎ 404-522-4226; 285 Peachtree Center Ave NE)
Germany (☎ 404-659-4760; 285 Peachtree Center Ave NE)
Italy (☎ 404-303-0503; 755 Mount Vernon Hwy NE)
Japan (☎ 404-892-2700; 100 Colony Sq, 1175 Peachtree St NE)
Mexico (☎ 404-266-0777; 3220 Peachtree Dr NE)
New Zealand (☎ 404-888-5196; 75 14th St NE)
Norway (☎ 404-239-0885; 3715 Northside Pkwy NW)
UK (☎ 404-524-5856; 245 Peachtree Center Ave NE)

MONEY

The US dollar is divided into 100 cents (¢). Coins come in denominations of 1¢ (penny), 5¢ (nickel), 10¢ (dime), 25¢ (quarter) and 50¢ (the rare half-dollar). There are also $1 coins. Keep a stash of quarters handy for vending machines, laundry machines and parking meters. Notes, commonly called bills, come in $1, $2, $5, $10, $20, $50 and $100 denominations – $2 bills are rare, but perfectly legal.

Exchanging Money

Most banks in major cities will exchange cash or traveler's checks in major foreign currencies, though banks in smaller cities and outlying areas don't do so very often, so it may take them some time. Although you'll get a better rate at a bank, exchange windows in airports also offer this service.

ATMS

Almost all ATMs accept cards from the Cirrus, Visa, Star and Global Access networks. They are found everywhere, especially at banks and convenience stores. Most ATMs charge a service fee of $1.50 or so per transaction for foreign bank cards, but exchange rates usually beat traveler's checks.

Traveler's Checks

American Express, Visa and Thomas Cook are widely known issuers of traveler's checks. Restaurants, hotels and most shops readily accept US-dollar traveler's checks, same as cash, but small businesses, markets and fast-food chains may refuse them.

Taxes

A state sales tax of 5% in South Carolina and 4% in Georgia is charged in addition to city and county taxes.

Tipping

Tip restaurant servers 15% to 20%. If the restaurant automatically adds a 'service charge' (usually for groups of six or more), do not double-tip. Bartenders get at least $1 for one or two drinks, or 15% when you're buying a round. Tip taxi drivers 10% of the fare, rounding up. Valet parking attendants get $2 when they hand you the keys to your car. Skycaps, bellhops and cloak-room attendants get $1 to $2 per item; hotel maids are tipped $1 to $2 per day.

POST

Postage rates for 1st-class mail within the USA are 37¢ for letters up to 1oz (23¢ for each additional ounce) and 23¢ for postcards.

International airmail rates (except to Canada and Mexico) are 80¢ for a 1oz letter and 70¢ for postcards. Airmail to Canada and Mexico costs 60¢ for a 1oz letter, 85¢ for a 2oz letter and 50¢ for a postcard. Aerogrammes are 70¢.

The cost for parcels airmailed anywhere within the USA is $3.50 for up to 1lb and $3.95 for up to 2lb; the cost increases per pound up to $7.55 for 5lb. For heavier items, rates differ according to the distance mailed. Books, periodicals, and computer disks can be sent by a cheaper 4th-class rate.

For 24-hour postal information, call ☎ 800-275-8777 or check www.usps.com. These services give ZIP (postal) codes for any given address, the rules about parcel sizes and the location and phone number of any post office.

You can have mail sent to you care of General Delivery at any post office that has its own ZIP (postal) code. These addresses are provided in the text. Mail is usually held for 10 days before it's returned to sender; you might request your correspondents to write 'hold for arrival' on their letters.

TELEPHONE

All phone numbers within the US consist of a three-digit area code followed by a seven-digit local number. The area code in Charleston, Myrtle Beach and the South Carolina coast is 843. In Savannah and along the Georgia coast, the area code is 912. If you are calling locally, just dial the seven-digit number. If you are calling long distance, dial 1 + the three-digit area code + the seven-digit number. If you're calling from abroad, note that the international country code for the US is 1.

For local directory assistance, dial ☎ 411. For directory assistance outside your area code, dial 1 + the three-digit area code of the place you want to call + 555-1212. For example, to obtain directory assistance for Charleston, dial ☎ 1-843-555-1212.

The 800, 888, and 877 area codes are designated for toll-free numbers within the US and sometimes Canada. Calling areas can be restricted to outside the local area or within the US. For toll-free directory assistance, call ☎ 800-555-1212. The 900 prefix is designated for calls for which the caller pays a premium rate – chat lines, horoscopes, sex lines etc.

Local calls usually cost 35¢ or 50¢ at pay phones. Long-distance rates vary. Don't ask the operator to put your call through, however, because operator-assisted calls are much more expensive than direct-dial calls. Generally, nights (11pm to 8am), all day Saturday and from 8am to 5pm Sunday are the cheapest times to call. Daytime calls (8am to 5pm Monday to Friday) are full-price within the USA.

To make a direct international call, dial 011, then the country code (found in the front of most phone directories), followed by the area code and the phone number.

Many hotels (especially the more expensive ones) add a service charge of 50¢ to $1 for each local call made from a room phone, and they also have hefty surcharges for long-distance calls. Public pay phones are always cheaper.

TIME

The region covered in this guide falls under Eastern Standard Time, five hours behind Greenwich Mean Time (ie, when it's noon in Savannah, it's 5pm in London). All Southeastern states observe daylight saving time (comparable to British Summer Time).

Transport

THINGS CHANGE...

The information in this chapter is particularly vulnerable to change – prices for international travel are volatile, routes are introduced or cancelled, schedules change, special deals come and go, and rules and visa requirements are amended. Check directly with the airline or travel agency to make sure you understand how a fare (or a ticket you may buy) works. Get opinions, quotes and advice from as many airlines and travel agencies as possible before you part with your hard-earned cash. The details given in this chapter should be regarded as pointers: they are not a substitute for careful, up-to-date research.

The two most common ways to reach this region are by air and by car, but you can also get there by train and by bus. Travelers coming from the Midwest, Northeast and Great Plains states don't have far to go if they want to drive – and in general, excellent highways connect the region to every part of the US. Travelers from farther afield usually fly in, then rent a car.

GETTING THERE & AWAY

AIR

US domestic airfares vary tremendously, depending on the season you travel, the day of the week you fly, the length of your stay and the flexibility the ticket allows for flight changes and refunds. Fares also vary depending on which airport you are flying into – no single airport in the region has a lock on the best deals.

Nothing determines fares more than demand, and when things are slow, regardless of the season, airlines will lower their fares to fill empty seats. There's a lot of competition, and at any given time, any one of the airlines could have the cheapest fare. In general, high season for nationwide airline travel rates in the US is mid-June to mid-September and the weeks before and after Christmas.

Airports & Airlines

Three main international airports serve the Georgia and South Carolina coasts and offer service from Atlanta, Charlotte, Miami, New York, Newark, Chicago, Washington DC, Cincinnati, Dallas and Houston – among others. Many indirect flights connect through Atlanta's Hartsfield International Airport (code ATL; www.atlanta-airport.com) or Raleigh-Durham International Airport (code RDU; www.rdu.com).

Brunswick-Golden Isles Airport (code BQK; www.glynncountyairports.com; p101) Served by Delta Connection, with flights to and from Atlanta.
Charleston International Airport (code CHS; www.chs-airport.com; p170) Located 12 miles outside of Charleston, in the city of North Charleston.
Hilton Head Island Airport (code HHH; www.hiltonheadairport.com; p132) Served by one airline, US Airways Express, which flies to Hilton Head from Washington, DC and Charlotte, North Carolina.
Myrtle Beach International Airport (code MYR; www.myrtlebeachairport.com; p188) Just two miles from the center of Myrtle Beach.
Savannah/Hilton Head International Airport (code SAV; www.savannahairport.com; p85) About 5 miles west of downtown Savannah, off I-16.

Airlines

The following are the major airlines that serve the region:

AirTran Airways (☎ 800-247-8726; www.airtran.com)
Continental Express (☎ 800-525-0280; www.continental.com)
Delta (☎ 800-221-1212; www.delta.com)

Hooters Air (☎ 888-359-4668; www.hootersair.com)
Flies to Myrtle Beach only.
Northwest Airlines (☎ 800-225-2525; www.nwa.com)
United Airlines (☎ 800-241-6522; www.ual.com)
US Airways (☎ 800-428-4322; www.usairways.com)

LAND
Bus
Greyhound (☎ 800-231-2222; www.greyhound.com) is the only nationwide bus company with good coverage in Southeastern cities and towns. Buses are air-conditioned, and most are decently maintained. In Georgia, relevant stations include Savannah and Brunswick; in South Carolina, stations are present in Beaufort, Charleston, Georgetown and Myrtle Beach.

Dealing with Greyhound on the telephone is often a major investment of time and patience, but their website is excellent for finding out schedules or buying tickets. Fares are not necessarily cheap and depend on the distance, day of the week and how far in advance the ticket is bought. The best deals are 'plan-ahead' specials that require ticket purchase two weeks prior to your departure date. Services can be infrequent, sometimes just once a day and at weird times. If you're planning on doing a lot of touring by bus, you might want to check out car rentals instead; you'd be surprised how much bus fares can add up. Some sample routes are as follows.

Depart	Arrive	Cost	Duration	Frequency
Atlanta	Savannah	$48	5½ hrs	25 daily
Atlanta	Charleston	$64	8 hrs	3 daily
Columbia	Charleston	$24	2¼ hrs	2 daily
Jacksonville	Charleston	$53	6 hrs	3 daily
Jacksonville	Savannah	$25	21 hrs	12 daily
New York	Myrtle Beach	$92	16 hrs	3 daily

Car & Motorcycle
Most travelers to the Georgia and South Carolina coasts either fly or drive, and on the interstates and highways you'll see plenty of RVs and cars with out-of-state license plates. Foreign drivers need their vehicle's registration papers, liability insurance and an international driving permit, in addition to their domestic driver's license.

From Atlanta, I-75 S connects to I-16 heading east to Savannah and the gateway to the Georgia barrier islands. From Atlanta to Charleston, the best route is I-20 east to Columbia, then I-26 southeast to the coast. Travelers coming from Northeastern states mainly use I-95, cutting over to the coast on I-26 near Charleston, or I-16 near Savannah. From Florida, I-95 parallels Hwy 17 up to cost to roughly Beaufort; though I-95 is faster, Hwy 17 is much more scenic.

Train
Amtrak (☎ 800-872-7245; www.amtrak.com) is the only railroad in the US that provides cross-country passenger service, with several lines running from New York down the east coast toward New Orleans or Florida. Trains tend to be infrequent, and the daily service may actually depart in the middle of the night. Fares vary according to type of seating; you can travel in coach seats or in various types of sleeping compartments. The child fare is half the adult fare (children must be traveling with an adult paying the full fare). A 15% student discount pass is available for $20 per year. Anyone over age 62 qualifies for a 15% discount. Special fares are also available for disabled travelers.

International travelers can take advantage of Amtrak's USA Rail Pass, available for travel agents outside of North America. Foreign-passport holders can purchase it from Amtrak once inside the USA. The pass offers unlimited coach-class travel within a specific region for either 15 or 30 days, with the price depending on region, number of days and season traveled. The 15-day East Coast pass costs $210 to $260, and the 30-day East Coast pass is $265 to $320.

The *Silver Meteor* and *Silver Palm* travel the coast from New York south to Jacksonville, Florida, with continuing service to Miami. The trains stop in Charleston and Savannah and in Florence, South Carolina, 70 miles west of Myrtle Beach. Fares from New York to Savannah and Charleston are about the same, starting at $190. Tickets from Savannah or Charleston to Jacksonville start at $22; to Miami, $54.

GETTING AROUND

There's no question about it: if you want to see the scattered rural attractions that lie between the cities of the Southeast, the best way is by car. The highways are good, and public transportation isn't as frequent or as widespread as in many other countries. Of course, a focused trip or tour can work nicely with air, train or bus transit between major destinations.

Very few tourists fly between small regional airports in this region, as all the major cities and attractions are within driving distance. Some private and charter planes use the small municipal airports that are scattered throughout the region.

BUS

Greyhound (☎ 800-231-2222; www.greyhound.com) is the way to get around up and down the coast. The bus stations are generally well maintained and staffed.

Tickets can be bought by phone or over the Internet with a credit card (MasterCard, Visa or Discover) and then received by mail (if purchased 10 or more days in advance) or picked up at the terminal with proper identification. Greyhound terminals also accept American Express, traveler's checks and cash. Note that all buses are nonsmoking, and reservations can be made with ticket purchases only.

Sample fares are as follows:

Depart	Arrive	Cost	Duration	Frequency
Atlanta	Myrtle Beach	$46	12 hrs	2 daily
Beaufort	Charleston	$26	2 hrs	2 daily
Brunswick	Savannah	$16	1½ hrs	26 daily
Charleston	Savannah	$27	3 hrs	2 daily
Myrtle Beach	Charleston	$26	2¼ hrs	2 daily

BICYCLE

Notwithstanding the odd hurricane, flood or snow flurry, the coast is amenable to cycling. You'll find brilliant trails all along this part of the Atlantic coast, from the removed peace of Georgia's St Simons Island to the neon glare of Myrtle Beach. Historic districts are great for a spin, too. In the heat, cyclists should carry at least two full water bottles, and it's a good idea to carry a pump and patch kit. Rentals are widely available along the coast; see destination chapters for details.

Though the region is flat and has many gorgeous backroads, few direct routes are conducive to long-distance road riding. There are, however, a lot of nice day rides on secondary and tertiary highways. See the Outdoors chapter (p000) for local organizations that put together maps and rides in the region.

CAR & MOTORCYCLE

Driving offers visitors the most flexibility at a reasonable cost. If you're planning on exploring beyond the main cities, a car is a must. Nothing in the region is more than a few hours away. If you are staying put in the historic districts of Savannah, Charleston or Beaufort, you can easily see all the sights car-free, as it's easy to get from one side of town to the other on foot. For folks who don't like to walk, horse-drawn carriages and motorized tours are widely available.

To get up and down the coast, you will get very familiar with Hwy 17, a mostly two-lane road that takes you to all the attractions, or at least to the roads that'll get you there. Hwy 17 is also referred to as the Savannah Hwy and the Coastal Hwy. Also running north–south along the coast is I-95, and though it's faster, it's much less scenic.

Car theft is not a big problem in the region, though it's wise not to leave desirable items visible inside the car. You're better off bringing valuables into your hotel or leaving them in the trunk.

Motorcycling is great along the coast, as the weather is usually warm. Rains can come vigorously but last only a little while. You must wear a helmet in Georgia, but in South Carolina, if you're over 21, you can ride helmet-free.

Rental

Major international rental agencies like Hertz, Avis, Budget and National have offices throughout the region, but there are also local agencies. Most rental companies require that you have a major credit card, that you be at least 25 years old, and that you have a valid driver's license.

The following car rental agencies have desks at the major airports:

Avis	(☎ 800-230-4898)
Budget	(☎ 800-527-0700)
Enterprise	(☎ 800-325-8007)
Hertz	(☎ 800-654-3131)
National	(☎ 800-227-7368)
Payless	(☎ 800-729-5733)
Thrifty	(☎ 800-367-2277)

TRANSPORT

Many rental agencies have bargain rates for weekend or weeklong rentals, especially outside the peak summer season or in conjunction with airline tickets. Prices vary greatly according to region, season and type or size of car. You might pay as little as $30 per day or as much as $70, with unlimited mileage included at the top end.

Be sure to ask for the best rate – discounts may be offered for renting on weekends, for three days, by the week or month – or even for renting a car in one place and returning it to another if the company needs to move cars in that direction. In any case, a 'one way' rental can be useful. The extra drop-off charge ranges from nothing to $200.

Take time to mull over the insurance angles. Liability coverage is required by law in most states but isn't always included in rental contracts, because many Americans are covered for rental cars under their regular car liability insurance policy. You need liability coverage, but don't pay extra if sufficient coverage is already included with the rental. Insurance against damage to the car, called collision damage waiver (CDW) or loss damage waiver (LDW), is usually optional ($8 to $12 per day), but you may have to pay a $100 to $500 deductible; this may be avoided by paying additional premiums. Credit cards often cover your CDW if you rent for at least 15 days and charge the rental to your card. Check with your credit card company to see what insurance coverage your card's benefits include.

Road Rules

The speed limit is generally 55mph or 65mph on highways, 25mph to 35mph in cities and towns, and as low as 15mph in school zones (strictly enforced during school hours). It's forbidden to pass a school bus when its tail lights are flashing. On the interstate highways in designated rural areas, the speed limit can get as high as 75mph. Always watch for posted speed limits. Some towns have started hiding surveillance cameras inside traffic lights, which will take a photo of your license plate if you run a red light. You'll receive the ticket in the mail.

Most states have laws against littering – if you are seen throwing anything from a vehicle, you can be fined as much as $1000. Penalties are severe for DUIs – driving under the influence of alcohol and/or drugs. Police can give roadside sobriety checks; if you fail, they'll require you to take a breath test, urine test or blood test. If you refuse to be tested, you'll be treated as if you'd taken the test and failed. In both South Carolina and Georgia, the maximum legal blood–alcohol concentration is 0.08%, roughly the alcohol content of two drinks. It's illegal to carry open containers of alcohol in a vehicle, even if they're empty or if only the passengers are imbibing. Containers that are full and sealed may be carried, but if they have been opened, they must be carried in the trunk.

LOCAL TRANSPORT

Getting around the major cities and islands is easily done on foot or by bicycle, though catching a horse-drawn carriage in Charleston, Savannah or Beaufort is highly recommended.

In Savannah, the Chatham Area Transit (CAT) runs a free shuttle bus throughout the Historic District, regularly stopping at the visitors center and area hotels.

In Charleston, the Downtown Area Shuttle (Dash) makes regular stops along five routes in the historic district. The city buses are operated by the Charleston Area Regional Transportation Authority (Carta), which services outlying communities.

Taxis are common in bigger cities, and can easily be flagged for a fare. In small towns you generally must phone for a cab. Hotels often provide free shuttles to/from the airport.

Health by David Goldberg, MD

The southern coastal region of the United States can get uncomfortably hot in the summer, but that's likely to be your biggest concern. Because of the high level of hygiene here, as in the rest of the USA, infectious diseases are rarely a significant concern for most travelers.

BEFORE YOU GO

INSURANCE

The United States offers possibly the finest health care in the world. The problem is that unless you have good insurance, it can be prohibitively expensive. If you're coming from abroad, you should buy supplemental travel health insurance if your regular policy doesn't cover you for overseas trips. (Check www.lonelyplanet.com/subwwway for more information.) If you are covered, find out in advance whether your insurance plan will make payments directly to providers or whether the company will instead reimburse you later.

Domestic travelers who have coverage should check with their insurance company for affiliated hospitals and doctors. US citizens who don't have regular health coverage can purchase domestic travel insurance, but be aware that most plans only cover emergencies.

Bring any medications you may need in their original containers, clearly labeled. A signed, dated letter from your physician describing all medical conditions and medications, including generic names, is also a good idea.

ONLINE RESOURCES

There is a wealth of travel health advice on the Internet. The World Health Organization publishes a superb book called *International Travel and Health*, which is revised annually and is available online at no cost at www.who.int/ith. Another website of general interest is MD Travel Health at www.mdtravelhealth.com, which provides complete travel health recommendations for every country, updated daily, also at no cost.

It's usually a good idea to consult your government's travel health website before departure, if one is available:

Australia www.dfat.gov.au/travel
Canada www.hc-sc.gc.ca/pphb-dgspsp/tmp-pmv/pub_e.html
United Kingdom www.doh.gov.uk/traveladvice/index.htm
United States www.cdc.gov/travel

IN THE REGION

AVAILABILITY & COST OF HEALTH CARE

In general, if you have a medical emergency, the best bet is to find the nearest hospital and go to its emergency room. If the problem isn't urgent, you can call a nearby hospital and ask for a referral to a local physician, which is usually cheaper than a trip to the emergency room. You should avoid stand-alone, for-profit urgent-care centers, which tend to perform large numbers of expensive tests, even for minor illnesses.

Pharmacies are abundantly supplied, but international travelers may find that some medications that are available over the counter at home require a prescription in the United States, and if you don't have insurance to cover the cost of prescriptions, they can be shockingly expensive.

INFECTIOUS DISEASES

In addition to more common ailments, there are several infectious diseases that are unknown or uncommon outside North

HEALTH

America. Most are acquired by mosquito or tick bites.

West Nile Virus

These infections were unknown in the United States until a few years ago but have now been reported in almost all 50 states. The virus is transmitted by mosquitoes of the Culex family, which are active in late summer and early fall and generally bite after dusk. Most infections are mild or asymptomatic, but the virus may infect the central nervous system, leading to fever, headache, confusion, lethargy, coma and sometimes death. There is no treatment for West Nile virus. For the latest update on the areas affected by West Nile, go the US Geological Survey website at http://westnilemaps.usgs.gov.

Lyme Disease

This disease has been reported from many states, but most documented cases occur in the northeastern part of the country, especially New York, New Jersey, Connecticut and Massachusetts. A smaller number of cases occur in the northern Midwest and in the northern Pacific coastal regions, including northern California. Lyme disease is transmitted by deer ticks, which are only 1mm to 2mm long. Most cases occur in the late spring and summer. The Center for Disease Control has an informative, if slightly scary, web page on Lyme disease: www.cdc.gov/ncidod/dvbid/lyme.

The first symptom is usually an expanding red rash that is often pale in the center, known as a bull's-eye rash. However, in many cases, no rash is observed. Flu-like symptoms are common, including fever, headache, joint pains, body aches and general malaise. When the infection is treated promptly with an appropriate antibiotic, usually doxycycline or amoxicillin, the cure rate is high. Luckily, since the tick must be attached for 36 hours or more to transmit Lyme disease, most cases can be prevented by performing a thorough tick check after you've been outdoors.

Rabies

Rabies is a viral infection of the brain and spinal cord that is almost always fatal. The rabies virus is carried in the saliva of infected animals and is typically transmitted through an animal bite, though contamination of any break in the skin with infected saliva may result in rabies. In the US, most cases of human rabies are related to exposure to bats. Rabies may also be contracted from raccoons, skunks, foxes and unvaccinated cats and dogs.

If there is any possibility, however small, that you have been exposed to rabies, you should seek preventative treatment, which consists of rabies immune globulin and rabies vaccine and is quite safe. In particular, any contact with a bat should be discussed with health authorities, because bats have small teeth and may not leave obvious bite marks. If you wake up to find a bat in your room, or discover a bat in a room with small children, rabies prophylaxis may be necessary.

Giardiasis

This parasitic infection of the small intestine occurs throughout the world. Symptoms may include nausea, bloating, cramps and diarrhea, and may last for weeks. To protect yourself from Giardiasis, you should avoid drinking directly from lakes, ponds, streams and rivers, which may be contaminated by animal or human feces. The infection can also be transmitted person-to-person if proper hand washing is not performed. Giardiasis is easily diagnosed by a stool test and is readily treated with antibiotics.

HIV/AIDS

As with most parts of the world, HIV infection occurs throughout the United States. You should never assume, on the basis of someone's background or appearance, that they're free of this or any other sexually transmitted disease. Be sure to use prophylaxis for all sexual encounters.

ENVIRONMENTAL HAZARDS
Dehydration

Visitors to the humid Lowcountry may not realize that they need to keep hydrated, but they do – they lose a lot of water by sweating. The prudent tourist will make sure to drink more water than usual – think a gallon a day if you're active. Parents can carry fruits and fruit juices to help keep kids hydrated.

Severe dehydration can easily cause disorientation and confusion, and even day hikers have gotten lost and died because they ignored their thirst. So bring plenty of water even on short hikes, and drink it!

Heat Exhaustion
Without heeding certain precautions, visitors not acclimated to a subtropical climate may experience discomfort from extreme summertime heat, humidity and overexposure to the sun. Avoid exposure to the midday sun and heat – have a plan to be indoors – and confine strenuous activity to early morning and late afternoon. Wear sunscreen and a hat. More sensitive types may want to carry an umbrella to shield themselves from the sun. Rent a car with air-conditioning and light-colored interiors. Drinking lots of water is also good. Note that many establishments overcompensate for the heat by cranking up the air conditioning – brace yourself for the bodily shock of alternating between the 100°F exterior and 70°F interiors.

Heatstroke
This serious, occasionally fatal, condition can occur if the body's heat-regulating mechanism breaks down and the body temperature rises to dangerous levels. Long continuous periods of exposure to high temperatures and insufficient fluids can leave you vulnerable to heatstroke.

The symptoms are feeling unwell, not sweating much (or at all) and a high body temperature (102°F to 106°F). Where sweating has ceased, the skin becomes flushed and red. Severe, throbbing headaches and lack of coordination will also occur, and the sufferer may be confused or aggressive. Eventually the victim will become delirious or convulse. Hospitalization is essential, but in the interim get victims out of the sun, remove their clothing, cover them with a wet sheet or towel and then fan continually. Give fluids if they are conscious.

Bites & Stings
Commonsense approaches to these concerns are the most effective: wear boots when hiking to protect yourself from snakes, and wear long sleeves and pants to protect yourself from ticks and mosquitoes. If you're bitten, don't overreact. Stay calm and follow the recommended treatment (below).

MOSQUITO BITES
When traveling in areas where West Nile (p210) or other mosquito-borne illnesses have been reported, keep yourself covered (wear long sleeves, long pants, hats and shoes rather than sandals), and apply a good insect repellent, preferably one containing deet, to exposed skin and clothing. In general, adults and children over 12 should use preparations containing 25% to 35% Deet, which usually lasts about six hours. Children between two and 12 years of age should use preparations containing no more than 10% deet, applied sparingly, which will usually last about three hours. Neurologic toxicity has been reported from deet, especially in children, but this appears to be extremely uncommon and generally related to overuse. deet-containing compounds should not be used on children under age two.

Insect repellents containing certain botanical products, including oil of eucalyptus and soybean oil, are effective but last only 1½ to 2 hours. Products based on citronella are not effective.

Visit the Center for Disease Control's website (www.cdc.gov/ncidod/dvbid/westnile/prevention_ info.htm) for prevention information.

TICK BITES
Ticks are parasitic arachnids that may be present in brush, forest and grasslands, where hikers often get them on their legs or in their boots. Adult ticks suck blood from hosts by burrowing into the skin and can carry infections such as Lyme disease (p210).

Always check your body for ticks after walking through high grass or a thickly forested area. If ticks are found unattached, they can simply be brushed off. If a tick is found attached, press down around the tick's head with tweezers, grab the head and gently pull upwards – do not twist. (If no tweezers are available, use your fingers, but protect them from contamination with a piece of tissue or paper.) Do not rub oil, alcohol or petroleum jelly on it. If you get sick in the next couple of weeks, consult a doctor.

ANIMAL BITES

Do not attempt to pet, handle, or feed any animal, with the exception of domestic animals known to be free of infectious disease. Most animal injuries are directly related to a person's attempt to touch or feed it.

Any bite or scratch by a mammal, including bats, should be promptly and thoroughly cleansed with large amounts of soap and water, followed by application of an antiseptic such as iodine or alcohol. The local health authorities should be contacted immediately for possible post-exposure rabies treatment, whether or not you've been immunized against rabies. It may also be advisable to start an antibiotic, since wounds caused by animal bites and scratches frequently become infected.

SNAKE BITES

There are several varieties of venomous snakes in the Lowcountry, including cottonmouth, copperhead and coral snakes, but unlike those in other countries, they do not cause instantaneous death, and antivenins are available. First aid is to place a light constricting bandage over the bite, keep the wounded part below the level of the heart and move it as little as possible. Stay calm and get to a medical facility as soon as possible. Bring the dead snake for identification if you can, but don't risk being bitten again. Do not use the 'cut an X and suck out the venom' trick; this causes more damage to snakebite victims than the bites themselves.

SPIDER BITES

Although there are many species of spiders in the United States, the only ones that cause significant human illness are the black widow, brown recluse and hobo spiders.

The black widow is black or brown in color and measures about 15mm in body length, with a shiny top, fat body and distinctive red or orange hourglass figure on its underside. It's found throughout the United States, usually in barns, woodpiles, sheds, harvested crops and the bowls of outdoor toilets. If bitten by a black widow, you should apply ice or cold packs and go immediately to the nearest emergency room. Complications of a black widow bite may include muscle spasms, breathing difficulties, and high blood pressure.

The brown recluse spider is brown in color, usually 10mm in body length, with a dark violin-shaped mark on the top of the upper section of the body. It's usually found in the south and southern Midwest, but it has spread to other parts of the country in recent years. The brown recluse is active mostly at night, lives in dark sheltered areas (such as under porches and in woodpiles), and typically bites when trapped. The bite of a brown recluse typically causes a large, inflamed wound, sometimes associated with fever and chills. If bitten, apply ice and see a physician.

Hobo spiders are found chiefly in the northwestern United States and western Canada. The symptoms of a hobo spider bite are similar to those of a brown recluse, but milder. Again, if bitten, apply ice and see a physician.

SCORPION BITES

The only dangerous species of scorpion in the United States is the bark scorpion, which is found in the southwestern part of the country, chiefly Arizona. If stung, you should immediately apply ice or cold packs, immobilize the affected body part, and go to the nearest emergency room. To prevent scorpion stings, be sure to inspect and shake out clothing, shoes, and sleeping bags before use, and wear gloves and protective clothing when working around piles of wood or leaves.

Glossary

A

antebellum – the period prior to the Civil War (Latin for 'before the war').

B

beach music – a relaxed, nostalgic form of pop music derived from R&B and soul; ostensibly from the South Carolina coast.

benne – a Gullah word for 'sesame'; benne crackers are popular in Charleston.

blackwater – swamps or rivers that contain high concentrations of tannic acid from the acidic roots of cypress trees, still water and decomposing leaves.

bluegrass – a form of folk music that evolved in the bluegrass region of Kentucky and, later, Tennessee.

blue laws – laws limiting business activity on Sundays in parts of the South, especially South Carolina and Louisiana; based on an English statute from the reign of Charles II.

boiled peanuts – peanuts in the shell are boiled in a big pot of salty water until the shells are soft; a favorite Southern snack.

Brunswick stew – an antebellum dish originally made with squirrel meat; today most cooks use rabbit or chicken and add potatoes, beans, tomatoes, okra and spices.

C

Carolina Gold – name of the rice cultivated by West African slaves and grown on plantations prior to the Civil War.

chicken-fried – a breaded and deep-fried piece of meat, usually steak or pork chops, served with gravy.

chitterlings – large intestine of a pig, boiled and then fried; locals pronounce them 'chitlins.'

collards – a shortened version of collard greens, a common side dish with many Southern meals.

cracklins – fried strips of pork skin and fat, considered a snack food.

D

dirty rice – white rice cooked with chicken giblets or ground pork, along with green onions, peppers, celery, herbs and spices.

F

fixing – used as in 'to prepare,' as in 'I'm fixin' to go fishin' later.'

French Huguenots – French ethnic Protestants who settled in the South in the late 17th century, especially in Charleston and South Carolina.

Frogmore stew – a one-pot dish that combines shrimp, sausage, corn, potato and spices; also called 'Lowcountry boil.'

G

grits – coarsely ground hominy, or white corn, prepared as a mush and served with breakfast throughout the South, often with butter, cheese or gravy.

Gullah – a culture that reflects strong African traditions, as well as a language that is a hybridization of English and African languages. It is still spoken on some coastal islands; the term also refers to cuisine.

gumbo – a Louisiana soup often recreated in Lowcountry kitchens, made with seafood, okra and spices.

H

haint – Gullah word for ghost or spirit.

hopping John – a hearty stew made with ham and cow peas or field peas.

hush puppy – a bread substitute served with many Southern meals; made from deep-fried balls of cornmeal and onion.

I

indigo – a tropical plant of the pea family once harvested along the coast, with fronds of pointed leaves and spikes of red or purple flowers; a source of indigo dye.

J

jambalaya – a one-dish meal of rice cooked with onions, peppers, celery, ham, shrimp, sausage and whatever else is on hand.

jim crow – an old pejorative term used for a black person; also, discrimination against African Americans by legal enforcement.

jim crow laws – in the post–Civil War South, laws intended to limit the civil or voting rights of blacks.

joggling board – a long bench on rockers used in the days of porch courting.

L

live oak – an evergreen oak indigenous to the US and Mexico.

Lowcountry boil – see 'Frogmore stew.'

M

meat-and-three – a set-price meal that includes a meat dish plus three side dishes.

mint julep – a Southern drink made with bourbon, sugar and ice and garnished with sprigs of mint.

P

pilau – a rice dish; corruption of 'pilaf.'

pluff mud – the name for the gooey, stinky mud of salt marshes at low tide.

po'boy – from New Orleans, a submarine-style sandwich served on French bread; fried oysters, soft-shell crabs, catfish and deli meats are offered as fillings.

S

shag – a form of dancing derived from the jitterbug, popularly danced to beach music in South Carolina.

she-crab soup – a creamy Charleston specialty made flavorful by the added roe from female crabs.

shotgun shack – a small timber house with rooms arranged so that you could (theoretically) fire a gun from front to back; once a common type of dwelling for poor people in the South.

single house – a type of building, found in Charleston, with piazzas facing south or west to collect the ocean breeze.

Spanish moss – an epiphyte found on live oaks in the South; it's not actually moss but is member of the pineapple family.

T

tabby – a bricklike material made from crushed oyster shells.

Trail of Tears – the route taken by Native American tribes who were forcibly removed to western reservations by the US federal government in 1838.

Behind the Scenes

THE LONELY PLANET STORY

The story begins with a classic travel adventure: Tony and Maureen Wheeler's 1972 journey across Europe and Asia to Australia. There was no useful information about the overland trail then, so Tony and Maureen published the first Lonely Planet guidebook to meet a growing need.

From a kitchen table, Lonely Planet has grown to become the largest independent travel publisher in the world, with offices in Melbourne (Australia), Oakland (USA), London (UK) and Paris (France).

Today Lonely Planet guidebooks cover the globe. There is an ever-growing list of books and information in a variety of media. Some things haven't changed. The main aim is still to make it possible for adventurous travelers to get out there – to explore and better understand the world.

At Lonely Planet we believe travelers can make a positive contribution to the countries they visit – if they respect their host communities and spend their money wisely. Since 1986 a percentage of the income from each book has been donated to aid projects and human rights campaigns, and, more recently, to wildlife conservation.

THIS BOOK

This is the first edition of *Savannah, Charleston & the Carolina Coast*. Randall Peffer researched and wrote the Getting Started, Itineraries, History, Culture, Savannah, Georgia Coast and Hilton Head chapters. Debra Miller researched and wrote Snapshot, Outdoors, Environment, Food & Drink, Charleston, Myrtle Beach & the Grand Strand, Directory, Transport, Glossary and the Beaufort sections of the Hilton Head chapter. David Goldberg, MD wrote the Health chapter.

THANKS from the Authors

RANDALL PEFFER First of all, thanks to my co-author Deb Miller for her enthusiasm in getting off the beaten track and uncovering fresh corners of the Lowcountry and bringing a Georgia resident's perspective to our text. Her boundless wit kept me emotionally afloat while I was adrift in a sea of computer files. Rock on, Scarlett! Our commissioning editor Kathleen Munnelly and project editor Wendy Taylor were equally supportive and went above and beyond the call of duty. Cartographers Bart Wright and Kat Smith have proven themselves wizards at their tasks. Thanks also to Elisabeth Cook and her staff of research librarians at Phillips Academy's Oliver Wendell Holmes Library for their magical ability to unearth rare and valuable sources at lightning speed. My field research would not have been as trouble-free nor as much fun without the support of Erica Bachus, of the Savannah Area Convention & Visitors Bureau; Charlie Clark, of the Hilton Head Visitors & Convention Bureau; and Patrick Saylor, of the Brunswick-Golden Isles Visitors Bureau. Most importantly, thanks to my family – Jackie, Jacob and Noah – for giving me the time, space and support to finish this project. The adventure of travel writing would be hollow indeed without having my family to share it.

DEBRA MILLER Many people, most of whom will never meet each other, came together to help my research. From the bartenders in Charleston to the booksellers in Beaufort, from boat captains to concierges, from tennis pros at Kiawah to waiters in Myrtle Beach, I owe most of my thanks to you, for the casual conversations full of insider scoops. Other folks who helped immesely: Holley Aufdemorte, at the Myrtle Beach Area Chamber of Commerce; Nicole Aiello; Helen Benso, at Brookgreen Gardens; Katie Chapman, at the Charleston Area Chamber of Commerce; the hep cats at *Barfly* magazine, in Charleston; Matt Owen, at Kiawah Island Resort; and the good folks at the visitors centers in Beaufort. Special thanks to my lovin' husband, Rob Landau, for hopping on his Harley and braving the torrential rains just to meet me halfway through my research trip. Your love and support rock my world. A special thanks to Kathleen Munnelly and the hardworking crew at Lonely Planet. Finally, a big thanks to my co-author Randy Peffer, an astonishing guy full of Rhett Butler's charm and wit, but with plenty of Bubba pizzazz. He's a guy as eloquent in a 5-star restaurant as he is on a sailboat swilling beer and deboning fish. Randy, your humor, ideas, professionalism and excellent craft have made this project a joy.

CREDITS

Savannah, Charleston & the Carolina Coast was commissioned and developed in the US office by Kathleen Munnelly. Series Publishing Manager Susan Rimerman oversaw the redevelopment of the regional guides series, and Regional Publishing Manager Maria Donohoe steered the development of this title. The guide was edited and proofed by Wendy Taylor. Cartographers Bart Wright and Kat Smith created the maps. Candice Jacobus designed the color pages and oversaw layout, which was done by Shelley Firth. Gerilyn Attebery designed and prepared the cover artwork. Ken DellaPenta compiled the index. Darren Burne helped with coding, and Alex Hershey provided invaluable support.

ACKNOWLEDGMENTS

Many thanks to the US Fish & Wildlife Service for the use of their content 'Packing for a Canoe Trip' (p113).

SEND US YOUR FEEDBACK

We love to hear from travelers – your comments keep us on our toes and help make our books better. Our well-travelled team reads every word on what you loved or loathed about this book. Although we cannot reply individually to postal submissions, we always guarantee that your feedback goes straight to the appropriate authors, in time for the next edition. Each person who sends us information is thanked in the next edition – and the most useful submissions are rewarded with a free book.

To send us your updates – and find out about LP events, newsletters and travel news – visit our award-winning website: www.lonelyplanet.com.

Note: We may edit, reproduce and incorporate your comments in Lonely Planet products such as guidebooks, websites and digital products, so let us know if you don't want your comments reproduced or your name acknowledged. For a copy of our privacy policy, visit www.lonelyplanet.com/privacy.

Index

000 Map pages
000 Location of color photographs

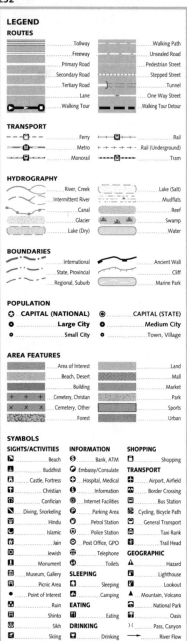

LEGEND

ROUTES

............Tollway
............Freeway
............Primary Road
............Secondary Road
............Tertiary Road
............Lane
............Walking Tour

............Walking Path
............Unsealed Road
............Pedestrian Street
............Stepped Street
............Tunnel
............One Way Street
............Walking Tour Detour

TRANSPORT

............Ferry
............Metro
............Monorail

............Rail
............Rail (Underground)
............Tram

HYDROGRAPHY

............River, Creek
............Intermittent River
............Canal
............Glacier
............Lake (Dry)

............Lake (Salt)
............Mudflats
............Reef
............Swamp
............Water

BOUNDARIES

............International
............State, Provincial
............Regional, Suburb

............Ancient Wall
............Cliff
............Marine Park

POPULATION

◎ **CAPITAL (NATIONAL)**
● ....**Large City**
● ....Small City

◉ ....CAPITAL (STATE)
● ....Medium City
● ....Town, Village

AREA FEATURES

............Area of Interest
............Beach, Desert
............Building
+ + + ...Cemetery, Christian
× × × ....Cemetery, Other
............Forest

............Land
............Mall
............Market
............Park
............Sports
............Urban

SYMBOLS

SIGHTS/ACTIVITIES
🅝 ....Beach
🅑 ....Buddhist
🅒 ....Castle, Fortress
🅒 ....Christian
🅒 ....Confician
🅝 ....Diving, Snorkeling
🅤 ....Hindu
🅒 ....Islamic
🅙 ....Jain
🅙 ....Jewish
🅜 ....Monument
🅜 ....Museum, Gallery
🅟 ....Picnic Area
● ....Point of Interest
🅡 ....Ruin
🅢 ....Shinto
🅢 ....Sikh
🅢 ....Skiing
🅣 ....Taoist
🅦 ....Winery, Vineyard
🅩 ....Zoo, Bird Sanctuary

INFORMATION
🅢 ....Bank, ATM
🅔 ....Embassy/Consulate
🅗 ....Hospital, Medical
🅘 ....Information
◎ ....Internet Facilities
🅟 ....Parking Area
🅟 ....Petrol Station
🅟 ....Police Station
⊗ ....Post Office, GPO
🅣 ....Telephone
🅣 ....Toilets

SLEEPING
🅐 ....Sleeping
🅐 ....Camping

EATING
🅔 ....Eating

DRINKING
🅓 ....Drinking
🅒 ....Café

ENTERTAINMENT
🅔 ....Entertainment

SHOPPING
🅢 ....Shopping

TRANSPORT
🅐 ....Airport, Airfield
🅑 ....Border Crossing
🅑 ....Bus Station
🅒 ....Cycling, Bicycle Path
🅖 ....General Transport
🅣 ....Taxi Rank
🅣 ....Trail Head

GEOGRAPHIC
🄰 ....Hazard
🅛 ....Lighthouse
🅛 ....Lookout
▲ ....Mountain, Volcano
🅝 ....National Park
🅞 ....Oasis
) (............Pass, Canyon
→ ....River Flow
🅢 ....Shelter, Hut
+ ....Spot Height
🅦 ....Waterfall

NOTE: Not all symbols displayed above appear in this guide.

LONELY PLANET OFFICES

Australia
Head Office
Locked Bag 1, Footscray, Victoria 3011
☎ 03 8379 8000, fax 03 8379 8111
talk2us@lonelyplanet.com.au

USA
150 Linden St, Oakland, CA 94607
☎ 510 893 8555, toll free 800 275 8555
fax 510 893 8572, info@lonelyplanet.com

UK
72–82 Rosebery Ave,
Clerkenwell, London EC1R 4RW
☎ 020 7841 9000, fax 020 7841 9001
go@lonelyplanet.co.uk

France
1 rue du Dahomey, 75011 Paris
☎ 01 55 25 33 00, fax 01 55 25 33 01
bip@lonelyplanet.fr, www.lonelyplanet.fr

Published by Lonely Planet Publications Pty Ltd
ABN 36 005 607 983

© Lonely Planet 2004

© photographers as indicated 2004

Cover photographs by Lonely Planet Images: Spanish moss–covered Live Oak trees at Wormsloe Historic Site, Savannah, Jeff Greenberg (front); Drayton Hall, Charleston, Jeff Greenberg (back). Many of the images in this guide are available for licensing from Lonely Planet Images: www.lonelyplanetimages.com.

Printed through Colorcraft Ltd, Hong Kong.
Printed in China